HERMAN MELVILLE

A Collection of Critical Essays

Edited by
Myra Jehl

D1445127

Prentice Hall, Englewood Cliffs, New Jersey 07632

813.36
M531yh

Library of Congress Cataloging-in-Publication Data

Herman Melville : a collection of critical essays / edited by Myra
  Jehlen.
      p.   cm. — (New century views)
  Includes bibliographical references.
  ISBN 0-13-573585-8
  1. Melville, Herman, 1819–1891—Criticism and interpretation.
I. Jehlen, Myra.   II. Series.
PS2387.H42   1994
813'.3—dc20

                                                        93–36344
                                                        CIP

Acquisitions editor: Alison Reeves
Copy editor: Ellen Falk
Editorial/production supervision and
  interior design: Joan Powers
Cover design: Karen Salzbach
Production coordinator: Patricia Kenny

Printed in the United States of America
10 9 8 7 6 5 4 3 2 1

ISBN 0-13-573585-8

Prentice-Hall International (UK) Limited, *London*
Prentice-Hall of Australia Pty. Limited, *Sydney*
Prentice-Hall Canada Inc., *Toronto*
Prentice-Hall Hispanoamericana, S.A., *Mexico*
Prentice-Hall of India Private Limited, *New Delhi*
Prentice-Hall of Japan, Inc., *Tokyo*
Simon & Schuster Asia Pte. Ltd., *Singapore*
Editora Prentice-Hall do Brasil, Ltda., *Rio de Janeiro*

Contents

Introduction

Myra Jehlen

When I saw the essays I had gathered for this volume in one group, I was surprised. The collection seemed more various than I would have predicted, but paradoxically also more united. It represented a wider range of critical approaches that, however, yield a more basic agreement. And when, in preparing my preface, I consulted Richard Chase's preface for *Melville* written thirty years ago for the Twentieth Century Views series, the predecessor to New Century Views,[1] the surprise grew. For Chase had found the same thing—a combination of divergent interpretations merging in an overall accord: "Although some of the essayists who contribute to this volume have reservations of various kinds about the art of Melville or the quality of his thought," he began, "none of them thinks it necessary to defend his greatness."

This division between "art" and "thought" on one side, and "greatness" on the other, did not trouble Chase. Relegating the particularities of Melville's art to a dependent clause, he projected the notion, characteristic of his critical generation, that "greatness" is a quality of literature outside its local characteristics, whereby certain works and authors transcend into universality and timelessness. But many in this critical generation, and I among them, have become skeptical of the very notions of the transcendent—the universal and the timeless—whose definitions we read instead as generalizing the values of the currently reigning culture.

Yet the essays assembled before me appeared to have followed those Chase had collected in not deeming it part of their critical task, as he put it, to defend Melville's greatness. In the current idiom, they did not query Melville's place in the literary canon, but seemed to take this place for granted. I had not imagined Melville deposed, certainly; but perhaps decanonized. I had thought that the canon debates of the last two decades would echo in the criticism of this central figure of the established tradition. That tradition, set out notably in F. O. Matthiessen's 1941 *American Renaissance*, has received a great deal of scrutiny in the last twenty-five years or so. It seemed logical to suppose that Melville's status would have become something at least to query; though perhaps at the same time, not an arena for the

---

[1] *Melville: A Collection of Critical Essays* (Englewood Cliffs, NJ: Prentice-Hall Inc., 1962).

sort of revisionist thinking that was engendering the critical upgrading of, for instance, sentimental novels and slave narratives.

Obviously, I was wrong on both counts. The writers of the essays presented here posit both Melville's centrality and his excellence. None reasons from the demonstration of either political or even artistic fallibility to a devaluation of his importance or brilliance. Edgar Dryden, Sacvan Bercovitch, Brian Higgins, and Hershel Parker find *Pierre* tortuous and overwrought but (unlike Melville's nineteenth-century reviewers who damned him for such textual sins) treat its difficulties as just more to analyze. Like their twentieth-century predecessors, Dryden, Bercovitch, Higgins, and Parker too seem to take Melville's "greatness" for granted.

My second supposition, that Melville—the very type of the white, male, and culturally elite writer—would not have inspired the most revisionist critics, was equally mistaken. For, on the evidence of this collection and the many other essays that could have been included, Melville has been as interesting and compelling a writer for New Historicists, Feminists, Deconstructionists, and African-Americanists as has any other American writer. He has been no less interesting to these critics than he ever was to those who propounded the Great Tradition. There is a perception abroad that the authors of the Great Tradition have been neglected as a result of inquiries into the making and legitimacy of the canon. This perception is erroneous in general,[2] and it is particularly false about Melville.[3]

Between 1940 and 1949, and thus before the effect of *American Renaissance* and its peers was evident, the Modern Language Association *Bibliography* listed 119 critical works about Melville, 8 about Harriet Beecher Stowe, and none about Frederick Douglass. The critics of the fifties were writing from within the newly assumed canon and Melville scholarship increased to 325 essays and books, while 30 were written about Stowe and still none about Douglass. Interest in Melville grew again in the sixties, to 606 essays; interest in Stowe was almost stationary judging by the modest increase of published works about her, from 30 to 36. One critic published on Douglass. In the seventies, Melville was still the center of critical attention—he was the subject of 1,174 listed works; at the same time, Stowe criticism grew a little more vigorously to 81 publications, and Douglass inspired 29. The depressed mood of academic life in the eighties is apparent in a general decline of publications, to 945 on Melville and 58 on Stowe; Douglass scholarship did increase, to 34. It continued to grow, to 21 works in 1990–91 alone, as did Stowe scholarship, with 26 works; but in the same two years, 188 people wrote about Melville. (All along, Hawthorne and Emerson kept pace with Melville; writings about them outnumbered those about Stowe and Douglass

[2]See Bettina J. Huber, "Today's Literature Classroom: Findings from the MLA's 1990 Survey of Upper-Division Courses," *ADE Bulletin*, no. 101, Spring 1992, pp. 36–60.

[3]I am very grateful to my assistant Elise Lemire for the research reflected here.

many times over.) Overall, in the half century from 1940 to 1991, the *Bibliography* lists 3,357 publications on Melville, 239 on Stowe, and 85 on Douglass.

Melville has remained canonical through the whole period of canon-busting. At the same time, for all that they continue to view him as a canonical writer, critics analyze his works in terms that intend to undermine the categories of canonical writing: They assume that he is a "great" writer even as they read him, one might say, against "greatness." Thus they depict Melville and his writings always engaged in a dialogue with his particular place and time, his authority thereby limited by its limited realm. But somehow, his authority within that limited realm appears unlimited, as if he were locally transcendent. I would like to speculate briefly about this paradox which I believe reflects interestingly on both of its terms: on the notion and possibility of "greatness," and on the meaning of its current questioning.

Matthiessen's essay on *Billy Budd* closes the Chase collection with a discussion that elaborates the author's stipulated "greatness." In his last, tragic novel, according to Matthiessen, Melville's despair is as absolute as his hope. Billy Budd is totally guilty and wholly innocent, and in those impossible adjuncts Melville has represented his society's moral collapse and its chance for redemption. Neither implementations nor defiances of the system of worldly justice can achieve this redemption, writes Matthiessen, but only "a radical affirmation of the heart." For Melville has "learned what Keats had, through his kindred apprehension of the meaning of Shakespeare, that the Heart is the Mind's Bible." This is the knowledge that inspired "the passionate humanity in Melville's own creation of tragedy" and enabled him to believe to the end "that though good goes to defeat and death, its radiance can redeem life." Historical conditions enter into this reading, but they seem oddly timeless and unrooted: The "rapaciously individualistic America" to which Melville is said to be reacting is hardly more an actual place than the radiance of the good is a real light. From among such abstractions and in the company of Keats, Shakespeare, and God, Melville himself rises transcendent. In a ringing affirmation that Leo Bersani and Donald Pease might be directly addressing in their essays, Matthiessen concludes: "Melville's endurance is a challenge for a later America."

This volume has been assembled in a twice-later America, later than Melville's and later again than Matthiessen's and Chase's. At the close of both the century and the millennium, phrases such as "though good goes to defeat and death, its radiance can redeem life" ring less definitively; indeed, they make one look about for definitions. "What 'good'?" the end-of-the-millennium critic is likely to ask. "Radiance?" "Redeem?" The Christian resonance of this vocabulary, which Matthiessen intends and finds unproblematical, would today require justification even from a declared Christian critic. Such terms have lost their innocent abstraction and are for us historically charged and accountable. On the other side, formulations such as "rapacious individualism" have also acquired more historical nuance. In *this* later America, the relevance of past good and evil lies rather in their history-making antecedence than in their transcendence.

The notion that Melville's "endurance" in his time could be a "challenge" to later times projects history as an allegory, when for many critics today history is thought of as the opposite—possibly plotless altogether but, at its most ordered, a cacophony of competing narratives. But if it seems unlikely, therefore, that a critic in an America widely dubbed "postmodern" in order to underline its differences from the past, would invoke Melville as a current master, in what terms (I wondered, surveying my group of essays) do these critics unquestioningly accord Melville his traditional distinction? What is a great writer today when the correct spelling of "greatness" includes the quotation marks? And how does Melville exemplify "greatness" such that no one here has found it necessary to spell it at all?

On the evidence of the essays themselves, it seems to me that one can say one or two things about literary "greatness" as it has surprisingly survived its fall from transcendence. Thus, one thing the essays imply is that Melville's stature has to do with a particularly penetrating way of seeing his world. They imply this in the way they set about reading various works as illuminations of the situations described: in a certain trust they evince in Melville's representation of a situation even when or, rather, precisely when they dispute it. Mitchell Breitwieser judges the representation of the colonization of the Marquesas as disingenuous, but argues with it from within *Typee*, questioning its interpretation, even its integrity, but not its adequacy. Wai-chee Dimock raises questions about Melville's account of the naval practice of flogging in *White-Jacket* and concludes that it is "a deceptive book." However, this deceptiveness testifies for her not to a limited understanding but to Melville's more basic knowledge of an untellable truth. Eve Kosofsky Sedgwick deciphers an account of homosexuality in *Billy Budd* that exposes a repressive sexual ideology; in the same story, Barbara Johnson decodes an allegory about knowledge and its communication revealing the fundamental duplicity of authorized knowledge. Robyn Wiegman brings out some assumptions that shape the author's invention of characters perhaps unwittingly. All five readings press on Melville's writing as one presses on the ground in walking, not thinking about whether it will hold but only of negotiating its contours.

In such analyses, the tacit recognition of Melville's "greatness" might be said to lie in a perception that his vision is wholly sufficient to his materials. Another set of readings, by Richard Brodhead, Bryan Wolf, and Philippe Jaworski, assume Melville's self-sufficiency. These readings sketch the processes by which Melville shapes his works as the unfolding of possibilities that he possesses even when he doesn't yet fulfill them—even if he never fulfills them. About Theodore Dreiser, for instance, critics often juxtapose the limits of the author's own vision and craft with the difficulties of his materials. About Melville, in these essays, there is only a sense of the difficulties of the materials shaping Melville's writing, and possibly of reluctance (Dimock), inexperience (Brodhead), duplicity (Breitwieser), overcomplication (Bercovitch), and ambivalence (Sedgwick), but not of *his* limits. How he represents the world seems to be a matter of will (albeit sometimes unconscious), not of capability or capacity.

None of this lessens the difference between the way Chase and Matthiessen understood Melville and the way he has been read more recently. Indeed, as I said earlier, the surprise of finding Melville still treated not just as an important, excellent, central writer, but beyond these, as a "great" writer, arises precisely in relation to the radical difference between other aspects of the earlier and later criticism. The most important component of this difference lies in the treatment of history that Matthiessen and Chase define occasionally, slavery and imperialism providing Melville with occasions for the demonstration of universal and eternal verities. On the contrary, Eric Sundquist places the movement to abolish slavery at the center of "Benito Cereno" (as Arnold Rampersad places Melville at the center of the movement for a black literature); and Bartleby illustrates for Gillian Brown a truth about mid-nineteenth-century America that distinguishes it in essential ways from other times and places. For most of the critics whose essays appear here, there are no universal and eternal verities, but only a variety of local veracities.

The solution to the puzzle of Melville's unquestioned greatness may lie in a parallel formulation: Few critics today believe that there is such a thing as universal literary "greatness." But they do seem to believe, if only implicitly in the way they read, in a variety of ways that writing may be "great"; and all these ways appear to participate in a certain recognizable, palpable quality of understanding and of art. *How* this quality is recognized or felt is difficult to say, impossible to say exactly; but this doesn't mean that it doesn't exist.[4] The recent attacks on the established literary canon have rarely sought to demote authors or titles; they have wanted to add, arguing that certain writers and works have been wrongly excluded from the lists of great literature because the arbiters of such lists held other literary values. Thus the canon revisers argued that sentimental novels are not of a lesser literary quality but of a different one; that for the very reasons Matthiessen found Melville a "great" writer, he could not appreciate Harriet Beecher Stowe. The objection to Matthiessen's exclusion of Stowe, therefore, does not imply rejecting his concept of "greatness," but only the parochialism of his definition.

Indeed, if one takes these essays as an indication, the objection to parochialism may even imply an enhancement of the notion of literary quality, because the expansion of the range of "greatness" frees literature from

---

[4]The Wittgensteinian distinction between saying and showing might be useful here: Although one can't describe literary "greatness" directly by naming its qualities, it is readily recognizable symbolically; Melville's writings constitute one of its symbols.

necessary service to a precise ideology, here of late—that of elite, white, male America. Chase linked Melville's "greatness" to his liberalism; the critics whose essays are collected here don't require or expect him to believe as they do. Indeed, many of them are dubious about systematic belief altogether, and find in Melville a welcome and reassuring disbelief that is, however, not anarchic or even disorderly. Melville's esthetic, freed from its ethical association with Chase's liberal humanism or Matthiessen's humanist Christianity, emerges more autonomous in these essays precisely for its engagement with a particular and untranscendable history. Michael Paul Rogin proposes a biographical source for Melville's characters and plots, in the form not of explanation but of juxtaposition, story to story. Their engagement with a reality that, as we tend today to view it, has no reliable narrative of its own lends Melville's stories power to make history even greater than the power to surpass it.

Indeed, a deepened autonomy is a major term in the reconstitution of "greatness" that emerges from these essays. There was an edge of defensiveness in the claims that critics such as Chase and Matthiessen made for the independence of literature's imagined reality, for they did not deny that historical reality was, objectively, more real. The world of fiction was, in Richard Poirier's elegant phrase, "a world elsewhere," but *this* world had precedence if only because it preceded. How much of objective reality precedes historical representations is no longer clear, and there are some who deny fact any precedence. As more of what we take to be real life is seen to be constructed by narratives, the self-consciously imaginary narratives of literature appear more independent than ever, possibly *more* true for exposing their invention.

Autonomy, sufficiency, power to create a complete world—these are terms whose past political affiliations have, in the past twenty years or so, rendered them almost fatally suspect. Yet they seem to me to describe the underlying assumptions even the revisionist critics in this collection make about Melville's writings. So doing, however, the critics do not unwittingly betray themselves—far from it. Rather, they move toward the culmination of their revisions to reclaim "greatness" in a substantively new form. Autonomy is now a function of historical engagement, sufficiency means adequacy rather than insulation, power sets differences in self-fulfilling motion rather than dissolving or appropriating them. And these qualities of great literature are thought to be mysterious without being otherworldly; being, on the contrary, the signs of an exceptional immanence.

When the current critical rethinking began, one of the clearest ways it explained the objection to traditional conceptions of literary "greatness" was in terms of the relation of "author" and "authority." Since roughly the eighteenth century, "authors" have had a heightened cultural status for being seen to embody a concept of the universal individual in possession of truths that apply to the entire society. To reject universal *authority*, it seemed for a time that the *author* would have to go with it; but, as I have been suggesting, with the concept of universal authority pretty well overthrown, Melville remains, and he remains "Melville." For contemporary critics, however, being Melville the "great author" no longer implies having authority: it implies having autonomy but not authority.

In a philosophical and literary culture in which representations of the world are by definition always problematical, author and authority have developed a contradictory relation. The greater the author, according to current readings, the *less* he confirms authority, even his own, for the more he reveals the making of his own authority. It is both tempting and easy, since one always reads from one's own perspective, to claim now that this contradiction has always been recognized and central to literary creation. Reading this way, the God of Genesis Himself might be the model for the current view of the author who has to point to chaos in order to make us appreciate the order that he, or she, creates. Ahab's fatal error can be described as a failure to understand this same contradiction; the captain of the Pequod believes in the authority of authors and determines to acquire it for himself, whereupon he forces the two mutually exclusive terms together to their mutual annihilation. Ishmael survives to tell the tale because he understands all along that a tale is just a tale; and that the first condition for telling is to recognize the unauthorized nature of tales. Ahab's error engenders a tragedy he could never have written. Belief in authority keeps one from being an author—see *Pierre*.

In this very current and dated (neither once nor future) sense—which of course informs this preface as surely as the individualist and imperial "new liberalism" of the forties and fifties informed the one Chase wrote—Melville is a "great" author precisely because he exposes the falsehood of authority; but also because, having exposed authority, he is able to establish himself as an "author" through the sufficient autonomy of his art.

This collection includes more essays than is usual for a volume of this size, and I begin this survey by warning readers that all the essays have been cut to the bone of their arguments. (The cuts, indicated by ellipses, are not only substantial but substantive, and I urge readers to seek out the complete versions. All but one[5] of the essays have been published previously at least once and are readily available.) It seems to me that a major interest of this collection as such lies in its representation of the range of recent critical thought. I decided, therefore, to present not so much a series of separate, self-sufficient readings as a general conversation among exponents of as many as possible of the current critical approaches. To the same conversational end, the collection includes a cluster of three essays each on *Moby-Dick* and on *Pierre*, the first Melville's best-known novel and the second currently his most controversial; as well as two on *Billy Budd*, Melville's last work and perhaps the one more people have actually read.

[5]Arnold Rampersad's "Melville and African-American Writers" appears here for the first time in print.

Typee was Melville's first novel, based on a real-life adventure and published when he was 27. The renewal of interest in Melville in the 1920s established *Moby-Dick*[6] as his masterpiece, which also set the terms for appreciating Melville's writing generally. From this perspective, codified in Matthiessen's *American Renaissance*, *Typee* appeared a preliminary exercise whose interest lay in its foreshadowings of greater things to come. As Charles Feidelson explained it in his *Symbolism and American Literature*,[7] Melville's decision following conversations with Hawthorne to revise *Moby-Dick* reflected a transformation of Melville's understanding of the very character of storytelling—from a descriptive, almost reportorial enterprise to a probing of the very nature of the universe through its symbolic representation. Today the distinction between realistic and symbolic writing is less clear to critics, who have been demonstrating that language, whatever its form, always reconstructs the world in describing it; at the same time, an explosion of interest in the subject of colonization has made *Typee*'s subject matter newly compelling. Mitchell Breitwieser opens this volume with an unmistakably late-twentieth-century discussion of the way Melville understood and represented the relationship of the West to its empires.

Although the action in *Moby-Dick* takes place all over the globe, actual locations remain strangely unimportant; the world the *Pequod* sails is always the New World, which is the United States. Not so the world the hero of *Typee* walks, which is a place made up entirely of borders between the specific national culture he has left and the other civilization he cannot bring himself to enter. Breitwieser reveals the importance of this first novel for Melville's opus but also raises questions about it: He finds Melville's much noted and at the time highly controversial "sympathy" for the colonized to be "false." Breitwieser has not only asked a new question that has had the likely effect of highlighting a new text, but has also brought this new question, along with the new text, into the center of the Americanist conversation: Tommo's attitude toward the Typees is seen to demonstrate the limits not only of his political understanding but of his philosophy of selfhood. With this recasting of a traditional issue, Breitwieser demonstrates once again that context is all. Stripped of his empire, the colonizer himself, whether as imperialist or as anti-imperialist, emerges no longer a global being.

After *Typee*, Melville wrote *Omoo*, which along with *Redburn* has been omitted from consideration in this volume for reasons of space. (The Chronology at the end of the volume lists all of Melville's works.) *Mardi*, Melville's third novel and probably the least read for reasons Richard Brodhead sets out,

---

[6]Raymond Weaver's *Herman Melville: Mariner and Mystic* (1921) reintroduced Melville to a reading public that had essentially forgotten him. At around the same time, the psychologist Henry A. Murray began a passionate lifelong study of Melville that also contributed to the author's revival and canonization. See Forrest G. Robinson's recent biography, *Love's Story Told: A Life of Henry G. Murray* (Cambridge, MA: Harvard University Press, 1993).

[7]Chicago: University of Chicago Press, 1953.

represents a conscious reversal of the realistic method of the first two. Brodhead quotes Melville's declaration that he was here writing a real romance, a mode he opposed to realism. Brodhead interprets this shift as the author's discovery of an ambition for creation as such, for invention. The distinction between Brodhead's analysis and previous accounts of Melville's unfolding art—for instance, Feidelson's in *Symbolism and American Literature*—is subtle and unheralded in the essay; but it is fundamental. In Melville's move from realistic description to romance, Brodhead chronicles a conscious change, the invention rather than the discovery of authorship. He describes a passage of literary self making that is not an unfolding but rather a series of choices that are far from self-evident; as there is nothing self-evident about *Mardi*.

In this sense of seeing authorship as a practice rather than a way of being, Brodhead's essay leads into Wai-chee Dimock's about *White-Jacket* and the way the established conceptions of authorship and of audiences comprise actual institutions and enter not only into the content of individual works but into their form, which has to negotiate the structures of cultural understanding and communication. Like Breitwieser, Dimock focuses on borders: between authors and texts, texts and audiences. These borders mark the limits of imaginative agency in the making of literature, but also register the force of the literary imagination.

The three essays on *Moby-Dick* by Donald Pease, Leo Bersani, and Bryan Wolf demonstrate three distinct but also distinctly post-Chase critical approaches. Pease shares Dimock's sense that the cultural setting in which it is written holds the key to a novel's basic terms, but his definition of this setting is a little different from hers. What he calls "the scene of cultural persuasion" is a more abstract setting than Dimock's political scene; Pease is less concerned with the content of Melville's culture than with its forms. He wants to understand how *Moby-Dick* works as much as what it says. But his is no formalist analysis—quite the opposite, for Pease reads form as the fuller realization of content. Neither in its writing nor in later readings does he see the novel's formal qualities and strategies as any less historically responsive than its subject matter and views. Thus, when mid-twentieth-century America reinterprets this mid-nineteenth-century novel, its rhetorical structures are as much at issue as its characters and plot. *Moby-Dick* then and now works most effectively not in dispensing abiding truths but in organizing the cultural discourse.

To this view of the novel as a continually evolving interlocution, Bersani opposes a reading of *Moby-Dick* that effectively denies that it means to say anything of what it seems to be affirming. The anti-message message of this "our mighty book" is, according to Bersani, a continual dissolution of meanings and even of knowledge in the repetition of "utopian negations" that embrace and celebrate, as the only genuine national identity, the country's culturally "impoverished beginning." Melville in *Moby-Dick* erases meaning as he goes, refuses rhetoric or shows it to be invalid. On one level, this view rejects recent reinterpretations that appropriate the novel to a current agenda. But on another level, the notion of a continual dissolution is also unmistakably of this time. Neither Matthiessen nor Chase would have read Melville as refusing to mean. He may (for them) fail to mean, but not refuse to mean, except as an expression of a despair that, of course, would make the refusal itself meaningful. For the refusal to create cultural forms or ongoing values to become a conceivable literary project, and for this refusal to be seen as historically inspired, literature and history both have to be seen not as builders of monuments but as being perpetually under construction. Or they have to be viewed more liminally, as always about to be constructed and therefore not less real for never being built. Bersani's reading of *Moby-Dick* is the opposite of Brodhead's reading of *Mardi*, but they are complementary opposites, in that both posit and demonstrate that writing novels is—before, during, and after—always a manipulation of contingency; never an inscription of truths such as God, Shakespeare, and Keats have already inscribed.

The third reading of *Moby-Dick*, by Wolf, seems at first unrelated to the other two. But a common membership in the current critical scene manifests itself when, while exploring the relation of Melville's writing in *Moby-Dick* to the paintings of his contemporaries Thomas Cole and Asher Durand, Wolf uncovers few positive echoes and many problematical ones. At first sight, early in the novel, Wolf finds *Moby-Dick* almost programmatically "sublime." But in a last paragraph that seems to foreshadow Bersani's own conclusion, Wolf describes the final defeat of the novel's sublime ambition which, to effect Ishmael's survival, "has been reduced from the motions of an omnivorous self to a grammar that reabsorbs all vision into its own circling vortex."

The three *Moby-Dick* essays are followed by three essays on *Pierre*. *Pierre* seems to have the distinction of having sold in the nineteenth century the fewest copies of any of Melville's books.[8] Appropriately, all three essays address themselves to the problem of the novel's readability. Edgar Dryden's depiction of an "entangled text" concludes that in the end no reliable account of the story can be derived from a "tangle of . . . inscriptions that seem at first to embody a presence but that actually condemn us to absence." Sacvan Bercovitch offers an interpretation that does make sense of the story, but the interpretation culminates in senselessness: On the last and prophetic level of its fivefold allegory, *Pierre*, writes Bercovitch, is "a failed book (entitled "Herman Melville Crazy") about the failure of symbolic art." (In relation to

---

[8]Harper's printed 2,310 copies. Of these, 1,423 were sold on publication in 1853; 133 more had found buyers by October 1854, after which, over the next 33 years, *Pierre* sold a total of 300 copies; and 150 were distributed to reviewers. This accounts for 2,006 when the plates were melted in March 1887. These figures come from the "Historical Note" of *Pierre, or the Ambiguities*, ed. Harrison Hayford, Hershel Parker, and G. Thomas Tanselle (Evanston and Chicago: Northwestern University Press and the Newberry Library, 1971). As this collection goes to press, *Pierre* is once again unavailable except in scholarly editions.

these essays, Brodhead's depiction of the genesis of *Mardi* as a turn toward art acquires a new poignancy.) Brian Higgins and Hershel Parker declare flatly that *Pierre* "failed disastrously on all levels" and take as their subject the problem of how it fails. Great failures, of course, are well-regarded in art and *Pierre* is not in that sense unusual. William Faulkner once remarked that all the great books were failures in that an author only did his best work when he tried to surpass himself. Samuel Beckett wrote that "to be an artist is to fail, as no other dare fail," and he might as well have had *Pierre* in mind.[9] But current critics don't just recognize *Pierre*'s failure, they actually focus on it and treat it as a (sometimes *the*) defining characteristic of the book. Though in this century it was the object of a cult among the writers of the Beat generation, *Pierre* is almost proverbial in the American tradition for its unreadability.

Is it less readable than *The Confidence Man*? and why do the difficulties posed by this novel not tend to attract attention for themselves as do those of *Pierre*? Daniel Hoffman observes at the end of his essay in Chase's collection that *The Confidence Man* is a formal failure. But until then he has been lucidly explicating this most convoluted and ultimately incoherent plot, treating its impenetrability as incidental. The terms of Michael Paul Rogin's reading suggest how the textual obscurity of *The Confidence Man* differs from that of *Pierre*, and why the former may therefore seem less literarily problematical.

Rogin interprets *The Confidence Man* with relation to Melville's family history. *Pierre* is certainly also about families, but there the drama itself is at issue, even before its resonances and legacies, preempting their examination. *The Confidence Man* warns us at the start not to believe what we read. We make our way through the thickening maze, therefore, in growing confusion but with a certain calmness of spirit; for never having suspended disbelief, we remain in possession of the theoretical possibility of true belief. But *Pierre* begins in just the opposite way, projecting an infinite vista of truths whose radical uncertainty coopts the entire universe of understanding. If critics read *Pierre* for its resistance to being read, this is because it tenders this resistance writ large as a problem about storytelling in general, as a paradoxical means of approach. And if students of Melville have been finding *Pierre* especially interesting recently (there are no *Pierre* essays in Chase's collection), this may be because resistance, both by the text and as the text's message, is a major theme of current literary scholarship. Implosion into anarchic ambiguity is a constant ultimate threat implicit in a definition of literature and language as together the original creators of order. Of course, few texts and critical approaches today are immune to this danger. And in the end, after showing

---

[9]"Three Dialogues," *Disjecta: Miscellaneous Writings and a Dramatic Fragment*, edited with a foreword by Ruby Cohn (New York: Grove Press, Inc., 1984), p. 145. Jim Hicks called this passage to my attention.

how Melville succeeded imaginatively where his father failed in real life, Rogin recalls the criticism of *Pierre* by concluding that "the anesthesizing price of his power as author is an absent self, and so the masquerade consumes both the confidence man and his creator."

Besides *Moby-Dick*, Melville's best-known works are perhaps the two stories "Bartleby the Scrivener" and "Benito Cereno." A third trio of essays addresses these stories: Gillian Brown discusses commerce in "Bartleby," Eric Sundquist slavery in "Benito Cereno," and, despite their major differences, both discussions illustrate the primacy that current criticism gives to the historical context; neither abstracts from context to text. For Philippe Jaworski, who brings to this collection one of two contributions from outside the United States, the problem posed by both protagonists is that they cannot enter the world of their ostensible stories because of economic and political identities that render them impenetrable or insignificant to their narrators. Bartleby is nothing to the lawyer; black Africans are nothing to Captain Delano. Melville writes about characters excluded from the literary universe and whose tales therefore cannot be told: Unreadable in some cases, Melville's stories are, in other cases, unwritable.

Arnold Rampersad also focuses on "Benito Cereno," but to reverse the perspective of the three earlier essays in order to examine not what Melville made of blacks, but what black writers made of Melville—how they have read Melville and used him for their own writing. Rampersad's conclusion that Melville "clearly saw something of . . . the ways [blacks] would become, or had already become, entangled in the apparatus of signification designed to keep them in perpetual servitude" posits the definitive role of history in Melville's writing. There is no question here of black characters representing more than themselves; Melville's achievement lies in his awareness that they can and should represent themselves.

The next two essays, the first on "The Paradise of Bachelors and the Tartarus of Maids" and the second on *Billy Budd*, explore a relatively recent concern in literary criticism—the cultural definition of sexual identity. Robyn Wiegman demonstrates the way the categories of feminist analysis can bring out latent aspects of Melville's writing. Once again there is an assumption about the definitive influence of context on text underlying this procedure. Eve Sedgwick finds in *Billy Budd* an illustration of the role played by the repression of homosexual desires in the construction of both social and cultural orders. Like Rampersad, she too stipulates the primacy of issues, persons, experiences, and events that an earlier mode of Melville criticism took as secondary—occasions for representing universalities.

Two related basic assumptions have emerged from this brief survey of the collected essays, one about history and the other about literature. About history, the critics here assembled seem as a group to think with new respect. They grant it a shaping force in defining even the most fundamental principles of Melville's literary vision. About literature, on the contrary, these critics are less confident than their predecessors. They read it for its self-exposures. Barbara Johnson's essay closes this volume in telling contrast with the last essay of Chase's collection. As we saw earlier, Matthiessen drew the moral of that earlier volume by attributing to even the despairing, dying Melville of *Billy Budd*, a sort of triumph of the moral will. Johnson, also writing on *Billy Budd*, reads it less affirmatively. Her essay is titled "The Execution of *Billy Budd*" and opens with a section called "The Plot against the Characters." It reads Melville's last novel as a dire warning *against* moral certainty, and against believing in the authority of knowledge and its literary accounts. Violence in *Billy Budd* is the final authority, Johnson suggests, because the assertion of authority is an act of violence.

History, in these essays, has gained more relative power, and literature has lost its absolute authority. Both developments express the same major modification in Western thought in the very late twentieth century: a tempering of ambition to control the world and transcend its limits, brought home as a limitation of individual potency. The indwelling of history in literature expresses itself here as a distinction between author and authority. At the same time, to return to the beginning of this preface, readers who do not expect and who indeed reject authorial authority continue to recognize something that literature achieves uniquely as art, not history. This achievement, insofar as one can glean its definition from this survey, transforms history without transcending it, and creates an autonomous reality that is simultaneously an exceptionally penetrating vision of the real world. The autonomy of this vision is no mere effect but a tangible existence built by language and inhabiting its own esthetic dimension: a palpable, mappable thereness not elsewhere but here, inside Melville's novels and stories.

Richard Chase had set out the position from which he collected his volume of Twentieth Century Views in a 1949 book-length study of his own.[10] This study had explicit political intentions. He named as its first purpose illuminating Melville's writings. But his second intention was "to contribute a book on Melville to a movement which may be described . . . as the new liberalism— that newly invigorated secular thought at the dark center of the twentieth century which . . . now begins to ransom liberalism from its ruinous sellouts, failures, and defeats of the thirties." My purpose in collecting these essays has been simply to represent the continuing resonance of Melville's writings in the most current of our current concerns. Yet it is evident that this very resonance and the desire to represent it also have political implications. For at the still darker end of the twentieth century, vision—just being able to see and possibly to understand—has acquired a surpassing urgency. The Enlightenment's light of reason now appears to have cast one of the deeper shadows

---

[10]*Herman Melville: A Critical Study* (New York: The Macmillan Company, 1949). Citations are from the preface, p. vii.

in human history; the ideal of equality and the revolutionaries who tried to institute it seem to have been particularly oppressive. We seem to be back at the beginning of imagining the world a better place, but with a terrible awareness of the worse places to which such imaginings can lead. I have suggested that the writers of these essays all seem to trust in Melville's imagination, even when they dispute his judgment. "I have the conviction that if our liberalism is serious about its new vision of life," Chase wrote, "it must come to terms with Herman Melville." Our skepticism, I would suggest, needs to come to terms with the way Herman Melville still, or again, commands belief.

The very close of this collection is a short piece by Antonio Tabucchi about which nothing need be said by me, except to express gratitude for the elegance with which it brings the volume together and concludes it.

False Sympathy in Melville's *Typee*

Mitchell Breitwieser

Typee (1846) is often viewed as a critique of the colonization of the Marquesas.[1] But to see it this way is to accept the narrator's claim to affinity with the Marquesans, and Melville made that claim eccentric and muddled, obliging us to look for underlying self-interest. For D.H. Lawrence, Tommo, the narrator, is so self-involved that he never sees the Typees, and he is no more compatible with them than are the colonialist powers he deplores. However, *Tommo's* unreliability does not imply *Melville's*: Tommo's unreliability circumscribes him within a critique related to but more acute than his own. A resentful romantic objection to conspicuous social power, Melville contends, is not necessarily true sympathy for the other victims of that power, however much it might announce that it is. Such sympathy may very well be complicit in what it denounces. Tommo and Melville are distinct: though Tommo's sentiments were once Melville's, and though Melville returned to them repeatedly, in the act of writing Melville put those sentiments at a distance that permitted an analytic exploration of the idea that the root of colonialism is so deep that even an apparent rebel may turn out to be an agent.

The first sign of Tommo's self-absorption is the absence of Marquesans from the first quarter of the book, though the story is supposedly written to bring their innocence and plight to the public's attention. Rather than observing this purpose, these early pages, recounting and justifying Tommo's escape from the whaler and his flight inland to elude recapture, keep Tommo on stage and the Typees in the wings, delineating his point of view and challenging its objectivity in advance. If we believe that the book is about Typees, rather than about the role Tommo will make them play in the drama of his

Reprinted from *American Quarterly*, 34.4 (1982), with the permission of the Johns Hopkins University Press.

[1]Charles Anderson, *Melville in the South Seas* (New York: Columbia Univ. Press, 1939); and T. Walter Herbert, *Marquesan Encounters: Melville and the Meaning of Civilization* (Cambridge Univ. Press, 1980). I would also like to acknowledge my debt to Edward Said, *Orientalism* (New York: Random House, 1979); and *Covering Islam* (New York: Pantheon, 1981). In preparing my essay for publication in the current volume, I have excised a number of discussions of Melville's later writing, of Melville criticism, and of various theoretical inspirations for my argument. The original essay appeared in *American Quarterly* 34, #4 (Fall, 1982), pp. 396–417.

grudge, this delay will seem pointless. But once we conclude that the book's topic is Tommo's self-conception as it is drawn into the open by his encounter with the Typees, these pages will seem justified.

Tommo believes that this preliminary narrative establishes his credibility. He presents himself as a *picaro* whose freethinking, though it may offend staid readers, proves he is not encumbered by the vested interest that biases other accounts of the Marquesas. But beneath his easygoing, skeptical humor, there is an active self-centered hostility toward his parent culture that complicates the objectivity the humor is supposed to certify. Tommo can champion the Marquesans only so long as he can assume that sharing an antagonist is the same as sharing an identity. When thinking of them as fellow victims, he excludes evidence of their actual life in order to construct an idyllic image in order to denounce those he detests without seeming self-serving. Tommo depicts Typee life in order to indict what he detests rather than to understand a culture that is comprehensively alien to *all* aspects of his own, including his own injured self-esteem. He is a sympathetic primitivist as long as he is left in charge of defining "primitive."

Melville distinguishes himself from Tommo by compelling Tommo to undergo the trauma that results from the encounter between his rhetorical primitive and the actual primitive, at which point Tommo's narrative falls into a bewildered vacillation between seeing the Typees as noble victims of colonialism and as blithe practitioners of an appalling depravity. In this vacillation, Tommo is failing to limit the alterity of the Typees, celebrating their lifestyle so long as it negates selected aspects of his culture, but detesting it once it begins to impinge on himself. Tommo's failures reveal his imaginative imperialism, his desire to use rather than to perceive. . . .

Melville shipped out in 1841 because the variety of experience and the imaginative independence promised by a long cruise to the end of the world would postpone the dreadful obligation of settling down to a regular but stultifying work life. This hope is recalled in the first pages of *Typee*, where Tommo conjures visions of boundless and exotic experience out of his readings in romantic travel literature. But ship discipline convinces Tommo that the sailor's life is even more enervating than the life he had left behind, and he jumps ship, as Melville did, when he realizes that the captain will not allow shore leave. The work chosen to escape tedium has turned out to be more oppressive, a sentiment intensified by interdicted opportunities within sight from the deck. So far, Tommo resembles the young Melville. But his turgid book-ridden language suggests an authorial irony, an irony that will eventually go after deeper targets than juvenile naiveté.

After he deserts, Tommo converts his antiauthoritarian resentment into sociological theory. By lamenting the imminent destruction of the Marquesan idyll, he will be able to criticize his society's subjugation of personality to mechanism with more impressive evidence than his private sense of injury. In one sense this makes Tommo an opponent to Jacksonian America, but is also typically Jacksonian in his desire for a self-mastering masterlessness that, alongside but separate from any concomitant prosperity, had become a compelling impulse for young men of Melville's and Whitman's generation, the crucial component of their notion of manhood.

Tommo echoes this legacy when he seeks to justify his desertion by updating the Declaration of Independence:

> Our ship had not been many days in the harbor of Nukuheva before I came to the determination of leaving her. That my reasons for resolving to take this step were numerous and weighty may be inferred from the fact that I chose rather to risk my fortunes among the savages of the island than to endure another voyage on board the Dolly. . . . I had made up my mind to "run away." Now as a meaning is generally attached to these words no way flattering to the individual to whom they are applied, it behooves me, for the sake of my own character, to offer some explanation of my conduct.[2]

Like Franklin recalling his escape from Boston, Tommo attempts to elude the moral dubiousness of desertion by detailing the abuses of authority that drove him to it. However, the more immediate textual precedent is the Declaration:

> When in the course of human events, it becomes necessary for one people to dissolve the political bands which have connected them with another, and to assume among the Powers of the earth, the separate and equal station to which the Laws of Nature and of Nature's God entitle them, a decent respect to the opinions of mankind requires that they should declare the causes which impel them to the separation.

Like Jefferson, Tommo lists, in grammatically parallel clauses, the complaints against his George III, the captain of the Dolly. And he concludes that "it was vain to think that he would either remedy them, or alter his conduct, which was arbitrary and violent in the extreme. . . . To whom could we apply for redress" (20–21)? This is the only place where Tommo adopts this expository tone, suggesting that the passage is a self-conscious appeal to the Declaration, an uneasy imitation that betrays rather than disguises the moral dubiousness of the desertion, using eighteenth-century notions of independence to consolidate outrage at nineteenth-century America's indifference to those notions.

Tommo is thus both anti-American and typically American in that he faces a society that forbids its members the freedom it nonetheless promises. To Tommo, America means both the superstructural promise of self-reliant masterlessness and the infrastructural reduction of persons into units of labor. Tommo's predicament is therefore not that he has two selves, but that his society presents him with two mutually exclusive modes of selfhood. Two

---

[2]Herman Melville, *Typee: A Peep at Polynesian Life* (1846; rpt. Evanston and Chicago: Northwestern Univ. Press and the Newberry Library, 1968), 20. Hereafter all page citations for material quoted from *Typee* will appear in the text.

years before *Typee* was published, Marx analyzed this "double existence" of nineteenth-century subjectivity:

> He lives in the *political* community, where he regards himself as a *communal being,* and in *civil* society where he acts simply as a *private individual,* treats other men as means, degrades himself to the role of mere means, and becomes the plaything of alien powers.

As a member of civil society, "he has been corrupted, lost to himself, alienated, subjected to the rule of inhuman conditions and elements, by the whole organization of our society. . . ." But as the heir of the Enlightenment, he is "the imaginary member of an imaginary sovereignty, divested of his real, individual life and infused with an unreal universality." In the mass society of the nineteenth century, such a sovereign is only abstract, artificial man, an "allegorical, moral person" rather than a reality.[3]

Tommo cannot realize personal sovereignty so long as he is connected with his society. Consequently, he posits that Typee society is entirely free from the oppressive structure of his own and so offers the purity he desires. *Typee* is therefore a romance, because Tommo attempts to use the culture of the South Seas as a situation that will permit him to realize what is only an "abstract, moral person[hood]" at home; but also a novel, because Melville makes the futility and egoistic imperiousness of such an attempt quite clear. Tommo's romance persists until experience compels him to discover that Typee life is as much a negation of the self-mastering masterless self as it is of the division of labor, at which point the romance degenerates into terror and loathing.

Tommo's contradiction first appears in his conflicting explanations of flaws in western representations of the Marquesans. In general, he is affably skeptical and facetious about the accounts written by missionaries and other official visitors because he considers them warped by xenophobia, literary convention, normative ethnocentrism, and self-justification. He feels special resentment toward the missionaries who, pretending to exercise Christian sympathy for the victims of power, are actually rendering the islanders pliable by shaming them out of indigenous and cultural traditions. In this passage, for example he poses as the Increase Mather of Polynesia:

> In truth, I regard the Typees as a back-slidden generation. They are sunk in religious sloth, and require a spiritual revival. A long prosperity of bread-fruit and cocoa-nuts has rendered them remiss in the performance of the higher obligations. The wood-rot malady is spreading among the idols—the ruin upon their altars is becoming offensive—the temples themselves need rethatching—the tattooed clergy are already too light-hearted and lazy—and their flocks are going astray. (179)

[3]Karl Marx, "On the Jewish Question," *Early Writings,* trans. and ed. T. B. Bottomore (New York: McGraw-Hill, 1963), 13, 20, 14, 30.

But jocular satire does not hide completely the bitterness beneath. Tommo believes that the motive for such specious representations is less spiritual concern than justification for cultural invasion:

> Among the islands of Polynesia, no sooner are the images overturned, the temples demolished, and the idolators converted into *nominal* Christians, than disease, vice and premature death make their appearance. The depopulated land is then recruited from the rapacious hordes of enlightened individuals who settle themselves within its borders, and clamorously announce the progress of the Truth (195).

Anticipating later critiques of colonialist edification, Tommo argues that those who pretend to offer relief and consolation in the midst of imperial cruelty are in fact advance-men, demoralizing the populace to prepare it for submission.[4]

But, when confronted with Marquesan indifference to the selfhood he seeks to realize, Tommo relocates representational flaw in the Marquesans, who deviously conceal the horror of the way they live from whites who would be rightly appalled:

> It is a singular fact, that in all our accounts of cannibal tribes we have seldom received the testimony of an eye-witness to the revolting process. The horrible conclusion has almost always been derived either from the second-hand evidence of Europeans, or else from the admissions of the savages themselves, after they have in some degree become civilized. The Polynesians are aware of the detestation in which Europeans hold this custom, and therefore invariably deny its existence, and, with the craft peculiar to savages, endeavor to conceal every trace of it (234).

The innocent, hedonistic savages of the first passage have become demonically crafty, and the idea of "becoming civilized" is no longer swathed in heavy irony. This radical alteration in tone and assertion demonstrates Tommo's unwillingness to accept the Marquesan culture as a complete and intact fabric. He champions it selectively, choosing instances of "innocence" that allow him to deride execrable dimensions of his own culture. But the mere possibility that the Marquesans are comprehensively, rather than conveniently, independent from white norms converts his affability into credulous horror.

Because Tommo never understands that the source of the ambiguity causing his oscillations lies in himself, he cannot stabilize his conflicting portraits of Polynesian life. In his first discourse on cannibalism, for example, Tommo reveals loathing: "These celebrated warriors appear to inspire the other islanders with unspeakable terrors. Their very name is a frightful one; for the word 'Typee' in the Marquesan dialects signifies a lover of human flesh" (24). On the next page, he admits he shares this terror, and his apprehension seems intense enough to make him forget his suspicion of Western reports about island life: "I could not but feel a particular and most unqualified repugnance to the aforesaid Typees. Even before visiting the Marquesas, I

---

[4]See for instance Frantz Fanon, "Algeria Unveiled," *A Dying Colonialism*, trans. Haakon Chevalier (New York: Grove Press, 1965), 35–68.

had heard from men who had touched at the group on former voyages some revolting stories in connection with the savages. . . ." However, a few pages later, his horror is gone and he is once again skeptical about transmitted stories, so skeptical that he dismisses all charges against the Marquesans:

> How often is the term "savages" incorrectly applied! None really deserving of it were ever yet discovered by voyagers or travellers. They had discovered heathens and barbarians, who by horrible cruelties they had exasperated into savages. It may be asserted without fear of contradiction, that in all the cases of outrages committed by Polynesians, Europeans have at some time or other been the aggressors, and that the cruel and bloodthirsty disposition of some of the islanders is mainly to be ascribed to the influence of such examples (27).

Though he claims that this may be "asserted without fear of contradiction," his early remarks contradict it. Other portions of his own narrative provide or at least hint at two reasons for disbelieving this assertion. First, the Polynesians practiced some cannibalism before the whites arrived, and the Typees, whom Tommo represents as the most cannibalistic, have had the least contact with the whites. And second, cannibalism is a ritual institution rooted in symbolic practice—the ingestion of the enemy's virtue—and thus not a commensurate revenge modeled after the interlopers' example. Cannibalism does not begin with the intervention of colonialism, and it cannot be understood as a just, equivalent return of blow for blow. Tommo is willing to forget his own understanding of cannibalism in this passage because he is eager to throw the innocence of the Polynesians in his society's face. When he hears the word "savages" applied to the Polynesians by others, he imagines himself hearing it from the same mouth that calls his self-liberation "running away," and righteous (if spurious) sympathy replaces revulsion.

Tommo's intuition of his own inconsistency leads him to represent it as a contradiction within the observed rather than within the observer. Soon after he leaves the Dolly, he begins to distinguish between two tribes of Marquesans, the Typees and their neighbors the Happars: "Typee or Happar? A frightful death at the hands of the fiercest of cannibals, or a kindly reception from a gentler race of savages? Which?" (66) The distinction between demonic and edenic primitives is presented as a distinction between two kinds of Nukuhevans. Tommo revives this strategy at the end of the book, where the Typees divide into the humanized, individualized, sentimentalized types who tearfully respect his homesickness and the undifferentiated mob of ferocious captors led by the one-eyed Mow-Mow. But his attempt to render his inner dissonance as a difference between Marquesans never becomes credible by developing into a persistent explanatory theme. Tommo presents it fitfully, and this fitfulness betrays its origin in his anxiety over his own indecision.

Tommo's ambivalence appears again in his feelings about nudity. When he can use Marquesan nakedness to satirize his countrymen, he is eager:

> When I remember that these islanders derived no advantage from dress, but appeared in all the naked simplicity of nature, I could not avoid comparing them

with the fine gentlemen and dandies who promenade such unexceptional figures in our frequented thoroughfares. Stripped of the cunning artifices of the tailor, and standing forth in the garb of Eden—what a sorry set of round-shouldered, spindle-shanked, crane-necked varlets would civilized men appear! Stuffed calves, padded breasts, and scientifically cut pantaloons would then avail them nothing, and the effect would be truly deplorable (180–81).

Earlier, Tommo had recounted the tale of some Marquesans who peeked beneath a missionary's wife's dress and were disgusted to find that she was a woman among others despite her affectation of difference. He had also told of a visit to a French frigate by a local queen who, admiring one sailor's tattoos, volunteered a view of the more extensive tableau on her back parts. In such episodes, the humor results from the contact between physical candor and some manifestation of Western ostentation. He is at ease with Marquesan nudity when he can place it next to signs of authoritarian prestige:

The next moment they stood side by side, these two extremes of the social scale—the polished, splendid Frenchman, and the poor tattooed savage. They were both tall and noble-looking men; but in other respects how strikingly contrasted! Du Petit Thouars exhibited upon his person all the paraphernalia of his naval rank. He wore a richly decorated admiral's frock coat, a laced chapeau bras, and upon his breast were a variety of ribbons and orders; while the simpler islander, with the exception of a slight cincture about his loins, appeared in all the nakedness of nature (29).

So long as naked nature stands next to some captain of the Western world, Tommo is delighted.

But the celebrated savage keeps a slight cincture: prudishness intrudes into ribaldry, a prudishness that becomes more prominent when naked nature stands next to Tommo. His first social gesture upon arriving in the Typee valley is to throw a cotton cloth over the shoulders of a young couple who emerge from some bushes to greet him and his companion. Fayaway, who "clung to the primitive and summer garb of Eden" (87), is the most conspicuously nude character in the book—in an orgy of discretion, Tommo remarks that her hair covers her breasts when she bends over. As long as he holds Fayaway's nakedness against his memories of home, Tommo is tranquil: "The easy unstudied graces of a child of nature like this, breathing from infancy an atmosphere of perpetual summer, and nurtured by the simple fruits of the earth; enjoying a perfect freedom from care and anxiety, and effectually removed from all injurious tendencies, strike the eye in a manner which cannot be pourtrayed [*sic*]" (86). But sexuality appeals to the free self only when it is subjected to an external interdiction; otherwise, it threatens that self with a confining absorption. Hence Tommo's prudery: "Out of the calico I had brought from the ship I made a dress for this lovely girl. In it she looked, I must confess, something like an opera dancer. The drapery of the latter damsel generally commences a little above the elbows, but my island's beauty began at the waist, and terminated sufficiently far above the ground to reveal the most bewitching ankles in the universe" (134–35). This odd coupling of salaciousness and inhibition, as in the remark on the slight cincture, visually epitomizes Tommo's indecision: as much is to be taken off as will satirize the overdressed West, but not so much as will undo repression entirely. For his part, Tommo always maintains a slight cincture, resisting various blandishments. He is for partial nudity, as he is for selective "decivilization."

As his sojourn is extended and his memory of oppression wanes, the delightfulness of Typee life is less frequently celebrated. Instead, he begins to see that even the slight cincture is torn away, that the Typees are also innocent of selfhood as he understands it. His growing horror and detestation accompany an ethnocentrically normative description of valley life that is remarkably coherent in its analysis of what is lacking in Typee thought. He observes that there is no such thing as a self there: the Typees do not understand personal identity as a freestanding entity that can assess the value of its participation in various moments of interest and desire and that can consequently conceive of itself as living a unified and internally teleological life. The history of a Typee's day, Tommo contends, is the history of a life. Without a free sense of his life's direction, the Typee's life is one long nap. Correspondingly, the culture has no history, either in a collective destination or a derivation from the past, which is embodied in the huge stone monuments that elicit Tommo's interest but to which the Typees are indifferent. Fish are eaten raw, so cooking does not differentiate the eater from the eaten. What little there is of native labor is sporadic, wastefully intense though brief, and collective, like the labor of bees in a hive, so self-interested work is ignored. Not only do the Typees worship idols, confining divinity to shape, but the idols are taken to be gods, rather than representations, and they are treated familiarly, even contemptuously. Typee heaven is a duplicate of the Typee valley, so Kory-Kory is in no hurry to get there. Leaders mingle with the led, from whom they are indistinguishable. Though this indifference to protocols of worship and prestige might have made good satire earlier in the book, it has become ominous: self, god, and political leader never separate into independence from their immediate context; the Typees are indifferent to abstraction and independent power *per se*, not just those forms of abstraction and independent power Tommo resented. Even their music is a kind of iterative, nonprogressive, unproductive chanting, and, though they are intrigued by melody in Tommo's songs, their most enthusiastic applause is reserved for the refrain.

Tommo comes to prefer a balked and dominated self to no self at all. Where he had quarreled with his own culture over his freedom to determine his own nature, he differs from the Typees in even having a sense of life as a unique, progressive whole. He is appalled and sickened by the thought that the Typees are indifferent to meaningful time itself, rather than just to the contemptible "progress of the Truth" preached by the missionaries. They are without story, and this nonnarratability infects Tommo's narration, provoking an entropic decline from suspenseful narration into disjointed observation. Though the sheer lazy chronicity of Typee life initially seems to be a good tonic for the corrupt teleology of colonialist "enlightenment," its indifference to Tommo's own vital plan nauseates him, at least in those increasingly rare moments when he can conjure enough sense of self to realize that identity is dissipating into isolated instants of sensation. Through the subtle influence of Typee lassitude, Tommo sees his own self-awareness relaxing into the incessant repetition of identical pleasures: "There are no roads of any kind in the valley—nothing but a labyrinth of footpaths twisting and turning among the thickets without end" (194). Though the Typees are *free to* do any number of things interdicted in America, they are not *free from* the entanglement of consciousness in the simplicity of here and now.

Vexed by this dissipation, Tommo begins to interrupt decayed narrative with ominous allusions to cannibalism and tattooing, using horror to induce disconnection and refocusing. Tommo glimpses first, shrunken heads, and then a skeleton in a box to which cling morsels passed over by sated feeders; and, on the old men in the Ti, the victory of gravity over flesh has pulled once distinct designs into repellent, shapeless groups of dull color. These disgusting visions secede from the surrounding chapters in order to re-collect and concentrate the self's proper *logos*.

Cannibalism whispers to Tommo that he is meat, that distinctive individuality is a self-consoling illusion, a reminder still more painful than the lesson of capitalism, for which one is at least animate meat—labor power. For Tommo, to eat something is to be its master, to reduce it to a quantity of material nourishment and thereby to accentuate one's transcendentality. To eat a man, however, is to acknowledge that one can play either part in this relation. Though the cannibal is momentarily supreme over his victim's subjectivity, his every bite tells him he may be eaten at a later date: as he eats, so he may be eaten; his throne at the apex of the foodchain is a provisional regime. One is only temporarily aloof from the circulation of calories: if eating establishes a difference from and supremacy over what is eaten, cannibalism confesses that the difference is not permanent or ontological, but only exists for the duration of the act and may be reversed in a moment.

This is a false understanding of cannibalism which, as Ishmael realizes, is less a response to hunger than a ritual ingestion of the antagonist's virtue and is therefore mindful of the individuality of the vanquished. The true difference between Tommo's and the Typees' views of cannibalism is that he considers individuality to be completely free of its vessel, and so concludes that to eat the body is to express contempt for the self: whereas they treat the body as a rich and necessary participant in the personality that is indissociably immured in its texture. Tommo never escapes his fear that he is being fattened, like Hansel and Gretel, and that cannibalism expresses only unrestrained hunger, "decivilization" rather than cultural difference.

Tommo's fear of radical inversion also lies behind his attitude toward tattooing, which shows him that the writer may be written upon. Tommo's act of writing about the Marquesans, like the missionary treatises, is an imposition of a shaping will onto the lives of others, and therefore an act of mastery, so being written upon would place the writer's self in the position of the victim. Made into a "human canvas," one is blank matter subject to another's will, and though the other inscribes rather than eats, the reversal is still repulsive: "I now felt convinced that in some luckless hour I should be disfigured in such a manner as never more to have the *face* to return to my countrymen, even should an opportunity offer" (219). Tattooed, his face would always say "Typee," the boundlessness of personal identity would be permanently sacrificed to a single mode of identity. This, of course, is tattooing's purpose: as a ritual practice, tattooing is an irreversible sign of the tribe's having stipulated, restricted, and directed the individuality of its members into a single channel: even if, like Queequeg, a member of the tribe wanders, he will remain tied to the self assigned to him. He can never be the anonymous stranger. Tattooing therefore represents an indelible and infinitely more penetrating determination of self by society than the various coercions Tommo has fled.

Cannibalism and tattooing are thus extreme versions of the lapse of self chronicled in the lazy narrative they interrupt. They usefully terrify Tommo with the thought that freedom as he understands it is among the Typees precarious and subject to reversal in a moment, that each individual is inescapably knower and known, eater and eaten, writer and written upon. In summoning loathing, Tommo attempts to suppress whatever part of his consciousness he imagines to correspond to the Typee way, denying it by dissociating himself from two unacceptable practices that are made to stand for the whole, struggling to reconstruct a difference that is absolute because grounded on being rather than on historical and material contingency.

At the very end, Tommo equivocates. Mow-Mow swims after the boat in which Tommo is escaping:

> Even at the moment I felt horror at the act I was about to commit; but it was no time for pity or compunction, and with a true aim, and exerting all my strength, I dashed the boat-hook at him. It struck him just below the throat, and forced him downwards. I had no time to repeat my blow, but I saw him rise to the surface in the wake of the boat, and never shall I forget the ferocious expression of his countenance (252).

Outwardly, escape requires that he strike the savage, who comes to the surface again; inwardly, escape requires that the memory of ferocity be stronger than pity for the savage, who will nonetheless surface in memory repeatedly. In this excruciating scene Tommo almost thinks of the grotesqueness of a mastery that requires denial, but he perceives no alternative, and the thought sinks with the savage. Though Tommo's horror thus successfully produces homesickness, the narrative ends not with home but with Tommo being picked up by a cruising whaler whose captain is shorthanded and happy for an able hand, ends, that is, with a restoration of the initial situation and its intrinsic condemnation of self to machine. Tommo is wholeheartedly gratified only once:

> We had left the beach early in the morning, and after an uninterrupted, though at times difficult and dangerous ascent, during which we had never once turned our faces to the sea, we found ourselves, about three hours before sunset, standing at the top of what seemed to be the highest land on the island, an immense overhanging cliff composed of basaltic rocks, hung round with parasitical plants. We must have been more than three thousand feet above the level of the sea, and the scenery viewed from this height was magnificent (40).

As if escaping Sodom, they do not look back, because pausing would risk being caught by the captain's searching eye. But once they are high enough to see without being seen—to be the subjects who compose the landscape rather than objects in a landscape composed by the eye of another—they stop. Tommo continues:

> The lonely bay of Nukuheva, dotted here and there with the black hulls of the vessels composing the French squadron, lay reposing at the base of a circular range of elevations, whose verdant sides, perforated with deep glens or diversified with smiling valleys, formed altogether the loveliest view I ever beheld, and were I to live a hundred years, I should never forget the feeling of admiration which I then experienced (40).

Tommo has attained the point from which a perfectly visible world emanates down: from here, he knows a whole world of his own composing that includes the power that had attempted to ingest or inscribe him. The descent to the Typee valley is yet to come, so the idyllized Eden of the imagination in which his self will be realized is not yet corrupted by actuality. He is lord not by the contingency of political entitlement but by imaginative, self-sufficient supremacy. This island's topography is an image of his desire gratified: from this apex, rock spokes slope to the sea; each valley, seen from the apex, is a rich possibility that culminates at the white beach that stretches between the ends of the spokes. Here, Tommo is a pure, boundless potentiality, distinct from its outcomes.

Such boundlessness is ritually constituted as anathema in the Typee world view. Though Tommo uses the taboos as testimony to the Typee's incoherence, there is a pattern. The taboos circumscribe things that do not fit into categories of classification: women prohibited from canoes, their menstruation a possible pollution of masculine martial implements; animals imported from outside the island; young men in the process of being tattooed, that is, in transition from boyhood to social manhood; Marnoo, an intertribal diplomat permitted to move from tribe to tribe because he is not a full member of any single tribe; and the alien Tommo himself. Tommo's inability to see the structure or symbolic logic of the taboo, his inability to see it as other than eccentric or bizarre, issues from his insistence on seeing Typee only as a negation of America, rather than as a separate culture with its specific rationality. Though his sentiments concerning Typee-as-negation oscillate, he never wavers in his deeper decision to see Typee *as* negation. This is not to fault Tommo for failing to be a Mauss or Levi-Strauss so much as to suggest that the discoveries of such thinkers reveal the not-seeing that consistently determines all of Tommo's inconsistencies. Understanding the function of taboo, one also understands that the real difference between the Typees and Tommo is that Tommo relishes a personal boundlessness because he feels oppressed by the categories with which his culture orders experience, whereas the Typees surround that which escapes ordering with the reverential suspicion of the taboo. Typee cognition incorporates an intense respect for the difference between the object and the representation that is made of it. Whereas Tommo sees escape from order as a relief, the Typees see it as a violation, a sacred threat to their slight hold on a mysterious universe.[5] The Typee world view is more distinctly ecological, but, though it is perhaps therefore culturally strong, it will nonetheless prove unable to respond effectively to the concentrated infusion of uncontained restless power represented by both the French frigates and Tommo.

As soon as Tommo begins his descent to Typee, his leg swells, a frightening malady that wanes and recurs regularly throughout his sojourn and restrains his flight. According to Ziff, this phlebitis signifies Tommo's inherent connection with America and his insuperable alienation from Typee.[6] However, it seems to me that, if the swelling is a symbol at all, it probably signifies his *attraction* to Typee, to that dim, half-conscious part of himself that holds him captive through captivation and has to be curbed with the repulsive visions of cannibalism and tattooing. This would be true if we accept the frequent observation that the swollen leg is a phallus, and so expresses an attraction to Typee by a part of Tommo's consciousness that is separate from his desire for supremacy. It would also be true if we accept Thomas P. Joswick's assertion that this immobilizing affliction signifies an autochthonic attachment to the life of one particular place.[7] The swollen leg speaks for a part of Tommo that does not equate identity with supremacy, the part willing to admit a world where the relation of subject to object is provisional and given to the interchange of reversal from moment to moment. Perhaps ultimately Tommo refuses Typee not because it happily welcomes the predicament of the real, but because it collectively performs acknowledgment of the predicament. If this were so, the refusal, for all of its intensity and finality, would nonetheless emit the odd glow of an unknown perception.

[5]See Claude Levi-Strauss, *The Savage Mind* (Chicago: Univ. of Chicago Press, 1966), esp. 53, 96–97, and his "Introduction a l'oeuvre de Marcel Mauss," in Mauss's *Sociologie et Anthropologie* (Paris: Presses universitaires de France, 1950).

[6]Larzer Ziff, *Literary Democracy*, 9.

[7]Thomas P. Joswick, "Typee: The Quest for Origin," *Criticism*, 17 (1975), 335–54 and Claude Levi-Strauss, *Structural Anthropology*, trans. Claire Jacobson and Brooke Grundfest Schoepf (New York: Basic Books, 1963).

Mardi:
Creating the Creative

Richard H. Brodhead

'If this book be meant as a pleasantry, the mirth has been oddly left out—if as an allegory, the key of the casket is "buried in ocean deep"—if as a romance, it fails from tediousness—if as a prose-poem, it is chargeable with puerility.' This is what the reviewer of *The Athenaeum* had to say about Melville's *Mardi* and his comments no doubt express the views of many intelligent readers, both at the time of the book's appearance and since. Even readers who are enthusiastic about *Mardi* tend to hedge their praise with reservations—Melville's French admirer Philarète Chasles, who judged it 'un des plus singuliers livres qui aient paru depuis long-temps sur la face du globe', also called it 'oeuvre inouie, digne d'un Rabelais sans gaieté, d'un Cervantes sans grace, d'un Voltaire sans goût'; Hawthorne wrote: ' "Mardi" is a rich book, with depths here and there that compel a man to swim for his life. It is so good that one scarcely pardons the writer for not having brooded long over it, so as to make it a great deal better.'

Every unkind thing that has been said about *Mardi* is more or less true. It is the loosest and baggiest of prose monsters, a book that changes direction freely on its way it knows not where, its ramblings held together only by the flimsy framework of a quest for an insubstantial maiden that would itself be completely forgotten if a boatload of phantom damsels did not appear every eighty pages or so to pelt the quester with symbolic flowers. The style of the book, with its addiction to bombast and the more mechanical sorts of poetic effects, is usually something to be endured, not enjoyed. Its metaphysical soarings, in which philosophical commonplaces are delivered as if they were newly discovered truths, are often enough to make a lover of Melville the deep diver blush. But the important thing is not that *Mardi* has flaws but that it has ones of such an order. The chaos of its narrative is not the petty fault of an author who has tried to make a work in a conventional form but failed for lack of skill, but the massive one of an author who has tried to construct a work in a radically new way. Similarly its more embarrassing passages of poetry and philosophy are products not of a simple stylistic or intellectual

From *New Perspectives on Melville*, edited by Faith Pullin. Copyright © 1978 by Edinburgh University Press.

deficiency—the author of *Mardi* is obviously equipped to do many sorts of things well—but of the fact that Melville is straining after effects that are so grand in them, and so far beyond what he has the powers to achieve. What is remarkable about *Mardi* is not its specific virtues or defects but the boldness of its endeavour. Where did Melville find the confidence to depart so completely not just from his own earlier works but from any easily recognizable formal model? How could he have dared to go on working at a project that required him to live so far beyond his artistic means? Melville never was a cowardly author, but the writing of *Mardi* was little less than an exercise in sheer audacity.

As Merrell Davis has demonstrated, many of *Mardi's* peculiarities are results of the peculiar way in which it was written. Melville's letters show that after finishing *Omoo* he planned a third work that would continue the story of his South Seas adventures where *Omoo* left off. But a report from his publisher on the sales of his books discouraged him from attempting another work in the same format. This coincided with an event of the first importance in Melville's inner life, an explosion of consciousness touched off by his discovery of great literary works of the past (in early 1848 he began reading Rabelais, Montaigne, Sir Thomas Browne, and Coleridge, among others) and by what he later called the 'burst[ing] out in himself' of a 'bottomless spring of original thought.' The combination of pressure from without and the activation of a powerful creative energy within him led to a series of changes in the plan of the book he was at work on. A letter to his English publisher, John Murray, on 1 January 1848, claims that 'the book now in hand, clothes the whole subject in new attractions & combines in one cluster all that is romantic, whimsical & poetic in Polynusia'. He is feeling his way toward a new mode of composition, one less tied to documentary fact and actual experience, but he has not yet made a complete break with his earlier works—'It is yet a continuous narrative', he hastens to add. But when he writes to Murray again, on 25 March, this break has been effected.

> I believe that a letter I wrote you some time ago—I think my last but one—gave you to understand, or implied, that the work I then had in view was a bona-vide narrative of my adventures in the Pacific, continued from 'Omoo'—My object in now writing you—I should have done so ere this—is to inform you of a change in my determinations. To be blunt: the work I shall next publish will (be) in downright earnest [be] a 'Romance of Polynisian Adventure'.

Melville goes on to explain here, as he does in the preface to *Mardi*, that his chief motive for writing such a work is to show readers who doubted the authenticity of *Typee* and *Omoo* that 'a *real* romance of mine . . . is made of different stuff altogether'. But another inducement to change his plans, he continues, is that Polynesia furnishes a rich poetic material

> which to bring out suitably, required only that play of freedom & invention accorded only to the Romancer & poet.—However, I thought, that I would

postpone trying my hand at any thing fanciful of this sort, till some future day: tho'
at times when in the mood I threw off occasional sketches applicable to such a
work.—Well: proceeding in my narrative of *facts* I began to feel an incurible
distaste for the same; & a longing to plume my pinions for a flight, & felt irked,
cramped & fettered by plodding along with dull common places,—So suddenly
standing [abandoning?] the thing alltogether, I went to work heart & soul at a
romance which is now in fair progress, since I had worked at it under an earnest
ardor.—Shout not, nor exclaim 'Pshaw! Puh!'—My romance I assure you is no dish
water nor its model borrowed from the Circulating Library. It is something new I
assure you, & original if nothing more. But I can give you no adequate idea, of it.
You must see it for yourself.—Only forbear to prejudge it.—It opens like a true
narrative—like 'Omoo' for example, on ship board—& the romance & poetry of
the thing thence grow continually, till it becomes a story wild enough I assure you
& with a meaning too.

This letter, surely one of the most extraordinary ever sent by a young
author to an established publisher, is a perfect expression of the audacity that
brought *Mardi* into being. I got tired of what I was doing, Melville tells
Murray, so I decided to do something else (without, of course, bothering to
start the book over); and if you don't think that's a proper way to compose a
book, you're wrong—'My *instinct* is to out with the Romance, & let me say
that instincts are prophetic, & better than acquired wisdom—which alludes
remotely to your experience in literature as an eminent publisher'. As
Melville tells the story, having started writing a book like his earlier ones, he
begins to feel the stirring of an urge that cannot find expression in that form.
As he continues writing this urge becomes stronger and stronger until it
begins to generate fragments of a second work, different in kind, alongside
the first. Finally it becomes so imperious that he can no longer resist it or
channel it off; at this point he discards his initial plans and allows this urge to
take over the writing of his book. The letter that chronicles this usurpation
marks a crucial turning point in Melville's career, the moment at which he
starts conceiving of his works not as a record of preexisting experience—a
narrative of *facts*—but as a creative imaginative activity. His letter suggests
that in its change of design *Mardi* itself acts out this shift, that as one sort of
book displaces another in it it bursts the fetters of conventional form ('true
narrative') and a reportorial tie to reality ('dull common place'), freeing the
imagination to soar into realms of beauty and strangeness.

Melville clearly feels that to be properly judged *Mardi* needs to be taken
on its own terms, seen as making its own formal model rather than imitating
an already available one, and that it needs to be read as a metamorphosis, a
growth through radical changes of state. I am interested in trying to understand the strange thing that *Mardi* is, and also what it means for Melville to
have undertaken such a work at this stage in his career; and it seems to me
that Melville's directions to Murray point to the way in which the book should
be approached. This is to pursue it through its changes—not to locate its
chapters and sequences in relation to an externally established chronology,

but to discover from within the book what sort of form it proposes for itself, and how this form evolves as the book unfolds.

As Melville's letters lead us to expect, the opening of *Mardi* does bear a direct resemblance to *Typee* and *Omoo*. Here again a sailor-narrator tells how he came to jump ship, with a companion, in search of adventure. He provides several reasons for his act, making sure that it seems plausibly motivated; he also provides a good deal of circumstantial information about nautical matters, taking care to locate his tale in a world that is solidly documented, if unfamiliar to us. But really *Mardi* is something quite different from *Typee* or *Omoo*, and it must be stressed that it is so from the first. While on watch in the masthead in the first chapter the narrator broods on the islands that lie westward in the Pacific, 'loosely laid down upon the charts, and invested with all the charms of dream-land', and that he will leave behind if he sails northward on the *Arcturion*.

> I cast my eyes downward to the brown planks of the dull, plodding ship, silent from stem to stern; then abroad.
> In the distance what visions were spread! The entire western horizon high piled with gold and crimson clouds; airy arches, domes, and minarets; as if the yellow, Moorish sun were setting behind some vast Alhambra. Vistas seemed leading to worlds beyond. To and fro, and all over the towers of this Nineveh in the sky, flew troops of birds. Watching them long, one crossed my sight, flew through a low arch, and was lost to view. My spirit must have sailed in with it; for directly, as in a trance, came upon me the cadence of mild billows laving a beach of shells, the waving of boughs, and the voices of maidens, and the lulled beatings of my own dissolved heart, all blended together.

Shipboard life is a plodding affair, its very tedium heightening the lure for the narrator of what Ishmael calls the wonder world. Although he begins by thinking of this fascinating alternative in terms of actual Pacific islands, what attracts him quickly changes from an exotic location in the real geographical world to a vista in a world beyond, and from a place to be reached by physical travel to a state to be attained through the heightening of desire, ecstatic transformations of consciousness, and the flight of the visionary spirit. The narrator shares Melville's aversion to dull commonplaces; his adventure, like his creator's, defines itself as an imaginative flight into a romance world of expanded possibility.

What follows from this opening is a voyage not to strange lands but into strangeness itself. The narrative mode of *Mardi*'s opening phase has less in common with that of *Typee* than with that of Edgar Allan Poe's *Narrative of A. Gordon Pym*, which uses the format of the nautical adventure story to lead the reader on a magical mystery tour. The narrator's jumping ship, like Pym's running away from home, is presented not just as a rejection of a settled way of life but as a rejection of ordinary reality. His desertion is not just a lark but a knowing act of 'moral dereliction' that is also an act of suicide, leaving him feeling like 'his own ghost unlawfully tenanting a defunct carcass'; like Pym denying his identity to his grandfather and descending into the coffin-like enclosure in the ship's hold, this narrator's adventure begins with a conscious rejection of the moral obligations of ordinary life and a willed dying to his own ordinary self. The chapters that follow, describing life on the ocean in an open boat and the sense of immobility and unreality induced by the calm, do not function simply as accounts of actual experience; like Pym's minute dissection of his feelings in the wildly accelerating boat or in the dark confinement of the hold, these are records of an extreme dislocation in the experience of space and time, a dislocation that is itself one of these characters' means for breaking out of ordinary reality. Similarly the chapters on sharks, swordfish, and marine phosphorescence are not merely informative; like Pym's discussions of the Galapagos turtle or the nests of penguins, they evoke a vision of nature as full of strange and alien forms. As nature becomes more marvellous in these books, marvels become more natural—the ship *Parki* in *Mardi*, like the ship of death in *Pym*, is experienced as a phantom craft; Samoa, like Dirk Peters, looks like a hitherto unknown form of human life.

The same patterns govern the actions of these books on their progress into strangeness. One of these patterns is the repeated overthrow of figures of authority. The narrator of *Mardi* gains through desertion the freedom from his captain's control that Pym gains through a mutinous rising of the crew of the *Grampus*. The massacre of the officers of the *Parki* by savages who have cunningly concealed their diabolical malice exactly repeats the fate of the captain and crew of Poe's ship *Jane Guy*. Another is a pattern of violation of taboos and sacred interdicts. *Mardi* has nothing to match the cannibal episode in *Pym*, but its narrator's most pronounced trait is his urge to pry into what he has been warned away from. These two patterns come together in *Mardi* when, after the *Parki* episode, the narrator murders the priest and father Aleema, and, having been told 'that it would be profanation', pierces the tent to seize the sacred maiden Yillah. In both books the violation of taboos and the destruction of authorities are the means by which the adventurer breaks into forbidden territory. The massacre of the crew of the *Jane Guy* and his disregard of the natives' dread of its sacredness bring Pym closer to the unutterable experience enshrouded by the Pole's white veil. By the same logic the conjunction of murder, sexual penetration, and profanation committed by the narrator of *Mardi* has as its immediate consequence the opening up before him of Mardi, the world beyond for which he sought.

The list of similarities between *Mardi* and the *Narrative of A. Gordon Pym* could be greatly extended, but these few examples suggest how like the books are in their procedures. What is important about this is not so much that it reveals particular debts on Melville's part as that it demonstrates what kind of a book Melville is writing in *Mardi*'s first fifty chapters—like Poe, he is using the form of the adventure narrative to conduct an exploration into other modes of reality. But, interestingly, when his book comes upon the islands of Mardi this seems to be as much a moment of discovery for the author as it is for his hero. The archipelago spreads before him a whole world of fictional possibilities, and at first he does not seem certain what he is going to do with them. He keeps alluding to Jarl, Samoa, and Yillah as if he thinks that his story's way might lie in continuing his narrator's earlier adventures; meanwhile he begins staging episodes on the island of Oro, and as it were testing what he can make of it. All at once he seems to see how he can go about exploiting Mardi in his book, and at this point he modifies his narrative in a drastic way. Samoa and Jarl become effectively invisible; Yillah vanishes, leaving the narrator to pursue her just half-heartedly enough to provide a pretext for a voyage; King Media, the historian Mohi, the philosopher Babbalanja, and the poet Yoomy join him for a tour through Mardi; then the narrator himself recedes, leaving the book to carry on not as the record of his adventures and speech but as a freewheeling island-hopping symposium.

The section of *Mardi* that follows takes as its model the anatomy form that Melville would have been familiar with in Swift and Rabelais. As in the third book of *Gulliver's Travels* or the fourth book of *Pantagruel*, Melville's island voyaging permits him to people a world with shapes of his own invention. Some of these mirror features of the actual world more or less directly, as Pimminee reflects social affectation, or Maramma the collective blindness of institutional religion. Others seem completely unreal, wildly imaginative, until, as in a caricature, we recognize in their grotesque distortion a previously concealed feature of reality: the bloody war games through which the lords Hello and Piko maintain the population of Diranda in equilibrium thus bring into focus the nightmare of human destructiveness unleashed by a cynically calculated appeal to abstract values. But although the island voyage enables Melville to mirror actuality and to mock the lighter and graver follies of human behaviour, satire is only one ingredient of this part of the book, not the controlling intention. In the imagining of these islands the desire to expose specific abuses is subservient to the free play of fantastic invention. In any case the islands are surrounded by a sea of talk, insets in a never-adjourning colloquy that passes freely from poetic recitations to nonsense to philosophical speculations to celebrations of food and drink.

As Melville closes his Poe and opens his Rabelais the kind of book he is writing undergoes a radical shift. But it is also worth noting that the metaphysical adventure narrative in the manner of Poe and the Rabelaisian anatomy have similarities as narrative models. They are, thus, both episodic in structure. In the early parts of *Mardi* as in *Pym* ships appear out of nowhere and then vanish again, and the narrator goes through experiences which, although they are vividly real while they last, disappear without a trace when they are ended. The sequences of action simply succeed one another, without being caused by what came before them and without causing what comes after. The essence of organization of the anatomy, whether we see it in *Mardi* or in *Gargantua and Pantagruel* or in *The Tale of a Tub* or in *Tristram Shandy*, lies in the weakness of its narrative line, its failure to give the book's ramblings the coherence of motion directed to an end. Each island in Mardi is by definition a separate occasion for Melville, and each reopening of discussion offers him a chance to pursue a new topic. The result is that in both parts of his narrative Melville is remarkably free to project an imaginative possibility, toy with it, develop it further if he likes, and then drop it when he is tired of it, going on to project another without having to consult the requirements of an overall plan.

Not only do they emphasize the independence of parts over the coherence of a cumulative design; both of the forms Melville is working with also permit major structural modifications to be made while they go along. One of the most striking resemblances between *Mardi* and the *Narrative of A. Gordon Pym* is that in both of them characters and scenes that are distinctly defined at one moment undergo dreamlike metamorphoses at the next. In both books, for example, it is impossible to make the narrator compose into a consistent personality as, from chapter to chapter, he exhibits not only totally different amounts of knowledge and sensitivity but even totally different traits of character. This instability means that, while ostensibly pursuing the story of someone's adventures, the books actually keep revising the nature of their adventure—what is a dream voyage into mental darkness at one point becomes a white imperialist's voyage among primitive peoples at another, and so on. The anatomy form, in addition to encouraging frequent modulations of mode, also allows Melville to define and redefine the terms of his action while in the middle of it—it permits him thus to turn the visit to Mardi's islands into a tour of the contemporary social world, and then to continue it as such for twenty-five chapters, without violating the logic of the book. Both of the genres Melville employs in *Mardi* maximize the author's on-going freedom within his projected form. They require nothing of him but that he improvise, that he keep making his book up as it goes along.

After he has pursued his voyage through the countries of Europe and the regions of the United States Melville again seems uncertain what he is going to do next. At first he solves his dilemma simply by carrying on with his device, extending his tour through Asia, Africa, and the Middle East. But the tour is yielding rapidly diminishing returns, and it is clear from its accelerated pace that Melville has little interest in its continuation. Then he sees another way to solve his problem. He simply puts his device aside and steps forward from behind his book's action, addressing us now in his own voice:

> Oh, reader, list! I've chartless voyaged. With compass and the lead, we had not found these Mardian Isles. Those who boldly launch, cast off all cables. . . . Hug the shore, naught new is seen; and 'Land ho!' at last was sung, when a new world was sought.

What appears to happen here is that the breakdown of his narrative device precipitates a moment of genuine self-recognition for Melville. He begins with what sounds like an explanation specifically of his present predicament—

I don't know where I'm going, I've been writing without a plan; his blustering invocations of New World explorers sound like pieces of bravado, attempts to present his directionlessness as a sign of courage. But having opened the subject, he now goes on to define more and more precisely how this book came to be written, and what it might mean to have written a book in this way.

> And though essaying but a sportive sail, I was driven from my course, by a blast resistless; and ill-provided, young, and bowed to the brunt of things before my prime, still fly before the gale;—hard have I striven to keep stout heart.
>
> And if it harder be, than e'er before, to find new climes, when now our seas have oft been circled by ten thousand prows,—much more the glory!
>
> But this new world here sought, is stranger far than his, who stretched his vans from Palos. It is the world of mind; wherein the wanderer may gaze round, with more of wonder than Balboa's band roving through the golden Aztec glades.
>
> But fiery yearnings their own phantom-future make, and deem it present. So, if after all these fearful, fainting trances, the verdict be, the golden haven was not gained;—yet, in bold quest thereof, better to sink in boundless deeps, than float on vulgar shoals; and give me, ye gods, an utter wreck, if wreck I do.

Here Melville brings to consciousness what he has been doing in writing *Mardi*, and as he does so he redefines his book from within one more time. He comes to see that its true action is not his characters' adventures but his own creative process: that its real voyage is the imaginative one he has undertaken in conceiving *Mardi*, that the real object of its quest is nothing his characters seek but the mental world he himself discloses through the act of creating his book. His metaphors of exploration lose their initial defensiveness and develop into a fully formed aesthetic of adventure, an aesthetic that validates his audacity in writing *Mardi* as the boldness necessary for new discovery, and that enables him to recognize the possibility of the book's failure and to accept it as proof that its attempt was bold enough.

After 'Sailing On' Melville continues with his symposium-cruise, and at the end of the book he even reaches back to pick up the thread of the narrator's progress through profanation into strange new worlds. But it is hard not to feel that *Mardi* reaches its real culmination in this chapter and the meditations that follow from it. Subsequent discussions are increasingly preoccupied with what Media calls 'the metaphysics of genius', and in Babbalanja's discourse on the poet Lombardo in chapter 180 *Mardi* renews its consideration of itself as its author's creation. The author who alluded to a blast resistless that led him prematurely to attempt such a work becomes even more candidly confessional here, taking us behind the curtain to reveal the financial and family pressures that are driving him to finish his book, and sharing what he has learned about the genesis of works of art and the experience of inspiration in composing it. He also formulates more clearly what the writing of *Mardi* signifies. Babbalanja tells King Abrazza:

> When Lombardo set about his work, he knew not what it would become. He did

not build himself in with plans; he wrote right on; and so doing, got deeper and deeper into himself; and like a resolute traveler, plunging through baffling woods, at last was rewarded for his toils. 'In good time,' saith he, in his autobiography, 'I came out into a serene, sunny, ravishing region; full of sweet scents, singing birds, wild plaints, roguish laughs, prophetic voices. Here we are at last, then,' he cried; 'I have created the creative'.

Where in 'Sailing On' he implied that there is some connection between chartless voyaging and coming upon new worlds of mind, Melville sees much more clearly here how writing and discovery are linked, and he is able to specify much more precisely what the 'world of mind' consists of. Writing spontaneously and without plan is the means by which Lombardo blazes a trail into the wilderness of his mind until, at its centre, he finds a paradise within. This paradise is not so much a place as a deep source of generative mental energy; and it is not something already existing yet concealed but something that needs to be brought into being. Through the act of writing, thus, Lombardo creates the creative.

In this chapter the novel that unfolded without direction and without a governing intention finds out where it was headed and why it followed the course it did. The novel that reveled in improvisation for five hundred pages discovers what improvisation is for—discovers that it is through the exercise of its freedom and invention, its unconstrained play of conception and articulation, that the creative imagination brings itself into being. Having, by means of it, created the creative, Lombardo can discard his first writing and begin a work of greatness. In the images of the chapter it is the trash that needed to be removed from the mine for the ore of genius to be reached, the callow form that the eagle had to pass through on its way to attaining maturity and power. Melville is similarly detached from his own writing in *Mardi*. Having lavished his inventive energy on them he shows no further interest in the book's individual episodes. He is the first to admit that it has deep flaws— Hawthorne's assessment of *Mardi*, for instance, echoes Melville's own, made in the book itself; ' "It has faults—all mine; its merits all its own;—but I can toil no longer. . . . My canvas was small," said [Lombardo]; "crowded out were hosts of things that came last. But Fate is in it" '. What sustains his equanimity in the face of its faults is the fact that the aim implicit in the book is not the production of the perfect work Hawthorne has in mind. What he intends to achieve in writing it is not really to be understood at the level of the work itself at all. If Lombardo expresses Melville's thoughts, as there is every reason to assume he does, the value of *Mardi* for its author lies not in what it is but in what his composition of it could bring into being—his own mature creative self.

Melville consistently thinks of *Mardi* in terms of a future attainment that it points toward. Shortly after finishing it he writes to Evert Duyckinck:

Would that a man could do something & then say—It is finished.—not that one

thing only, but all others—that he has reached his uttermost, & can never exceed
it. But live & push—tho' we put one leg forward ten miles—it's no reason the
other must lag behind—no, *that* must again distance the other. . . .

The writing of *Mardi* is a step; even though he longs for it to be a final
achievement he recognizes that it is truly only a stage in the ongoing process
of realizing his creative potential. In a letter to *Mardi*'s English publisher,
Richard Bentley, Melville speaks of the book in terms of germination and
maturing: 'you know perhaps that there are goodly harvests which ripen late,
especially when the grain is remarkably strong'. In another letter to Duyckinck he speaks of it in terms of education: 'I admit that I learn by experience
& not by divine intuitions. Had I not written & published 'Mardi', in all
likelihood, I would not be as wise as I am now, or may be.' We know, as
Melville at this point could not, what the author of *Mardi* would go on to
achieve. Since he himself conceives of it as pointing forward we might now
look back at *Mardi* from Melville's later works, and try to discern what
relation it actually has to what comes after it.

In terms of his career as a whole perhaps the most striking thing about
Mardi is the emergence in it of the Melville who compulsively engages in
ontological heroics. In *Mardi* Melville meets metaphysics and succumbs to its
charms. The symposium format enables him to stage his first comedy of
thought, to play with intellectual puzzles and explore the paradoxes of
intellectual positions. The figure of Babbalanja embodies for the first time in
Melville's fiction an obsession with cosmic riddles and a resolution to uncover
'that which is beneath the seeming'. Certainly one of the main functions of the
anatomy form that he adopts midway through the book is that it permits him
to speculate, with varying degrees of seriousness, on questions like what man
is, what truth is, and what happens after death.

What Melville has to say about the problem of the universe in *Mardi* is
often trite and naive. . . . But even at their feeblest *Mardi*'s philosophical
excursions are not without importance. In them Melville is appropriating a
kingdom of thought. If he repeats ideas without having assimilated them,
nevertheless *by* repeating them he begins to possess them, to make them his
own. Thus as his writing proceeds his thought grows in depth. He keeps
returning to subjects like the relation of belief to truth, considering it once in
terms of religious belief, another time in terms of storytelling, another time in
terms of our knowledge of the physical world—he never stops to treat it
systematically, but with each return to it he extends the range of its implications. As he goes along ideas seem to be pressing up into his mind, making
themselves felt in a number of places until finally, by grasping and articulating
them, he brings them fully to the surface. Thus he discusses at one point how
the alternating domination of his psyche by 'contrary impulses, over which he
had not the faintest control' makes King Peepi incapable of 'moral obligation
to virtue'; at another Babbalanja broaches a psychological theory based on
demonic possession; at another the narrator, rapt in an ecstasy of inspiration,

describes his mastery by 'this Dionysius that rides me'. All of these are partial versions of a notion that finally gets fully explored in chapter 143, where, discoursing on 'the incomprehensible stranger in me', Babbalanja develops the idea that an instinctive, involuntary energy lies beneath the conscious rational self, governing and impelling it—a pioneering expression of an idea Melville can then take further in *Moby-Dick* and *Pierre*.

There is a similarly teasing likeness between the images of *Mardi* and those of Melville's later books. . . . This is Melville's description of Aleema:

> The old priest, like a scroll of old parchment, covered all over with hieroglyphical devices, harder to interpret, I'll warrant, than any old Sanscrit manuscript. And upon his broad brow, deep-graven in wrinkles, were characters still more mysterious, which no Champollion nor gipsy could have deciphered.

It is impossible to read this without thinking of Queequeg's tattooing, those 'hieroglyphical marks' in which a departed seer 'had written out on his body a complete theory of the heavens and the earth, and a mystical treatise on the art of attaining truth . . . but whose mysteries not even himself could read, though his own live heart beat against them'. It is echoed even more precisely by the end of the chapter 'The Prairie' in *Moby-Dick*:

> Champollion deciphered the wrinkled granite hieroglyphics. But there is no Champollion to decipher the Egypt of every man's and every being's face. Physiognomy, like every other human science, is but a passing fable. If then, Sir William Jones, who read in thirty languages, could not read the simplest peasant's face in its profounder and more subtle meanings, how may unlettered Ishmael hope to read the awful Chaldee of the Sperm Whale's brow? I but put that brow before you. Read it if you can.

To put it alongside these passages from *Moby-Dick* is to see how undeveloped Melville's image is in *Mardi*. He has got so far as to link Polynesian tattooing, wrinkles, hieroglyphics, and the deciphering achievements of Champollion and Sir William Jones, but he appears unaware of the symbolic content the resultant image could carry—the undecipherable hieroglyph has yet to become his preferred figure for a cosmic mystery that invites but perpetually thwarts the human effort to solve it. Describing a calm at sea in chapter 16 of *Mardi* Melville images a process by which the totality of elements fuse with one another to produce a nothingness, a 'blank', a 'vacuum', 'colorless', 'gray chaos in conception'. We are on the verge, here, of *Moby-Dick*'s 'colorless, all-color of atheism from which we shrink'; all that is missing is a perception of the metaphysical condition such a fusion could symbolize. With these images as with his philosophical throwaways Melville produces out of nowhere something that will be saturated with significance in his future work, but that has yet to acquire that significance.

How is it that 'The Prairie' manages so to intensify and extend the implications of the figure through which Aleema's brow is described in *Mardi*? Certainly part of the answer lies in Ishmael's (and the Melville of *Moby-*

Dick's) universalizing habit of mind. While *Mardi* keeps focusing on Aleema's face Ishmael moves from the Whale's brow to 'every being's face', and from the face physically understood to the face 'in its profounder and more subtle meanings'. But this difference is itself a function of the different ways in which they handle figurative language. Melville's prose in *Mardi* keeps the image and the reality it describes rigidly separate. It isolates the precise points (like, harder, more) at which comparisons between the face and a scroll of mysterious writing are being established. Further, it establishes comparisons only between features the two already share—the face's lines already are hieroglyphical devices; it is not the analogy of the scroll that makes them so. In the passage from *Moby-Dick*, by contrast, analogy becomes a dynamic process, and a process of genuine transfiguration. Features associated with faces and features associated with writing continue to interfuse with one another. The result of this fusion is that each of these normally separate areas of experience provides a new idiom in which the other may be expressed (wrinkled granite hieroglyphics, the Egypt of the face, the awful Chaldee of the brow) and a new set of terms in which the other may be understood— here legibility or illegibility is not a property already possessed by the face but one it acquires by virtue of being conceived of in terms of language. The essential difference between the two passages is that in the one from *Moby-Dick* Melville commits himself to metaphor, allowing the play of figuration to generate meaning as it evolves.

Mardi is full of restricted images, images that have not undergone such a genuinely metaphorical development. King Uhia, a moody aspirer who lunges through the present toward future achievements and who feels intolerably confined by the limits reality imposes on his will, clearly prefigures Captain Ahab, as his perception of the human cost of his aspiration—'Here am I vexed and tormented by ambition; no peace night nor day; my temples chafed sore by this cursed crown that I wear'—looks forward to Ahab's in 'Sunset' and 'The Symphony'. But only when the crown and the experience of wearing it are imagined in an expanding series of particularized details, details that are allowed to stand for ambition's self-inflicted pain, will Uhia's lament open out into Ahab's 'Is, then, the crown too heavy that I wear? . . . 'Tis iron—that I know—not gold. 'Tis split, too—that I feel; the jagged edge galls me so, my brain seems to beat against the solid metal'. The ending of 'Sailing On'—'yet, in bold quest thereof, better to sink in boundless deeps, than float on vulgar shoals'—links pressing off into the ocean with heroic intellectual questing as Melville will again in 'The Lee Shore', and it even establishes the rhythms of 'The Lee Shore's' prose—'so, better is it to perish in that howling infinite, than be ingloriously dashed upon the lee, even if that were safety!' The difference is not that 'The Lee Shore' celebrates such questing more ardently than 'Sailing On' but that, by allowing the opposition of sea and shore to develop itself ('the port is pitiful; in the port is safety, comfort, hearthstone . . .') and by allowing the figures thus generated to define the opposition between independence and spiritual timidity, it gives such questing an increasingly rich and precise content. . . .

So many passages in the later books resemble *Mardi* in some way as to suggest that Melville is rewriting rather than writing. As he comes to realize in it, the true significance of *Mardi* is that it is the first draft of all his subsequent works. Not a draft in the sense that it consciously undertakes to produce a rough version of a work whose subject or form is defined, however vaguely, in advance—as we have seen, Melville refuses to build himself in with plans, asserting his right to improvise without constraint. Rather, it is a draft in the sense that, without attempting to foresee what it is a preparation for, it nevertheless gives initial formulation to the work that comes after it— without being directed toward any end, Melville's improvisational act generates themes, thoughts, characters, images, narrative forms, and stylistic features out of which other creations can then be made. In giving him the particular materials and skills that their composition required, and more generally in making him capable of conceiving and expressing them, the writing of *Mardi* made Melville the author who could then go on to write *Moby-Dick, Pierre,* and *The Confidence-Man.* To use Keats's words, *Mardi* is the form in which the Genius of Poetry in Melville worked out its own salvation. Its spirited performance is the necessary prelude to the mature career of an author who always gained in power by exercising his power—who grew imaginative by exerting his invention, who grew profound by diving after deep thoughts, and who grew creative by engaging in the act of creation. . . .

White-Jacket:
Authors and
Audiences

Wai-chee S. Dimock

In a letter to Judge Lemuel Shaw in 1849, Melville made the well-known disparaging remark about two books he had just completed, *Redburn* and *White-Jacket*: "But no reputation that is gratifying to me, can possibly be achieved by either of these books. They are two *jobs*, which I have done for money—being forced to it, as other men are to sawing wood."[1] The following year, writing to Richard Henry Dana, Jr., Melville similarly complained that he had written "these books of mine almost entirely for 'lucre'—by the job, as a woodsawyer saws wood" (*Letters*, p. 106). These statements deserve our attention because they reveal a less exalted but no less important side of Melville: Melville as a professional writer, a disgruntled professional writer who writes not for pleasure but for a living. William Charvat has long urged us to recognize not only the literary artist but also the professional writer behind works of literature.[2] In the case of Melville this recognition is especially pertinent, since he himself was outspoken about it. Even though Melville defended *White-Jacket* on one occasion and in 1849 asked Dana to defend it also (*Letters*, p. 93), the circumstances of professional authorship made him openly disdainful of his book. One wonders whether this disdain is woven into the text, whether it is a shaping force behind the composition. Certainly, between the book's lofty humanitarian rhetoric and the lowly function ascribed to it there is a marked discrepancy which raises many questions about Melville's intentions. As I see it, *White-Jacket* is a deeply divided book,

[1]Melville to Shaw, 6 Oct. 1849, in *The Letters of Herman Melville*, ed. Merrell R. Davis and William H. Gilman (New Haven: Yale Univ. Press, 1960), p. 91; hereafter referred to in the text as *Letters*.

[2]This is a persistent concern behind Charvat's works. For an explicit statement, see, for example, the introduction in *The Profession of Authorship in America, 1800–1870: The Papers of William Charvat*, ed. Matthew J. Bruccoli (Columbus: Ohio State Univ. Press, 1968), p. 3.

divided not only in mood, aim, and manner of narration but, most fundamentally, in the implied relation between author and reader.[3]

At first glance *White-Jacket* reveals nothing but goodwill and camaraderie. Melville is careful to establish a genial partnership from the outset, and the opening sentence proceeds on precisely this understanding. "It was not a *very* white jacket, but white enough, in all conscience, as the sequel will show."[4] The declaration is imperious, but also implicitly sociable, for it already presupposes an audience—one that is kindly disposed and receptive. Melville talks about the jacket with great familiarity and a kind of chummy gruffness, as if he were addressing a circle of seasoned confidants accustomed to his impulsive moods.

The curt, offhand opening of *White-Jacket*, and the brief "Note" to the American edition, differ quite markedly from the careful introductions that characterize the genre. Most sea authors find it advisable to dilate on their past history, their motives for going to sea, and their reasons for writing a book. Among the identified sources for *White-Jacket*, Samuel Leech's *Thirty Years from Home* contains no less than a preface, testimonials from several ministers, and finally, an entire first chapter devoted to the author's early life. Implicit in these laborious beginnings is the assumption that the reader is as yet unacquainted, indifferent, and that he needs to be informed, persuaded, won over. In *White-Jacket*, however, all such formalities are dispensed with. From the very first the audience is assumed to be on good terms with Melville, a party to his personal complaints, and the unceremonious opening sentence actually serves as a gesture of fraternity. It generates a congenial climate, projects a mutual enterprise, and both solicits and rhetorically creates a sympathetic audience.

Comradeship is easily the dominant mode of intercourse between author and reader in *White-Jacket*. Certainly it is the informing spirit behind the well-known antiflogging chapters. Here, the polemical voice addresses the reader directly from the text, hortatory and sermonlike, without any mediation or any imposition of distance. It is an unimpeded discourse, unimpeded by any reserve on the part of the speaker or by any recognition of difference between the advocate and his audience. Melville the reformer is confident and relentless because presumably there exists a bond of shared sentiments and beliefs between him and his readers which gives him the license to speak out. . . .

3By "reader" I am referring to the implied or internalized reader in *White-Jacket*, the reader as conceived by Melville. Distinct from the implied reader, but also intimately related, is the actual historical audience, who will be referred to as Melville's *contemporary* readers.

4*White-Jacket; or, The World in a Man-of-War*, ed. Harrison Hayford, Hershel Parker, and G. Thomas Tanselle, Vol. 5 of *The Writings of Herman Melville*, Northwestern-Newberry Edition (Evanston and Chicago: Northwestern Univ. Press and Newberry Library, 1970), p. 3. Subsequent references to this work appear in the text.

Given the popular appeal of Melville's antiflogging passages, it is not surprising that these are the passages in which the relation between author and reader is most genial, least problematic, and in which the discourse takes on the confidence and directness of a speech delivered to kindred minds in a common cause. Melville makes no bones about where he stands. In his impassioned plea he bares his soul, as it were, to his readers. Surprisingly, a few months after completing *White-Jacket*, Melville confided to Evert Duyckinck: "What a madness & anguish it is, that an author can never—under no conceivable circumstances—be at all frank with his readers" (*Letters*, p. 96). And yet he had also declared that in writing *White-Jacket*, "I have not repressed myself much" (*Letters*, p. 92). When we put together Melville's comments on *White-Jacket*, we find, not a single judgment, but a welter of conflicting and mutually qualifying views, which themselves require commentary. Given Melville's scathing exposé of the navy, where has he not been "at all frank"? And if *White-Jacket* is not frank, how has Melville avoided repressing himself?

The precise degree of Melville's candor will always be a subject of speculation for us. However, one aspect of his writing does contradict the hearty and comradely ambience that characterizes other parts of the book. In the narrative persona we encounter an element of uncertainty, an element of resistance. Like several other Melvillean narrators, notably Taji and Ishmael, White-Jacket seems oddly disembodied, as if he were not meant for human contact. Except for a handful of specific exploits, he remains incorporeal, unelaborated. He is a narrative voice and not a human character, a verbal surface that calls attention to what it says rather than what it is. A polemicist and a reporter, he makes his opinions and observations freely available to us, and yet his psychology remains stubbornly unknowable. This impersonal quality prompted Evert Duyckinck to remark—with evident approval—that *White-Jacket* is "simply a clear reflecting mirror" rendering the "objective life of the sea."[5] For Melville's contemporaries, the self-effacing narrator is praiseworthy. All the same, White-Jacket's insubstantiality directly contradicts the camaraderie of his public discourse. After all, how can we be chummy with someone who is merely the sum of his verbal professions, who is faceless, intangible, about whose life we know next to nothing?

If White-Jacket is unobtrusive for the most part, there is one notable exception. In his numerous literary and historical allusions he draws attention to himself and his unseamanlike erudition. This is done so frequently, and with so much emphasis, that almost all contemporary reviewers noticed it. English reviewers tended to be skeptical about Melville's true identity. The London *Daily News*, for instance, believed that *White-Jacket* was "the romance of the quarter-deck, with a dive now and then into the hold of the middies. But it ignores the forecastle, in which Mr. Melville lives, and sleeps,

[5]*Literary World* (New York), 16 Mar. 1850, p. 271.

and devours his grub."[6] American reviewers, on the other hand, were generally impressed. The *Literary World* applauded Melville for his "union of culture and experience" and noted that "the sharp breeze of the forecastle alternating with the mellow stillness of the library . . . distinguishes the narratives of the author of *Typee* from all other productions of their class."[7] The *Southern Literary Messenger*, in a similar vein, suggested that "this practical experience from the 'fo'k'sle' uniting with a love of elegant learning and with an educated taste . . . has distinguished Melville from all other writers of his class. . . . It is not often that the stains of the tar-bucket and inkstand are seen upon the same fingers."[8] Interestingly, both reviewers used the word "class," and even though the word probably was not used as a socioeconomic category, it seems appropriate to read it in that light, for in his learned allusions White-Jacket has indeed transcended the "class" of common sailors. He has combined the plebeian and the aristocratic, the forecastle and the library. To further the effect, Melville refers to Hawthorne and to "my friend Dana" (p. 99), and finally, by interjecting an event which actually takes place *after* the cruise is over, in which White-Jacket chances upon the Commodore at a "ball given by the Russian Minister, the Baron de Bodisco" (p. 290), Melville puts White-Jacket in a milieu far removed from the lowly station he occupies on the *Neversink*. . . .

Curiously, these disclosures do not make us more familiar with the narrator; they do not even make him more distinct. Instead, they merely outline a *class* to which the narrator belongs. Paradoxically, personal revelations lead to impersonal generalizations, which forces us once again to question the closeness between author and reader. Even more crucially, the role of the reader is beginning to change. If he is elsewhere hailed as a comrade, a trusted companion, here he becomes an external source of constraint which Melville has to reckon with. To impress his readers favorably, he must preserve a cautious distance from the scene of action. Unqualified intimacy with lower-class life is finally neither commendable nor edifying, and at some point Melville must step back, withdraw from direct contact, cultivate a margin of inexperience and personal exception—even to the extent of singling out himself in class-affiliated disclosures—before he can carry on his narrative with impunity. One might notice, in this context, that even though White-Jacket cites numerous instances of flogging, he himself remains unmolested. Why is he never flogged? Surely his story would have gained immeasurably in power and persuasiveness if he himself had undergone the ordeal. But the convention governing the respectable narrator is perhaps even more powerful than the temptation toward experience. (In *Thirty Years from Home*, Samuel Leech includes no less than three incidents of "hair-breadth escape from the

[6]London *Daily News*, 11 Feb. 1850.
[7]*Literary World* (New York), 16 Mar. 1850, p. 271.
[8]*Southern Literary Messenger*, April 1850, p. 250.

lash," but also escapes uninjured.)[9] *White-Jacket* is torn between subject and audience, between fictional experience on the one hand and regard for the reader on the other. These rival claims come to a head in chapter 67, "White-Jacket arraigned at the Mast."

As Howard Vincent convincingly shows, chapter 67 is in part derived from John Sherburne Sleeper's *Tales of the Ocean*.[10] Sleeper's story is an eyewitness report in which a vengeful sailor, unjustly flogged, kills both the captain and himself, while the narrator comments from a distance. When Melville comes to use the story, he appropriates the main action for White-Jacket himself. Melville's choice is significant because it lends itself to a conflict between subject and audience that Sleeper has managed to avoid. Sleeper's story, it seems to me, embodies a clear alliance with the readers. Like them, the narrator stays outside the scene of action, observes, sympathizes, formulates moral and philosophical opinions, but never directly experiences the emotions of the crisis. Melville is apparently too interested in the subject to settle for such detachment. To explore the full potential of the crisis, he puts the narrator where the story is most immediate and most compelling, as an active participant. And yet, by the same token, he also forfeits the narrative safeguard that Sleeper preserves. Whereas Sleeper's narrator comments safely on the action of another man, White-Jacket is personally endangered. There is now no graceful exit. If he had been flogged, he would have pushed the narrative into a realm offensive to the reader. And if he had tried to revenge himself, he would have brought an end to himself and foreclosed the narrative. At some point, then, Melville must check his fascination with the subject and return the narrative to a more manageable, as well as more socially acceptable course. In short, the narrator must come close to being flogged, must experience the anguish of it, and yet in the end he must escape unharmed, to keep the company of his readers.

The resulting plot is precarious, and Melville is obviously uncomfortable with it. On the verge of martyrdom, White-Jacket is rescued just in the nick of time and by a totally unexpected agent. The plot reverses itself as if by miracle:

"Captain Claret," said a voice advancing from the crowd. I turned to see who this might be, that audaciously interposed at a juncture like this. It was the same remarkably handsome and gentlemanly corporal of marines, Colbrook, who has been previously alluded to, in the chapter describing killing time in a man-of-war.

"I know that man," said Colbrook, touching his cap, and speaking in a mild, firm, but extremely deferential manner; "and I know that he would not be found absent from his station, if he knew where it was." (pp. 280–81)

The intervention is not only unprecedented, it is altogether unearned. Nothing in *White-Jacket* has prepared us for this astonishing development. Corpo-

[9]Leech, *Thirty Years from Home*, p. 94. See also pp. 78–79, 86, 93.
[10]*The Tailoring of Melville's "White-Jacket,"* pp. 150–53.

ral Colbrook is hardly a memorable character, having appeared only once before, in a minor portrait. Furthermore, in that previous scene he bears no relation to the heroic role Melville now assigns him. Far from being a logical candidate for this honorable deed, he was formerly vain, dandyish, sentimental, a "complete lady's man" (p. 172), hardly someone to risk his neck on a common sailor's behalf.

Colbrook is clearly a problem. If nothing in the past entitles him to his new heroic stature, an even greater danger is that he might not be remembered at all. Melville evidently feels a strong need to defend himself and to justify the new development in his story. Lest the forgetful reader accuse him of fraud, he hastens to remind us that Colbrook is indeed an authentic character and a legitimate choice, since he "has been previously alluded to, in the chapter describing killing time in a man-of-war."

Surely this is a most unusual bit of information to emerge from a narrative climax. . . .

In the thick of an explosive crisis the story suddenly comes to a halt, and the author steps forward to reiterate certain facts about his composition. At this exciting juncture Melville seems to have lost interest in the story, and rather than worrying about his narrator (whose fate is still undecided) he worries instead about his own credibility and about the possible incredulity of his readers. In the most vivid way, the authorial reminder illustrates the powerful effect of audience on Melville and on *White-Jacket* as a whole. As it arrests the dramatic action, the narrative moves precipitously from the self-confident world of fiction, where events just occur and require no authentication, to the exacting world of audience, where every step needs to be justified.

However, if the uneasy authorial gesture acknowledges the supremacy of the reader, it also catches the reader in a much less congenial light. No longer the chummy confidant of the opening sentence or the like-minded comrade of the reformist chapters, he is now a source of anxiety to the author. He is careless, forgetful, not to be trusted with details. Even worse, he is also a censor, a judge who requires explanations and apologies. Twice in a single chapter the reader registers his presence in the narrative. On a large scale he is responsible for the reversed plot, for White-Jacket's miraculous rescue. More particularly, he dominates the text in Melville's anxious reminder. In both instances, pressure from the reader works to the detriment of the plot. Not only does it interrupt the story, it also holds in check Melville's fictional energy and curtails his attempt to explore a potentially harrowing experience. . . .

What makes *White-Jacket* so interesting, and perhaps so perplexing in the end, is that it embodies not only a sociable but also a misanthropic spirit. Against the Melville of the reformist chapters, there is another Melville, ill-contented and acrimonious, a Melville eager not to befriend his readers but to disconcert them. The disparity between these two Melvilles is most vividly felt in those odd moments when the narrative language somehow fails to square with the character of the narrator. White-Jacket is projected as a genial, hearty fellow, and for the most part Melville writes in a genial, hearty style. . . .

Occasionally, however, Melville does stand apart, and his distance is measured not by irony toward the narrator but by the use of certain phrases and details which seem at odds with the genial character of White-Jacket. In these instances Melville steps outside his narrative persona and assumes a new voice, at once grating and unfamiliar.

These jarring notes often appear in the most pleasant context. For example, when Jack Chase is first introduced to us, Melville enumerates a list of obligatory virtues: Jack was "tall and well-knit, with a clear open eye, a fine broad brow, and an abounding nut-brown beard. No man ever had a better heart or a bolder. He was loved by the seamen and admired by the officers. . . . No one could be better company in forecastle or saloon; no man told such stories, sang such songs, or with greater alacrity sprang to his duty." In short, Jack Chase is the luckiest of mortals. But suddenly the tenor of the passage changes: "Indeed, there was only one thing wanting about him; and that was, a finger of his left hand" (p. 13). This casual reference shocks and offends us, not only because a missing finger is in itself an ugly detail, but also because it violates our sense of fictional compatibility and mutilates the entire description. A missing finger is the last thing we would expect of Jack Chase, and, in fact, except for this isolated instance, it is never mentioned again. Missing limbs and digits belong to a different kind of fictional reality. Often grotesque, sometimes tragic, they invoke the world of Samoa and Ahab, a world of grim necessity, of misshapen forms and warped spirits, and have nothing to do with the lighthearted, rosy-hued, idealized picture of the "handsome sailor." Such a carefree portrait puts us in a carefree mood, and yet the next moment Melville turns around and rebukes us for our facile sentimentality. The cliché "the one thing wanting" turns out to be shockingly literal, shockingly tangible, and jostles us precisely because we *have* paid it no serious attention, because we *have* expected it to be a cliché. The jarring wordplay reveals a hidden violence, a barbed hostility, which seems inexplicable, uncalled for, and altogether out of place in its context. Certainly it is not directed against Jack Chase, whom Melville truly loves and admires. One can only surmise that this violence is directed outward, toward an external source of irritation. These strange and disconcerting interludes crop up again and again in *White-Jacket*. . . .

However sporadic, Melville's ill-natured assaults on the reader directly contradict *White-Jacket*'s dominant fraternal mood. They also make us wonder anew about the character of the reader as conceived by Melville. Who, after all, are the people Melville has in mind when he composes these spiteful passages? Already, the implied reader in *White-Jacket* has assumed a number of guises. He may be a buddy, a comrade, addressed confidently and directly, or he may be a censor, a critic, viewed with apprehension and mistrust. Who, then, is this other reader, despised and rudely put out of countenance?

The despicable reader is most vividly reflected, I think, in the battle scenes. These are interesting episodes, and not the least interesting fact about them is that they might not have been in the story at all. The *Neversink* never engages in any actual combat and, properly speaking, has no war stories of its own. Battle scenes in *White-Jacket* are strictly gratuitous, strictly interpolations, and to accommodate them Melville uses a number of devices—"told stories," recollections by war veterans, or simply fantasies. These episodes are badly integrated, and in aim and emotion they contradict the rest of the book. Above and against Melville's humanitarian concerns, the war stories proclaim man's fascination with bloodshed. What comes through is less the inhumanity of war than the intoxicating excitement it affords. In the long run, Melville's war stories are celebrations of the spectacle of atrocity. They accept the gory details of war, accept them and relish them, turn them into the stuff of fiction, and glorify them with a kind of garrulous ebullience. In substance and by implication the war stories stand apart. They exercise a different emotional appeal and, most crucially, they cast the reader in a far less flattering role than the high-minded reformer he is allowed to be in the antiflogging sections. Melville's bloody stories have a way of including the reader in their company. Like the storyteller, we too are excited by the unleashed forces, by the magnitude of destruction, by the world of sudden and violent death, at once abominable and exhilarating. . . .

White-Jacket is full of chatty metaphors about war and other occasions of bloodshed. Wads for gun-carriages, for example, are "big as Dutch cheeses"; a cannister shot is "packed in a tin case, like a tea-caddy" (p. 68); guns smoke "like rows of Dutch pipe-bowls" (p. 318); sailors scrambling up the ladder to their respective guns are "like eating-house waiters hurrying along with hot cakes for breakfast" (p. 68); and the surgeon's steward presiding over the amputation table is "like an over-conscientious butler fidgeting over a dinner-table just before the convivialists enter" (p. 256). In each case the metaphor welds together two incongruous realms of existence, the man-of-war's and the reader's, and in each case the effect is to domesticate war, to naturalize it within the landscape of civilian America. Because war is talked about with so much homeyness and so little astonishment, and in such comfortable language, it becomes a pedestrian affair, a routine diet, something that can be talked about without raising an eyebrow. If readers of war stories are able to tolerate atrocity to an unconscionable degree, Melville gives ironic utterance to their callousness by his gastronomic metaphors, which turn the war into a regular feast for ordinary Americans. In this convivial mood, in the familiar setting of pleasure and comfort, injustice and brutality become tame and acceptable.

Melville's relation to the reader in *White-Jacket* is finally much less comradely and much more calculating than one is led to think. A humanitarian advocate, he does not neglect to feed us many unnecessary gory details. By his reckoning, the reader is not only a morally vigilant reformer but also an unscrupulous war addict—no different, in this respect, from the officers on board the *Neversink*—whose blood quickens at the sign of combat. Melville's cynical view of readers turns out to be historically justified. His contemporaries *did* indeed enjoy lurid stories no less than lofty sermons, a fact well understood and exploited by other authors besides Melville. Samuel Leech, every bit as ardent as Melville on the subject of naval reform, is even more graphic in his depiction of the bloodshed on the *Macedonian*. In his alternate use of moralism and sensationalism, Melville is merely following an accepted and expedient convention among sea writers. However, if he knows his readers well enough to meet their taste, he also knows them well enough to scorn them. His metaphors ironically give vent to his distaste, and parody his readers in their complacency and hard-heartedness.

Whether affable or abusive, *White-Jacket* labors under an acute consciousness of its audience. Often Melville has to court his readers, sometimes he lashes out at them, but in one way or another they command his attention and govern his narrative. Aside from the actual merit of the book (of which Melville is no reliable judge), the sense of subservience, of cramped necessity, must have oppressed him throughout the composition of *White-Jacket*. No wonder he spitefully dismisses the book as a "job." In a more relenting mood he decides that he has "spoken pretty much as I feel" (*Letters*, p. 92). However, the manner in which he has to communicate these feelings and the compromises and concessions he has to make on the way cannot be anything but exasperating. *White-Jacket* is finally an embittered book bearing the full burden of its author's disaffection. It is, as Melville himself admits, in a letter to Dana in 1849, "rather man-of-*warish* in style—rather aggressive I fear" (*Letters*, p. 93).

Melville's freedom as a writer finally lies in this truculent energy. Even though much of the aggression in the book is targeted, directed toward the reader, and inversely acknowledges the reader's importance, there is another kind of aggression, not only occasionless but also objectless. This aggression is purely linguistic, a verbal onslaught that easily overwhelms the world of objects it purports to describe. In these moments Melville impresses us not as a cautious practitioner dutifully and grudgingly plying his trade but as a heady swimmer, just short of being carried away by his own verbal torrents.

This linguistic liberty was apparently resented by some contemporary reviewers, several of whom found fault with Melville's verbosity and his lack of purpose. *Atlas*, for instance, objected to Melville's "descriptive flights"; *Britannia* complained that the book "labours under the defect of want of motive" and that "the elaborate descriptions lead to no end." The *Globe and Traveller* regretted that the "elaborate description" and fanciful "conceits" in *White-Jacket* resulted "in a dissension of taste between writer and reader, palpable enough to the latter to diminish materially his enjoyment" of the book. The London *Morning Post*, angered by the "incongruous mass of illustration" and "disgusting details" of the amputation chapter, singled it out for censure. Even favorable reviewers sounded apologetic when they were confronted with Melville's verbal excesses. The *Home Journal*, for instance, explained, "[Melville's] elaboration of trifles, his redundancy and often incongruity of metaphor, his quaintness of expression, what are they but parts of his suggestiveness? the fulness, the fun and humor of his soul?" In a way, contemporary reviewers were right to be critical, for if one accepts Melville's stated humanitarian goals, chapter 63 is indeed worthless and excessive, a sheer act of authorial indulgence. Overwrought descriptions, as much as overblown theories, become an end in themselves, become self-sustained and self-generated, and ill-serve any didactic end. And yet these descriptive excesses also give Melville the license to be most at home with himself. In the delight of verbal activity, the reader is left behind. The "descriptive flight" is a solitary adventure for the author.

In spite of the dominant fraternal mood, *White-Jacket* is finally a deceptive book. Much of the complication arises, I think, from the fact that there are not one but several Melvilles in the book, and not one but several fictive audiences. The multiplicity of implied authors and implied readers accounts for the incongruity between the declamatory and the descriptive sections; it also accounts for the disjunctions, excesses, and reversals that make the book baffling to read. Out of his need for readers Melville presents himself as a genial companion and an ardent advocate, sharing the same beliefs and the same language with his audience. However, this necessity disenchants him and biases his view of the book. There is another Melville operating just beneath the surface of the text—a morose, sardonic Melville, the exact opposite of his sociable self. Caught between these conflicting authorial attitudes, the reader in *White-Jacket* also takes on different roles. Most conspicuously he is the trusted friend and like-minded comrade of the reformist chapters. More obscurely, he is an external source of anxiety and restraint, an unrespected arbiter whom Melville bows to but also resents. At his most contemptible, the reader is a target for Melville's virulence. By parodic metaphors, self-abusive rhetoric, and occasional moments of expository violence, Melville ruptures his reasonable discourse and revenges himself on us. However, the very act of revenge attests to the dominance of the reader. Melville is truly free only when he becomes self-sufficient in his fiction, only when the reader ceases to matter to him in one way or another. In certain moments of verbal excess Melville achieves this rare indifference. The most exuberant sections of *White-Jacket* are also the most readerless.

Melville and
Cultural Persuasion

Donald E. Pease

The broad topic of this discussion will be the scene of cultural persuasion at the time of the publication of *Moby-Dick*. Some of the more powerful moments in literature occur when characters are persuaded to see reality in a form they would otherwise reject, as when Othello is persuaded by Iago to distrust Desdemona; when the serpent persuades Eve that God has denied her knowledge; or when Ahab persuades the crew to embark on a mission unlike any they had signed on for. And in each of these moments, the means of persuasion involves terms crucial to the organization and maintenance of the differing cultures. The famous quarterdeck scene in *Moby-Dick* exemplifies the dynamics of cultural persuasion in mid-nineteenth-century America, and I begin accordingly with an analysis of Ahab's means of persuasion in that scene.

As it happened, Ahab's first mate voices the only opposition, pointing out, with a sure sense of the persuasive power of marketplace rationality, that he has signed on to hunt whales for the Nantucket market and not to hunt them for his captain's vengeance. Vengeance on a dumb brute motivated only by instinct, Starbuck righteously concludes, constitutes a form of blasphemy. The terms of Starbuck's dissent, grounded as they are in a strong faith in the American system of free enterprise, with the religious piety in that common ground underscored by the accusation of blasphemy, a designation usually reserved for religious controversy, could, out of their own persuasive power, initiate a mutiny. But they do not.

An understanding of why they do not requires an analysis of Ahab's response:

"Hark ye yet again—the little lower layer. All visible objects, man, are but as pasteboard masks. But in each event—in the living act, the undoubted deed—there, some unknown but still reasoning thing puts forth the mouldings of its features from behind the unreasoning mask. If man will strike, strike through the mask! How can the prisoner reach outside except by thrusting through the wall? To

From *Ideology and Classic American Literature*, edited by Sacvan Bercovitch and Myra Jehlen. Copyright © 1986, Cambridge University Press. Reprinted with the permission of Cambridge University Press.

me, the white whale is that wall, shoved near to me. Sometimes I think there's nought beyond. But 'tis enough. He tasks me; he heaps me; I see in him outrageous strength, with an inscrutable malice sinewing it. That inscrutable thing is chiefly what I hate; and be the white whale agent; or be the white whale principal, I will wreak that hate upon him. Talk not to me of blasphemy, man. I'd strike the sun if it insulted me. For could the sun do that, then could I do the other; since there is ever a sort of free play herein, jealously presiding over all creations. But not my master, man, is even that fair play. Who's over me? Truth hath no confines. Take off thine eye! more intolerable than friend's glaring is a doltish stare."[1]

In responding in this way, Ahab does not so much answer Starbuck's charges as invest those charges with a power Starbuck is unable to command. Starbuck's words resound with righteous indignation; Ahab relocates righteous indignation in a context capable of converting it into the full-fledged wrath of a prophet. In taking Starbuck down a little lower layer, in other words, Ahab also deepens the context for Starbuck's indignation. Implicitly, however, Ahab in this dive also chastens Starbuck for the shallow purposes to which he puts his religion. If Starbuck is willing to kill whales for the capital their oil will bring in Nantucket, he is not willing to see them as representative of any purpose other than his need for capital. His profit motive makes it necessary for him to see the whales as dumb brutes. Ahab's vengeance, in informing the whale with a deeper cosmic design, turns Starbuck into the blasphemer. In treating the whale as a pasteboard mask for his profit motive, Starbuck necessarily confirms the other alternative in Ahab's apocalyptic either/or. For the Christian whose rationality is equiprimordial with the profit motive, there is indeed "nought beyond" this market context. Ahab speaks with all the rage of a man who can no longer be satisfied with this conception. So instead of responding in terms sanctioned by Starbuck's context, Ahab declaims with all the rage of a man who experiences Starbuck's context as a further source for his sense of lost freedom.

In other words, Ahab does not respond either in or to the terms of Starbuck's argument; rather, he displaces Starbuck as well as the terms of his argument onto another scene. On this other scene, however, Starbuck cannot continue his argument with Ahab. For Ahab has cast the terms (the profit motive, the Nantucket market, the instrumental reason) informing Starbuck's argument into the role of oppressive agents. Ahab's recasting of the terms of his argument with Starbuck from a marketplace context into an apocalyptic realm, converts his public argument with Starbuck into Ahab's private argument with the cosmic plan. And this *conversion*, in its turn, reverses the positions of the combatants. Instead of remaining the cruel captain whose exploitation of his crew would justify Starbuck's mutiny, Ahab, in turning into

---

[1]Herman Melville, *Moby-Dick*, ed. Harrison Hayford and Hershel Parker (New York: Norton, 1967), p. 144. Subsequent references are to this edition.

the enraged victim of a cruel cosmic design, lays claim to the right to mutiny. In taking Starbuck down onto *his* little lower layer, he *acts out* Starbuck's motive for mutiny, but does so on a *scene* that has at once co-opted the terms of Starbuck's potential mutiny but also virtually eliminated any part for Starbuck to play. On this other scene, in other words, Ahab idealizes the impulse to mutiny. By elevating defiance onto an apocalyptic scene where it appears utterly coincident with his character, Ahab, instead of remaining a force to be defied, gives defiance its most noble expression.

In laying prior claim to Starbuck's defiance, however, Ahab does not lessen Starbuck's anger. In bringing Starbuck up against his own rage, Ahab further exploits the resources in this other scene. As an enraged man who now feels all the rage he needs to kill Ahab, Starbuck no longer can claim the character of a rational, Christian man. Whereas formerly he could oppose Ahab precisely because of the clear distinction between Ahab's rage and his own moral identity, Starbuck now knows a state of mind enabling him to identify Ahab's rage with an impulse of his own inner life.

After provoking Starbuck to "anger-glow," Ahab, in the most remarkable move in this extraordinary scene, does not bring Starbuck up against his apocalyptic rage but gently chides Starbuck to let go of the anger Ahab *has agreed to embody alone.*

> "So, so, thou reddenest and palest; my heart has melted thee to anger-glow. But look ye, Starbuck, what is said in heat, that thing unsays itself. There are men from whom warm words are small indignity. I meant not to incense thee. Let it go. Look! see yonder Turkish cheeks of spotted tawn—living, breathing pictures painted by the sun. The pagan leopards—the unrecking and unworshipping things, that live; and seek, and give no reasons for the torrid life they feel! The crew, man, the crew! Are they not one and all with Ahab, in this matter of the whale? See Stubb! he laughs! See yonder Chilean! he snorts to think of it. Stand up amid the general hurricane thy one tost sapling cannot, Starbuck. And what is it? Reckon it. 'Tis but to help strike a fin; no wondrous feat for Starbuck. What is it more? From this one poor hunt, the best lance out of all Nantucket, surely he will not hang back, when every foremast-hand has clutched a whetstone? Ah! constrainings seize thee; I see! the billow lifts thee! Speak, but speak!—Aye, aye! thy silence, then, *that* voices thee." (p. 144)

In this passage Ahab completes his elimination of Starbuck from the scene of persuasion in which the motives for action are determined. Earlier, Ahab provoked his own reaction to the universe, a defiance grown out of rage, in Starbuck. In this passage he recovers defiance as *his trial* and not the burden of a man who can now recover his rightful place—not in Ahab's world but with the rest of the crew.

In his encounter with Starbuck, Ahab has elicited his inner life, the rage against a potentially nihilistic universe, which Starbuck must deny in order to remain himself. And Ahab acts out that inner life as his means of dominating the Starbuck who can *free himself from rage* by finding it thoroughly perfected in Ahab's extraordinary character. Once located on his scene of persuasion, Ahab ceases to be a locus for Starbuck's dissent; instead, he elevates Starbuck's dissent into apocalyptic status where dissent and a final reckoning become indistinguishable from each other. In this elevation, however, Ahab also utterly separates what we might call the *ideological motives for action*, the struggle between an utterly self-reliant man and oppressive cosmic forces, from the individual's action. Once he has voiced *his* rationale for hunting the whale, Ahab does not expect Starbuck to hunt for the same reasons alluded to in Ahab's scene, but expects him to return to a scene more in keeping with his character. After revealing the powerful forces at work in his inner world, Ahab releases Starbuck from the need to "stand up amid the general hurricane" and enables him to return to his appropriate position with the crew, where instead of hunting whales for either cosmic revenge or for the profit motive he will merely "help strike a fin." Having established the world of motives onto the scene where he will control the resolution, Ahab converts the crew into a realm *informed* and *determined* by this other scene but, as is the case with the world of the pagan leopards, living and seeking without the need to understand the motives for their actions. Ahab's scene of persuasion collapses the space of argument, where dissent would otherwise be acknowledged, into an opposition—that between him and cosmic forces—whose terms carry the conclusion within their organization.

That Ahab manages all this in cadences borrowed from Shakespeare only underscores the "scenic" character of his separation from the crew. If he talks to the men at all, he talks to them in a language that immediately encloses him in a theatrical frame: a theatrical frame, moreover, claiming all the "unapproachable" cultural power that Melville, in his review of Hawthorne's *Mosses from an Old Manse*, claimed Shakespeare wielded over the mob.[2] Thus, Ahab not only "acts out" and "ideally resolves" the principle of rebellion he evokes in the crew, but he does so in a language so invested with cultural power that they can only be inspired by the cultural heights to which Ahab elevates their will to rebel. In short, Ahab embodies not only the crew's inner life but also the best means of articulating it.

In transforming Starbuck's dissent into a pretext for the demonstration of the force of his character, Ahab effectively silenced any opposition from the crew. As if to supply the opposition the crew did not, the formulators of the American canon, from F. O. Matthiessen to the present, have set the freedom they find displayed not in Starbuck's dissent but in Ishmael's narrative against the totalitarian will at work in Ahab's polity. Now, although I began by claiming the broad topic for this discussion would be the scene of cultural persuasion at the time of *Moby-Dick*, I must confess to a more personal motive—a failure to remain persuaded by the reading of *Moby-Dick* that has become canonical, the one in which Ishmael proves his freedom by opposing

[2]See "Hawthorne and His Mosses," in *The Literary World*, August 17 and 20, 1850.

Ahab's totalitarian will. I do not wish merely to prove the superiority of an alternative reading but to argue that the reading to which I was not persuaded appropriated *Moby-Dick* to quite a different scene of cultural persuasion, the global scenario popularly designated as the "Cold War." The Cold War may initially seem an unfit context for a discussion of *Moby-Dick*, but I shall argue that the Cold War is crucial both for the canonical reading of that narrative and for its ongoing placement within the rationalist context F. O. Matthiessen called the "American Renaissance." . . .

In what follows I wish to use the term "scene of cultural persuasion" to designate the ideological work performed in two different cultural contexts: that at work in the culture of the time of *Moby-Dick*'s publication and that at work in the culture that has elevated *Moby-Dick* into a masterwork of the American canon. The conception of the difference in the ideological work performed by these two different scenes releases a context sufficiently alienated from the Cold War to make *Moby-Dick* susceptible to another reading.

The scenes of cultural persuasion generated by the Cold War and by Captain Ahab both work through a form of radical displacement—one in which the specific terms of conflict or dissent are recast in other terms and on another scene. Captain Ahab, when confronted with Starbuck's commonsense argument against his revenge quest, converts the commonsense opposition into a scenario in which Ahab's belief in his right to utter self-reliance has been violated by cosmic design. Ahab, in other words, embodies nineteenth-century faith in the self-made, self-reliant man. And in embodying this faith, the ideological ground for Starbuck's right to dissent, Ahab cannot be perceived as opposing Starbuck's right to dissent. Instead he speaks *as* the ideological principle, the belief in absolute freedom, justifying Starbuck's right to dissent. As the enabling ground for Starbuck's dissent, Ahab cannot be responsive to the specific terms of Starbuck's dissent; instead he provides Starbuck with an occasion to witness what sanctions this right: Ahab's embodiment of *absolute freedom.* . . .

But the problem with the appropriation of *Moby-Dick* by critics who have written with a Cold War consensus is that they have converted Ahab into a figure whose totalitarian will opposed the freedom displayed in Ishmael's narrative formulations, rather than, as we suggested in our discussion of the quarterdeck scene, the figure whose belief in absolute freedom constituted the basis for any of his crew's—whether Starbuck's or Ishmael's—exercise of freedom. The Cold War frame, in other words, flattens into an opposition between two different characters, a contradiction between absolute and individual freedom, displayed in Ahab. In Melville's time, Ahab's need for absolute power over the crew was interpreted in the psychological terms of *monomania*[3] rather than the political term "totalitarianism." And, as I will

---

[3]See, for example, the review "Cause for a Writ de Lunatico," *The Southern Quarterly Review* 5 (January 1852), 262; or William Harrison Ainsworth, "Maniacal Style and Furibund Story," *New Monthly Magazine* (July 1853), 307–8.

suggest, it is not at all clear that for Melville, Ishmael was any more immune to the contradictory pulls between individual and absolute freedom than was Ahab. Although they represented two different rhetorical traditions, neither these traditions nor the characters representing them quite contradicted so much as they complemented one another in the formation of a national character quite different from that of postwar America.

In coming to terms with the difference between these two cultural periods, it is best to begin with a document on the American Renaissance written in 1941, the year of America's entrance into a world war that would make necessary the Cold War scenario as a means of postwar containment.[4] I refer to the criticism of F. O. Matthiessen, whose work on the cultural period in which Melville wrote *Moby-Dick* would establish American literature as a discipline and America as a culture, at a time America needed such a self-consensus to acknowledge the great tradition it stood to lose to a totalitarian power as different from the Soviet Union as Nazism was from Communism. At a time when America needed to be educated to the global duties of renaissance men whose loyalty was to America as a nation with a national tradition great enough to enable it to take its place as a free nation among free nations, Matthiessen would meet what he called the need of every great civilization, "like the Renaissance," to create "its own heritage out of everything in the past that helps it to transcend itself,"[5] with the publication of *American Renaissance: Art and Expression in the Age of Emerson and Whitman*. His choice of an age was timely. For those were the years when the United States, in confronting the issues of slavery, union, and expansionism, would decide to wage a just war destined to establish its identity as a nation among nations.

Curiously, however, as if not to threaten the coherence of the cultural space called the *American Renaissance*, Matthiessen, although he did not completely eliminate them, at least discounted such political questions informing his own earlier work as class inequality and the extension of democracy to economic as well as political levels, even as he reduced the political questions informing the age he called the American Renaissance to the opposition between what he called the Emersonian will to virtue and Ahab's will to power. Yet in 1941 Matthiessen could exclude certain political issues, for the political questions were as clearly defined then by the international arena as the Cold War claims to define them today: in both cases, as the struggle of the free world against a totalitarian power. What was needed was what *American Renaissance* provided: the designation of a cultural power morally superior to that of any totalitarian power with which the free world was then at war. And

---

4I realize that Matthiessen was not writing during the time of the Cold War, but I wish to argue that his American Renaissance helped to create the postwar consensus on American literature as Cold War texts.

5F. O. Matthiessen, *American Renaissance: Art and Expression in the Age of Emerson and Whitman* (New York: Oxford University Press, 1941), p. 656.

not the least sign of that cultural power was the American Renaissance's claim
for a canonical place among the American masterworks for a work that had
only recently been discovered: a survivor from the period of greatness in
America's past, and a text that in its plot enacted the survival by a free man of
the destructive actions of a totalitarian figure. *Moby-Dick*, in getting into the
American Renaissance, seemed to prefigure America's power to get the free
world through a war.

Acting as a means of consensus formation as well as canon definition,
Matthiessen's American Renaissance *displaced* the need to acknowledge dissenting political opinions from the past onto the power to discover an
unrecognized masterwork that guaranteed a future for a free world. . . .

Writing as he did at a time in the international political arena marked by
Nazi hegemony, when national self-consciousness could not appear merely
locally political, Matthiessen separated politics from a cultural politics indistinguishable from consensus formation. But, writing in the years when the
Vietnamese War made national self-consciousness appear indistinguishable
from the political rhetoric of the Cold War, Sacvan Bercovitch found the Cold
War rhetoric supported by another tradition that he called the tradition of the
American jeremiad.[6] And he found a broad-based locus for this form precisely
in the rhetoric Emerson and Whitman shared with the orators and politicians
of the American Renaissance. If for F. O. Matthiessen the American Renaissance proved its power as a cultural consensus by silencing dissenting political
opinions, for Bercovitch the American jeremiad derived all its cultural force at
precisely that moment in the nation's history when dissenting *political* opinions over such explosive issues as union, slavery, and expansionism would
make a difference in the very form of the nation handed over from the past.

But, like the Cold War paradigm it prefigures, the American jeremiad did
not quite come to terms with these issues. Rather, it put them into other
terms: other terms, moreover, that made these issues indistinguishable from
those surrounding the single event—the American Revolution—that, once
resolved, seemed to have made up the nation's mind once and for all. Seeing
issues in terms of the American Revolution, that is, precluded them from
becoming explosive political issues. For the Revolution, in its office as the
fulfillment of the Puritan Divine Mission, lost its status as a historical event
that took place and turned into a perpetual national resource, a rhetorical
means for making up the nation's mind over whatever issue presented itself.
Displaying the same power to *alienate opposition* we found at work in the
Cold War scenario, the jeremiad compels any listener intent on issuing his
own dissenting opinion to discover that his dissent has, in the American
Revolution, already achieved its ideal form. So dissent becomes indistinguish-

[6]See Sacvan Bercovitch, *The American Jeremiad* (Madison: University of Wisconsin Press,
1978).

able from a national revolutionary ideal, which, Bercovitch argues, has in its turn become the ideological representation of the free enterprise system. . . .

[According to the model proposed by Bercovitch,] political issues turn into great public occasions for displacment of scenes of present troubles by scenes in which those troubles have already been solved. And the same figures who made up the public's mind for it in the past, in acting out potentially divisive public issues, can in the present separate the issue from the anxiety attending it; in place of the anxiety over political events in the present, these figures foreground a threat that seems to have a greater claim to public attention: the loss of a relation with a past. These same figures then allay the anxiety they have aroused by returning from a past, a past become all the more gratifying because of its claim to fulfill all present political aspirations. . . .

Although the concept of the American jeremiad is quite resourceful in disclosing the way in which the distinction between consensus and compulsion, always a difficult one to maintain, disappears altogether, nevertheless it cannot quite account for what we might call crises in coercion occasioned by those moments in American cultural history when identical figures in nearly identical forms of the jeremiad were used to represent opposing opinions on related questions. When scenes of cultural persuasion work, they are able to return all the potentially disruptive contradictions in political debate to their ideological ground, which, as we have seen, is capable of functioning as the ideal resolution for these contradictions. But the scenes of cultural persuasion became themselves a source of contradiction at times, and a threat to the ideological ground could result. Such a threat clearly appeared when Theodore Parker, speaking against slavery, John Calhoun, speaking against Union, and David Lee Childs, speaking against expansionism, could all write variations on the same line: "If I am rightly informed, King Ahab made a law that all the Hebrews serve the idol Baal." When this same line could be used by different orators to represent such violently opposed views on such explosive issues, King Ahab could not be said to have made up his mind on these matters. And with the recognition of Ahab's confusion, Americans lost their traditional way of feeling compelled about what to do.

Given our analysis of the unique cultural apparatus brought into existence by the consensus formations we have by turns called the American jeremiad and the Cold War, we cannot simply dismiss such moments as manifestations of cognitive dissonance on a massive scale. In the national economy of the representation of dissent we have been describing, the figures who idealized dissent into final, resolved form existed in a world we called the other scene, in which everyday dissenting opinions, doubts, and contradictions existed only in a fully resolved state. And the relation between the everyday world of indecision and the other scene of *The Decision* was an overdetermined and compensatory one. This everyday world could function precisely because that other world hedged its bet, converting all of its irresolution into a resolved form. It is not simply that doubts and indecisions do exist in local, contingent form, but that they exist *free from the need for decisive resolution* precisely because this other world exists as *The Resolution.* Dissent exists free from the need for resolution in the everyday world because the jeremiad can resolve dissent of its indecision by wording it into an indubitable final reckoning on the Other Scene. Not only does the other scene permit indecision and doubts; it demands them as ongoing proof of its authoritative power to judge.

Now, with this relation between words as a context, imagine one of the rhetorical figures used to free the individual of the consequences of doubt (that is, the need to decide on a course of action)—such as Ahab in Parker's sermon—himself become human enough to experience indecision. What results is a confusion of realms on an apocalyptic scale. When the Ahab who exists to absolve this world of its conflicts himself experiences on that other scene the irresolvable doubts of this world, the other scene reverses its relation to this world. Whereas before, actual indecision discharged itself through symbolic resolution in the other scene, now a form of symbolic resolution from the other scene demands actualization of its indecision in the everyday world. Whereas before, *The Decision* in the other scene was an overdetermined form of the indecisions of everyday life, with this confusion of realms everyday decisions get invested with the overdetermined energy of decision.

Unless one were an orator who actually experienced himself as a figure brought into existence by the words uttered in that other scene, it is difficult to imagine a rhetorical figure (like the Ahab used by different orators to justify expansionism, slavery, and union) who can come into the actual world full of the conflicting demands the other scene can no longer resolve. If Ahab, who was formerly used as an ideal resolution of conflicting demands in the public sphere, now appears in his multiple representations as an ideal expression of the conflicting demands in that same public sphere, it might be said that Ahab, as a means of making up the mind of the public sphere, has come to life as the "character" of that mind. As the "lived experience" of its *betrayed* resolution, he expresses what we call the "national character" as a desperate need to convert conflicting demands back into a decisive form. . . .

The Ahab who feels the compulsive need to persuade utterly separated from the form sanctioning persuasion appears not in anyone's jeremiad but in Melville's novel *Moby-Dick.* And should we follow Melville's lead and remain attentive to the demands not of the American jeremiad but of the figure who is not persuaded by it, we can turn to another American Renaissance. This time, however, we should not be guided by the figure who organized it into an ideal consensus formation. Rather, we should be prepared (by the figure of Ahab) to hear that other F. O. Matthiessen, whose own dissenting opinions were silenced by what we can now recognize as the jeremiad force of *American Renaissance: Art and Expression in the Age of Emerson and Whitman.*

When guided by Matthiessen's opinions in conflict with the consensus formed by the *American Renaissance,* we can revalue the use of Whitman and Emerson. In using Coleridge's organicist aesthetic to distinguish the political rhetoric of such orators as Parker from what he called the "vitally" aesthetic writings of Emerson and Whitman, *American Renaissance* (as a consensus formed at the expense of Matthiessen's own dissenting position) strategically promotes Whitman's and Emerson's rhetoric, in which national self-consciousness becomes indistinguishable from personal self-consciousness, into a cultural asset. Moreover, this act of promotion constitutes the historical power of consensus formation in 1941. For in order to sanction America's national right to a free culture at a time when that right was threatened less by national than international politics, *American Renaissance* locates a cultural past so united that even the political issues surrounding the Civil War seem petty. When viewed in this context, Whitman and Emerson perform the same function for Matthiessen, in his politics of consensus formation, that they performed for the politicians used to the consensus formed by the American jeremiad in their time. They silence the conflicting claims in that form by replacing the politicians' forensic motives with motives open to the more rarified concerns of aesthetics. Seeming, then, to distinguish Emerson and Whitman from the politicians, *American Renaissance* in fact locates in their writings an organicist aesthetic justification for the rhetoric of national individualism at precisely the moment when the politicians seem to be losing the Divine justification for that rhetoric. As we have seen, this bracketing out of politics through a turn to aesthetic questions in fact served Matthiessen's "higher" political purpose—to devise a national consensus. Now we might best sense the cultural power of his "higher" purpose if we imagine F. O. Matthiessen coming after Sacvan Bercovitch to convert the "mere rhetoric" of the American jeremiad into the achieved art of the American Renaissance.

When conceived in terms of this "higher" purpose, however, Emerson and Whitman lose their purely aesthetic characters and reveal the explicitly rhetorical use to which *American Renaissance* put them. Nowhere does Emerson lose this character and Matthiessen lose control of the working of his consensus formation more definitely than in the midst of an analysis of the tyranny of Captain Ahab in the quarterdeck scene in *Moby-Dick.* Curiously, Matthiessen presents this analysis in what we could call a scene of critical persuasion. When considering Ahab's compelling domination of the men in the quarterdeck scene, Matthiessen pays no attention to specific lines but reads the compulsion in Ahab's language as a "sign" of Shakespeare's "power over" Melville. Then, in a monodrama intended ultimately to reveal Melville's artistic power, he transcends lines exchanged by Ahab and Starbuck into their blank-verse form and observes that "the danger of such unconsciously compelled verse is always evident. As it wavers and breaks down into ejaculatory prose, it seems never to have belonged to the speakers but to have been at best a ventriloquist's trick."[7] Having first *posited* Shakespeare's language as the rhetorical power informing Ahab's exchanges, Matthiessen then rediscovers this power Shakespeare wields *through* Ahab at work in the spell Shakespeare cast *over* Melville's prose. This dramatic conflict ends only after Melville "masters" the power Shakespeare's rhetoric wields over him by discovering the secret of his own dramatic power.

Of course, all the power in this drama inheres less in Melville's discovery than in the dramatic use to which Matthiessen puts it. When Matthiessen's drama, which should have concluded with an example of Melville's triumphant "mastery" of Shakespeare, comes to its close, Melville's "mastery" of Shakespeare neither reveals itself through one of Melville's own characters nor represents one of Melville's own themes. Instead, Melville's "vital rhetoric" is said to "build up a defense of one of the chief doctrines of the age, the splendor of the single personality."[8] In other words, Melville's recovery from Shakespeare's rhetoric becomes a means for Emerson to defend his doctrine of self-reliance.

That Matthiessen sees the need for this defense gives pause. But the cause for the defense is implicit in the drama that builds up to it. Although he mentions Hitler only in his account of Chillingworth, the figure whose totalitarian position Matthiessen wrote *American Renaissance* to oppose is everywhere present in his discussion of Ahab. By staging the textual appearance of the doctrine of self-reliance within the scenes of Melville's recovery from a compulsive rhetorical principle, Matthiessen defends its rhetoric in advance from the charge that it may be as compelling in its excesses as Hitler was in his. When Matthiessen writes, "living in the age of Hitler, even the least religious can know and be terrified by what it is for a man to be possessed,"[9] it is clear that compulsive rhetoric, in all of its forms, is what figures from Matthiessen's *American Renaissance* exist to oppose. Consequently, when Melville dramatically achieves independence from the compulsive hold of Shakespeare's rhetoric, in eyes trained to see by the *American Renaissance*, he earns the *authenticity* of the doctrine of self-reliance by literally realizing its *doctrine* as his defining aesthetic action.

The compelling logic of this dramatic sequence is clear. Matthiessen wants to *see* the doctrine of self-reliance at work, but when Matthiessen "hears" this doctrine enunciated by Ahab, he loses all the benefits accrued by the rest of his drama. Indeed, Matthiessen's own earlier treatment of Ahab as the "dummy" through whom Melville performs ventriloquist's tricks with Shakespeare's language posits Ahab as the principle of mere rhetoric rather than authentic art. And this earlier treatment releases troubling questions. If Ahab served as the dummy figure through whom Matthiessen could reveal

[7]See Matthiessen, *American Renaissance*, p. 426.
[8]Ibid., p. 430.
[9]Ibid., p. 307.

Melville's act of "working through" his possession by Shakespeare's rhetoric, does he not, once Matthiessen hears him speaking Emerson's rhetoric of self-reliance, disclose Matthiessen's unstated fear that compulsion might be at work in the doctrine of self-reliance? In short, doesn't the quarterdeck scene become Matthiessen's pretext for the articulation of a felt need—not the need to defend but the need to defend himself against Emerson's ideology of self-reliance, which informs the consensus formation he called the American Renaissance? . . .

Emerson states the doctrine [of self-reliance] with a simplicity that almost conceals its power. "Self-reliance is precisely that secret," he writes, "to make your supposed deficiency redundancy. If I am true, the theory is, the very want of action, my very impotency, shall become a greater excellency than all skill and toil."[10] When revealed, the secret is as simple as the doctrine; it makes a promise to convert powerlessness into a form of power. Before the reader can wish to find this doctrine appealing, however, she needs as her prior experience to feel powerless. The doctrine, in other words, presupposes a disproportion between a secret inner self and an outer world that it works to maintain. Actually, the doctrine of self-reliance doesn't simply presuppose such a disproportion between inner self and outer world but demands it as the context for its display of power.

By definition, a self-reliant individual cannot rely on an outer world but only on an inner self, experienced as superior to the external world. But she can create this inner self only by first reducing the outer world to the level of an abstract externality, as arbitrary as it is merely contingent. Such a reduction cuts two ways. A world that is viewed as *arbitrary at best* allows for a retreat from it without too much regret. And this separation from the mere contingencies of the external world can, out of sheer contrast, be experienced from *within* as the first *authentic* choice in an otherwise arbitrary world.

But at least two problems attend the appearance of this inner self. If its authenticity is derived from a prior experience of contingency, then the inner self has not replaced but only internalized the contingency of an outer world. What results, moreover, is what Ishmael, at the beginning of *Moby-Dick*, calls a bad case of the hypos: that is, a wish for intense action but, given the contingency of internal as well as external worlds, without any incitement to act. The self-reliant individual, then, feels empowered to act but is disconnected from any world that can validate action.

In addressing these two problems, Emerson devised two distinct roles for self-reliance to perform. In its role as a doctrine, self-reliance encouraged a sense of withdrawal from the world; but in its role as an address, self-reliance converted this withdrawal into the appearance of power. In this second role, self-reliance acts less like a doctrine corroborating any particular inner self

10See *Selections from Ralph Waldo Emerson*, ed. Stephen Whicher (Boston: Houghton Mifflin, 1960), p. 146.

and more like one of those rhetorical figures of will we saw at work on the Other Scene of the American jeremiad, capable of providing the private person with the freedom in relation to the external world denied by the doctrine. We begin to understand the power inherent in this division better when we discover what happens when Emerson declares this doctrine as an address. As a figure of address effected by the self-reliance he evokes, Emerson can presume to speak to another individual, not from an external position but with all the power of that "secret" inner life to which each self-reliant individual aspires. And so effective is this power to speak the inner life that such public figures as John Jay Chapman, James Garfield, and Moncure Conway will declare after listening that Emerson's words have become their "secret" character.[11]

When speaking *as* what we might call the sovereign figure of the will released by the doctrine of self-reliance, however, Emerson does not encourage the individual either to act in the world or to will action. Instead he encourages the individual to discover power in this inability to act: "If I am true, . . . my very impotency shall secure a greater excellency than any skill and toil." In what we could call a compensatory unconscious, the inability to perform any particular action recovers the sovereign *capability* to perform *all* actions. And through this remarkable turn, the sovereign will can recover the motivation lost after the devaluation of the external world. The individual will recovers its motivation, however, not by bridging the gap between motive and action but by enlarging it to the point where the motivating power, the sheer impulse to action, assumes priority over any particular action.

Thus the doctrine of self-reliance fulfilled the private will, but only through an address by a figure effected by a sovereign will, who relocates *within the abstract capability of the alienated individual* the Other Scene of *Final Reckoning* we discovered in the form of the American jeremiad. If the jeremiad separated the individual from the need for political decision by providing the scene on which everything had already been decided, self-reliance alienated individual action from individual motives for action by providing an internal sovereign will whose abstract capability to do what "might be done" was all the action there could be. When addressed by a spokesman, like Emerson, for this sovereign, the private person could feel persuaded not to perform any particular action but to experience the sheer force of the motivation to act—resounding in such imperatives as "trust thyself, every heart vibrates to that iron string"—as if it were already the only fulfillment needed.

If the doctrine of self-reliance justified the individual's alienation from a world of action, the power of address it made possible justified the separation

---

[11]Garfield's account is cited in Ralph Leslie Rusk's *The Life of Ralph Waldo Emerson* (New York: Scribner, 1949), p. 385. Conway's can be found in *Remembrances of Emerson* (New York: Cooke, 1903) and John Jay Chapman's in "Emerson," in *The Shock of Recognition*, ed. Edmund Wilson (New York: Doubleday, 1943), p. 615.

of self-reliant individuals from one another. In replacing the merely private will with the "sovereign will," self-reliance also allowed for a great economy of discussion in the public sphere. For it eliminated first and third persons altogether and turned everyone into representations of what we could call a national "second person," an empty discursive slot to be filled in by a figure addressing the nation. Although this second person seems to address "you," he derives all of his power by presuming to speak *as* "your" inner life. Thus, in listening to him, "you" can believe you are investing yourself with executive power. . . . Whenever an individual "acted out" the inspiring power of the orator's motives, he became a figure of will indistinguishable from the inner life of the self-reliant man and earned, as was the case with Ahab, the right to speak as the national second person he, in his personal life, had already become. He could motivate others, in short, because he had already equated their inner motivation with his public action.

Such national second persons as Ahab were the subject not only of legends that assimilated the excesses of the orator's rhetoric into human shape but also of tall tales that . . . de-created these legendary figures by exposing their apparently heroic deeds as mere "stretchers." Here the distinction needs to be made between demystifying a rhetorical position and telling a tall tale. For the latter—telling a tall tale—displaces the need to do the former. Instead of wishing to acknowledge the rhetorical status of a tall tale, the teller never wants to get outside its format. For if he did, he would not have the pleasure of "taking in" a third person. This third person, in his turn, does not recognize what it is that has taken him in, but simply experiences the pleasure of "taking in" another third person with another tall tale. The legend and the tall tale, then, establish what we might (in our memory of the national second person) call a "second first" and a "second third" person who never become skeptical or even self-conscious about the rhetoric of pure persuasion, but who wish instead to claim their second person privileges and remain in the position of persons addressed by the nation's second person.

But if narrativity functions as a motive to remain within the form of address of the nation's second person, reading narratives became an occasion to locate the power of this will to address. Reading, in other words, offered an occasion to turn what is read—that is, words as motive forces—into what does the reading. Or, what is the same thing, reading became a means of internalizing and so, following the logic we found at work in the doctrine of self-reliance, making sovereign, what we have called the nation's second person.

The interrelationship between Americans engaged in the activities of listening, speaking, arguing, and reading—activities valued most, on at least one cultural level, when most indicative of a certain independence of mind— and what we have called the sovereign will of mind, releases an alarming recognition. When accompanying the "democratic" operations acclaimed as proof of the power of individual Americans to make up their own minds, the sovereign will turned these operations into expressions of a national compulsion. When turned toward the national scene on which compulsion could do its work, individual Americans did not make up their own minds but witnessed the scene on which their minds were made up for them as an "experience" of each American's self-reliance.

Perhaps this recognition will have its greatest value if we imagine it stated by the F. O. Matthiessen who led us to it: not the one who used Emerson's doctrine of self-reliance to form the consensus he called the *American Renaissance*, but the one whose dissenting political opinions were silenced by *Art and Expression in the Age of Emerson and Whitman*. Because we began to hear this Matthiessen who was not persuaded by the scene of cultural persuasion in his reading of the quarterdeck scene of *Moby-Dick*, perhaps we can use this scene as an oppositional one. And because the narrative of *Moby-Dick* offers an occasion for Matthiessen to signal opinions in conflict, we should expand the context of this oppositional scene by differentiating Melville's narrative vision from *Art and Expression in the Age of Emerson and Whitman*.

At around the time of the composition of *Moby-Dick*, Melville imagined a reading experience utterly at odds with what we have described as the internalization of the sovereign will. Moreover, he discovered what he called the "will of the people" by reading not Emerson or Thoreau but a figure Matthiessen included as another (subsidiary) voice in the American Renaissance. Reading Hawthorne's *Mosses from an Old Manse*, a work attentive enough to the value of different opinions to provoke in the reader a series of conflicting attitudes, Melville conceived a review in which he *staged* the release of conflicting reactions. Recorded over a two-day period by a Virginian vacationing in Vermont, the review dramatizes a protocol the reverse of what we have called a scene of public persuasion. Instead of finding *his* mind already made up in the figure of Hawthorne's tales, this southerner vacationing in the heart of the abolitionist Northeast discovers a whole range of conflicting reactions to these tales: with each reaction possessed of sufficient self-consciousness to organize itself into an articulate opinion and each opinion accompanied by a second thought—the shocking recognition of the limits of that single opinion. In an intricate series of moves, Melville reads neither as an individual nor quite as a general will but as the conflicting opinions within a reading public—not a ready-made consensus in the process of formulation, or what Melville calls a "plurality of men of genius" released in reading Hawthorne's twice-told tales.

In other words, Melville, at the time of his composition of *Moby-Dick*, imagined the release of the reading public from the sovereign will of the national second person. Moreover, he released that public by giving multiple voices, each with the possibility of "parity," to the conflicts silenced by that sovereign will. We got some indication of the dimensions of those conflicts when we analyzed what resulted when the rhetorical figure of Ahab was used to voice opposed political views. But as Alan Heimert in the past and Michael

Paul Rogin in the present have pointed out, the other two principles in *Moby-Dick*—the figures of Ishmael and the Leviathan—were also deployed, in all their rich biblical allusiveness, to voice contrary political positions on the issues of abolitionism, secession, and manifest destiny in the form of the American jeremiad.[12]

If we can imagine, in the broad context of a scene of cultural persuasion, the political conjuncture elemented by the different issues of slavery, secession, and expansionism, then if we imagine the three Ahabs, three Ishmaels, and three Leviathans used to word these issues into jeremiads, we can see how conflicted had become the space that was used to achieve consensus. If such cultural forms as the jeremiad, pure persuasion, the legend, and the tall tale had been used to "work through" the conflicts in the general will, Melville, in characterizing the contradictory relations among these forms, released the conflicts at work in the general will.

The "great tradition" of American literature founded by the *American Renaissance silenced* these contradictory relations by converting all of them into the opposition between Ishmael's freedom and Ahab's totalitarian will. And this contradiction resolves the felt force of the contradiction by converting it into an "ideal conflict," a (Cold) War whose appropriate outcome has already been determined. In his analysis of the quarterdeck scene, however, Matthiessen displays a contradictory relation, a contradictory attitude unresolvable by the ideal opposition between Ahab and Ishmael. In his analysis, Matthiessen identifies Ahab as both totalitarian will and the freedom a self-reliant man must use to oppose it. Put another way, through the figure of Ahab, Matthiessen reads the feared compulsion at work in what he formerly regarded as the sovereign freedom of the self-reliant man.

He reads the compulsion, but, as we'll recall, he reads it in terms of Shakespeare's blank verse. And whereas Melville represented Ahab's use of Shakespearean language as a sign of his power over the crew, Matthiessen treats this language as a sign of Shakespeare's power over Melville. By reading Ahab's silencing of Starbuck's dissent as a disclosure of the power Shakespeare wielded over Melville's prose, Matthiessen of course acknowledges the political power of Shakespeare's language. (Shakespeare, in the politics of canon formation, had, after all, functioned as Matthiessen's means of securing English Renaissance validity for American Renaissance figures.) But he displaces the context for the display of this power, moving it from the relation between Ahab and the crew to the relation between Melville and Shakespeare. And in doing so, Matthiessen simultaneously praises (through his mastery of Shakespeare's language) the Ahab he condemns (as the proponent of a totalitarian will). More specifically, Matthiessen in his one-dimensional

---

[12]See Alan Heimert, "*Moby-Dick* and American Political Symbolism," *American Quarterly*, 15 (Winter 1963): 498–534, and Michael Paul Rogin in *Subversive Genealogy: The Politics and Art of Herman Melville* (New York: Knopf, 1983).

reading of Ahab's totalitarian will, also reenacts Starbuck's scenario. For Ahab performs for Matthiessen the same function he performs for Starbuck: In embodying compulsion as his inner life alone, he releases Matthiessen from the need to find compulsion at work in the doctrine of self-reliance, the Emersonian will to virtue informing the body of his work.

We might say that the contradictory attitudes released by Matthiessen's reading disclose his doubts about, rather than the effectiveness of, both scenes of cultural persuasion. Earlier we suggested that the scene of cultural persuasion exists to displace political dissent experienced in the public sphere onto another scene, where the contradiction disappears into the ground terms, or where the principles sanctioning the right to dissent replace the specific terms of dissent. In Matthiessen's reading, the political contradictions existing at the time Melville wrote (between democratic ideals and the principle of self-reliance) turn into the opposition (between the totalitarian will and individual freedom) sanctioned by the Civil War. But Matthiessen's discovery of the agency of individual freedom (Emerson's "will to virtue") within Ahab's totalitarian will indicates only the failure of the scene of persuasion to resolve the contradiction.

The contradictions released by Matthiessen's reading, however, do not simply point up his conflicting responses to the character of Ahab. Because these contradictions appear at the point at which Matthiessen fails to remain persuaded in the scene (*American Renaissance*) he used to appropriate nineteenth-century America, these same contradictions opened up a cultural space, answerable neither to the scenes of persuasion operative in Melville's nor Matthiessen's (nor, by extension, our own) time. Since these contradictions are released within the character of Ahab's totalitarian will and are concerned by extension with his canonical opposition to Ishmael's "freedom," perhaps we should conclude with a consideration of that relation.

Let us begin with an observation missing from Matthiessen's concentration on Ahab's totalitarian will. Ahab's very power to silence dissent also causes him to reexperience his sense of loss. Unlike the spokesmen for the American jeremiad, Ahab cannot depend on Divine Writ to sanction his words. Consequently, a dual recognition accompanies his every act of persuasion: the terrible doubt that it may be without foundation, and the "experience" of his separation from another. Both recognitions remind him of the loss of his leg. And it is Ahab's need to justify this sense of loss—to make it his, rather than God's or Fate's—that leads him to turn his will, which in each act of persuasion repeats that separation of his body from his leg, into the ground for his existence.

Indeed, all of Ahab's actions—his dependence on omens, black magic, thaumaturgy—work as regressions to a more fundamental power of the human will. They constitute his efforts to provide a basis *in* the human will for a rhetoric that has lost all other sanction. Ahab, in short, attempts to turn the coercion at work in his rhetoric into Fate, a principle of order in a universe without it. But since this will is grounded in the sense of loss, it is fated to perfect that loss in an act of total destruction.

That final cataclysmic image of total destruction motivated Matthiessen and forty years of Cold War critics to turn to Ishmael, who in surviving *must*, the logic would have it, have survived as the principle of America's freedom who hands over to us our surviving heritage. When juxtaposed to Ahab, Ishmael is said to recover freedom in the midst of fixation; a sense of the present in a world in which Ahab's revenge makes the future indistinguishable from the past; and the free play of indeterminate possibility in a world forced to reflect Ahab's fixed meanings.

Given this juxtaposition, we should take the occasion to notice that if Ahab was a figure who ambivalently recalled the scene of persuasion in the American jeremiad, Ishmael recalls nothing if not the pure persuasion at work in Emerson's rhetoric. As does Emerson, Ishmael uncouples the actions that occur from the motives giving rise to them, thereby turning virtually all events in the narrative into an opportunity to display the powers of eloquence capable of taking possession of them. Indeed, nothing and no one resist Ishmael's power to convert the world that he sees into the forms of rhetoric that he wants. The question remains, however, whether Ishmael, in his need to convert all the facts in his world and all the events in his life into a persuasive power capable of recoining them as the money of his mind, is possessed of a will any less totalizing than Ahab's. Is a will capable of moving from one intellectual model to another—to seize each, to invest each with the subjunctive power of his personality, then, in a display of restlessness no eloquence can arrest, to turn away from each model as if it existed only for this ever-unsatisfied movement of attention—is such a will any less totalitarian, however indeterminate its local exertions, than a will to convert all the world into a single struggle?

Because, in a certain sense, Ishmael puts his will to work by converting Ahab's terrifying legend into cadences familiar from the tall tales, we might take this occasion to differentiate Ishmael's tall tale from those we have analyzed earlier in the chapter. In telling his tale, the Ishmael who was taken in by Ahab's rhetoric does not, as was the case with other narrators of the tall tales, use the tale to work through the excesses in Ahab's rhetoric. Instead, the extraordinary nature of Ahab's words and deeds legitimizes elements of Ishmael's narrative that might otherwise seem inflationary. As the figure whose excesses in word and deed cause him literally to be read out of Ishmael's narrative, Ahab turns into the figure who enables the reader to rule out the charge of excess in Ishmael's rhetoric. Ishmael occupies three different spaces in his narrative. As the victim of Ahab's narrative, he exists as a third person. As the narrator of his own tale, as a first person. And as the subject of such urgent addresses as "Call Me Ishmael," a second person. But because, as a first-person narrator, he turns Ahab into the figure who has victimized Ishmael, Ishmael does not have to be perceived as taking anyone else in. Ishmael turns Ahab into both the *definitive third-person* victim and the perfect *first-person* victimizer. In perfecting both roles, Ahab becomes Ishmael's means of exempting his narrative in advance of the charge of trying to victimize anyone. Moreover, because, in Ishmael's case, first-person narratives always turn into pretexts for second-person sermons, Ahab, the locus for all false rhetoric, also becomes Ishmael's means of redeeming *his second person* by exempting it in advance from all charges of mystification.

As Ishmael's means of purifying his individual acts of persuasion of any actantial component, Ahab, in his conflation of victim and agent, motive and deed, also turns out to be the second-person *power*: the figure of will who performs actions absolutely indistinguishable from the motive powers (released by an orator's address) within Ishmael's rhetorical exercise. In Ishmael's rhetoric, each individual act of perception turns into the occasion for an exercise of persuasive power. Through Ahab's death, Ishmael of course exempts these occasions from any charge of coercion (which has been perfected by Ahab).

The sensed loss of Ahab, however, results in another, less desirable state of affairs. Through Ahab, Ishmael experiences the one figure in his narrative capable of realizing inspired words in matching deeds. Buried within Ishmael's display of remarkable oratorical power is his reiterated demand that the world be indistinguishable from the will of his words: Buried within Ishmael's narrative is the one figure capable of making these words consequential. In reaction to the fate befalling Ahab, the man who would make deed as consequential as his words demanded, Ishmael retreats into endless local performances of rhetorical exercises, with each performance invested with the desperate complaint that the world will not be consequential enough. Each of these performances—these momentary indulgences in a sense of power superior to the given structures of the world—becomes Ishmael's means for recovering the force if not the person of Ahab.

In speaking with the force of Ahab's demand for a world indistinguishable from human will but *free of* the consequences of that will, Ishmael can discover pleasure not quite in another world but in a *prior world,* in which the endless proliferation of possible deeds displaces the need for any definitive action. The pleasure in this *prior* world results from the economization of ends over means, and the capacity to experience this economy as pleasure (rather than frustration) also derives from Ahab. The fate befalling Ahab's decisive conversion of word into deed determines Ishmael's need for a realm in which the indeterminate play of endless possible reactions overdetermines his *in*decision.

We can begin to understand all of this better when we turn to the crucial distinctions that critics during the Cold War drew between Ishmael and Ahab. In their view, Ishmael, in his rhetoric, frees us from Ahab's fixation by returning all things to their status as pure possibilities. What we now must add is that Ishmael has also invested all the rest of the world of fact with possibility, then invests possibility with the voice of conviction. And when all the world turns out to be invested with the indeterminate interplay of possibility, it does not seem free but replicates what Ishmael called the hypos and what we call boredom (the need for intense action without any action to perform) that motivated the Ishmael who felt the "drizzly November in his soul" to feel attracted to Ahab in the first place. This interpolation of an excess of indeterminancy between motive and act displaces Ahab's fixation but in doing so causes Ishmael to develop a need for Ahab. In short, Ishmael's form of freedom does not oppose Ahab but compels him to need Ahab—not only as the purification of his style, but as the cure for a boredom verging on despair. Only in Ahab's final act can the Ishmael who has in his rhetoric converted the external world into an exact replica of the restless displacements of endlessly mobile energies of attention that we formerly identified with the sovereign will, find a means to give all these energies a final, fatal discharge. Ahab's fatal, decisive deed permits Ishmael to feel that the excessive force of *Ahab's decision over*determines his exercises in indecision. Put more simply, Ahab's compulsion to decide *compels* Ishmael *not* to decide.

At this point, however, Ishmael cannot be said to oppose Ahab as freedom would totalitarianism. But the form of his narrative does anticipate the totalizing logic we saw at work in the Cold War scenario. For in identifying all coercion as the work of Ahab's totalitarian will, and not say his own boredom, Ishmael is free to multiply his scenes of persuasion with the knowledge that all of them will be free in advance of the charge of coercion. Because in Ishmael's rendition it is Ahab alone who controls us against our will, we are "free" to read Ishmael's own obsessive multiplication of occasions to compel our attention as the work of Ahab.

Thus *Moby-Dick* does not limit its exposure to that of the scene of cultural persuasion in its own time. Ever since Matthiessen's reading of it as the sign of the power of the freedom of figures in the American Renaissance to oppose totalitarianism, *Moby-Dick* has been a Cold War text, one that secures in Ishmael's survival a sign of the free world's triumph over a totalitarian power. But Melville, in the organization of the narrative relation as a self-conflicted will, instead of letting Ishmael remain in opposition to Ahab, reveals the way in which Ishmael's obsession depends on Ahab's compulsion. Nor does he alienate opposition by positioning all opinions within the conflict between Ishmael and Ahab. Instead he "works through" the vicious circulation informing the conflicted will at work in Ishmael and Ahab. If the Cold War consensus would turn *Moby-Dick* into a figure through which it could read the free world's survival in the future struggle with totalitarianism, Melville, as it were, speaks back through the same figure, asking us if we can survive the free world that Ishmael has handed down to us.

Incomparable America*

Leo Bersani

In his essay "Hawthorne and His Mosses," Melville argues that American originality will write a glorious new chapter in the history of world literature only if it rejects its place in that history. Is it possible to write *like* nobody—without, however, eliminating the possibility of writing *better* than anyone else or being favorably compared with those to whom one owes nothing?

Moby-Dick, in extraordinary ways, accepts and struggles with the pressure of these contradictions. It is clear that Melville has no intention of waiting for those men just being born on the banks of the Ohio to prove their genius. *Moby-Dick is* the great original American book invoked in "Hawthorne and His Mosses"; or, at the very least, it squarely meets the challenge of that essay. Melville will take an American subject—even a provincial American subject: the industry of whaling—and show that the greatest literature can be made from that subject. It is not a question of proving that a lot can be made out of a little, but rather of showing that what may seem to be a little is already a lot. "To produce a mighty book," Ishmael declares, "you must choose a mighty theme. No great and enduring volume can ever be written on the flea, though many there be who have tried it."[1] Whaling is inherently a mighty subject, and to embrace it is to try to hold something that itself reaches out and connects to everything else in human time and cosmic space. Ahab may be crazy to assign evil intentions to a dumb brute, but the pursuit of Moby Dick can't help being a hunt for sense. A whaling expedition is inevitably an adventure in reading; the whale is a primary text of nature itself. Not only that: even as Melville's novel goes along, it is constantly being submitted to a vigilant comparison to other cultural models. There is a cultural encyclopedism in *Moby-Dick* as well as a cetological encyclopedism. It is not that the entries exhaustively treat any subject, but the encyclopedic intention—which is perhaps all the encyclopedic novel ever gives us in any case—is obvious with respect to foreign cultures as well as to whaling. It is as if the great American novel had constantly to be measuring itself against the

*For permission to photocopy this selection, please contact Harvard University Press. Reprinted by permission of the publishers from *The Culture of Redemption* by Leo Bersani, Cambridge, MA: Harvard University Press, Copyright © 1990 by the President and Fellows of Harvard College.

[1]Herman Melville, *Moby-Dick*, ed. Harrison Hayford and Hershel Parker (New York: Norton, 1967), p. 379. Further page references to this edition are given in the text.

highest achievements of other cultures, and in *Moby-Dick* this means testing the American book's capacity to appropriate a vast field of cultural reference. Melville's splendidly arrogant claim is that almost everything in world culture might be made to serve his subject. The "comprehensiveness of sweep" of Ishmael's thoughts of Leviathan reaches out, most notably, to the Bible, to Shakespeare, and to Greek tragedy, and these illustrious references lose some of their autonomous worth in order to serve *Moby-Dick*, to become mere aids to intelligibility—analogical satellites—in an American drama. It is not merely that *Moby-Dick* is worthy of being compared to either *King Lear* or *Oedipus Rex*. Instead it must be compared to both at the same time; only an encyclopedic range of cultural reference can do justice to Melville's mighty theme. His book reenacts several biblical dramas (Ahab, Ishmael, Ezekiel, Rachel, and others), the Greek tragedies of fatality, and Lear's tragic intimacy with nature and madness. *Moby-Dick* is therefore not only as great as any one of these references; in needing them all to explain itself, it also proposes to surpass them all. Cetological erudition in *Moby-Dick* is only the first step in an enterprise of cannibalistic encyclopedism. Like its monster-hero, Melville's novel opens its jaws to devour all other representations from Lear's Fool to Vishnoo the Hindu god.

And yet all this is something of a joke (although one that can also turn on itself and make another kind of joke of joking):

> Friends, hold my arms! For in the mere act of penning my thoughts of this Leviathan, they weary me, and make me faint with their outreaching comprehensiveness of sweep, as if to include the whole circle of the sciences, and all the generations of whales, and men, and mastodons, past, present, and to come, with all the revolving panoramas of empire on earth, and throughout the whole universe, not excluding its suburbs. (379)

"Not excluding its suburbs"? Something, obviously, has gone awry. The hyperbole of the first part of this passage may already have made us somewhat suspicious, but how are we to place that phrase about the universe's suburbs in a serious claim about *Moby-Dick*'s mighty theme? Much has been written about the humor in Melville's novel, especially as a counterpoint to Ahab's monomaniacal pursuit of the whale. The possibility of sinister and far-reaching significance in the whale is often dissipated by all the mocking allusions to the philosophical profundity necessary to uncover that significance. Besides, the last thing a whaling ship needs is a serious philosophical mind. Indeed, this is the explicit lesson of "The Mast-Head" chapter, where Ishmael warns Nantucket shipowners to beware that "sunken-eyed young Platonist [who] will tow you ten wakes around the world, and never make you one pint of sperm the richer" (139). The cultural appropriations meant to authenticate *Moby-Dick*'s claim to greatness are exposed as both laughingly inappropriate to the book's subject and even somewhat ridiculous in themselves. Not only that: in spite of what might seem like a heavy dose of cetology for a work of fiction, Ishmael actually encourages us to be distrustful of his research and presumed knowledge about the whale. The book's cetological erudition—based on remarkably partial sources—is often nothing more than a parody of the erudition of others, and the "proofs" offered of the whale's extraordinary powers most frequently consist (as in "The Affidavit" chapter) of hearsay and assertion. More is at stake here than Ishmael's resistance to Ahab's monomania, more than a presumably viable humanistic alternative to interpretive madness. It is as if the writing of *Moby-Dick* became for Melville the eerie process of dismissing the very ambitions that the novel also seeks so strenuously to realize, as if a kind of leveling indifference had taken over or—most interestingly—as if the notion of American literary greatness were dropped in order to be reinvented, but reinvented *as* something lost, indefensible, abandoned.

What is it, in *Moby-Dick*'s primary project, that might explain Melville's apparent indifference toward it, even his subversion of it? In *Moby-Dick* the political implication of the contradictions hinted at in "Hawthorne and His Mosses" becomes inescapable. More exactly, the notion of American literary greatness is politically represented in *Moby-Dick*, and this means trying to give some coherence or plausibility to the idea of a democratic greatness. The "august dignity I treat of," Ishmael writes in the early section introducing Ahab and his mates,

> is not the dignity of kings and robes, but that abounding dignity which has no robed investiture. Thou shalt see it shining in the arm that wields a pick or drives a spike; that democratic dignity which, on all hands, radiates without end from God; Himself! The great God absolute! The center and circumference of all democracy! His omnipresence, our divine equality!
>
> If, then, to meanest mariners, and renegades and castaways, I shall hereafter ascribe high qualities, though dark; weave round them tragic graces; if even the most mournful, perchance the most abased, among them all, shall at times lift himself to the exalted mounts; if I shall touch that workman's arm with some ethereal light; if I shall spread a rainbow over his disastrous set of sun; then against all mortal critics bear me out in it; thou just Spirit of Equality; which hast spread one royal mantle of humanity over all my kind! (104–105)

Nothing in this passage suggests a rejection of the principle of aristocratic privilege. On the contrary: Ishmael promises a multiplication of the signs and accoutrements of a society based on privilege. He will ascribe "high qualities" to the heroes of his narrative, "weave around them tragic graces," touch them with "ethereal light" and lift them to "exalted mounts"; "pearl" and "finest gold" translate the genius of Bunyan and Cervantes, and Andrew Jackson is imagined as having been "thundered" higher than a throne. "Democracy" here consists in the fact that none of this preeminence is predetermined: in a democratic society, anybody can be lifted to royalty. The principles that determine places within a hierarchy have been changed, but the hierarchical structure has remained intact. It is simply that now the "champions" will come from "the kingly commons." In *Moby-Dick* the rhetoric of democracy has become oxymoronic: in a democracy, equality founds and legitimates inequality.

Ahab's "irresistible dictatorship" perfectly represents this conversion of democracy into royalism. His absolute domination of the crew provides a democratic sanction of despotism. It is true that to a certain extent "the paramount forms and usages of the sea" reinforce a captain's authority independently of his intrinsic merit. In this sense a ship is less like a democracy than a monarchy, and can even call to mind those "royal instances" when "external arts and embellishments" have "imparted potency" to "idiot imbecility." But having granted this, Ishmael insists that the greatness of Ahab owes nothing to the prestige of inherited forms, that—and we can add: like the greatness of America itself or that of the American literary works invoked in "Hawthorne and His Mosses"—it is a wholly original greatness, one without history or traditions. Unlike the "tragic dramatists" who, wishing to "depict mortal indomitableness in its fullest sweep and direct swing," never forget to lend their heroes the persuasive power of "external arts and embellishments," Ishmael sees his captain Ahab as moving before him

> in all his Nantucket grimness and shagginess; and in this episode touching Emperors and kings, I must not conceal that I have only to do with a poor old whale-hunter like him; and, therefore, all outward majestical trappings and housings are denied me. Oh, Ahab! What shall be grand in thee, it must needs be plucked at from the skies, and dived for in the deep, and featured in the unbodied air! (129–130)

Far from being a democratic rejection of emperors and kings, *Moby-Dick* proposes a unique expansion of the monarchic principle. Ahab will earn his right to be called King Ahab, to have his meals with his three mates compared to "the Coronation banquet at Frankfort, where the German Emperor profoundly dines with the seven Imperial Electors." Ahab embodies and realizes the ambition of the novel itself: to have a royal preeminence over European literature without borrowing anything from European models of literary greatness.

And yet the very condition of this success is of course a massive borrowing from those models. The justification of Ahab's kingship is perhaps original and democratic; but the implicit argument for kingship itself comes from abroad, and this condemns Ishmael to analogical proofs of Ahab's greatness. That is, his royal nature will be confirmed by both passing (the German emperor) and sustained (Lear) comparisons between him and other royal natures, by continuous assertions that no royal example is too high to describe him. Melville defines the idea of greatness itself—both for his book and his tragic hero—by constant appeals to our cultural recognitions, thus destroying the argument for originality with its proofs. Or, to put this another way, originality turns out to be nothing more than multiplication of the same. *Moby-Dick's* greatness is unlike that of any other book, and Ahab's royal nature is not to be thought of as comparable to that of other kings and emperors precisely because they can be compared to so many other books and kings. Originality occurs, as it were, after a certain threshold of absorption has been passed, and *Moby-Dick's* cultural encyclopedism is a peculiarly American attempt to quantify quality, to produce originality through mass. Once again we are forced to recognize the novel's oxymoronic argument: democracy produces the greatest kings, and analogy authenticates originality. Thus Melville wins his argument for Ahab by destroying the very reason for making the argument in the first place: the unassimilable, incomparable uniqueness of the democratic personality.

If the democratic ideas of intrinsic worth, and of equal opportunity to assert that worth, are shown to have oligarchic consequences, these consequences are also vindicated in the novel's metaphysical terms. Although Ahab's monomania is most explicitly defined as his transferring the idea of (and, in an even madder way, the responsibility for) "all evil" to Moby Dick, there are hints in the novel that he may also see the whale in terms closer to those used by Ishmael in the central chapter on "The Whiteness of the Whale." Then Moby Dick would not only embody "that intangible malignity which has been from the beginning" (160); more subtly, and more terrifyingly, he would figure the absence of any intentionality whatsoever outside the human mind. This, as we shall shortly see, is the basis for what I will call the crisis of interpretation in *Moby-Dick*. Ahab's defiant invocation to fire in "The Candles" best indicates this shift of metaphysical emphasis: "In the midst of the personified impersonal, a personality stands here. Though but a point at best; whencesoe'er I came; whereso'er I go; yet while I earthly live, the queenly personality lives in me, and feels her royal rights" (417). From this perspective, the pursuit of Moby Dick is perhaps less mad; it is precisely because the whale *is*, as Starbuck says, merely a dumb brute that its power to do so much harm is intolerable. It may *unintentionally destroy*. To be attacked by the whale is not to encounter an enemy; rather, as Ahab at least suggests, it is to have the catastrophic experience of personality's contingency in the universe. Even more intolerable than Moby Dick's intelligent malignity would be its lack of any design at all, for then Ahab's pursuit would be a madly (and comically) incongruous motivation in a universe where purely physical laws govern the movements and meetings of objects. Ahab's assertion of personality—even more, his assertion of royal prerogatives for his "queenly personality"—would then be at once senseless and heroic, a necessarily unheard protest against his having been thrown into the wrong universe, against *this* universe's metaphysical uncongeniality.

Self-assertion is, then, vindicated in *Moby-Dick* as the most profound manifestation of a metaphysical pathos. The value given to personality in a democratic society might be thought of as the political corollary of the novel's philosophical bias in favor of political and metaphysical and literary self-assertions. Against those aristocratic societies where individual personality is largely irrelevant to a hierarchy of power determined by inherited privileges and reinforced by external arts and embellishments, Melville argues for a society (if not a universe) where the individual personality counts, indeed is determinant, in the distribution of power. But it is the very assertion of the rights of self which risks destroying those conditions allowing for it in the first place. In the terms of an unrelenting logic enacted by *Moby-Dick*, democracy ultimately promises the unintended and politically tragic consequence of its own extinction. Melville persuasively expresses the thrill of the democratic promise, both for the individual and for literature, but that thrill is perhaps inseparable from the prospect of unlimited power. The excitement *about* Ahab in *Moby-Dick* is provoked by the spectacle of what might be called an earned despotism. The *Pequod* is the social realization of a fantasy of intrinsic kingship. The opportunity for self-expression and self-assertion in a democratic society is, Melville's novel suggests, existentially translated as a will to power; despotism is the social logic within an argument for the rights of personality.

But we also have Ishmael and the *Pequod's* crew. Another type of society is—or so it appears—constituted in the margins of Ahab's rule. There seems to be a social space in *Moby-Dick* outside the circle of fascinated subjugation to Ahab's monomania. And this space would be defined by a kind of democratic camaraderie in shared work.[2] There is, for example, the convivial atmosphere during the hoisting, cutting, and lowering of the whale's blubber, a task accompanied by fraternal swearing and the transformation of part of the crew into a "wild" operatic chorus. See especially the famous description of the men squeezing lumps of sperm back into fluid, an activity that frees Ishmael "from all ill-will, or petulance, or malice of any sort whatsoever":

> Squeeze! squeeze! squeeze! all the morning long; I squeezed that sperm till I myself almost melted into it; I squeezed that sperm till a strange sort of insanity came over me; and I found myself unwittingly squeezing my co-laborers' hands in it, mistaking their hands for the gentle globules. Such an abounding, affectionate, friendly, loving feeling did this avocation beget; that at last I was continually squeezing their hands, and looking up into their eyes sentimentally; as much as to say,—Oh! my dear fellow beings, why should we longer cherish any social acerbities, or know the slightest ill-humor or envy! Come; let us squeeze hands all round; nay, let us all squeeze ourselves into each other; let us squeeze ourselves universally into the very milk and sperm of kindness. (348–349)

---

[2]This argument is made in C. L. R. James's stirringly personal book, *Mariners, Renegades and Castaways: The Story of Herman Melville and the World We Live In* (New York: C. L. R. James, 1953). The *Pequod's* crew, James writes, "owe no allegiance to any body or anything except the work they have to do and the relations with one another on which that work depends" (p. 20). "The contrast is between Ahab and the crew"; Melville endowed the crew with "the graces of men associated for common labor" (p. 30).

The fraternal warmth engendered by this communal activity seems to be the best antidote to Ahab's mad isolation. It is, in terms of the book's major metaphorical opposition, a return from the dangers of sea to the security of land. Ishmael goes on to interpret what he has just described in precisely such terms. Having learned that "man must eventually lower, or at least shift, his concert of attainable felicity; not placing it anywhere in the intellect or the fancy; but in the wife, the heart, the bed, the table, the saddle, the fire-side, the country," he is "ready to squeeze ease eternally" (349). But this is a tame and pious conclusion to what we have just read, and it is difficult to see what wife, fireside, and country have to do with the "strange sort of insanity" that leads Ishmael—made drunk by the touch of "those soft, gentle globules of infiltrated tissues" and the "uncontaminated aroma" of "that inexpressible sperm"—to begin squeezing his comrades' hands and gazing "sentimentally" into their eyes, dreaming of an ecstatic loss of self in a universal melting squeeze. I don't mean simply that the need to place happiness in wife and fireside seems a strangely inappropriate lesson to be drawn from such an obviously homoerotic experience, but rather that the homoeroticism itself is merely the secondary expression of a comically anarchic sensuality. Ishmael's coworkers allow for the momentary focusing and socializing of a sensuality that is so idiosyncratic, so frankly irreducible to any viable social bond—in Ishmael's own words, so insane—that it can only be *described*— accommodated by language—as a joke. The joke is emphasized by the corny, decidedly nonpious vision at the end of the passage: "In visions of the night, I saw long rows of angels in paradise, each with his hands in a jar of sperma-ceti."

Much has been made of homoeroticism in *Moby-Dick*, and this is not astonishing in view of the novel's hints in this direction.[3] The major piece of presumed evidence is of course the Ishmael-Queequeg relation, in which Ishmael seems not at all reluctant to portray himself as the huge savage's contented wife. On the one hand, as a couple Ishmael and Queequeg both prefigure and personalize the fraternal feelings in such tasks as cutting into the whale's blubber and reconverting its sperm into liquid. On the other hand, Ishmael gives a highly eroticized account of the friendship. After their first night together in the same bed at the Spouter Inn in New Bedford, Ishmael awakes to find Queequeg's arm thrown over him "in the most loving and affectionate manner," as if he "had been his wife" and were being held in a "bridegroom clasp" (32–33). The next night they seal their friendship, once again in bed, with "confidential disclosures," just as man and wife often choose

---

[3]To mention two ends of a kind of moral spectrum of perspectives on homosexuality in *Moby-Dick*: Leslie Fiedler, in *Love and Death in the American Novel* (New York: Stein and Day, 1966), finds Melville (and other American writers) unable to deal with adult heterosexual love. Robert K. Martin, in *Hero, Captain, and Stranger: Male Friendship, Social Critique, and Literary Form in the Sea Novels of Herman Melville* (Chapel Hill: University of North Carolina Press, 1986), reinterprets this failure as an accomplishment of the highest order.

their bed to "open the very bottom of their souls to each other." "Thus, then," this passage ends, "in our hearts' honeymoon, lay I and Queequeg—a cosy, loving pair" (54). During the voyage, when they are both tied to the same monkey rope (in the "humorously perilous business" of Queequeg's going over the side of the ship to insert a blubber hook into the whale's back, where he must remain during the whole stripping operation), they are not simply "inseparable twin brother[s]" but are "for the time . . . wedded" (271).

There is no ambiguity whatsoever in all these eroticizing allusions. They clearly instruct us to think of the bond between Ishmael and Queequeg as not unlike marital bonds, and it can be argued that they do this with no suggestion of homosexual desire. I say this somewhat tentatively because we might also say that homosexual desire is precisely what is signified by those conjugal signifiers. But where exactly is the signified? Is there a *subject* of homosexual desire in *Moby-Dick*? Far from representing either unequivocal homosexuality or surfaces of heterosexual desire troubled by repressed homosexual impulses, Melville's characters have no sexual subjectivity at all. Critics readily admit how little the wholly improbable soliloquies of Melville's characters conform to the discursive parameters of realistic fiction; they have more difficulty recognizing that those soliloquies adequately represent the essence of the characters. Interiority in *Moby-Dick* is almost entirely philosophical; each character is a certain confluence of metaphysical, epistemological, and social-ethical positions. Homoeroticism can enter the novel so easily because, psychologically, there is nothing at stake. In Balzac, Gide, and Proust, homosexual desire is a fact of great psychological significance, whereas it may be a peculiarity of American literature—Cooper, Twain, and Hemingway come to mind—that it frequently presents homosexual situations that are psychologically inconsequential, unconnected to characterization. Ishmael's marital metaphors reveal nothing about him because there is nowhere in the novel an Ishmael about whom such metaphors can be revealing.

This does not mean that they are unimportant: their very significance depends on *not* providing an intelligible alternative to Ahab's despotism. Each time the novel spells out any such alternative, it is in terms that do little more than negatively repeat what they oppose. Thus the land is opposed to the sea, and Ahab's unhappy solitude is set against the quiet joy of domestic ties. Starbuck is the principal advocate of intelligible alternatives to Ahab, such as wife and family, the land, fraternal compassion, and a democratic respect for the rights of others. But if Ahab's tyrannical rule enacts the ultimate logic of the privileges that democracy would accord personality, then perhaps the very principle of oppositional couplings cannot be trusted. Only something that does not enter into logical opposition can be "opposed" to Ahab. Politically this means that in order to escape the antidemocratic consequences inherent in the democratic ideal, a type of social relation must be imagined that is neither autocratic nor democratic.

Ishmael's response to Queequeg and the crew is the testing of this other relation, although each time he tries to analyze it he also banalizes it, as in the Starbuck-like contrast between the intellect and the fireside. But, just as Ishmael's insane ecstasy while squeezing blobs of sperm is irreducible to any of these terms, so the introduction of homoeroticism into the novel prevents his representation of Queequeg and the crew from being one of a society united in the bonds of friendship created by communal work. This homoeroticism, however, never settles into what would be merely another type of oppositional grouping. By figuring what I have called a nonpsychological homosexuality, Melville proposes a social bond based not on subordination to the great personality embodied by Ahab, not on the democratic ideal of power distributed according to intrinsic worth, not on those feelings binding either two friends or the partners in a marriage, not, finally, on the transgressed homage to all such legitimated social bonds in conventional images of homosexual desire. . . .

The casual humor of both the early section on Ishmael's "marriage" to Queequeg and the description of sperm squeezing helps to transform the representation of both friendship and homoeroticism into an inconceivable social bond. In so doing it evokes, in an unexpected way, the originality of American society, which Melville is both attached to and unable to describe. Ishmael's humor is a way of simultaneously proposing and withdrawing definitions and identifications, of using what are, after all, the only available categories, social and linguistic, to coax into existence as yet unavailable terms. Even the most inappropriate descriptions can serve this dislocating function. Thus, though I may have been right to argue that the reference to wife, heart, and fireside is a taming irrelevance in the squeezing-sperm chapter, the terms also disturbingly suggest an unformulated relation between a kind of anarchic sensuality and a socially viable domesticity. Similarly, far from being a parodistic version of normal marriage or a domesticating of homosexual bonds, the Ishmael-Queequeg marriage enacts a sensuality that cannot be reduced to the psychology of either heterosexual or homosexual desire, a sensuality at once nontransgressive and authorized by nothing beyond Ishmael's mode of addressing it.

Lest this begin to sound like an argument for the socially unthreatening nature of homoeroticism, I want to insist on the absence of authorization. Melville makes it clear that the society in which these new relations are being tested is a society wholly outside society. From the very first pages, going to sea is presented as a letting go of all social, conceptual, and sexual familiarity. The first chapter of *Moby-Dick* is an extraordinarily haunting invocation of seagoing as a "substitute for pistol and ball," a deliberate removal from life itself. A whole city is transformed into a collective suicidal longing when Ishmael evokes thousands of men "posted like silent sentinels all around the town" and "fixed in ocean reveries." We should keep in mind this powerfully oneiric image of a humanity thronging "just as nigh the water as they possibly can without falling in," anxious to abandon the ship of society for the magnetizing and original death promised by the sea. The first chapter clearly warns us not to consider any bonds or fellowship that may develop or, in the case of Ishmael or Queequeg, be confirmed on board the *Pequod* as compatible with the society of the land.

Is the *Pequod*, to the extent that it functions outside Ahab's domination, the image of an authentically democratic work society? Perhaps—but the workforce is constituted by a hybrid collection of exiles and outcasts. Not only does the biblical name by which the narrator invites the reader to address him in the novel's first line resonate with such connotations; the latter aptly describe the crew of the *Pequod*. Ishmael's emphasis on all the countries and races represented on the ship invites us to see the crew as a kind of international fraternity of men united in harmonious and useful work. But there is an equally strong emphasis on the wild, untutored, asocial nature of the men in that fraternity. "They were nearly all Islanders in the Pequod. *Isolatos* too, I call such, not acknowledging the common continent of men, but each *Isolato* living on a separate continent of his own" (108). It is, as Starbuck says, "a heathen crew . . . whelped somewhere by the sharkish sea" (148), a crew, as Ishmael puts it, "chiefly made up of mongrel renegades, and castaways, and cannibals" (162). Indeed whalers in general are "floating outlaws," manned by "unaccountable odds and ends of strange nations come up from the unknown nooks and ash-holes of the earth" (198).

Ishmael himself must be thought of as belonging to that group; he is its expression. He is so casual in his dismissals of ordinary assumptions about social bonds that we may easily miss his readiness to reject the values of the land. "For my part," he announces in chapter one, "I abominate all honorable respectable toils, trials, and tribulations of every kind whatsoever." In context, this is playfully perverse hyperbole; but it also belongs to what amounts to a systematic rejection of the civilized ethics of a democratic and Christian land society. Honorable respectable toils are abominated; the chapter on Fast-Fish and Loose-Fish is a Swiftian mockery of legal systems in which rights to ownership are often identical to the brute force necessary to claim possession; and Christianity itself is implicitly dismissed in the comparison of images of physical "robustness" in art ("in everything imposingly beautiful, strength has much to do with the magic") to "the soft, curled, hermaphroditical Italian pictures" of Christ, which "hint nothing of any power, but the mere negative, feminine one of submission and endurance, which on all hands it is conceded, form the peculiar practical virtue of his teaching" (315). The *Pequod* is not, however, a reconstitution of politics, morality, or religious beliefs on some presumably more natural basis. Queequeg's religion is as unsatisfactory as Christianity, and Ishmael's infinite tolerance, far from being grounded in a faith where tolerance is preached as a virtue, merely expresses his unwillingness to be intolerant in the name of any faith whatsoever. Nor is Ishmael willing to swear allegiance to the *Pequod*'s society of savages as a type of social organization. "I myself am a savage, owning to no allegiance but to the King of the Cannibals, and ready at any moment to rebel against him" (232).

Is the *Pequod* an image of America?[4] It is the settlement of America reenacted, but uncompromisingly radicalized. The "unaccountable odds and ends" from all over the world who ended up in America were of course not only castaways and cannibals; nor were they all, for that matter, unaccountable. But by insisting on the *Pequod*'s nearly total break with the land and the past, Melville simultaneously evokes the origins of America as a house for exiles from everywhere and makes those origins absolute. That is, he evokes the possibility of exile as a wholly new beginning and brutally deprives it of the comforting notion of loss. There is no dream that has been frustrated, no second chance for forms of life imagined, but then blocked in their realization, somewhere else. The sea is wildness and anarchy; it opposes to both Ahab's despotism and the democratic vision a kind of social suicide. Thus Melville's novel dreams metaphorically of that absolute break with Europe which of course never took place, of a risky willingness to "come to America" with no social vision at all, with nothing but an anxious need to die to society and to history. Far from fulfilling a European dream, America would therefore have to be invented by those "thousands upon thousands of mortal men" who at first wanted nothing more than to flee from the land but who, having joined the crew of exiles and renegades from all over the hated world, now find themselves suspended in their dying and are obliged to redefine the social itself.

I have argued that, principally through Ahab, *Moby-Dick* dramatizes the oxymoronic impasse of democracy: the great man's despotism realizes the democratic dream of equality. But *Moby-Dick* also reinvents that politically infernal rhetoric as a political promise: it dreams a society owing nothing whatsoever to known social ideas. What this society after social death might actually be, we can say no more than Melville (or Ishmael) himself can. What can be said is only what has already been said, and Ishmael's way of coercing all that used speech into unimagined significances is to withdraw humorously from nearly all his propositions. He can say what he means only by refusing to mean what he says. America's history will take place in the space at once cluttered and blank where all imaginable social bonds have been simultaneously figured and dissolved. Melville's America is a historical meta-oxymoron: it defeats the defeating oxymoron of a democracy ruined by the fulfillment of

---

[4]The distance between this America and historical America is also suggested, from another perspective, by the ship's name. The Pequod Indians, a reputedly bloodthirsty Connecticut tribe, were massacred by militia from Hartford in 1637. If Melville's *Pequod* is an image of America, it is an America expelled from America and eliminated by America. Rogin writes that in naming Ahab's ship *Pequod*, Melville paid ironic homage to a process in which "the conquest of savages and the acquisition of their power" is implicitly seen as "regeneration through violence." Michael Paul Rogin, *Subversive Genealogy* (New York: Alfred P. Knopf, 1983), p. 124. For a study of this process, see Richard Slotkin, *Regeneration Through Violence* (Middletown: Wesleyan University Press, 1973).

its own promise by erasing all promises in order to make the wholly unauthorized promise of an absolutely new society.

The representation of Melville's America is thus inseparable from a crisis of meaning. On the one hand, the interpretive faculty is associated with madness. It is not only that "all evil" is personified in Moby Dick, but also that Ahab sees evil omens and portents everywhere. The mass of information given to us about whales and whaling is obviously designed to counteract this madness; here the encyclopedia functions as an antidote to overreading, as a source of reliable facts, as a comfortable and necessary myth of a collection of knowledge unaffected by the collector's passions. "So ignorant are most landsman of some of the plainest and most palpable wonders of the world, that without some hints touching the plain facts, historical and otherwise, of the fishery they might scout at Moby Dick as a monstrous fable, or still worse and more detestable, a hideous and intolerable allegory" (177).

But this is somewhat disingenuous. The most persistent and extravagant sign reader in the novel is Ishmael. His allegorical wisdom, it is true, is of fairly modest quality; nor does he hesitate to mock it himself. What is interesting, as others have noted, is the interpretive habit itself or, more strangely, the inability to stop reading, even though the object to be read may be unreadable. *Moby-Dick* is full of enigmatic texts. First and foremost, there is the whale, both as a species and in its individual features and behavior. There is also the doubloon, with its "strange figures and inscriptions"; in chapter 99, Ahab, Starbuck, Stubb, Flask, the Manxman, Queequeg, Fedallah, and Pip all perform interpretively—producing little more than self-characterizations—in front of the gold coin. If Ahab interprets "in some monomaniac way whatever significance might lurk" in the doubloon's markings, "some certain significance," Ishmael nonetheless adds, "lurks in all things, else all things are little worth, and the round world itself but an empty cipher, except to sell by the cartload, as they do hills about Boston, to fill up some morass in the Milky Way" (358). Even Queequeg's tattoos are described as hieroglyphics containing "a complete theory of the heavens and the earth, a mystical treatise on the art of attaining truth"; and looking at that unsolvable riddle, Ahab wildly exclaims: " 'Oh, devilish tantalization of the gods!' " (399). Most remarkably, however tragically frustrated or humorously tentative all such readings may be, the very course of events in the novel spectacularly confirms the power of reading. Not only do all the omens and portents turn out to be omens and portents of what actually happens to the *Pequod* and its crew; Elijah's dire prophecy also accurately prefigures the voyage's tragic end (" 'Good bye to ye. Shan't see ye again very soon, I guess; unless it's before the Grand Jury' " [91]); and the demonic Fedallah's prediction—one doesn't even know what text he reads—of how he and Ahab will die is fulfilled with uncanny precision.

Moby-Dick is a chaos of interpretive modes. As a drama of interpretation,

Melville's novel appears to center on Ahab. But Ahab represents only one type of interpretive activity, and in a sense it is the crudest and the easiest to discredit. For him, Moby Dick is a symbol of evil that, in its vicious attacks, fittingly partakes of the nature of what it symbolizes. Ahab is guilty of a double mistake of logic: he unjustifiably infers an agent or course of evil from the observable phenomenon of human "sufferings and exasperations," and then he identifies a possible manifestation of that evil with its essence. Having done that, he—and with him now the crew—begins to see all things as signs. Although the symbolic reading is particular to Ahab (nothing indicates that the crew shares Ahab's philosophically sophisticated madness of attributing the sum of human woes to the whale they are chasing), a degraded form of symbolic interpretation manifests itself as the superstition of signs. Instead of symbols, we have portents: the darting away of "shoals of small harmless fish . . . with what seemed shuddering fins," the "tri-painted trinity of flames" when the ship's three masts are set on fire by lightning during the typhoon, and the seizing of Ahab's hat from his head by a savage sea hawk. Symbolism is a vertical mode of interpretation (Moby Dick is transcended by the metaphysical reality he points to), but the ominous sign can be thought of as a metonymic slip. It is as if part of a pattern of catastrophe had been detached from the pattern and moved ahead of its realization in time. The omen announces the events to which it belongs; it is the beginning of a catastrophe that has not yet begun.

There is, more generally, the interpretation of the entire novel as a philosophical parable in which going to sea figures the risky movement of speculative thought, of thought unanchored, set loose from all evidential "land" securities. . . .

The consequence of all this is that *Moby-Dick* becomes a novel unavailable to the culture it still manages to define (while making the generous, even utopian assumption that such readings as the one I am proposing *are* available to that culture). Melville's novel is the literary equivalent of that "dumb blankness full of meaning" which is what Ishmael finds so awesome in that whale's whiteness. We may continue to speak of *Moby-Dick* (as the novel itself demonstrates, criticism is unstoppable), but we can at least hope for an appropriately impoverished reading, one that principally describes how the narrative anticipates, entertains, and withdraws its assent from all our interpretive moves. The chapter on "The Whiteness of the Whale" analyzes the symptoms of a mind afflicted with an oxymoronic perception of the universe. Reality is an infinitely meaningful absence of meaning, and *Moby-Dick*—a novel of metaphysical realism—repeats that textuality in its own apparently unlimited capacity to entertain unauthorized interpretations. But this type of textuality—in which unreadability is identical to a limitless availability to interpretation—may be the condition of the novel's originality. American literature can be great not by being as good as or even better than European literature; it must be, in the full force of the term, incomparable. Thus

Ishmael will not only destroy the terms of comparison; he will also invalidate the very process of comparison—the unrelenting analogical habit—to which he appeals in order to validate his project of writing a "mighty book." *Moby-Dick* outdoes the cultural references it appropriates by dismissing itself; the simultaneous proposal and erasure of sense produces a book bloated with unaccepted sense. The extraordinary originality of Melville's work is that it somehow subsists—materially—as a book orphaned by its content.

The only surviving analogy of this shipwreck of sense is the analogy with America itself. Not only does the *Pequod*'s crew reenact the origin of American society as a break with the very idea of the social; the hermeneutic suspension of every interpretive move in the novel gives a kind of plausibility to the difficult idea of an historical originality.[5] It suggests that the originality of America cannot consist in a chimerical absolute break with its European past, but rather in what might be called an encyclopedic nonendorsement of that past. In America, as in Melville's novel, the massive borrowing from other cultures is identical to a self-distancing from other cultures. Sense is borrowed without being subscribed to, and the very indiscriminacy of the borrowing should produce a society without debts, one that never holds what it nonetheless greedily takes. *Moby-Dick* is at once politically, aesthetically, and economically utopian in that it invites America *to dissipate its capital*. This is not, I believe, merely another capitalistic or liberal mystification: far from merely offering the illusion of a break with established orders (an illusion so comforting that it would actually weaken our resistance to those same orders), *Moby-Dick* proposes no object of loyalty or of desire except the continuously repeated gesture of not receiving the wealth it appropriates.

The encyclopedism of *Moby-Dick* is, then, in no way redemptive. Never using either its cetological erudition or its cultural borrowings to monumentalize the truly raw materials of the American life, Melville's novel takes the same risks as the country it finally honors, not by taking the lead in world literature but by repeating its impoverished beginning, its utopian negations. *Moby-Dick* is indeed our mighty book, not because it makes a whole of the fragments of America but rather because, in its sheer massiveness, it never stops demonstrating (as if to inspire courage) the sustaining, self-renewing powers of historical and cultural orphanhood.

---

[5]In *Pierre* Melville himself will satirize the illusion of literary originality. A critique of the possibility of originality from the perspective of a post-structuralist ideology of textuality can be found in Edgar Dryden, "The Entangled Text: Melville's *Pierre* and the Problem of Reading," reprinted in this volume.

When Is a Painting Most Like a Whale?: Ishmael, *Moby Dick*, and the Sublime

Bryan Wolf

On October 6, 1847, the young Herman Melville, newly arrived upon the New York literary scene, attended the opening night celebration of the Art Union. The Art Union, which represented virtually every aspiring American painter of the period, had moved to new quarters on Broadway, and Melville, together with his publisher and mentor, Evert Duyckinck, joined at least "five hundred invited guests" who sampled the art and the fine wine that accompanied it. Among the many "clergymen, literary men, editors and artists" present, Melville met William Cullen Bryant, dean of American nature poets, and William Sidney Mount, a leading genre painter of the period.

Two years later, Bryant reappeared as a figure in a painting undoubtedly seen by Melville, Asher B. Durand's *Kindred Spirits*. The painting is a memorial tribute to Thomas Cole, father of the Hudson River school of landscape art. Cole had died unexpectedly in 1848, and Durand eulogized the painter by placing him next to Bryant in an imaginary Catskill landscape. The title of the painting . . . reminds us how close painters and writers were to each other in the early nineteenth century. . . . Both were engaged in the creation of an American version of the sublime. If *Moby-Dick* is our national tale of questing, an account not just of boats and whales but of the imagination and its limits, then it also shares with the writings of Emerson and the landscapes of Cole and Durand an impulse toward the sublime. Whether in prose, poetry, or pigment, American art of the 1850s fermented with the energies of a visionary character it could barely contain. What began in eighteenth-century England as a taste for the wild and destructive concluded in mid-nineteenth-century America as a national way of seeing. And Melville was a part of that ferment.

1

Melville provides many warnings in *Moby-Dick*, some of them quite humorous, against a form of romantic revery associated with Emerson and his followers. In the chapter "The Mast-Head," Ishmael cautions an imaginary "young Platonist," more given to "unseasonable meditativeness" than to searching for whales, against standing watch on the perilous height of the mast-head. The problem involves more than a question of philosophy. It concerns the law of gravity and its untoward consequences for those who mistake the roll of the sea for the rhythms of their soul.

> But while this sleep, this dream is on ye, move your foot or hand an inch; slip your hold at all; and your identity comes back in horror. Over Descartian vortices you hover. And perhaps, at midday, in the fairest weather, with one half-throttled shriek you drop through that transparent air into the summer sea, no more to rise for ever. Heed it well, ye Pantheists! (Chap. 35)

Ishmael cautions the visionary pantheist, caught in an Emersonian moment of "midday," the "fairest weather," and "transparent air," not to mistake the pleasantries of nature for the realities of his own soul. The peril of such confusion is that the young philosopher risks, quite literally, losing his grip on reality and plunging, unwittingly, to the waiting seas below. Ishmael's warning represents more than an insight into the dangers of a particular strand of American thought. It is a good-natured form of self-admonishment, a caution against his own visionary penchants, and we do well to take Ishmael seriously on the matter. For the very confusion of nature and self that he warns against is precisely the stance he takes in the chapter. . . . But Ishmael shares far more with the bard of Concord than his comic caveat acknowledges. . . .

The famous "transparent eyeball" passage of Emerson's *Nature* commences, as previous commentators have noted, not in the countryside but on the Boston Commons:

> Crossing a bare common, in snow puddles, at twilight, under a clouded sky, without having in my thoughts any occurrence of special good fortune, I have enjoyed a perfect exhilaration. I am glad to the brink of fear. In the woods, too, a man casts off his years, as the snake his slough, and at what period soever of life is always a child. In the woods is perpetual youth. . . . In the woods, we return to reason and faith. There I feel that nothing can befall me in life,—no disgrace, no calamity (leaving me my eyes), which nature cannot repair. Standing on the bare ground,—my head bathed by the blithe air and uplifted into infinite space,—all mean egotism vanishes. I become a transparent eyeball; I am nothing; I see all; the currents of the Universal Being circulate through me; I am part and parcel of God. . . . In the wilderness, I find something more dear and connate than in streets or villages. In the tranquil landscape, and especially in the distant line of the horizon, man beholds somewhat as beautiful as his own nature.

The key to this passage can be found in its opening lines, and especially in the manner in which Emerson situates himself in space. The passage begins in a state of transition: The speaker is in the process of "Crossing a bare common." He is already in motion when we first observe him, and his movements carry with them the suggestion of a moral geography. To cross a bare common is not only to initiate a process of change, a pilgrim's progress, but to fill the emptiness of the common with significance: to cross it, to place it under the sign of the cross. Both "crossing" and "common" are puns. The former has religious overtones, whereas the latter suggests a vernacular world, the common realm of everyday experience. "Crossing a bare common," then, is not only an act of secular faith, an investment of the vernacular with significance, but also a negating of the everyday, a crossing out of the ordinary in the name of that which is to follow, the extraordinary. This second meaning of "crossing," an allusion not just to theology but to the negation, the emptying out that must precede salvation, is reinforced by the description of the common as "bare." It has been denuded, emptied of its color by the "clouded" "twilight" hour of the day, and shorn of its relation both to nature (it is no longer a wilderness, but the heart of a city) and to society (where are the people?).

We encounter the term "bare" again several lines later in the description that immediately precedes the "transparent eyeball" experience. "Standing on the bare ground,—my head bathed by the blithe air and uplifted into infinite space,—all mean egotism vanishes." The "bare common" has become the "bare ground" here. It is both more anonymous than in the previous description and, for that very reason, more central to the experience that follows. The bare ground exists as a precondition, rhetorically and metaphysically, for the "uplifted" head. The act of vision depends upon a previous moment of negation. Before the speaker can *see*, before he can "dilate and conspire" with the universe around him, he must first reduce its otherness to a manageable form. And that happens as early as his initial "crossing" of the common.

What we learn from the earlier episode—what the later description confirms—is a process of displacement in which the speaker situates himself at an ever greater remove from nature. To cross a bare common is to cross out nature, to eradicate it as a scene of anything but the author's own vision. When two lines later we enter the woods at last, we arrive by force of analogy: "In the woods, too, a man casts off his years, as the snake his slough, and at what period soever of life is always a child." The transition from bare commons to the woods is effected by the word "too": "In the woods, too . . ." The "too" tells us that we have moved in analogous fashion from the commons to the woods, that in the woods *as on* the commons, a certain experience of divestiture occurs. "Too" then functions as a hidden simile. It reminds us that we move from one location to another only imaginatively, *as if* the commons were the woods, *as if* we were there. We learn that crossing any bare commons, when it is an act significantly done, requires motion no greater than a metaphor, and nature is simply that which is emptied out, erased, crossed over.

Childhood, then, is the endpoint of a twofold experience: the emptying out of the old, like a snake shedding his slough, and the creation in its stead of an imaginative self empowered by its own rhetoric. Childhood is rhetoric rightly learned, the capacity of tropes and language to fill nature's vacuum. It is little wonder that Emerson should subsequently find himself a transparent eyeball. It is a trope that not only combines in oxymoronic fashion the visual and cerebral (like trying to imagine what thought *looks like*) but defines visionary experience as a form of self-aggrandizement. The loss of "all mean egotism" requires more than a mystical congruence of self and world. True power occurs only in a moment of *representation* when vision and language are conjoined and the self is at its "ocular" best ("I *see* all"). The ego is not so much dissolved as concentrated in a state of heightened awareness, its perceptual possibilities intensified rather than transcended (why else be a transparent *eyeball?*). What Emerson provides us with, then, is not a metalinguistic event, an experience of union with nature outside language and time, but a moment of epiphany informed by the possibilities of perception.

That, I take it, is the force of Emerson's perceptual pilgrimage. Nature is fitted to the mind's shape, it circulates through us, and our own powers of seeing come to substitute for the common void of reality. The dualistic rhythms of Emerson's prose—"I am nothing; I see all,"—simply repeat the pattern of negation and plentitude supplied by the opening passage. And *what*, we may ask after all this, do we actually *see?* Why, ourselves, of course. Emerson concludes his experience of power and vision with a line as sweet and smooth as country butter: "In the tranquil landscape, and especially in the distant line of the horizon, man beholds somewhat as beautiful as his own nature." The allusion to the "line of the horizon" is meant to suggest an image of expansion that defines the self's rather than the world's boundaries. For as Emerson tells us at the conclusion of his sentence, "man beholds somewhat as beautiful as his own nature." Nature has become "his own nature," not just a possession of the visionary self ("*his* own nature"), but a version of himself: It is his *own* nature that we behold. The experience of the transparent eyeball has become a study in self-portraiture. The story behind the story is how one comes to possess nature as a version of oneself.

And this returns us to Ishmael and his young Platonist. What Ishmael shares with Emerson . . . is a rapaciousness of vision that swallows reality whole and converts it into a version of the self. The dreamy-eyed Platonist, you will recall, was doing the opposite: He was flowing with the ocean of life in mystical oneness. Or at least that is what he *thought* he was doing. . . . In the guise of warning us against pantheistic reveries, [Ishmael] was actually steering us away from the *real* danger: a form of visual and intellectual self-aggrandizement that reduces reality to a cipher at the same time as it renders man the cipher maker. The Emerson Ishmael implicitly satirizes exists nowhere but in Ishmael's text. He is a vacant-eyed worshipper of nature. But the real Emerson, the dangerous because sublime Emerson, is the true subject of Ishmael's concern. And that Emerson, *our* Emerson, exists not in Ishmael's satire but in his rhetorical doings, his metaphoric comings and goings. What Ishmael is not telling us is that he is our most Emersonian of narrators.

2

There is another way to define Ishmael's relation to Emerson, and that is to say that each represents an American version of the sublime. This is not the sublime of Burke and his eighteenth-century followers, who preached a power in nature, and a corresponding faculty of appreciation in man, that over-whelmed all of our usual notions of order. Burke's sublime was a transgressive one: It viewed nature as a punishing father and then transformed that punishment into a spectacle that could be safely viewed—and enjoyed—from a distance. By the time of Melville in the mid-nineteenth century, the sublime had undergone radical surgery. The presiding "physician" had been Immanuel Kant, the philosopher from Koenigsberg, who grafted large por-tions of Burke's sublime from nature as an external power to the *observer* within nature. The result was a new emphasis on perception itself. To behold the sublime in nature was not simply to witness the elements in all their grandeur but to appropriate that grandeur as a *metaphor* for consciousness. The question was no longer when is a landscape most like a father (and an angry one at that), but how is the horizon only another version of thought, a boundary to consciousness?

Kant's ideas underwent many transformations in the early nineteenth century. They surfaced in altered form in the writings of the English roman-tics and appeared, ghostlike, to haunt the literary corpus of Samuel Taylor Coleridge. Where they took deepest root, however, was in America, and here they grew at a prodigious pace, breathed to life in the writings of Emerson and nurtured by a certain cultural imperialism that was always happy to convert, in Emerson's terms, the NOT ME into the ME.

For that is what the sublime in the nineteenth century meant: an astonish-ing capacity of mind, an ability to consume the world as nothing more than a plenum of nutrients in that characteristically American project of self-making. At its most audacious, the sublime entailed a virtual substitution of self for world; it was an egotistical affair conceived in pride and consummated in an incestuous twining of nature back into the self, the NOT ME into the ME. The key to this project was language, the uncanny talent of words to usurp the place of things and to define possession as only another manner of speaking. As Thoreau, another of Emerson's disciples, wrote of his relation to the Yankee farmer on a neighboring farm, "I took his word for his deed, for I dearly loved to talk." The sublime artist deeded himself primogeniture over all the world, for it was his to inherit at a price no greater than words. The strategy was as brilliant as it was simple. Convert nature into language: Render that which is other, prior to, or outside the self into a version accessible to the self and you shall reign as a (figurative) monarch over all you see. . . .

Ishmael's story represents a test of the proposition that the world may be brought under the sway of language. His relation to events around him depends upon his use of words. In "Cetology," we catch Ishmael at his favorite labor: transforming his observations and arcane learning into a form of word play. He tells us at the outset:

> It is some systematized exhibition of the whale in his broad genera, that I would now fain put before you. Yet is it no easy task. The classification of the constituents of a chaos, nothing less is here essayed. (Chap. 32)

The term "essayed" alerts us to the design of Ishmael's project. He will not only attempt (essay) to comprehend the whale, but he will do so as a literary exercise (essay). Ishmael commences his cetological observations with a bow toward objectivity. He hurls every scrap of knowledge available to him at the unnamed significance of the whale, hoping to overcome nature's silence by the force of his learning. "Cetology" thus begins with what might be termed a "shotgun" approach to whaling: Ishmael loads his metaphoric gun with the fodder of human knowledge, takes aim at whales in particular and the universe in general, and then gently lets go. For the next several pages, we see scattered over the text the debris of human knowledge mingled with fragments of whale.

On the whole, it is a rather messy approach. Ishmael later admits that "As yet . . . the sperm whale, scientific or poetic, lives not complete in any literature. Far above all other hunted whales, his is an unwritten life." The effort to capture the whale within the hunt of knowledge is a failure. Ishmael accordingly rejects the classifications of Linnaeus and modern science and asserts, on the advice of some of his old sea friends and the biblical book of *Jonah*, that "a whale is a spouting fish with a horizontal tail. There you have him." He abandons science altogether and substitutes for natural history the Gospel of Whales according to Ishmael.

What follows is a transformation of whales into books grouped according to printers' conventions. In language redolent of biblical rhetoric and epic formula, Ishmael proclaims "the grand divisions of the entire whale host."

> First: According to magnitude I divide the whales into three primary BOOKS (subdivisible into CHAPTERS), and these shall comprehend them all, both small and large.
>
> I. THE FOLIO WHALE; II. the OCTAVO WHALE; III. the DUODECIMO WHALE. (Chap. 32)

Ishmael's strategy here is to replace learning with laughter—not *any* laughter, but his own deconstructive version of laughing. He undercuts the myths of objective knowledge with which he began and playfully proceeds to textualize his world, measuring reality according to the dimensions of books. His conversion of leviathans into folio sizes shifts the focus of "Cetology" from whales (what we thought Ishmael was talking about) to language (what in fact the chapter is about). In the process, Ishmael domesticates what is foreign in nature into a version of the familiar. . . .

Of course, Ishmael is not always so loquacious. When he first encounters Queequeg in the book's opening chapters, he finds himself speechless. In a scene full of comic happenstance, the most curious incident of all is Ishmael's momentary loss of language. Ishmael, as you will recall, has been sitting in bed, watching with amazement the rituals of a bald-headed stranger who is unaware of his presence. With growing horror, Ishmael realizes that the figure he is gazing at behaves suspiciously like a South Seas savage. "Had not the stranger stood between me and the door, I would have bolted out of it quicker than ever I bolted a dinner."

Ishmael doesn't bolt. What he does instead is observe, a comic witness to Queequeg's inscrutable rituals. The bolting, when it comes, is entirely Queequeg's. He grabs his tomahawk, puffs out "great clouds of tobacco smoke" and leaps into bed, unaware that Ishmael is anything more than an unruly fold of the sheets.

And that is where the curiosity lies. Ishmael is invisible to Queequeg; when Ishmael wants to talk, he can't. Realizing that Queequeg is about to leap into bed, Ishmael decides that it is time to announce his presence. "I thought it was high time, now or never, before the light was put out, to break the spell in which I had so long been bound." But he misses his chance. Queequeg pounces into bed while Ishmael is still deliberating what to do.

> But the interval I spent in deliberating what to say, was a fatal one. . . . The next moment the light was extinguished, and this wild cannibal, tomahawk between his teeth, sprang into bed with me. I sang out, I could not help it now; and giving a sudden grunt of astonishment he began feeling me. (Chap. 3)

Ishmael's response to this heathen invasion is as inarticulate as Queequeg's "sudden grunt."

> Stammering out something, I know not what, I rolled away from him against the wall, and then conjured him, whoever or whatever he might be, to keep quiet, and let me get up and light the lamp again. But his guttural responses satisfied me at once that he but ill comprehended my meaning. (Chap. 3)

Ishmael's invisibility at this point is tied to his momentary lack of language. He cannot be seen by Queequeg because he has no voice. His silence before Queequeg's leap into bed robs him of any opportunity to assert his presence or retain even modest control over a situation where bad yields quickly to worse.

Were we to diagram Ishmael's story, we might divide it into parts labeled "before" and "after." *Before* Queequeg's great leap forward, Ishmael is a mock-visionary self alone in the bed; *after* Queequeg jumps into the bed, Ishmael is an awkward body, subject both to Queequeg's surprise and to his unintended advances ("he began feeling me"). What separates the two is language. Language is what allows Ishmael to retain his visionary status, or, to be more precise, it is the *lapse* of language that subjects Ishmael to Queequeg's bodily interrogation. Language is what defends the visionary self, however comically presented, against its own bodily status.

We have seen this situation before in *Moby-Dick*, or rather, in the context of the book's chronology, we will see it again. In "The Mast-Head," Ishmael relies upon language—his own visionary powers—not only to dilate with the universe but to protect himself against the consequences of too bodily a response to gravity. "The Mast-Head" represents a rewriting of Ishmael's initial encounter with Queequeg; it is the same tale with a different ending. In both, the focus is upon visionary action, whether set comically in a dark bed at night or, more plausibly, on the mast-head of a whaling vessel. And in both, the moment of vision yields to its attendant dangers. In "The Spouter-Inn," Queequeg represents as real a bodily threat to the discombobulated Ishmael as the ocean depths do to the bleary-eyed Platonist. What distinguishes the two chapters is the nature of the threat presented and the manner in which it is resolved. And here the chapters work antithetically: What appears to threaten Ishmael with bodily harm in "The Spouter-Inn" proves to be a boon instead. Queequeg becomes Ishmael's closest friend and alter ego. In "The Mast-Head," to the contrary, what appears benign and inviting—the blue of the sky and ocean—leads to the possibility of death, that unsanctified plunge to the ocean floor.

What do we learn from all this? That Ishmael's encounter with Queequeg, like the "mystick's" oceanic feelings, are studies in the limits of consciousness. Each episode carries us from a visionary state to a moment of bodily threat, and when we arrive there, when we find ourselves at the margins of thought and language, we are confronted with two alternatives. We may, like the young Platonist, ignore the limits before us and plunge headlong into the sea (did you ever see a Platonist dive *feet* first?). Or, like Ishmael with Queequeg, we may discover in the very lapse of language the possibility of new experiences. The real threat, in effect, comes not from language but from ourselves: It lies in our inability to discriminate limits, to recognize where our discourse ends and someone else's begins. What we learn from Ishmael is not to take our own vision too exclusively. We need to make our peace with the *lapses*. For that is where Queequeg dwells.

What does all this have to do with the sublime? A great deal, for Ishmael's story represents an egotistical sublime continually testing its own limits. Ishmael is surrounded by things that go bump in the night, a world that repeatedly asserts its otherness to him. Whether that otherness takes the form of a South Seas savage, a wounded captain, a hunted whale, or an inscrutable universe, it is always there. Ishmael's response, in turn, is consistent. He affirms the very lapses that hem in a figure like Ahab—lapses that define the boundaries of his own discourse. When Ishmael speaks, two things happen. Whatever he touches turns to language (Ishmael as sublime narrator), and whatever he touches touches him back (the sublime discovering its limits). The first of these two moments represents Ishmael's effort to convert the world into a version of himself, whereas the second characterizes those instances of rupture in the text when we lose Ishmael's voice altogether. The question is: How do we reconcile the idea of the sublime with the idea of limits—don't the two represent a contradiction in terms? Or, in terms of Ishmael's story, what do we learn about the sublime from Ishmael's silences?

3

To answer our questions, we [turn] to mid-nineteenth-century American painting. We have been dealing with the sublime thus far as an egotistical event that operates through the medium of language. We haven't considered, however, the prices language exacts for its services. Language was not a neutral medium for Melville and his contemporaries. It came with certain tendencies and imperatives of its own. To understand Ishmael, we need to know not only how he converts the real into a form of language game, but what rules the game imposes upon its players. And nowhere is the tension between the sublime as an egotistical affair and the sublime as a form of language more evident than in the landscapes of Frederic E. Church. Church was a student of Thomas Cole. His landscapes of the 1850s commanded prices higher than those previously paid for any American painting. Church's flair for melodrama together with his tendency to paint exotic scenery made him the most prominent figure in the second generation of Hudson River school painters. His art provides us with a chronicle of the sublime as it negotiates its own contradictory imperatives. We discover in his canvases both the evasions and the affirmations that undergird a narrative like Ishmael's.

[In *The Andes of Ecuador* of 1855, Church depicts a South American sunrise. He fills the foreground of the canvas with mountain ranges rising to the sky and then places a small, round sun at the center of the painting. The sun animates the entire canvas with its vortex of light.] Church provides the viewer with an allegory of American national destiny, [harnessing] the traditions of the sublime for New World purposes. He renders a local, if idealized, landscape into an almost religious vision of birth and resurrection (a way of seeing that Church shared with many of his contemporaries). The painting effects its transformation of secular into sacred by two means: iconographically, [by juxtaposing a series of] crosses in the lower left of the canvas with the . . . cross of light [implicit] in the center, and in more painterly fashion through its use of overpowering light. The sun presides over a world in which matter is converted into energy and each day begins with the promise of new creation.

Church loved to pun: He occasionally signed letters with a picture of a church. . . . [In] *The Andes of Ecuador*, [Church includes] not only a church or monastery nestled in the foreground hills to the left of center, but also a recurrent series of light-filled crosses emanating downward along a vertical axis that literally inscribes the painter (or his iconic surrogate, the cross) into the landscape. We need not avail ourselves of the pun to appreciate the way in which the painter places *himself* at the center of his canvas. The painting subjugates matter to the laws of light and allows no refuge from its spellbinding energy. It celebrates in sublime fashion the powers of consciousness over the natural world, a world where light almost literally dematerializes the landscape that reflects it.

Church subordinates nature to the monopoly of mind in two ways: graphically, through the unifying efforts of color, tone, and composition; and verbally or iconically, through those puns that place the painter at the heart of his world. The canvas is composed of a series of concentric circles (or semicircles) around the organizing presence of the sun. This drive toward unity is counterpointed by a progression of rectangular planes, which in their movement from foreground to middle ground transform the landscape visually into a sequence of steps culminating in altarlike fashion before the regal and enthroned sun. To move from foreground to background is to undergo a progressive spiritualization, a dematerialization, that dissolves matter into light and renders all nature subject to the laws of the sun. Church's cross of light not only crosses out nature as anything more than a reflection of itself but proceeds, in Emersonian fashion, to fill the vacuum left through nature's negation with its own image. The impression of unity is reinforced by the monochromatic palette and muted colors that bind together Church's world.

But there is a problem, perhaps we might even say a *repression*, afoot, and we do well to note it. A deep chasm runs from the right foreground to the lower center of the painting, where it intersects with the vertical axis of Church's cross of light. This chasm announces, or at least suggests, a bifurcation of reality larger than the artist's monism would allow. The foreground breach in the landscape reminds us that Church is attempting to repair by color what has been sundered by composition, and that the covert drama of the painting so intent upon its own monistic unity concerns that hidden but lingering hint of dualism present in the canvas's foreground.

A brief bit of detective work brings us to Church's teacher, Thomas Cole, who had painted three decades earlier *Expulsion from the Garden of Eden*, 1827. [Cole's painting contrasts the beauty of Eden, seen on the right side of the canvas, with the terrors of a dark and fallen world on the left. The two realms are connected in the painting by a natural bridge which spans the distance between them.] In both paintings an angled chasm . . . divides the foreground into separate realms, a mated pair of palm trees [frames] the composition on the left, and a sloping series of waterways . . . eventuates on the right in a quiet lake whose water plunges into the chasm. *The Andes of Ecuador* not only alludes to Cole through its deployment of a foreground space adapted from the *Expulsion* but proceeds to rewrite—or repaint—Cole in two ways: first by naturalizing Cole's more allegorical landscape, and then by replacing Cole's chiaroscuro and dualism with its own monochromatic unity. The painting moves from a bifurcated Colean foreground to a dazzling vision of unity in the background.

What we witness in these images of birth and creation (Church) and the fall and expulsion (Cole) are alternative accounts of the sublime. To appreciate Church's painting, we must understand the contrast it invokes between Cole's radically divided landscape and Church's all-encompassing monism, his ability to restore that Edenic light in the right *half* of Cole's painting to the *whole* of his canvas. By rendering Cole a painter of dualisms and identifying himself, through the sun and cross in the sky, with the powers of a lost Eden, Church creates an image of Paradise regained. Church's painting provides an answer to Cole's *Expulsion*: It restores the light of Eden to the whole of the canvas. It is as if the pupil has not only memorialized the master [(there are a cross and a shrine in the left foreground)] but substituted for the latter's vision an image of self-repair and ultimately self-origination that claims for itself the sole power of creation. There is nothing in Church's sky to compete with his sun. He presides self-sufficient over his own light-infused world.

Or to phrase the matter alternatively, Church creates [in *The Andes of Ecuador*] an image of the egotistical sublime. He converts the past (Cole's *Expulsion*) into a version of himself at the same time as he renders nature as a metaphor for consciousness in general and the artist in particular. What begins publicly as a study of national destiny concludes privately as a portrait of the artist as a young man. Church thus resembles Ishmael (and, behind him, Emerson). For each figure, vision is always a two-step affair: an act of negation followed by a rewriting of the negated as a version of oneself, an absorption of nature into the language of the self.

Several years later, however, in *Cotopaxi*, 1862, [Church again depicts an Andean landscape, only this time the sky is divided into two realms: the sun presides over the right half of the canvas while a distant volcano punctures the horizon line on the left, filling the sky with its black smoke. Church returns in this painting to his relation to Cole. But the terms have been altered.] His composition is now divided into dual realms in a manner reminiscent of Cole's *Expulsion*. The X-shaped or chiastic structure of the landscape denies the viewer the security of the fixed-point perspective that characterized *The Andes of Ecuador* and requires instead that we reverse our original orientation to the painting in moving from the foreground cliffs to the volcano or sun diagonally opposite in the background. The sky, like the land, is divided and uncentered; volcano and sun serve as dual foci for an unstated parabola.

Cotopaxi marks a turning point in Church's conception of the egotistical sublime. If we understand Church's volcano to echo Cole's own use of volcanic imagery, then *Cotopaxi*, in both its iconography and its chiastic composition, represents a belated recognition of Church's indebtedness to Cole. *Cotopaxi* acknowledges what *The Andes of Ecuador* had attempted to suppress: the knowledge that all art is born from the traces of past art. The sublime, then, is an intertextual affair, conceived, if not in sin, then at least in its painterly equivalent, a world crowded with past images that permits no more than reactions, reinterpretations, of itself.

We know this in *Cotopaxi* because of the relation of sun to volcano. The two are united by a plume of dark smoke that forms, in its arc around the sun, the upper lid of an eyeball. The lower lid is defined by the curved line of the horizon. This is not Emerson's transparent eyeball but a bloody and apocalyptic organ, locked into a world it must share with others and dependent for its very definition upon a peak set to its side. To see is to *share* in this canvas, to construct a world distinguished not by its promise of newness, as in *The Andes of Ecuador*, but by its entanglement with the residue and debris of the past: that serpentine trail of volcanic smoke. In the fiery relation of volcano to sun, Colean trope to Churchian icon, we encounter an allegory of indebtedness that belies the myth of originality. *Cotopaxi* thus demythologizes what *The Andes of Ecuador* held to be central: that image of a new day, a new creation, untarnished by ties to the past. *Cotopaxi* thematizes instead, through its dual foci and chiastic construction, its own intertextual indebtedness. Without revision, the painting tells us, there is no vision.

And this returns us to Ishmael, whose narrative lapses resemble those moments of suppression in Church's canvases. What we learn from each is that language is a haunted medium. It comes with its own echoes and conventions. The ghost in Church's art is Cole. His compositions echo throughout Church's work, belying the very possibility of a sublime so egotistical that it can be sustained by nothing beyond itself. Queequeg similarly is Ishmael's spook (one of many), a figure of foreignness who intrudes upon Ishmael's comic narration. Queequeg, we should remember, is not only a person but a living system of representation. His most salient characteristic— the thing Ishmael notices about him first—is the network of hieroglyphic markings that cover his body. These markings return us to the linguistic dimension undergirding his relation to Ishmael; they are reminders that the sublime entails more than thought in confrontation with its bodily limits. The sublime is also an action of texts upon past texts. Ishmael's genius lies in his ability to read Queequeg, not as a specific text, for he can never fully decode Queequeg, but as a *prior* text. What Ishmael recognizes in Queequeg is a system of language different from his own. Ishmael's moments of silence, then, are like suture points in his narrative where other texts, other voices, make their presence felt. Ishmael's ability to bed down with Queequeg, whom he will later decide "was on the whole a clean, comely looking cannibal," represents a recuperation of the sublime in the face of its own limits.

Those limits, in turn, are imposed by the very otherness of language, its refusal of originality as anything more than an act of quotation. The egotistical sublime, from this point of view, is a clever act composed of equal amounts of quotation (for that is all language allows) and the suppression of one's sources (for that is what self-origination requires). What we learn from Ishmael, as from Church, is the capacity of the sublime both to affirm and to evade its boundaries by recognizing its own textual status. The sublime, then, is more than an egotistical event. It is an act of language predicated upon a recognition of otherness: an understanding that all writing, like all reading, stems from other and prior texts.

4

The dilemma of the sublime, then, lies in its need to balance two contradictory claims. On the one hand, it crosses out all of that which is other in order to re-create it in its own image; on the other hand, it harbors within itself, like an ill-digested meal, traces of past texts that refuse to be assimilated. Queequeg is one such text for Ishmael, as Cole was for Church. Queequeg represents the mystery of language itself, and Sphinx-like, he will not be answered. Yet it is not Queequeg who is to be feared in *Moby-Dick*; his cannibalism is relatively benign. It is Ishmael who is the book's ultimate cannibal, for what he devours are words, sentences, and paragraphs: whole systems of representation. And the reason he survives, the reason we love him, is that he doesn't care what he eats. The chewing is all.

Ishmael's endless capacity of incorporation, his ability to find nourishment from the most unlikely sources, sustains him throughout *Moby-Dick*. He is a cannibal of all texts, all experiences, a Zarathustrian joymaker for whom the pleasure of the game far exceeds all issues of gain or loss. His ability to garner life from the most unlikely sources, to buoy himself up at the novel's conclusion upon Queequeg's mystically inscribed coffin, renders him a figure of the fullest intertextuality, at once original and derived. His identity is both centered and dispersed, held together by the centripetal pull of the sublime toward an egotistical center and dissolved again by the centrifugal tendency of language to unravel into a cacophony of foreign voices. He thus embodies that tension within the romantic sublime between the negation of the other into the self and the emptying out of the self into a sea of intertextual echoes. He differs from Church in his ability to embrace what the painter can only suppress. For Church the lesson of intertextuality is a tragic one: It is knowledge of the price that language exacts from us all. Such knowledge comes only at the expense of one's artistic ego. For Ishmael, on the contrary, the otherness of language, its inhuman mockery of originality, is no more than a momentary threat, for what is foreign can still be embraced, and what can be embraced can be redeemed as yet another version of the self. The difference between Church and Ishmael, then, lies in the difference between a sublime that denies the conventionality of its own language and one that affirms it. . . .

[Ishmael] personifies not only the older dreams of the egotistical sublime, the attempt from Emerson to Church to render reality a version of the self, but also that second moment in sublime discourse when language takes an inward turn and stumbles upon its own conventions. Ishmael's power lies in his ability to turn that stumble into a soft-shoe: to dance where others fall. By embracing Queequeg, he embraces the mystery of language and affirms his ability to dwell within the margins of his own text.

There is an underside to Ishmael's story, a moment when all egotism, mean or otherwise, stumbles upon its linguistic origins and fails to recover. The scene is the famous "Doubloon" chapter, when assorted members of the *Pequod*'s crew stop to gaze at the coin nailed to the ship's mast-head. Each of the novel's central figures reads the Spanish doubloon before him according to his own disposition. Ahab sees in it demonic and narcissistic energies; Starbuck finds in the doubloon the possibilities of a moral imagination; Stubb has to haul out an almanac to interpret it; and Flask reduces it to a piece of currency and wishes that he could spend it.

What interests us about the chapter, however, are not the stereotypical views of the crew that it presents but the sequence of readings that structure the narrative. For we move in this chapter from the sublime (Ahab) to the moral (Starbuck) to the rote and mechanical (Stubbs) to the material and economic (Flask). The "Doubloon" thus follows a reductive pattern, a sequence that we might call anti-idealistic. . . .

[This] is the last interpretation that we overhear:

> This way comes Pip—poor boy! would he had died, or I; he's half horrible to me. He too has been watching all of these interpreters—myself included—and look now, he comes to read, with that unearthly idiot face. Stand away again and hear him. Hark!"
>
> "I look, you look, he looks; we look, ye look, they look."
>
> "Upon my soul, he's been studying Murray's Grammar! Improving his mind, poor fellow! But what's that he says now—hist!"
>
> "I look, you look, he looks; we look, ye look, they look."
>
> "Why, he's getting it by heart—hist! again."
>
> "I look, you look, he looks; we look, ye look, they look." (Chap. 99)

Pip is the only observer who does not attempt to interpret the scene before him. He does not try to understand the relation of the three peaks to the valleys and sky of the doubloon. He focuses our attention instead on the interpretive process itself: "I look, you look, he looks; we look, ye look, they look." Pip represents the endpoint of that devolution and regression that haunts all Emersonian idealism. Only he brings us to an end different from what we might have expected. It is not commodity or materialism with which we conclude, but the act of perception itself. Pip gives us the grammar of seeing with no visionary truth, no epiphanies, no egotistical aspirations. He reminds us of what happens to the Emersonian transparent eyeball when it gets trapped by its own rhetoric. For Pip represents a form of seeing with nothing to see but itself.

Emerson had described the problem in "Experience," his essay of 1844 where the light of *Nature* had darkened into a tangible obscure. The sublime heroism of the transparent eyeball hardens into solipsism in the later essay, and the culprit is Emerson's own self-consciousness: . . .

> Do you see that kitten chasing so prettily her own tail? If you could look with her eyes you might see her surrounded with hundreds of figures performing complex dramas, with tragic and comic issues, long conversations, many characters, many ups and downs of fate,—and meantime it is only puss and her tail. How long before our masquerade will end its noise of tambourines, laughter and shouting, and we shall find it was a solitary performance? A subject and an object,—it takes so much to make the galvanic circuit complete, but magnitude adds nothing. What imports it whether it is Kepler and the sphere, Columbus and America, a reader and his book, or puss with her tail?

This is a passage that begins and ends with a cat and her tail, and its project, between its opening and closing images, is to unveil life's "masquerade." . . . Emerson plunges through "complex dramas" and "conversations" in order to arrive at that single and simple motion that is the visionary self. What he finds is a "galvanic circuit," an image of motion without substance where "magnitude adds nothing." The image is repeated in the structure of his own prose, which begins and ends with puss in pursuit of her tail. It is an image of language, or rather, we might say, of the self as a grammar: a movement of tropes, none of which is significant by itself, along a signifying chain that we may term fate or God, but that finally is nothing but a perennial parade of images.

Emerson is left here not with the solipsistic self—that would be a comfort, for it would still possess "magnitude"—but with Pip's grammar of seeing. The threat posed to the visionary self is that it is a puffery of motion, a conceit and investment woven from the barest of rhetorics. Emerson's fear is that the visionary self reduces to its own language, and all promises of sublime circulation remain fanciful embroideries upon the barest grammar of seeing: "I look, you look, he looks." Pip is like puss with her tail. He is a grammar, the sheer movement of language for its own sake, selfhood reduced to its rhetorical underpinnings. . . .

Nor is Ishmael finally immune to the tragic force of Emerson's insight. Ishmael succumbs by the end of the novel to the power of the tale that he tells. He survives at last as an "orphan": "And I only am escaped alone to tell thee." *Moby-Dick* concludes with Ishmael displaced from the center of his story to its circumference. He survives not because of that centripetal pull of the ego to incorporate everything into itself, but because he can float "at the margin of the ensuing scene, and in full sight of it." He is saved by the centrifugal tendencies of language to disperse the self into a sea of tales. Ishmael becomes a witness to others' stories. The world he inhabits in the Epilogue is a world denuded of both its narcissistic investments and its egotistical aspirations. The sublime has been reduced from the motions of an omnivorous self to a grammar that reabsorbs all vision into its own circling vortex.

At the end of the story, the "devious cruising *Rachel*" returns to the scene of the *Pequod*'s destruction, searching for "her missing children." She finds no children of her own, but stumbles instead upon Ishmael. *Moby-Dick* thus concludes with an image of displacement. The *Rachel* grafts onto her original mission a new one, as unforeseen as it was inevitable. She comes to bear an unrecognized stranger and his tale. She is a trope finally for the workings of language: for its indirection, its refusal of original purpose, its repetitions of others' stories. Language has become a mode of witness by the end of *Moby-Dick*. It is a medium haunted by drowned men, whose voices are dispersed across a text (or sea) never wholly one's own. In search of our missing children, we discover, like Emerson, that we know ourselves *too* well, for the voice we hear within the whirlwind was only puss with her tail.

The Entangled Text:
Melville's *Pierre* and the Problem
of Reading

Edgar A. Dryden

Pierre is a book about reading and writing, about the consumption and production of literary texts—a double problem that fascinates Melville from the beginning to the end of his writing career. For unlike some of his romantic contemporaries he does not regard reading as a passive and parasitical activity that is the pale complement of the original and glamourous act of creation itself. Melville is free of the Hawthornian nostalgia for a "Gentle," "Indulgent," appreciative reader who graciously accepts unquestioningly the beautiful tapestry "woven with the best of the artist's skill, and cunningly arranged with a view to the harmonious exhibition of its colours."[1] For Melville the writer is himself originally a reader: indeed his creative powers depend on the depth and breadth of his reading, "spontaneous creative thought" being a process whereby "all existing great works must be federated in the fancy; and so regarded as a miscellaneous and Pantheistic whole."[2] The fabric of *Moby-Dick*, for example, is woven more from the threads of the texts that fill Ishmael's library than it is from the lines and ropes of the whaling world. Indeed Ishmael's relation to that world he seeks to represent is that of a reader to a text, and he tries to organize and arrange it as he previously has done his library by establishing a bibliographical system. Productive reading, however, is not an easy or casual activity; "no ordinary letter sorter . . . is equal to it."[3] In "Hawthorne and His Mosses," Melville distinguishes between that reader

Dryden, Edgar. "The Entangled Text," *Boundary 2*, 7:3. Copyright 1979, Duke University Press, Durham, NC. Reprinted by permission.

[1]Nathaniel Hawthorne, *The Marble Faun*, ed. William Charvat and Roy Harvey Pearce (Columbus: Ohio State Univ. Press, 1968), pp. 2, 455.

[2]Herman Melville, *Pierre; or, the Ambiguities*, ed. Harrison Hayford, Hershel Parker and G. Thomas Tanselle (Evanston: Northwestern Univ. Press, 1971), p. 284. All subsequent references to *Pierre* will be to the Northwestern edition, and the novel will be designated in the text by the abbreviation P.

[3]Herman Melville, *Moby-Dick*, ed. Harrison Hayford and Hershel Parker (New York: Norton, 1967), p. 118. All subsequent references to *Moby-Dick* will be to the Norton edition, and the novel will be designated in the text by the abbreviation MD.

who sees Shakespeare as a "mere man of Richard-the-Third humps, and Macbeth daggers," who responds only to the "popularizing noise and the show of broad farce, and blood-besmeared tragedy," and the more discriminating reader who seeks out the "still rich utterances of a great intellect in repose."[4] In the place of "blind, unbridled" (HHM, 542) reading Melville proposes a deeply committed one that is capable of discerning those truths that the writer "craftily says," or "insinuates" in his text. As Ishmael demonstrates when he tells the "Town Ho's Story" by "interweaving in its proper place the darker thread [the secret part of the tale] with the story as publicly narrated on the ship" (MD, 208), story-telling is a process of representing a dark truth that will only be available to the readers whose response is in the form of deep and probing examination.

At first glance, then, the Hawthorne essay seems equally to celebrate reading and writing, to regard both as distinguished and difficult but non-problematic activities. Composed during the period when Melville was hard at work on *Moby-Dick*, the essay implies a direct and unambiguous link between Shakespeare and Hawthorne and more importantly, records the positive effects of both writers on Melville. These effects are clearly discernible in the novel he was about to dedicate to Hawthorne. However, important if unacknowledged problems exist in the essay. At the same time that Melville records the way in which the "soft ravishments of [Hawthorne] spin [him] round about in a web of dreams" (HHM, 537-38) and celebrates Shakespeare's "great Art of Telling the Truth" (HHM, 542), he also "boldly contemn[s] all imitation, though it comes to us graceful and fragrant as the morning; and foster[s] all originality, though, at first, it be crabbed and ugly as our own pine knots" (HHM, 546). The essay, in other words, raises and then ignores the problems of derivation: authority and priority, tradition and the individual talent, literary fathers and sons. But his consideration of these issues is postponed only until *Moby-Dick* is completed, for in *Pierre* Melville focuses on them with an almost desperate insistence.

> "Dearest Lucy!—well, well;—'twill be a pretty time we'll have this evening; there's the book of Flemish prints—that first we must look over; then, second, is Flaxman's Homer—clear-cut outlines, yet full of unadorned barbaric nobleness. Then Flaxman's Dante;—Dante! Night's and Hell's poet he. No, we will not open Dante. Methinks now the face—the face—minds me a little of pensive, sweet Francesca's face—or, rather, as it had been Francesca's daughter's face—wafted on the sad dark wind, toward observant Virgil and the blistered Florentine. No, we will not open Flaxman's Dante. Francesca's mournful face is now ideal to me. Flaxman might evoke it wholly,—make it present in lines of misery—bewitching power. No! I will not open Flaxman's Dante! Damned be the hour I read in Dante! more damned than that wherein Paolo and Francesca read in fatal Launcelot!" (P, 42)

[4]Herman Melville, "Hawthorne and His Mosses," in *Moby-Dick*, pp. 541, 542. The essay will be designated in the text by the abbreviation HHM.

Woven and entangled in this passage are most of the thematic strands of
Pierre: the problem of reading; the question of relatedness, of genealogical
continuity and intertextuality (family structures and narrative forms); and
linking them all the larger issues of repetition and representation. The
generative energy of the passage (and the novel) is a story, the "story of the
face," a story that Pierre can narrate but cannot read because it exists for him
in the form of a "riddle" (P, 37) or "mournful mystery" whose meaning is
"veiled" behind a "concealing screen" (P, 41). Nevertheless, he is determined
to understand it fully, to confront its meaning, as he says, "face to face" (P, 41).
But as the labyrinthine quality of the passage suggests, the meaning of the
story is difficult to decipher, and Pierre's attempt to read it will generate a
second and even more entangled and problematic narrative, that of the novel
itself. . . .

[A]lthough the face "was not of enchanted air" but had been "visibly beheld
by Pierre" (P, 43), it nevertheless exists for him in an ambiguous representational mode. The "wretched vagueness" (P, 41) that haunts his memory stands
not in the place of its "mortal lineaments" (P, 43) but in the place of something
else: in this instance Dante's description of Francesca's face, or, perhaps, in
the place of Flaxman's graphic representation of Dante's description, or, more
problematically, in the place of Pierre's imaginary conception of Francesca's
daughter's face. Pierre's initial encounter with Isabel, then—an encounter he
is later to see as the central and authenticating one of his life—is cast in terms
of signs rather than substances. It is derived, not immediate. Any sense of the
face as a living reality dissolves before the "long line of dependencies" (P, 67)
implied in the passage. The focus here is on purely textual entities, on
questions of the relations between literary works (the chivalric tale, Dante's
poem, Melville's novel), between graphic and linguistic signs (Flaxman's
illustrations, Dante's poem) and on the bewitching power these entities
possess to produce others that displace and represent them. In this sense the
story of the face, and by extension Pierre's own story, is necessarily written
and read from the perspective of the "already written." The Paolo and
Francesca episode implies that not even passion itself is natural in the sense of
being an underived and spontaneous emotion (it comes from books)[5] and
hence suggests an entangled relation between one's natural genealogy and the
inherited texts of one's culture.

This problem of relatedness raised by Pierre's imaginative creation of
literary parents for the mysterious face is the first one to appear in the novel.
It begins with the celebration of the apparent differences between the "great
genealogical and real-estate dignity of some families in America" (P, 12) and
the "winding and manufactured nobility" of the "grafted families" (P, 10) of the
old world. Unlike the English Peerage, which is kept alive by "restorations

5I am indebted here to Roland Barthes, *S/Z*, trans. Richard Howard (New York: Hill and
Wang), pp. 20-21, 73-74.

and creations" (P, 10), Pierre's pedigree seems straight and unflawed. We meet the young hero "issuing from the high gabled old home" of his father and entering a world where the "very horizon [is] to him as a memorial ring," where all the "hills and swales seemed as sanctified through their very long uninterrupted possession by his race" (P, 8). Unlike the orphaned Ishmael, he seems to find himself in a world where he truly belongs, a world where his identity, place and destiny are confirmed by the self-reflected environment of a "powerful and populous family" (P, 7). Moreover, his position as the only "surnamed Glendinning extant" and the "solitary head of his family" seems to assure him that his only "duplicate" is the "one reflected to him in the mirror" (P, 8). Pierre, in other words, seems to enjoy the security of a family circle within which he can define and fix himself and at the same time remain free of the fear of any challenge to his originality or authority. He can possess at once the feeling of belonging enjoyed by the son and the procreative power of the father as well, hence his dream of achieving a "monopoly of glory in capping the fame-column, whose tall shaft had been erected by his noble sires" (P, 8).

However, this is a dream based on the assumption of an absolute correspondence between the natural and the human, on the notion that institutions and language possess the characteristics of the biological structure of generation. Families, however, are not trees, even though they may seem to "stand as the oak" (P, 9), for they do not originate and develop in the same way. The permanence, stability, and order implied by a genealogical chart or by the metaphor of the family tree conceals a host of discontinuities, disjunctions, entanglements, and desires that mark human relationships. The seemingly unentangled lines of the Glendinning genealogy are actually twisted and interwoven by the young heir's problematic relation to his family. Pierre's relation to his mother, for example, equivocates the orderly process whereby the father and mother produce a son who marries and continues the line: "In the playfulness of their unclouded love, and with that strange licence which a perfect confidence and mutual understanding at all points, had long bred between them, they were wont to call each other brother and sister" (P, 5). The entangling and confusing of relationships implied by this behavior is further complicated by their domestic practice that anticipates the "sweet dreams of those religious enthusiasts who paint to us a Paradise to come, where etherialized from the drosses and stains, the holiest passion of man shall unite all kindred and climes in one circle of pure and unimpairable delight" (P, 16). Pierre's relation to his mother, in short, is an only partially disguised expression of a set of inhibited desires generated by a genealogical system that condemns the son to a derived and secondary existence. These desires, partially displaced here by the religious language in which they are manifested, are more concretely expressed in Pierre's "strange yearning . . . for a sister" as well as by the narrator's smug observation, "He who is sisterless, is as a bachelor before his time. For much that goes to make up the deliciousness of a wife, already lies in the sister" (P, 7). This barely concealed expression of brother-sister incestuous desire, like the more deeply displaced mother-son relationship, suggests the extent to which Pierre unconsciously resists the defining authority of the father as well as the sense that he is no more than his father "transformed into youth once again" (P, 73). Both his relation to his mother and the nature of his longing for a sister constitute a challenge to the paternal role: they subtly entangle the genealogical line by disrupting its temporal development. The "striking personal resemblance" between Pierre and his mother—she sees "her own graces strangely translated into the opposite sex"—makes it seem as if the mother has "long stood still in her beauty, heedless of the passing years" and Pierre seems to "meet her half-way," to have "almost advanced himself to that mature stand-point in Time, where his pedestaled mother so long had stood" (P, 5).

But it is Pierre's response to the phantom face haunting him and enchanting him with its suggestions of dark foreignness that is the most obvious expression of his suppressed desire to free himself from a family prison. Its magnetic quality derives in part from the fact that it is at once "wholly unknown to him" (P, 49) and yet somehow familiar, thus making him aware of a "certain condition of his being, which was most painful, and every way uncongenial to his natural, wonted self" (P, 53). The nature and speed of Pierre's response to Isabel's disruptive note, of course, make explicit the status of these hidden desires. In Pierre's mind the note completely undermines the dignity and authority of the father and forces him to abandon all the "hereditary beliefs" (P, 87) he has been unconsciously resisting all along. "I will have no more father," he says, as he rejects all "earthly kith and kin" and "orphan-like stagger[s] back upon himself and find[s] support in himself" (P, 89). "Henceforth, cast-out Pierre has no paternity and no past . . . twice disinherited Pierre stands . . . free to do his own self-will and present fancy to whatever end" (P, 199). Because he feels himself "divinely dedicated" he decides that he can abandon all "common conventional regardings," including his "hereditary duty to his mother" and his "pledged worldly faith and honor to the hand and seal of his affiancement" (P, 140). Personal faith will replace hereditary beliefs and the result will be a more orderly as well as more authentic life; for the genealogical tradition that seems to promise continuity and unity is actually interwined in the "infinite entanglements of all social things" (P, 191). From the "long line of dependencies" that constitute it come the "thousand proprieties and polished finenesses" (P, 83) that characterize the social. Like Christ, Pierre believes that he can free himself from these "myriad alliances and crisscrossings" (P, 191) and disentangle himself from "all fleshy alliances" (P, 164) by substituting for the genealogical imperative a new and celibate enterprise.

> Not that at present all these things did thus present themselves to Pierre; but these things were foetally forming in him. Impregnations from high enthusiasms he had received; and the now incipient offspring which so stirred, with such painful, vague

vibrations in his soul; this, in its mature development, when it should at last come forth in living deeds, would scorn all personal relationship with Pierre, and hold his heart's dearest interests for naught.

Thus, in the Enthusiast to Duty, the heaven-begotten Christ is born; and will not own a mortal parent, and spurns and rends all mortal bonds. (P, 106)

In the place of inherited values and relations Pierre places an orphaned, self-begotten identity and that in turn generates a miraculous conception. In effect a spiritual genealogy supplants the physical one, apparently making possible a new family structure.[6] For both Isabel and Lucy, Pierre seems capable of fulfilling all the traditional familial roles. " 'I want none in the world but thee' " (P, 312), Isabel tells him, and Lucy insists that he is " 'my mother and my brother, and all the world, and all heaven, and all the universe to me—thou art my Pierre' " (P, 311). Moreover, the new relationships, as Pierre sees them, are free from the ambiguities of the more traditional ones: he and Isabel are " 'wide brother and sister in common humanity' " (P, 273) and he and Lucy spiritual cousins with " 'no declaration; no bridal' " (P, 310) who " 'love as angels do' " (P, 309).

Pierre, then, seems to have made himself his "own Alpha and Omega," to have reached a point where he can "feel himself in himself, and not by reflection in others" (P, 261). Moreover, having freed himself from the defining relationships of the paternal tradition, he has also made himself independent of its economic imperatives. When he abandons his "fine social position" and "noble patrimony" he boldly asserts that he will "live on himself" (P, 261); that is to say, he will become an author and support himself by putting his "soul to labor . . . and pay his body her wages" (P, 261). In the place of fathering a natural son who will be his unwilling copy even as he was his father's, he will give the world a book, "a child born solely from one parent" (P, 259), that through its radical originality will "gospelize the world anew" (P, 273).

Pierre assumes that as an author he will wield an authority that is not subject to confining and restricting definitions from the past. However, behind the differences that seem to separate the act of authoring from that of physical engenderment is a notion common to both, that what one makes is one's off-spring, legacy, and representative. This element of sameness puts into question Pierre's claims of absolute authority and originality.[7] As the Paolo-Francesca passage implies, the process of representation involves questions of inherited tendencies as well as originating intentions. These issues appear in their most obvious form in the novel's focus on painted images of the father, an especially likely association, for, as Paul de Man has shown, it is

---

[6]I am indebted here to John T. Irwin's discussion of the difference between the Judaic and Christian concepts of genealogy in *Doubling and Incest/Repetition and Revenge: A Speculative Reading of Faulkner* (Baltimore: The Johns Hopkins Univ. Press, 1975).

[7]I am indebted here to Edward Said's discussion of the problem in *Beginnings: Intention and Method* (New York: Basic Books, 1975), pp. 263-64.

in painting (and especially in eighteenth-century theories of painting) that the process of representation appears in its most unambiguous aspects. Conceived of as imitation, painting (as de Man points out) has the effect of seeming to restore the represented object to view as if it were present, miraculously bringing back into existence a presence that existed in another time and in another place. This duplication of the objects of perception, however, does not exhaust the power of the painted image. Even more impressive is its apparent ability to transform inward and ideal experiences into objects of perception and, by making them visible, confer upon them the ontological stability of objective existence.[8] The military portrait of Pierre's grandfather, for example, at once captures the image of the original so completely that the young Pierre feels a "mournful longing to meet his living aspect in real life," and it possesses the "heavenly persuasiveness of angelic speech; a glorious gospel framed and hung upon the wall, and declaring to all people, as from the Mount, that man is a noble, god-like being, full of choicest juices; made up of strength and beauty" (P, 30). This description, of course, equivocates Pierre's decision to "gospelize the world anew" by associating it with a related and prior originating act, but it also undermines the assumption that imitation duplicates presence. The "mournful longing" which the painting generates in Pierre is a reminder of one problematic aspect of representation since it points to the absence of the represented entity, and the disquieting effects of that absence are strengthened by the irony implicit in the fact that a military portrait seems to the young man to be a concrete expression of the ideals of Christ's Sermon on the Mount.

The painted image of the old Pierre Glendinning points to an absence rather than a presence, to "once living but now impossible ancestries in the past" (P, 32), and raises the problem of genealogy as representation by illustrating what the narrator calls the "endless descendedness of names" (P, 9). Not only is Pierre his father's "namesake" (P, 73) but his grandfather's as well, hence from one point of view doubly derived, the copy of a copy and as such a diminution, a smaller, weaker version of the authoritative original:

> The grandfather of Pierre measured six feet four inches in height; during a fire in the old manorial mansion, with one dash of his foot, he had smitten down an oaken door, to admit the buckets of his negro slaves; Pierre had often tried on his military vest, which still remained an heirloom at Saddle Meadows, and found the pockets below his knees. . . . (P, 29)

Pierre in his "most extended length measures not the proud six feet four of his John of Gaunt Sire," and as the "stature of the warrior is cut down" so is the "glory of the fight" (P, 271).

Pierre's assumption, however, is that his position in the genealogical chain is a matter of "empty nominalness," not "vital realness" (P, 192); for if his name

8Paul de Man, *Blindness and Insight* (New York: Oxford Univ. Press, 1971), pp. 123-27.

on the one hand seems to bind him to his paternal precursors, on the other it suggests a means of escape. The French origins of his Christian name allow him through a series of substitutions to link himself to another tradition that counters the democratic, revolutionary one represented by his ancestors. This is the one suggested by the mysterious "foreigner" of "noblest birth" and "allied to the royal family" (P, 76) of France who enchants Pierre's father and perhaps becomes the mother of Isabel. Although the signs of this "foreign feminineness" (P, 76) are less objective, less concrete, than the portrait of Pierre's grandfather—they consist of a "subtle expression of the portrait of [Pierre's] then youthful father" (P, 112), the word "Isabel" written in the interior of a guitar, and a "touch of foreignness in the accent" (P, 113) of the mysterious Isabel—Pierre is so convinced of her reality and her spiritual link to him through Isabel that he willingly breaks the lines linking him to his forefathers and, by a process of substitution based on the French meaning of his Christian name, becomes Peter, the rock on which Christ builds his church rather than the grandson of the old warrior.[9]

At first glance his progress seems significant. Replacing the authority of the grandfather and the father is that of Christ as expressed in "those first, wise words, wherewith [he] first spoke in his first speech to men" (P, 91), the Sermon on the Mount. Although Christ's words come to Pierre in the secondary form of the Biblical text, he at least no longer has to receive them indirectly and ambiguously by way of the military portrait of his grandfather. And just as he seems to have replaced a physical genealogy by a spiritual one and an interpreted, metaphoric "gospel" by the actual one, so he seems to have turned from the socially and conventionally determined aspects of his name toward its literal meaning. . . . [That is], he attempts to resist being no more than Pierre Glendinning the Third by dedicating himself to what he perceives as a Christ-like duty and associating himself with Peter, the rock on which Christ builds his church. However, this act as well as his assertion that " 'I am Pierre' " (P, 373) calls attention to the literal meaning of his name, and it becomes his fate to live out that meaning, to become at the end a rock "arbored . . . in ebon vines" (P, 362).

The implications of this movement from name to thing, from the signifier to the signified, are important concerns of *Pierre*, and they are symbolized most clearly in the related figures of the mountain and the pyramid, a natural object and an intentional representation of it. As I have noted elsewhere, the mountain is a recurring image in *Pierre*. The novel is dedicated to the "magestic mountain, Greylock," the "sovereign lord and king" of the "amphitheatre over which his central majesty presides," and important roles are given to Mount Sinai, meeting place of God and Moses; the "divine mount,"

---

[9]H. Bruce Franklin focuses on this process of substitution in his admirable analysis of *Pierre*. See his *The Wake of the Gods: Melville's Mythology* (Stanford: Stanford Univ. Press, 1963), pp. 99-125.

site of Christ's famous sermon; Bunyan's Delectable Mountains, from which the Celestial City may be seen; and Pelion and Ossa, mountains of Thessaly used by the Titans in the war against the gods' stronghold on Mount Olympus. These "crude forms of the natural earth" are the "cunning alphabet, whereby selecting and combining as he pleases, each man reads his own peculiar lesson according to his own peculiar mind or mood" (P, 342). Hence divine speech is associated with mountain tops as first Moses and then Christ, following their pagan predecessors, interpret that "profound Silence," that "divine thing without a name."

This process is emblematized in the figure of the pyramid, regarded by Melville as the source of the idea of Jehovah as well as the first work of art. Metaphysically the pyramid seems to suggest permanence, to proclaim a tenacious resistance to the pillages of time, and yet inside it contains decayed human ruins, or, more frighteningly, absolutely nothing: "By vast pains we mine into the pyramid; by horrible gropings we come to the central room; with joy we espy the sarcophagus; but we lift the lid—and no body is there . . ." (P, 285). Like Hegel, Melville is fascinated by the pyramid because it offers him an external man-made form that represents the "forms of the natural earth." It has the appearance of a natural product and yet conceals as its meaning a hollow void, the sign perhaps of the "horrible interspace" (P, 134) of the Memnon stone and the "Hollow" (P, 139) of God's hand. For as Hegel points out, this is the "realm of death and the invisible." The pyramid, in other words, aptly symbolizes the process of representation itself, for it points to the absence that all signs carry within them. Contained within language is a "Silence" that "permeates all things" (P, 204) and within all man-made objects and inscriptions a hollow void. Hence that "all-controlling and all-permeating wonderfulness, which, when imperfectly and isolatedly recognized by the generality, is so significantly denominated The Finger of God" is not "merely the Finger, it is the whole outspread Hand of God; for doth not Scripture intimate, that He holdeth all of us in the hollow of His Hand?—a Hollow, truly!" (P, 139).

It is the Finger of God, of course, that inscribes the Tablets of Stone given to Moses on Mount Sinai (Exod. 31:18) and that furnishes Christ with the power to give speech to the dumb (Luke 11:14-20). Inscribed within all cultural constructs, then, and within language itself is a radical absence suggesting an original loss. It is the pyramid situated in the cradle of civilization and the birthplace of the gods that marks the point beyond which it is impossible to go and that at the same time indicates that the moment of origin is not one of plenitude and presence but the sign of a loss. At the beginning for Melville there is already an unrecoverable past signified by the empty sarcophagus, and it is the burden of present and future architects that no matter how hard they may seek to establish an original relation to the forms of the natural earth, they must inscribe that empty tomb within all their monuments. Implied in the voice of culture is the silence of the tomb.

What then of the acts of reading and writing? How does the reader in the silence of his solitude define his relation to the verbose narrator of *Pierre* and to his "book of sacred truth" (P, 107)? This is a problem that is inscribed in the text of *Pierre*. The life of its hero is the story of a reader who attempts to become a writer. His growth is rendered in terms of the development of his interpretive faculties and his maturity is defined by his decision to "give the world a book" (P, 283). As a youth Pierre is a naive, unquestioning reader of novels, impatient with the "sublime . . . Dante" because his "dark ravings . . . are in eternal opposition to [his] own free-spun shallow dreams" (P, 54) and incapable of understanding even the "superficial and purely incidental lessons" of *Hamlet*, much less of glimpsing the "hopeless gloom of its interior meaning" (P, 169).

The extent to which the content and mode of Pierre's reading constitute his world is suggested by the fact that the act of reading provides the grid through which all aspects of his early life are seen. His life is an "illuminated scroll" (P, 7); love is a "volume bound in rose leaves, clasped with violets, and by the beaks of humming birds printed with peach juice on the leaves of lilies" (P, 34); grief is "still a ghost story" (P, 4); and human relations are intertextual: " 'Read me through and through,' " says Lucy to Pierre, " 'I am entirely thine' " (P, 40). The arrival of Isabel's letter, "the fit scroll of a torn as well as a bleeding heart" (P, 65), of course, reveals to Pierre the artificial and conventional structure of this world and produces a new understanding of reading and interpretation: " 'Oh, hitherto I have but piled up words: bought books, and bought some small experiences and builded me in libraries; now I sit down and read' " (P, 91).

One result of Pierre's new view of things is that he is able to recuperate a number of memories that to this point in his life have existed as unreadable and meaningless details of his inner world. His dying father's delirious ravings, his mother's ambiguous reaction to the chair portrait, and other "imaginings of dimness" that "seemed to survive to no real life" (P, 71) are suddenly rendered intelligible by Isabel's letter, the pre-text that "puts the chemic key of the cipher into his hands; then how swiftly and how wonderfully, he reads all the obscurest and most obliterate inscriptions he finds in his memory; yea, and rummages himself all over, for still hidden writings to read" (P, 70). Nor is the effect limited to the inscriptions of memory. The letter also allows Pierre to read Dante and Shakespeare in a deeper, more profound way, and this re-reading leads him to see that "after all he had been finely juggling with himself, and postponing with himself, and in meditative sentimentalities wasting the moments consecrated to instant action" (P, 170).

Isabel's letter, then, seems to provide a context or model that renders intelligible textual details which to this point have been unreadable or misread. The full implications of this complicated process, however, are not immediately obvious. But a number of them are illuminated by the narrator's account of Pierre's reading of two apparently contradictory texts: the gospel of

Matthew and the pamphlet "Chronometricals and Horologicals." Matthew, of course, is an important text for Pierre since in his enthusiasm he has decided to model his life on Christ's, to be directed by "those first wise words, wherewith our Savior Christ first spoke in his first speech to man" (P, 91), the Sermon on the Mount. His "acts" then will be a "gospel" (P, 156) perfectly intelligible and natural if read in the context of his scriptural model. However, in the darkness and silence of the coach that carries him and his "mournful party" (P, 104) away from his ancestral home, Pierre begins to question his conduct, and to escape from the "evil mood" that becomes "well nigh insupportable," he "plunge[s] himself" (P, 207) into a mysterious pamphlet that he has found:

> There is a singular infatuation in most men, which leads them in odd moments, intermitting between their regular occupations, and when they find themselves all alone in some quiet corner or nook, to fasten with unaccountable fondness upon the merest rag of old printed paper—some shred of a long-exploded advertisement perhaps—and read it, and study it, and re-read it, and pore over it, and fairly agonize themselves over this miserable, sleazy paper-rag, which at any other time, or in any other place, they would hardly touch with St. Dunstan's long tongs. So now, in a degree, with Pierre. But notwithstanding that he, with most other human beings, shared in the strange hallucination above mentioned, yet the first glimpse of the title of the dried-fish-like, pamphlet-shaped rag, did almost tempt him to pitch it out of the window. . . . (P, 206-07)

Here reading appears as a form of "infatuation" or "hallucination" the nature of which is "strange" and "unaccountable." Nevertheless, its function is to fill the voids of doubt, silence, and loneliness; for it is either that which we do to escape the "dark realities of things" or that which we do in the face of nothing to do. . . . Here then is a situation that seems to promise a totally naive and innocent reading: on the one hand a displaced reader seeking only relief from the loneliness and boredom of everyday life; on the other an orphaned and abandoned text picked up unconsciously and accidentally: a situation, in other words, that seems removed from the vicious cycle of a return of repressed and inhibited desire that previously has marked Pierre's reading.

Once Pierre becomes absorbed in the pamphlet, however, he discovers that he cannot "master [its] pivot idea" (P, 292). Indeed, the "more he read and re-read, the more [his] interest deepened, but still the more likewise did his failure to comprehend the writer increase. He seemed somehow to derive some general vague inkling concerning it, but the central conceit refused to become clear to him" (P, 209). Moreover, not only is the pamphlet unreadable but the reason for its being so is itself undecidable.

> If a man be in any vague latent doubt about the intrinsic correctness and excellence of his general life-theory and practical course of life; then, if that man change to light on any other man, or any little treatise, or sermon, which unintendingly, as it were, yet very palpably illustrates to him the intrinsic incorrectness and non-

excellence of both the theory and the practice of his life; then that man will—more or less unconsciously—try hard to hold himself back from the self-admitted comprehension of a matter which thus condemns him. . . . Again. If a man be told a thing wholly new, then—during the time of its first announcement to him—it is entirely impossible for him to comprehend it. For—absurd as it may seem—men are only made to comprehend things which they comprehended before (though but in embryo, as it were). Things new it is impossible to make them comprehend, by merely talking to them about it. . . . Possibly, they may afterward come, of themselves, to inhale this new idea from the circumambient air, and so come to comprehend it; but not otherwise at all. It will be observed, that neither points of the above speculations do we, in set terms, attribute to Pierre in connection with the rag pamphlet. Possibly both may be applicable; possibly neither. (P, 209)

Two possible explanations are offered here for Pierre's inability to comprehend the pamphlet, but neither is presented as absolutely applicable. Worth noticing, however, is that both have the effect of seriously limiting the dimensions of reading as an activity. We can read only the old and the familiar, the narrator seems to suggest, that which confirms and supports our normal assumptions and expectations. This is an insight that is confirmed later in the novel when Pierre meets Plotinus Plinlimmon, the "ostensible author" (HHM, 536) of the pamphlet, and seeks to re-read and understand it by the "commentary of [his] mystic-mild face" (P, 239). For now having found the "author" he has "lost" (P, 293) the text:

Pierre must have ignorantly thrust it into his pocket, in the stage, and it had worked through a rent there, and worked its way clean down into the skirt, and there helped pad the padding. So that all the time he was hunting for this pamphlet, he himself was wearing the pamphlet. . . .

Possibly this curious circumstance may in some sort illustrate his self-supposed non-understanding of the pamphlet, as first read by him in the stage. Could he likewise have carried about with him in his mind the thorough understanding of the book, and yet not be aware that he so understood it? (P, 294)

To say that Pierre wears the pamphlet even as he searches for it and that his understanding is an unconscious one is to imply that the act of reading is not so much one of recovery or discovery of an original meaning as it is one of becoming aware of relationships between texts. This is an insight confirmed by the fact that the narrator interrupts and delays his account of the fascinating pamphlet in order to discuss what appears to be another kind of reading and a completely different sort of text:

the earnest reperusal of the Gospels: the intense self-absorption into the greatest real miracle of all religions, the Sermon on the Mount. From that divine mount, to all earnest-loving youths, flows an inexhaustible soul-melting stream of tenderness and loving-kindness; and they leap exulting to their feet, to think that the founder of their holy religion gave utterance to sentences so infinitely sweet and soothing as these; sentences which embody all the love of the Past, and all the love which can be imagined in any conceivable Future. Such emotions as that Sermon raises in the enthusiastic heart; such emotions all youthful hearts refuse to ascribe to humanity as their origin. This is of God! cries the heart, and in that cry ceases all inquisition. (P, 207-08)

Here of course the focus is on a sacred text rather than a "sleazy pamphlet"; here reading seems an activity directed toward action in the world rather than a mystified escape from the "dark realities of things" (P, 207). The particular text in question is the gospel of St. Matthew, and within it, the account of Christ's "first wise words . . . in his first speech to men" (P, 91), words that Christ speaks "as one having authority, and not as the scribes" (Matt. VII:29) and that are transcribed by the author with unusual instructions: "whoso readeth, let him understand" (Matt. 24:15). The written text is presented, in short, as the authoritative and unambiguous record of speech, thereby restoring for the reader the full presence of Christ's words. Christ, however, presents himself as Son, as the re-presentative of God the Father, who speaks through him. In that sense his words have a secondary quality and this aspect of his message is underlined when it is given printed form. As Melville is well aware, Matthew, like the other gospels, was written years after the death of Christ; our knowledge of its author is skimpy at best; and there is some question as to whether the Greek text is the original or a translation from an earlier Hebrew text. All of these aspects signal non-presence and remind us that Christ, like Moses, his Old Testament precursor, insists that he can get a voice out of silence and hence resembles certain philosophers who pretend to have found the "Talismanic Secret" that will reconcile man's desire for full presence with the fact of his orphaned existence:

That profound Silence, that only Voice of our God, which I before spoke of; from that divine thing without a name, those impostor philosophers pretend somehow to have got an answer; which is as absurd, as though they should say they have got water out of stone; for how can a man get a Voice out of Silence? (P, 208)

The sacred text, then, has inscribed within it the very silence and absence that motivates Pierre to plunge himself into the sleazy pamphlet he finds in the coach, a text that seems to offer a model for human action directly contradicting that of the Sermon on the Mount since it emphasizes the incompatibility of Christian ideals and the practical demands of life in this world. However, as the narrator points out, the pamphlet is more of a "restatement of a problem, than the solution to the problem itself" (P, 210). And, indeed, the apparent differences between the two texts are equivocated by a set of ironic similarities that exist between them. The pamphlet's parabolic structure—based on a "strange conceit . . . apparently one of the plainest in the world; so natural a child might almost have originated it" and yet "again so profound, that scarce Juggalarius himself could be the author" (P, 210)—and the fact that it exists not as the product of the author who appears to have signed it but is rather his "verbal things, taken down at random, and bunglingly methodized by his young disciples" (P, 210), tie it to its Biblical pretext. This knotted relationship, moreover, appears to be inevitable rather than accidental since it is the product of a law as basic as that of gravity itself:

> thus over the most vigorous and soaring conceits, doth the cloud of Truth come stealing; thus doth the shot, even a sixty-two pounder pointed upward, light at last on the earth; for strive we how we may, we cannot overshoot the earth's orbit, to receive the attractions of other planets; Earth's law of gravitation extends far beyond her own atmosphere. (P, 261)

All words and conceits are subject to an "insensible sliding process" (P, 7) that mixes and entangles their paths and destines them to return at last to their silent source.

Reading consequently is an activity controlled by conceits that promise both wonder and enlightenment but produce disenchantment and confusion by entangling man in such a complex web of relationships that the "three dextrous maids themselves could hardly disentangle him" (P, 175). Such is Isabel's experience when she reads a "talismanic word" (P, 147) inscribed in the center of a book-like handkerchief. Before she can decipher the mysterious inscription, she must teach herself to read, and that process radically changes her relation to the world. To this point in her life her relation to the man who calls himself her father has been a special and unconventional one:

> "The word father only seemed a word of general love and endearment to me—little or nothing more; it did not seem to involve any claims of any sort, one way or the other. I did not ask the name of my father; for I could have had no motive to hear him named, except to individualize the person who was so peculiarly kind to me; and individualized in that way he already was, since he was generally called by us *the gentleman*, and sometimes *my father*." (P, 145)

For Isabel at this point "father" is simply the "word of kindness and kisses" (P, 124), a word that raises neither the problem of origins nor of authority for it implies only the "tenderness and beautifulness of humanness" (P, 122). Although when she looks in the pool of water behind the house she sees the "likeness—something strangely like, and yet unlike, the likeness of his face" (P, 124), the play of images does not generate sinister ambiguities but simply confirms her sense of the value of the human "in a world of snakes and lightenings, in a world of horrible and inscrutable inhumanities" (P, 122). Her father, however, on the last visit to her before his death, leaves behind a handkerchief bearing in its middle a "small line of the fine faded yellowish writing" that becomes for her a "precious memorial":

> "But when the impression of his death became a fixed thing to me, then again I washed and dried and ironed the precious memorial of him, and put it away where none should find it but myself . . . and I folded it in such a manner, that the name was invisibly buried in the heart of it, and it was like opening a book and turning over many blank leaves before I came to the mysterious writing, which I knew should be one day read by me, without direct help from any one. Now I resolved to learn my letters, and learn to read, in order that of myself I might learn the

meaning of those faded characters. . . . I soon mastered the alphabet, and went on to spelling, and by-and-by to reading, and at last to the complete deciphering of the talismanic word—Glendinning. I was yet very ignorant. *Glendinning*, thought I, what is that? It sounds something like *gentleman*;—Glen-din-ing;—just as many syllables as gentleman; and—G—it begins with the same letter; yes, it must mean *my father*. I will think of him by that word now:—I will not think of the *gentleman*, but of *Glendinning*. . . . as I still grew up and thought more to myself, that word was ever humming in my head; I saw it would only prove the key to more." (P, 146-47)

The inscribed handkerchief that is abandoned by "chance" and found "lying on the uncarpeted floor" (P, 146) is an object totally separated from its originating source, cut loose from the authority who could testify to the meaning of the "faded yellowish writing" on it. (Is its author the gentleman's wife, his sister who initials his neckcloths, or some anonymous seamstress like those who sew "in concert" at the Miss Pennies' house?) Consequently, the meaning of the word does not lie behind or within it but in its relation to other words and social conventions. For Isabel the word "Glendinning" does not stand first in the place of a person but in the place of another word, "gentleman," which it echoes, supplements, and particularizes. Ironically, it is this orphaned sign that leads Isabel to the second and even more problematic key to her origins, the word "Isabel" "gilded" in the "heart of [her] guitar" (P, 148). Even more than the handkerchief the guitar, having been purchased by Isabel from a peddlar who had "got it in barter from the servants" (P, 152) at the Glendinning estate, is a free-floating object, and the origins and meaning of the word in its interior are more mysterious than that of the one written on the handkerchief. Does it refer to the guitar's maker, to its owner, or to neither? As a given name rather than a patronym it is more clearly an object in its own right, its signification determined completely by the circumstances in which it functions, a truth that is confirmed by the fact that Isabel claims the name as her own only after she has read it in the guitar, having to that point "always gone by the name of Bell" (P, 148).

These two words, then, concealed in the interiors of the handkerchief and the guitar and associated by Isabel with her absent parents, function for her as keys that unlock and reveal a previously hidden set of relationships. These keys, however, are ambiguously inside the objects whose meanings they are supposed to unlock and their significance derives from a set of purely arbitrary associations. In this sense Isabel as a reader may be said to be the author of her own parentage; she has arrested the motion of two free-floating words and placed them within a genealogical order that is partially discovered, partially invented. And Pierre, through his reading and interpretation of the note that proclaims Isabel's relation to this order, entangles himself in a "fictitious alliance" (P, 175) that will lead him at last to his decision to become a writer and to "gospelize the world anew" (P, 273).

This process is the one the narrator refers to when he insists that "to a mind bent on producing some thoughtful thing of absolute truth, all mere reading is apt to prove an obstacle hard to overcome" (P, 283). Since the only non-textual reality is the silence of the crude forms of the natural earth, any act of speaking and writing is bound to be a repetition, a displacement or a representation of a purely textual entity, and necessarily derived, secondary and inessential. This is the perception that marks the text of *Pierre*, a text that is written against the "countless tribes of common novels and countless tribes of common dramas" as well as against those "profounder emanations of the human mind" (P, 141); yet it is doomed to contain and repeat them. Empty conventions from the domestic sentimental novel—the country-city setting, the incest theme, the dark and light ladies, the romantic symbols of guitar and portrait—combine with references to Dante, Spenser, Shakespeare, Milton, and others to produce a text that undermines the notion of writing as original creation and reading as an authentic act of discovery. "Had Milton's been the lot of Casper Hauser," the narrator insists, "Milton would have been as vacant as he" (P, 259). Hence the writer is portrayed as a whore who sells herself for money—"careless of life herself, and reckless of the germ of life she contains"; as an actor in an empty melodrama performing a part not written by him— "only hired to appear on the stage, not voluntarily claiming the public attention" (P, 258); and as an improvisator, echoing the music of others and creating off hand, on the spur of the moment, variations on any proposed subject—"it is pleasant to chat ere we go to our beds; and speech is further incited, when like strolling improvisators of Italy, we are paid for our breath" (P, 259). Correspondingly, the reader is portrayed as the victim of this "lurking insincerity . . . of written thoughts," the enchanted dupe of books whose leaves "like knavish cards" are "covertly packed" (P, 339). For that "wonderful" and mysterious "story" of the illegitimate and orphaned child may have been "by some strange arts . . . forged for her, in her childhood, and craftily impressed upon her youthful mind; which so—like a mark in a young tree— had enlargingly grown with her growth, till it had become the immense staring marvel" (P, 354). Her story like all stories is inevitably genealogical; it resembles a family tree that "annually puts forth new branches" (P, 9), but it also bears a "mark" that at once implies the activity of an originating intention and signifies our distance from it. For it points not to the authoritative source but to the tangle of other such inscriptions scattered throughout the text of *Pierre*, inscriptions that seem at first to embody a presence but that actually condemn us to absence.

How to Read Melville's *Pierre*

Sacvan Bercovitch

Melville's *Pierre* is a book that is very much in need of recovery. It is the pivotal work in Melville's career, an enormously ambitious and carefully planned novel, one that offers an extraordinarily rich perspective on his achievement as a whole, and of all his works the one that has proved least accessible. So my purpose here is evangelical as well as scholarly. . . . I want to make the novel accessible . . . by exploring, layer by layer, the difficulties it presents (in my experience) to graduate and undergraduate students. And to bring all this within the scope of an hour, I shall focus on a single passage, the author's Dedication, "To Greylock's Most Excellent Majesty":

> In old times authors were proud of the privilege of dedicating their works to Majesty. A right noble custom, which we of Berkshire must revive. For whether we will or no, Majesty is all around us here in Berkshire, sitting as in a grand Congress of Vienna of majestical hilltops, and eternally challenging our homage.
>
> But since the majestic mountain, Greylock—my own more immediate sovereign lord and king—hath now, for innumerable ages, been the one grand dedicatee of the earliest rays of all the Berkshire mornings, I know not how his Imperial Purple Majesty (royal born: Porphyrogenitus) will receive the dedication of my own poor solitary ray.
>
> Nevertheless, foreasmuch as I, dwelling with my loyal neighbors, the Maples and Beeches, in the amphitheater over which his central majesty presides, have received his most bounteous and unstinted fertilizations, it is but meet, that I here devoutly kneel, and render up my gratitude, whether, thereto, The Most Excellent Purple Majesty of Greylock benignantly incline his hoary crown or no.[1]

What's wrong with this passage? Let me count the complaints: excess, cliché, pasteboard dramatics—everything that makes the novel so hard to get through, as those of you who have read it know. For those of you who have not, it's an opportunity to rehearse the plot. To begin with, the sentimental setting: noble young Pierre, the natural aristocrat, on his country estate near

From *Amerikastudien*, 31 (1986): 31–49. Reprinted by permission of the author.

[1] All references to *Pierre, or the Ambiguities* are from Herman Melville, *Pierre, Israel Potter, The Piazza Tales, The Confidence-Man, Uncollected Prose, Billy Budd,* ed. Harrison Hayford, Library of America (New York, 1984). This paper is an expanded version of a talk I gave in October 1983 at Harvard University.

Greylock, alias the Delectable Mountain, with his adoring mother, Mary, and Lucy, his angelic, blue-eyed, blond-haired bride-to-be. Then, the gothic reversals: impassioned letters; an ambiguous portrait of Pierre's revered dead father; division between mother and son; and the cause of all this trouble, a dark lady, Isabel, who claims to be Pierre's illegitimate half-sister. That's Part I. In Part II, there are the melodramatics of Pierre's and Isabel's flight to New York, their many mishaps in the city, and most elaborately, Pierre's attempts to become a great writer, which result in utter failure, murder, and suicide.

The first point to make about all this is also the basic point in reading *Pierre*: Melville knew what he was doing. Clearly, the reason for the purple prose, in the Dedication and throughout *Pierre*, is that he wanted the book to sell. In fact, the Dedication is a rather crafty appeal for patronage. It links art to nature, and nature to natural aristocracy, extending local pride into a hymn to the country's purple-mountained majesty. If these sentiments seem commonplace, that is precisely their intent. Melville was trying to please. How well he succeeded may be gauged by two items in the September, 1852, issue of the New York *Day Book*, facing each other (on adjoining pages) like author and mountain in the Dedication. One is a review of *Pierre* entitled (in capital letters) "HERMAN MELVILLE CRAZY." The other is an essay on how to make it in the literary market. Basically, it says, what's needed is "a sufficient quantity of sighs and tears, along with a murder, and, if convenient, a suicide. Present the women in symbolic pairs, blonde and brunette, seraph and sensualist. The hero should be a perfectionist, an enthusiast for Truth and Virtue, and should come to a predictably melancholy pass."[2]

So Melville knew what he was doing, but the American public did *not* incline its hoary crown. And for good reason. As you have no doubt noticed, the Dedication really ridicules its subject. It makes fun of Greylock, of majesty, of the very notion of a man addressing a mountain; and the ridicule extends throughout the novel, in what amounts to a savage satire of American culture, pastoral and urban. Reviewers were understandably outraged. "He strikes with an impious . . . hand at the very foundations of our society"; such "antagonism . . . to all the recognized laws of social morality" can only "be supposed to emanate from a lunatic hospital." "His fancy is diseased," declared the influential critic George Washington Peck in the prestigious *American Whig Review*; we must "freeze him into silence."[3] But on this issue our sympathies lie with Melville, and our sense of the satire in his style is an incentive to return for a closer analysis of the text.

[2]New York *Day Book* (Sept. 7, 1852), IV, no. 948.
[3]Evert and George Duyckinck, unsigned review, New York *Literary World* (Aug. 21, 1852); rpt. in Hershel Parker, *The Recognition of Herman Melville* (Ann Arbor, MI, 1967), pp. 51–56; anonymous review, Boston *Post* (Aug. 4, 1852); rpt. in Brian Higgins, *Herman Melville: An Annotated Bibliography* (New York, 1979), p. 118; Peck, unsigned review, *American Whig Review*, 16 Nov. 1852; rpt. in *Melville: The Critical Heritage*, ed. Watson G. Branch (London, 1974), pp. 314–21.

Notice, first, that the Dedication sets out a number of cunningly inter-
linked themes, which in fact turn out to be the novel's main concerns. I refer
to the Romantic correspondence of mind and nature, to the patriotic contrast
between Europe and America, to the problems of perspective, interpretation,
and naming, and to the troubled relation of authorship to authority. Second,
the Dedication sets out the major symbolic pattern in *Pierre*. I refer now to
the novel's persistent reference to mountains, hills, rocks, and stones—
through analogy, image, and allusion; through the names of characters and
places; and through the events that drive Pierre from Saddle Meadows, his
country estate named for Saddleback Mountain nearby—alias Mount Greylock, or the Delectable Mountain, as the local inhabitants have renamed it—
from "the sweet purple airs of the hills round about . . . Saddle Meadows" to
the "mortar and stone" city, a "wilderness" of "stony roofs and seven-fold stony
skies" (pp. 316, 269, 418), where Pierre settles with Isabel in the stone-carved
Church of the Apostles, as though to fulfill the promise of his name: Pierre,
Peter, Christ, the rock of our salvation. Finally, there is the satiric element I
mentioned. The Dedication is an homage to royalty that declares the author's
independence, an act of defiance made in a posture of humility, a plea for
patronage that celebrates isolation, and a tribute to nature's nation which, in
its allusion to the Congress of Vienna—the "grand repression" of 1814, as
Melville termed it, comparable to the Reaction of 1848, when "all the world
around, these kings, they had the casting vote, and voted for themselves"[4]—
in its *grim* allusion to Old World repression effectually equates Europe and
America and the present with the past.

A rich and intricate piece of rhetoric, perhaps more intricate than necessary, as some readers have complained. Which brings us to the next step in
reading *Pierre*. The problem is not Melville's lack of control, but, if anything,
just the reverse. The language seems *too* controlled, overdetermined, self-
consciously elaborated to the point of impasse. It is as though two narrators
were speaking simultaneously—one, the proud author who is dedicating the
book; the other, the humble "I" inside the Dedication—one building up the
tribute, the other tearing it down. And neither of these, be it noted, is
necessarily Melville himself. Nor is it, necessarily, the official author of
Pierre, for whom Melville wanted an anonymous or (as he told his publisher)
"an assumed name—'By a Vermonter' say."[5]

Obviously, we need a clear and simple route into this prose, and parody is
the obvious way to start. Whatever else may be said about it, the Dedication
is meant to be funny, and so it is; and so is the novel. *Pierre* is a tragicomedy
of downward mobility, the story of a rich and pretentious country boy who
makes a mess of things at home, moves to the big city, and quickly falls from
riches to rags. The fall is moral as well as material. Pierre is an inversion not

---

[4]Melville, "The Piazza," in *Melville*, ed. Hayford, p. 623.
[5]Melville, Letter to Richard Bentley, April 16, 1852, in Jey Leyda, *The Melville Log: A
Documentary Life of Herman Melville, 1819–1891* (New York, 1951), I, 448.

only of the self-made man but of the self-reliant idealist. His revolt against convention ends in shambles—family destroyed, morality abandoned, not even a book produced—and through it all Pierre hardly seems to know what he's doing, let alone what he wants. His characteristic mode is the rhetoric of self-deceit. One example must suffice. Pierre pretends to marry the supposedly illegitimate Isabel because, he tells us, he wants to uphold the truth, protect his mother from the knowledge of his father's supposed sins, and redeem his father by himself atoning for those sins. In fact, of course, he is perpetuating a lie, punishing his mother (who soon dies of grief), and concealing his father's crime (if crime there was), all because he has been overcome by a passion that he needs to conceal from himself. . . .

But parody is only one element, an engaging way into the text. . . . I spoke earlier of two narrators in the Dedication, one naive and mystifying, the other sardonic, demystifying. . . . Now I would call attention to a third level of narration in the Dedication. I refer to the author who hears the stoney silence that elicits the Dedication in the first place—the self-conscious author who recognizes the ambiguity but cannot resolve it, and so insists on the process of symbol-making, whether the symbol has meaning or not. In the conversation between Pierre and Isabel, this narrative voice takes the form of a mind that's unable to reconcile duty and desire, virtue and truth—unable to reconcile these, but unable to acknowledge that failing in itself—and so keeps talking on and on, until it finds refuge in silence. In terms of the novel at large, it is the narrator who admires Pierre's resolve to find answers, whether the world responds or not, although he already knows, what Pierre himself never learns, that "Silence is the only Voice of our God" (p. 240).

So we come to the third step in reading *Pierre*: the novel's self-conscious psychological dimension. And here as before, the Dedication offers an excess of possibilities. Those three narrative voices I spoke of—praising, ridiculing, unresolved—constitute an endlessly interpretable commentary on a primal Oedipal confrontation. Think of the varieties of emotions implicit (in the Dedication) in the eight-times-repeated "majesty," "majestic"—and of how that image of overbearing authority turns into a measure of distance, a figure of alienation, and finally a trope 'for mere absence ("whether His Majesty incline his hoary crown or no"). Or think of the parallels between Greylock and Pierre's father as objects of contemplation (including the dizzying turns of perspective: "we must," "but," "whether or no," "I know not," "nevertheless"). Or again, think of the principle of symbolic inversion inherent in the dualisms that shape the Dedication (aggression-humility, deference-contempt, etc.) particularly as that principle informs the novel's events and characters. Isabel and Lucy, for example, oppose each other as (respectively) dark versus light, truth versus appearance, eros versus caritas, caritas versus eros, and so on in endless (because self-generating) reversals of meaning, until the two women, considered separately or together, come to seem a figure of ambivalence incarnate, like hoary Greylock. . . .

For my general purpose, a general and familiar point will do: this is a book about self-discovery. A familiar point which begins with a stylistic observation: psychologically considered, the subject of the Dedication is not Greylock, but the complex authorial "I." Starting with the external, the Not-Me—nature, history, and society ("Pines and Maples," ancient customs, "we of Berkshire")—the narrator moves gradually inward, toward subjectivity and the sole self. . . . He describes the self as a man-made mountain, a pyramid with a secret buried at its center; in that secret lies the meaning of identity. Hence our obsessive self-involvement: "By vast pains we mine into the pyramid; by horrible gropings we come to the central room; with joy we espy the sarcophagus; but we lift the lid and no body is there!—appallingly vacant as vast is the soul of a man!" (p. 332).

Since critics leap to read such passages as philosophic nihilism, it is worth remarking that something is discovered here by somebody. The descent into the pyramid is a metaphor not of absolute futility, but of the futility of absolute independence, the vast and vacant promise of the God within. *Pierre* is an incisive critique of various theories of the mind—Romantic, Lockean, and Protestant—and common to all aspects of the critique is the theme of narcissism. Indeed, images of Narcissus recur throughout the novel, and they are connected throughout to another of its main themes, the theme of incest. The connection is central to each step in Pierre's descent into self-discovery, so let me take a moment to summarize the link here between narcissism and incest. In Saddle Meadows, the implicit sexuality between Pierre and his mother—the first extended treatment in our literature of Oedipal desire—is nourished by an admiration of those qualities in themselves that each sees reflected in the other. Isabel serves to draw out both these elements in Pierre, sexuality and self-love. She is unmistakably his obscure object of desire. But she attracts him especially for what he can read into her about himself. She functions first as his *anima*, guide to the dark night of his soul, and then as his Pygmalion's model, on whom he projects what he desires for himself.

Vivia, the autobiograhical hero of Pierre's book, is the last stage of that voyage to the end of the self. He is Pierre's self-begotten Pygmalion and fullest self-reflection, the last in a series of doubles (mother-sister-fictional hero) that may be said to begin even before the novel does, with the Dedication. For in some sense, clearly, the mountain out there is a projection of the writer's anxieties and aspirations; and in that sense, the great stone face of Greylock which we know will finally *not* respond, is his own. In other words, the Mount Greylock of the Dedication is in some sense a shadowy image of Vivia, Pierre's self-made-word that never materializes. . . .

Beyond the psycho-drama, *Pierre* is a book about books, and more broadly, a book about art. The novel's structure is a Chinese box of narrators: Melville writing about an author (or authors), writing about Pierre, writing about Vivia, writing about himself, the autobiographical hero-author of Pierre's would-be novel. The main characters are artists: Pierre a writer, Isabel a musician, and Lucy a painter. The central problem is the interpretation of a portrait, or rather a series of portraits: first, a pair of conflicting family portraits, ostensibly of Pierre's father; then a portrait of Pierre (by Lucy); still later a fraudulent copy of Guido Reni's portrait of Beatrice Cenci (which we now know, and Melville would not have been displeased to learn, is neither by Guido Reni nor of Beatrice Cenci); and climactically, near the end of the novel, the portrait of a young man resembling Isabel, we're told, or perhaps Pierre's father, or else Lucy, though the painting is an avowed counterfeit—an "imported daub," bearing the "impotent scope" of a "mutilated torsoe"—a portrait numbered 99 (the number of the canto where Dante sees "the visage most resembling Christ")[6]: "*No. 99. A stranger's head, by an unknown hand*" (pp. 405–06).

Most striking of all in this respect is Pierre himself. If Vivia is the self-made-word, Pierre is the word made self, a sort of Frankenstein's monster of literary references. The narrator describes him as a mountain-climber trying to scale Parnassus with "a pile of folios on his back" (p. 330). And though Pierre claims to shed his burden as he mines into himself, the allusions keep piling up—Bulwer-Lytton's Glenn and Scott's Glendinning, Milton's Christ (as well as Satan), Spenser's Red Cross Knight and Keats's Melancholy, Goethe's Werther (and Goethe himself in his Autobiography), Aeschylus's Orestes and Prometheus (and Shelley's Prometheus too), Byron's Childe Harold (along with Cain and Manfred), Dante's Paolo (conflated with Shakespeare's Romeo), William Gilmore Simms's Beauchamp, Carlyle's Teufelsdröckh, and many others, including various mythic figures, from Apollo to Sisyphus, and several forgotten heroes of popular fiction.[7]

So we come to the fourth step in reading *Pierre*, the novel as a discourse on rhetoric. A fashionable subject, and the truth is that *Pierre* lends itself wonderfully to semiotics, deconstruction, and reader-response theory. The Dedication presents a mountain-*scape*, a de-centered, self-reflective verbal portrait of Greylock in the process of being interpreted. Words about words. An implied reader of mountains dangling in an aporia between achievement and anticipation, precariously suspended in the simultaneity of the mutually exclusive. *Pierre* may become too appealing on this level, and it's useful to recall that Melville was not modernist, much less post-modernist, except insofar as he was the most probing critical mind among the American

---

[6]*The Vision of Dante, Paradise,* ed. Clay, XXXII, p. 564.

[7]All of these references have been documented in a host of articles, ranging from the antiquarian—e.g., George Mower, "The Kentucky Tragedy: A Source for *Pierre*," *Kentucky Folklore Record,* 15 (1969), 1–2—to the sophisticated revisionist survey in Leon Howard and Hershel Parker, "Historical Note" to the Northwestern Edition of *Pierre, or the Ambiguities,* ed. Harrison Hayford, Hershel Parker, and G. Thomas Tanselle (Evanston, IL, 1971). In addition to the allusions and citations I have cited above, Howard and Parker list references to Dickens, Disraeli, Godwin, Mary Shelley, Thackeray, Cooper, Poe, Longfellow, Lamartine, DeQuincy, Browne, Martin Farquhar Tupper, Mme. de Staël, Eugène Sue, and Jean-Paul Richter (pp. 369–70).

Romantics. Indeed, the Dedication offers a commentary of sorts on Romantic aesthetics—as in the image of the sun through which the author claims his autonomy. Greylock, the "grand dedicatee" of Berkshire's "earliest rays," is now to receive light, whether he likes it or not, from the Romantic sun (or lamp) of the creative imagination. One thinks in this regard of Whitman's grand assertion of authorship in "Song of Myself": "Dazzling and tremendous how quick the sun-rise would kill me,/If I could not now and always send sunrise out of me." The difference, of course, is that in Melville's case the conflict turns inward, dissolves into ambiguities about the self, and those ambiguities reveal, among other things, that *this* creative sun draws its light (rather un-Romantically) from many other sources: for instance, Shelley's poem to "inaccessible" Mont Blanc, surrounded by "Its subject mountains"; Coleridge's earlier "magnificent hymn of Mont Blanc" (as *The Democratic Review* of 1848 described it); Sylvester Judd's odes to Mons Christi (and "the Delectable Way" that leads to it) in his best-selling novel of 1845 (revised and enlarged for republication in 1852); perhaps Poe's "Haunted Palace," where "Wanderers in [a] happy valley" see from afar, "sitting/(Porphyrogene!)/In state his glory well befitting,/The rule of the realm . . ."; perhaps even Poe's then well-known "Letter to B——," which images an Andes of the mind leading "ascendingly, to a few gifted individuals who kneel around the summit, beholding, face to face, the master spirit"; and almost certainly Thomas Gray's tribute to the bard Modred, "whose magic song/Made huge Plinlimmon"—the highest mountain in Wales, after Snowdon—"Made huge Plinlimmon bow his cloud-cap't head." In short, interpretation directs us not to an authorial self, but into a pyramid, "surface stratified upon surface" (p. 332), of literary reference. The empty sarcophagus has its double in a Pandora's box of intertextuality.

Still, there is a structure to the flow of allusions. . . .

In all cases, interpretation means regression: paradigmatically, a regression from current literature to the classics, and from the classics back through "innumerable ages" (as the narrator says of Greylock) to legend and myth. And in all cases, this process parallels the one I traced earlier, from social identity to cultural ideals to the primal self. It also parallels the process of Pierre's literary career: from writer of popular fiction (in Saddle Meadows), to an enthusiast of the classics (after he meets Isabel), to the autonomous author of Vivia. "O hitherto I have but piled up words," he declares, in deciding to flee with Isabel; "now I sit down and read" (p. 110). When later he begins to write, Pierre finds himself "transplanted into a new and wonderful element," where "books no more are needed." Standing there upon the Mont Blanc of the mind, overlooking the "full awfulness" of the Alps within, and—beyond these, across "the invisible Atlantic"—of our interior Berkshires and Rocky Mountains, he realizes that "all the great books in the world are but the mutilated showings-forth of invisible and eternally unembodied images of the soul; so that they are but mirrors, distortedly reflecting to us our own things; and never mind what the mirror may be"—Don Juan, Hamlet, Orestes—"if

we would see the object, we must look at the object itself, not its reflection"
(pp. 330–31).

The object itself: it is not intertextuality that undermines Pierre's romantic
heroics; it is (to repeat) the interdependence between textuality and the self.
Melville's critique in this respect may be understood most directly in contrast
with Emerson's doctrine of originality, which makes intertextuality (along with
multiple interpretation) the source of personal empowerment, the very
ground of self-reliance:

> What can see, read, acquire, but ourselves? Cousin is a thousand books to a
> thousand persons. Take the book, my friend, & read your eyes out; you will never
> find there what I find. . . . It occurred last night in groping after the elements of
> that pleasure we derive from literary compositions, that it is like the pleasure
> which the prince LeBoo received from seeing himself for the first time in a
> mirror,—a mysterious & delightful surprise. A poem, a sentence causes us to see
> ourselves. I be & I see my being, at the same time.[8]

These fragments from the Journals could be elaborated with excerpts from
Emerson's entire corpus. They constitute what remains the boldest claim of
American individualism: that all history is not only at but for one's disposal;
that the true individual, as the heir of the ages (like "America" at large), must
freely use the great books of the (Old World) past—applying what is relevant,
discarding the outmoded, improving upon the imperfect—as a standing
advertisement, till disproved, of his spiritual independence, his inalienable
authenticity, and his original relation to nature. . . .

So I come to the fifth and final step in my reading of *Pierre*: the American
connection. It is perhaps the novel's most comprehensive aspect, and surely
its most conspicuous. The Dedication pointedly appeals for American patronage; Greylock is unambiguously a symbol of American nature; the novel's
central movement, from agrarian family estate to urban society, reflects the
main transition of Jacksonian America; and Pierre is first and last an exemplary national figure, the *American* Enceladus, the natural aristocrat who
dreams of becoming what Melville celebrated in his essay on Hawthorne as
"the literary Shiloh of America." Everything about Pierre confirms this representative quality: his buoyant youthfulness, his fixation on the future, his
vaunted independence, his effort simultaneously to reject and redeem the
past, and above all his incredible faith in words. Pierre is the product of a
culture founded on rhetoric—a nation invented *ex verbo*, by the word, in a
long procession of covenants, declarations, written constitutions, statements
of principle and purpose, interpretations and re-interpretations of so-called
sacred texts. Pierre is also the product of history. He is heir to his family
estate; in the author's words, determined to cap "the fame column whose tall
shaft had been erected by his sires" (p. 12), as a sort of porphyrite monument
to American nationhood.

---

[8]Emerson, *Journals and Miscellaneous Notebooks*, ed. Merton M. Sealts (Cambridge, MA,
1965), III, 327 and V, 278.

The story of the Glendinnings is the story of how the land was won; and Isabel, the hidden and excluded daughter—the immigrant working-class girl in what we come to see is an oppressive class hierarchy—embodies the illegitimate deeds of the Glendinnings, past and present. In short, the father's taint is symbolic: the legacy of the fathers, Pierre's in particular and the country's in general. Again, one example must suffice. And since *Pierre* revolves around the interpretation of portraits, I would like you to think of this as the last in a procession of paintings, one fading into the other: Mount Greylock; Pierre's father; Pierre and Isabel in the stone-carved church of the Apostles; Pierre climbing the Mount of Titans; Pierre entombed in the massive stone city jail—and lastly, this portrait of Pierre's namesake—"grand old Pierre," as the narrator calls him, the founder of Saddle Meadows:

> Pierre's grandfather [was] an American gentleman . . . ; during a fire in the old manorial mansion, with one dash of his foot, he had smitten down an oaken door, to admit the buckets of his negro slaves; . . . in a night-scuffle in the wilderness before the Revolutionary War, he had annihilated two Indian savages by making reciprocal bludgeons of their heads. And all this was done by the mildest hearted, and most blue-eyed gentleman in the world; . . . a gentle, white-haired worshiper of all the household gods; the gentlest husband, and the gentlest father; the kindest of masters to his slaves; . . . a sweet-hearted, charitable Christian; in fine, a pure, cheerful, childlike, blue-eyed, divine old man . . . fit image of his God. . . . The majestic sweetness of this portrait was truly wonderful . . . a glorious gospel framed and hung . . . and declaring to all people, as from the Mount, that man is a noble, god-like being, full of the choicest juices. . . . (pp. 37–38)

The satire is excessive, especially considering that this American demigod, Pierre Glendinning the first, is modelled on Melville's grandfather, Peter Gansevoort, the hero of Fort Stanwix, after whom Melville had just named his son. But then, the same tone of excess may be found in all the other passages I have quoted, including the view of majestic Greylock, flowing with "bounteous fertilizations." In all cases, it is the tone of a betrayed idealist, an excess of outrage bred in an excess of hope. And in all cases it reflects the extremes of mood and action in the novel: the perfectionist demands that Pierre heaps on himself and others, the self-destructive fury with which he dashes himself against the "stony walls" closing in to "crush" him (p. 273). *Pierre* is a great commentary on the relation of violence to myth in America: the spiral of promise and frustration, rededication and further frustration, which seems always at the edge of explosion, and which has often sought release in dream-visions of apocalypse. . . .

Moby-Dick is Melville's American apocalypse. *Pierre* is an inside narrative of the myth-making process. It is a story based on the rhetoric of Apocalypse that works itself out in an apocalypse of rhetoric.

I mean apocalypse now in its primal sense: "to unveil or disclose, to reveal." In this sense, the first reviewers were right. As an inquiry into the ways that rhetoric deceives, traps, and maddens, *Pierre* really does strike with an impious hand at the very foundations of American society. It is also a self-immolating inquiry into Melville's commitment to America, and the most scathing review ever written of his own ill-fated literary career. This latter aspect of *Pierre* lies outside the scope of my paper, since it begins after the Dedication. . . . Insofar as the Dedication to *Pierre* recalls the one to Hawthorne, it evokes (through its different narrative voices) the process of Melville's creative unfolding, from 1846 to 1851, from popular fiction (in *Omoo*) to novels of self-discovery (like *Mardi*) to what he termed (in his review of Hawthorne, but thinking, too, of his own work in progress on *Moby-Dick*) "the great Art of Telling the Truth."[9] So considered, the portrait of Mount Greylock might well be seen as a commentary on the energizing tensions behind that astonishing development, connecting as it does the unfathomable otherness of Typee to the mute, majestic white whale. It is one of the terrible ironies of our cultural history that that interpretation should first have been suggested in the bitter five-fold allegory of *Pierre*: literally, the story of a provincial enthusiast; psychologically, the self-discovery of a Fool of Truth; aesthetically, the un-writing of *Moby-Dick*; culturally, the betrayal of Young America in literature; and prophetically, a failed book (entitled "Herman Melville Crazy") about the failure of symbolic art.

[9]Melville, "Hawthorne and His Mosses," in *Melville*, ed. Hayford, p. 1160.

The Flawed Grandeur of Melville's *Pierre*

Brian Higgins and Hershel Parker

Pierre was not conceived as a lesser effort, a pot-boiler like *Redburn*, which Melville disparaged as something he wrote to buy tobacco with. His response to Hawthorne's praise of *Moby-Dick* in mid-November, 1851, makes plain that Melville intended his next book to be as much grander than his last as the legendary Krakens are bigger than whales. Never a novelist or romancer within the ordinary definitions, Melville in *Moby-Dick* had attempted to convert the whaling narrative, a flourishing division of nautical literature, into a vehicle for the philosophical and psychological speculations a pondering man like him was compelled toward. *Pierre* is his comparable attempt to convert the Gothic romance (in one of its late permutations as sensational fiction primarily for female readers) into a vehicle for his speculations, the psychological now looming larger than the philosophical. . . .

While *Moby-Dick* succeeded for many of its first readers, even if only as a reliable source of cetological information, *Pierre* failed disastrously on all levels. Yet Melville's basic preoccupations are almost identical in both, except that in *Pierre* he shifted considerably from metaphysics toward psychology. Many of the themes of *Moby-Dick* recur, among them the determinant power of wayward moods over human destiny and the tragic necessity that loftier souls hurl themselves against the unresponsive gods in order to assert their own godhood; many of the images recur, especially the sliding, gliding aboriginal phantoms which link Fedallah and Isabel as embodiments of the Unconscious. Stirred by these or other powerful elements, whether or not related to *Moby-Dick*, the best readers of *Pierre* have paid tribute to the heroic intellectual tasks Melville undertook in it. Yet of them only E. L. Grant Watson thought those heroic tasks had been successfully accomplished,[1] while others more often admired the endeavour, whatever they construed it to be, but praised only one aspect or another of the performance. . . . Scholars and critics have not been able to define the precise nature of the book's grandeur

From *New Perspectives on Melville*, edited by Faith Pullin. Copyright © 1978 by Edinburgh University Press.

[1]'Melville's *Pierre*', *New England Quarterly*, 3 (April 1930) 195–234.

or the precise nature of the flaws which prevent it from being the masterpiece which *Moby-Dick* indisputably is. The problem of how *Pierre* fails can be answered only by rigorous attention to both biographical and aesthetic evidence. Our answers derived from documentary evidence are presented elsewhere; here we focus on evidence from within the book itself. . . .

For a several-week period of almost uninterrupted concentration after he began *Pierre*, Melville exerted an intellectual power which he had previously manifested only in *Moby-Dick* and a sustained control over his plot which was new to him. Very possibly that power and control carried him through to the conclusion of *Pierre* as a short novel, the shortest book he had written since *Typee*. Since the Harpers had rebuffed him the last time he had negotiated concerning a work-in-progress, the manuscript of *Pierre* which he took to them around New Year's Day of 1852 was probably complete or almost complete. The publishers accepted *Pierre* promptly enough, estimating it to take up some 360 pages, but their terms were ungenerous: rather than the usual 50¢ on the dollar after expenses Melville was to receive only 20¢. Stung by the implications for his career (the terms meant he might have to give up any hope of supporting his family by his writing), Melville was further distressed by reviews of *Moby-Dick* in the January magazines, for among them were scathing attacks on him personally as well as on his books. Brooding over the ironies of his literary career—initial fame with *Typee* from little effort or merit, financial failure from the ambitious *Mardi*, new condemnation for *Moby-Dick*, ill omens for his latest brainchild, Melville seems to have done what he did with *Mardi* after it was 'finished'—worked a previously unplanned plot line into the latter part of his manuscript. Almost surely . . . what Melville added to make *Pierre* swell by some 150 or 160 pages was the plot involving Pierre as a juvenile author and a young author immaturely attempting a mature book. The first half of *Pierre* as we know it probably survives pretty nearly intact from the original phase of composition, while the second half consists of more or less altered remnants of approximately the last third of the original version intermixed with sections written in January and February 1852. Signs of Melville's careful initial planning remain evident throughout the first half: to the end of Book XIV, 'The Journey and the Pamphlet,' action taking place in the novel's present occupies just four days, with Pierre and his companions leaving Saddle Meadows early on the morning of the fifth; lengthy flashbacks to different periods in the past illuminate developments in the present. Some signs of such careful planning survive even later, the heavy emphasis on the first and third nights in the city, for instance, suggesting that Melville may have originally written that section with a similarly controlled time scheme. A few awkwardnesses can be adduced, aside from those which are due to the insertion of the new plot, but by and large the plotting in *Pierre* is intricate and accurate and of a novelistic expertise new to Melville, extending to consistency of detail, just where he had never manifested anything approaching a compulsive tidiness. Care in plotting is especially obvious—indeed, deliberately over-obvious—in the elaborate predictions of events to come and in the complex set of cross references which lace parts of the book together.

The predictions come thick and fast at the outset, where they would naturally come if they are going to come at all. We are led to expect that the lives of Pierre and his mother will divide (5),[2] and that after Pierre's interior development he will not prize his ancestry so much (6). His aspirations clearly will be thwarted by Time (8), and his 'special family distinction' will be important to his singularly developed character and life career (12). Fate will very likely knock him off his pedestal (12), he will become philosophical (13), and will become a thoroughgoing democrat, even a Radical one (13). The predictions continue: Nature will prove ambiguous to Pierre in the end (13); Lucy will long afterwards experience far different 'flutterings' from those at Saddle Meadows (26); Pierre will never regain his lost sense of an undisturbed moral beauty in the world (65); his crawling under the Memnon Stone will later hold immense significance for him (135); in aftertimes with Isabel, Pierre will often recall his first magnetic night with her (151); Pierre, Isabel, and Delly will never return to Saddle Meadows once they leave (203). After the departure from Saddle Meadows the predictions diminish, as they naturally would past the middle of the book, when predictions are being fulfilled, not made. . . .

If the early chapters now stand roughly in order of their composition, they indicate that Melville had much of the basic plot well outlined from the beginning. The rather thick-strewn predictions do not, however, prove that no radical new elements were introduced into the plot. Curiously enough, despite all the fulfilled predictions there is nothing which conclusively proves that Melville intended from the outset to have Pierre become a writer once he was exiled from his home. In fact, the pattern of predictions makes it seem most likely that if Melville had had any such plan he would have signalled it at intervals throughout the Saddle Meadows section. Moreover, Melville may not have let stand some of the city episodes in the ways he had once intended. These limitations aside, the predictions do furnish at least some evidence as to the unusual degree of Melville's control over his material. . . .

Unusual though it was for Melville, control of such details obviously does not of itself lead to great fiction. Indeed the excessive emphasis on predictions early in *Pierre* reflects Melville's satirical playing with one of the routine conventions of popular fiction. His real triumph of control in *Pierre* is the way he leads the reader into fascinated engagement with his remarkable thematic preoccupations. At the outset he risks failing to achieve any such engagement at all, for he strangely idealizes the social rank and superior natures of the characters, who feel extraordinary emotions and speak an extraordinary lan-

---

[2]This essay cites *Pierre* in the Northwestern-Newberry edition (Evanston and Chicago, 1971), edited by Harrison Hayford, Hershel Parker, and G. Thomas Tanselle.

guage. In Book I, 'Pierre Just Emerging from His Teens', the first words of dialogue are ludicrous, by realistic standards, and there seems some fairy-tale quality about the whole situation. The style is often pseudo-Elizabethan bombast, often near the cloying romanticism of female novels of Melville's own time. Yet rapidly the reader begins to feel the tension created between the idealization of the characters and the constant predictions of disaster: the novel is to be a grand experiment in which Fate will take a hand in the life history of a rare specimen of mankind. With daring and often outrageous stylistic improvising Melville is in fact mocking Pierre's adolescent heroics, his unearned sense of security, and his unwillingness to face those dark truths that are to be the burden of the novel. The reader is led to view Pierre with amused, objective condescension and even slight contempt at the same time that he feels concern for the approaching crash of Pierre's illusions. After the early sense of impending calamity, Melville moves into another way of engaging his readers, by giving his hero unbidden inklings of a darker side of life. Events within and without impel Pierre toward maturer thought, yet he is reluctant to become philosophic (which in this novel means to awaken to a tragic sense). At the end of Book II, 'Love, Delight, and Alarm', Grief is still only a 'ghost-story' to Pierre (41). He resists the 'treacherous persuasiveness' (42) of the mournful pine tree and curses his reading in Dante (42), rejecting even imagined, not felt, experience of the darker aspects of reality, thinking, in juvenile pugnaciousness, that deprived of joy he would find cause for deadly feuds with things invisible.

In Book III, 'The Presentiment and the Verification', as Melville begins to develop Pierre's deeper side, his narrative voice becomes more restrained and sombre. He portrays the stirrings of Pierre's Unconscious, from which 'bannered armies of hooded phantoms' (49) disembark and attack his conscious mind. Yet Pierre still shrinks 'abhorringly from the infernal catacombs of thought' when beckoned by a 'foetal fancy' (51); he fights against his new sensations as a 'sort of unhealthiness' (53) when stirred 'in his deepest moral being' (as he thinks) by the sight of Isabel's face (49). But after receiving Isabel's letter his reluctance to face Truth when he does not know what he is evading turns into overeagerness to face Truth when he does not know what he is inviting (65). Hereafter Melville continues to trace the process of Pierre's mental growth, so that the reader becomes privy to the seemingly 'boundless expansion' (66) of the young hero's life. Previously engrossed and perhaps intermittently baffled by the stylistic virtuosity with which Melville reveals Pierre's absurdities, the reader is now impelled to follow the murky courses of Pierre's mind through all the ambiguous consequences of his absolute behaviour.

Book IV, 'Retrospective', as the title suggests, interrupts Melville's analysis of Pierre's current mental state. Now Melville announces explicitly a major theme present from the beginning but not emphasized before: that of the supersubtle complexity of psychological motivations and indeed of all psychological processes. We had been told (7) that tracing out 'precisely the absolute motives' which prompted Pierre to partake of the Holy Sacraments at the age of sixteen would be needless as well as difficult; merely, Pierre seemed to have inherited his ancestors' religion 'by the same insensible sliding process' that he inherited their other noble personal qualities and their forests and farms. But the stress had been more on Pierre's immaturity than on the subtlety of the processes by which he behaved as he did. Post-adolescent love-extravagancies are associated with 'subterranean sprites and gnomes' (34), but Melville does not then reveal that these quaint monstrosities emerge from the same Unconscious whence hooded phantoms are soon to embark (49). Early in the novel various images of mental processes as gliding and sliding prefigure Melville's full portrayal of the oblique workings of the mind, but not until the first chapter of 'Retrospective' does he confront the theme directly: 'In their precise tracings-out and subtle causations, the strongest and fieriest emotions of life defy all analytical insight. . . . The metaphysical writers confess, that the most impressive, sudden, and overwhelming event, as well as the minutest, is but the product of an infinite series of infinitely involved and untraceable foregoing occurrences. Just so with every motion of the heart' (67). The rest of Book IV uncovers the extremely complex combination of suddenly recalled events and stories and unbidden night-thoughts which leads to Pierre's immediate conviction that Isabel is his father's daughter. Hereafter, treatment of Pierre's inward development is inseparable from the theme of the shadowiness of all human motivation, the 'ever-elastic regions of evanescent invention' through which the mind roams up and down (82).

Moreover, by the end of Book IV Melville has gone beyond the super-subtlety of all human psychology to assert the *autonomy* of those subtler elements of man, as we first see in the description of the adolescent Pierre sometimes standing before the chair portrait of his father, 'unconsciously throwing himself open to all those ineffable hints and ambiguities, and undefined half-suggestions, which now and then people the soul's atmosphere, as thickly as in a soft, steady snow-storm, the snow-flakes people the air' (84). The imagery suggests an evanescence of thought which the individual no more controls than he does the snow-storm, and Melville distinguishes these 'reveries and trances' from the 'assured element of consciously bidden and self-propelled thought' (84). With similar intimations of forces beyond Pierre's control, Melville refers to the 'streams' of Pierre's reveries over the chair portrait of his father which did not seem 'to leave any conscious sediment in his mind; they were so light and so rapid, that they rolled their own alluvial along; and seemed to leave all Pierre's thought-channels as clean and dry as though never any alluvial stream had rolled there at all' (85). In Book V, 'Misgivings and Preparatives', Fate irresistibly gives Pierre an 'electric insight' into 'the vital character of his mother' so that he now sees her as unalterably dominated by 'hereditary forms and world-usages' (89). As

Melville says, 'in these flashing revelations of grief's wonderful fire, we see all things as they are' (88). Such use of images of natural phenomena to suggest the involuntary processes of the mind continues with added intensity after Pierre has had time to reflect on the letter from Isabel, when the thought of Lucy 'serpent-like . . . overlayingly crawled in upon his other shuddering imaginings' (104). These other thoughts, we are told, would often 'upheave' and absorb the thought of Lucy into themselves, 'so that it would in that way soon disappear from his contemporary apprehension' (104). The serpent image and the image of upheaval imply, once again, an independent vitality in the thought, free of Pierre's conscious control. Natural imagery now becomes more complexly elaborated as Melville portrays an expansion of Pierre's interior dimensions during the mental turmoil into which his reading of the letter has plunged him: 'Standing half-befogged upon the mountain of his Fate, all that part of the wide panorama was wrapped in clouds to him; but anon those concealings slid aside, or rather, a quick rent was made in them' (105). Through the 'swift cloud-rent' Pierre catches one glimpse of Lucy's 'expectant and angelic face', but 'the next instant the stormy pinions of the clouds locked themselves over it again; and all was hidden as before; and all went confused in whirling rack and vapor as before'. Yet while thus 'for the most part wrapped from his consciousness and vision', the condition of Lucy 'was still more and more disentangling and defining itself from out its nether mist,[3] and even beneath the general upper fog' (105). This passage portrays a rapidly expanded mental terrain but still a chaotic and uncontrollable one.

What Melville has achieved is an extraordinary conversion of Gothic sensationalism—mysterious face prefiguring revelation of dark family secrets—into profound psychological exploration. Isabel, Pierre's presumed half-sister, is identified either as his Unconscious or as a product of it, so that his closer involvement with her parallels his gradual opening to incursions from the Unconscious. His after-reveries on her face (41) are associated with his dawning half-admission that Grief may be more than merely a 'ghost-story'. Without 'one word of speech', her face had revealed 'glimpses of some fearful gospel' (43). Within an hour of first seeing Isabel, Pierre felt that 'what he had always before considered the solid land of veritable reality, was now being audaciously encroached upon by bannered armies of hooded phantoms, disembarking in his soul, as from flotillas of specter-boats' (49). After reading Isabel's letter, Pierre 'saw all preceding ambiguities, all mysteries ripped open as if with a keen sword, and forth trooped thickening phantoms of an infinite gloom' (85). Prior to his first interview with her in Book VI, 'Isabel, and the First Part of the Story of Isabel', Pierre gives himself up to 'long wanderings in the primeval woods of Saddle Meadows' (109); formerly sunny and Arca-

---

[3]The word 'nether' is Parker's recent emendation for the first edition's 'nearer'. The emendation will be incorporated in subsequent printings of the Northwestern-Newberry edition. See Parker's "Conjectural Emendations: An Illustration from the Topography of Pierre's Mind," *Literary Research Newsletter,* 3 (Spring 1978), pp. 62–66.

dian, the landscape now mirrors his new sense of the world: in the 'wet and misty eve the scattered, shivering pasture elms seemed standing in a world inhospitable'. . . .

One immediate aftereffect of reading Isabel's letter is that Pierre suddenly sees his father as morally corrupt, although he had always idolized him to the point of sacrilege (68), and the narrator emphasizes that the extreme of Pierre's idealization was possible only because at the age of nineteen he 'had never yet become so thoroughly initiated into that darker, though truer aspect of things, which an entire residence in the city from the earliest period of life, almost inevitably engraves upon the mind of any keenly observant and reflective youth' (69). To be sure, during the four years that he had possessed the chair portrait of his father, Pierre had felt 'ever new conceits come vaporing up' in him (83), so that the portrait seemed to speak with his father's voice: 'I am thy father, boy. There was once a certain, oh, but too lovely young Frenchwoman, Pierre'. Then, 'starting from these reveries and trances, Pierre would regain the assured element of consciously bidden and self-propelled thought' (84), promising never again to fall into such midnight reveries, suppressing suspicions of his father even as he begins to diffuse his own sexual feelings. In his agonized hours following the reading of Isabel's letter, Pierre feels that 'his whole previous moral being' (87) has been overturned. But though he is no longer free to worship his father, he still does not apply to himself the lesson earlier intimated by the chair portrait and apparently confirmed by Isabel's letter, that 'Youth is hot, and temptation strong', that beneath seeming innocence sexual impulses may be stirring (83). His sense of his own immaculateness is chronic. In sublime delusion he feels Christlike, as if 'deep in him lurked a divine unidentifiableness, that owned no earthly kith or kin' (89). While the narrator offers us 'hell-glimpses' (107), reminding us that Pierre was championing 'womanly beauty, and not womanly ugliness', Pierre himself is asking heaven to confirm him in his 'Christ-like feeling' (106).

More mental contortions follow as the deluded Christian knight begins to respond to Isabel's attractiveness. Accustomed from adolescence to a certain falseness in the relationship of mother-son, and more recently exposed to the new artifice by which Mrs Glendinning had converted Lucy into her little sister, Pierre blames Fate for his bewildered feelings about Isabel: 'Fate had done this thing to them. Fate had separated the brother and sister, till to each other they somehow seemed so not at all. Sisters shrink not from their brother's kisses' (142). Pierre begins 'to seem to see the mere imaginariness of the so supposed solidest principle of human association'—an incipient dis-crediting of the taboo against incest—yet feels 'that never, never would he be able to embrace Isabel with the mere brotherly embrace; while the thought of any other caress, which took hold of any domesticness, was entirely vacant from his uncontaminated soul, for it had never consciously intruded there' (142). In this state of mind, and just because his latent incestuous feelings are now stirring, Pierre is compelled, all ignorantly, to sublimate: 'Isabel wholly soared out of the realms of mortalness, and for him became transfigured in the highest heaven of uncorrupted Love' (142). Even as Lucy's bedroom had represented Love's 'secret inner shrine' for Pierre, at his second interview with Isabel the 'deep oaken recess of the double-casement' seems to him the 'vestibule of some awful shrine' (149), though Isabel's power over him is by now more obviously erotic: Pierre feels himself (150) 'surrounded by ten thousand sprites and gnomes, and his whole soul was swayed and tossed by supernatural tides'. (Here the narrator's word 'soul' merely reflects Pierre's own self-protective instinct toward sublimation.) Aware of an 'extraordinary physical magnetism' in Isabel, Pierre nevertheless generalizes his sexual attraction by associating it with a 'Pantheistic master-spell, which eternally locks in mystery and in muteness the universal subject world' (151). Just as he had pledged to Lucy 'the immutable eternities of joyfulness' (36), Pierre now makes extravagant loverlike declarations to Isabel, wishing that his kisses on her hand 'were on the heart itself, and dropt the seeds of eternal joy and comfort there' (154). In egregious delusion of immaculate magnanimity, his pledges to Isabel become as extravagant as his recurrent threats to the gods: 'we will love with the pure and perfect love of angel to an angel. If ever I fall from thee, dear Isabel, may Pierre fall from himself; fall back forever into vacant nothingness and night!' (154). By reinforcing his sense of his own Christlikeness, calling him a 'visible token' of the 'invisible angel-hoods', and praising the 'gospel' of his acts (156), Isabel aids Pierre in sublimating the passion increasingly evident in his words. . . .

The threats and bargains with the gods culminate in the scene with Pierre and Isabel at the Apostles' the third night after their arrival in the city. Once again Pierre makes pledges, inviting the 'high gods' to join the devils against him if he deceives Isabel (272). Once again he invites instant punishment if he fails in Virtue: 'then close in and crush me, ye stony walls, and into one gulf let all things tumble together!' (273). Once again he warns the gods, this time to 'look after their own combustibles': 'If they have put powder-casks in me— let them look to it! let them look to it!' (273). But in a crucial difference from earlier scenes Pierre now suspects that man himself, instead of the gods, may be a 'vile juggler and cheat' (272). Incapable now in Isabel's presence of denying to himself her erotic appeal, he fears that 'uttermost virtue, after all' may prove 'but a betraying pander to the monstrousest vice', and finally declares that the 'demigods trample on trash, and Virtue and Vice are trash!' (273). Declaring that Virtue and Vice are both nothing, and having already rid himself of the chair portrait, the most tangible reminder of Isabel's link to his father, Pierre is now free to commit incest, though whether or not actual sexual intercourse occurs that night at the Apostles' remains ambiguous but hideously possible.

Up to Pierre's arrival in the city with Isabel and Delly, everything has worked together to enhance the attentive reader's sense that he is in the hands of a profound thinker and innovative craftsman who will convey him through yet more hazardous regions of psychological and aesthetic experience. Melville has not only managed to put sensational Gothic plot elements to the service of an acute analysis of a tortuously complex mind; he has also managed to convert analysis into very vivid action, repeatedly portraying Pierre's psychological states and processes in extended metaphors and images, passages that are short, graphic, and frequently intense narratives in themselves. In these highly-charged passages, Melville combines penetrating analysis of his hero's states of mind with the enunciation of general truths, so that the record of Pierre's particular experience is continually expanding to include human experience at large. By the beginning of Book XVI, 'First Night of Their Arrival in the City', the reader wants nothing more than to follow 'the thoughtful river' of Pierre's mind through all the ambiguous consequences of his sublimely absolute and miserably deluded behaviour. Yet despite the brilliance of the scene on the third night at the Apostles', the wish goes mainly unfulfilled. Melville's primary concerns in the first half of the novel only intermittently engage his attention in the second half, and at times he seems lamentably unaware of the direction the first half was taking.

Symptomatic is the flaw in the first paragraph of Book XVII, 'Young America in Literature':

> Among the various conflicting modes of writing history, there would seem to be two grand practical distinctions, under which all the rest must subordinately range. By the one mode, all contemporaneous circumstances, facts, and events must be set down contemporaneously; by the other, they are only to be set down as the general stream of the narrative shall dictate; for matters which are kindred in time, may be very irrelative in themselves. I elect neither of these; I am careless of either; both are well enough in their way; I write precisely as I please. (244)

Earlier Melville had talked bluntly about his demands on the reader: 'This history goes forward and goes backward, as occasion calls. Nimble center, circumference elastic you must have' (54). He had called attention to his apparent disregard of rules in a passage that might strike the reader as 'rather irregular sort of writing' (25), and had announced that he followed 'the flowing river in the cave of man' careless whither he be led, reckless where he land (107). In these instances he had been in superb control, knowing exactly what he was doing with his stylistic absurdities in Books I and II, then knowing that his simultaneous exploration of Pierre's mind and his own might lead him into unknown winding passages (even as he kept to the outline of his plot), but confident that he could bravely follow that flowing river wherever it ran. Not reckoning where he landed was a way of proclaiming his determination to tell everything 'in this book of sacred truth' (107); he was not abandoning a point of view but asserting his determination to hold to it. The beginning of 'Young America in Literature' marks a drastic change in Melville's authorial purpose, a deep draining off of his control over the relationship between narrator and reader. The change is due to what happened in Melville's life between the last days of 1851 and the first days of 1852, but our concern here is with the effects on the manuscript, not the biographical causes.

After his claim to write precisely as he pleased, Melville continues with this remarkably inexact passage: 'In the earlier chapters of this volume, it has somewhere been passingly intimated, that Pierre was not only a reader of the poets and other fine writers, but likewise—and what is a very different thing from the other—a thorough allegorical understander of them, a profound emotional sympathizer with them' (244). On the contrary, we had been told, by Pierre himself in a moment of insight, that he had *not* been that sort of reader: 'Oh, hitherto I have but piled up words; bought books, and bought some small experiences, and builded me in libraries; now I sit down and read' (91). Furthermore, Melville had also asserted that before Pierre was enlightened by the flashing revelations of Grief's wonderful fire, he had *not* been a thorough allegorical understander of the poets:

> Fortunately for the felicity of the Dilletante in Literature, the horrible allegorical meanings of the Inferno, lie not on the surface; but unfortunately for the earnest and youthful piercers into truth and reality, those horrible meanings, when first discovered, infuse their poison into a spot previously unprovided with that sovereign antidote of a sense of uncapitulatable security, which is only the possession of the furthest advanced and profoundest souls. (169)

When he began Book XVII, Melville had simply forgotten this crucial aspect of his characterization of Pierre. But even in the process of crediting Pierre with being 'a thorough allegorical understander' of and 'a profound emotional sympathizer' with poets and other fine writers, Melville seems to have recognized his blunder and attempted an immediate recovery:

> Not that as yet his young and immature soul had been accosted by the Wonderful Mutes, and through the vast halls of Silent Truth, had been ushered into the full, secret, eternally inviolable Sanhedrim, where the Poetic Magi discuss, in glorious gibberish, the Alpha and Omega of the Universe. But among the beautiful imaginings of the second and third degree of poets, he freely and comprehendingly ranged. (244–5)

In these rapid second thoughts Melville ends up saying quite another thing from what he had just said: in fact, he reverts to saying something very like what he had denied at the outset of the paragraph, that Pierre was no more than a normally alert reader. The bitter fun Melville has with his mockery of the rules of writing comes at the considerable cost of jeopardizing the reader's trust in the narrative voice. . . .

Bad as these lapses are, by far the worst failure lies in Melville's altered treatment of Pierre. In the first half of the book, one of the most remarkable features had been the scrupulous and often brilliant presentation of the hero's motives and states of mind. In the last Books, Melville not only fails to provide certain contemplative scenes which were earlier implied if not directly promised (such as scenes in which Pierre thinks about the episode of the Memnon Stone after reaching the city or in which he remembers his first evening with Isabel), he also fails to devote sufficient analysis to Pierre's present states of mind, especially as they involve Isabel. Pierre had vowed to cherish and protect her, to treat her as an artisan handles 'the most exquisite, and fragile filagree of Genoa' (189). But he does not fulfill his pledges; instead, in a few days after reaching the city he becomes almost entirely preoccupied with the book he suddenly begins to write. Isabel is not allowed to participate in his labours (except much later to read aloud proofs to him) and is no longer at the centre of his thoughts. After the arrival in the city, in fact, Isabel is absent from the narrative for long periods. Apart from the scene on the third night at the Apostles' (271–4), she scarcely figures in the story at all until the reintroduction of Lucy. Henry A. Murray aptly comments: 'Pierre, having devoured what Isabel had to give him, is withdrawing libido (interest, love) from her as a person and using it to fold, and warm, and egg round embryoes of thought and to feed a precipitant ambition'.[4] Such an outcome is perhaps credible enough, considering the trauma and the 'widely explosive' mental development Pierre has experienced, but it does not receive from Melville the close analytical scrutiny that is typical of the first half of the book. . . .

The more emotionally involved Melville becomes in his portrayal of Pierre as author, the more he loses his grasp on the implications of other parts of his narrative. As Pierre's suffering and degradation in his attempt to be a profound writer worsen, Melville's rhetoric starts to exalt him: 'In the midst of the merriments of the mutations of Time, Pierre hath ringed himself in with the grief of Eternity. Pierre is a peak inflexible in the heart of Time, as the isle-peak, Piko, stands unassaultable in the midst of waves' (304). Implicitly approving Pierre's commitment, in spite of the self-destructiveness of his attempt to write a great book, Melville speaks of the 'devouring profundities' that have opened up in his hero: 'would he, he could not now be entertainingly and profitably shallow in some pellucid and merry romance' (305). In the next passage on Pierre as author, it is in his 'deepest, highest part' that he is 'utterly without sympathy from any thing divine, human, brute, or vegetable' (338). The mental distance between author and character diminishes appreciably; 'the deeper and the deeper' that he dives, Pierre perceives the 'everlasting elusiveness of Truth' (339), an elusiveness that Melville as narrator had postulated earlier (at page 165 and page 285). Pierre's scorn of the critics now is clearly Melville's: 'beforehand he felt the pyramidical scorn of the genuine loftiness for the whole infinite company of infinitesimal critics' (339). As the distance between author and hero narrows, the hero is increasingly exalted, and Melville speaks of Pierre in the same terms as Pierre sees himself. Pierre begins to feel 'that in him, the thews of a Titan were forestallingly cut by the scissors of Fate' (339); Melville comments: 'Against the breaking heart, and the bursting head; against all the dismal lassitude, and

4Pierre (New York: Hendricks House, Inc. 1949), p. lxxxiii.

deathful faintness and sleeplessness, and whirlingness, and craziness, still he like a demigod bore up' (339). Shortly afterwards Melville writes that the 'very blood' in Pierre's body 'had in vain rebelled against his Titanic soul' (341). In focusing on his hero as author, Melville loses sight of Pierre the young man attempting to be Christlike but undone by human flaws. Now he portrays Pierre the embattled demi-god, whose degradation is an inevitable part of his Titanic greatness: 'gifted with loftiness' he is 'dragged down to the mud' (339), even literally (341). Pierre is identified with Enceladus, 'the most potent of all the giants', one with 'unconquerable front' and 'unabasable face' (345). Melville approves the 'reckless sky-assaulting mood' of both Enceladus and Pierre: 'For it is according to eternal fitness, that the precipitated Titan should still seek to regain his paternal birthright even by fierce escalade. Wherefore whoso storms the sky gives best proof he came from thither! But whatso crawls contented in the moat before the crystal fort, shows it was born within that slime, and there forever will abide' (347). . . .

Yet for all Pierre's status as a profound, deep-diving author, he never consciously understands the relevance of the pamphlet to his life, though he has glimmerings of understanding (and Melville says that unconsciously he understood its application by the end of his life). He does not recognize the danger of Lucy's imitation of his sacrifice of self for another, in spite of his own experience. He reads Lucy's letter and is certain that 'whatever her enigmatical delusion' she 'remained transparently immaculate' in her heart (317), without even recognizing the possibility of a sexual motive in her decision to join him, as in his own deluded resolve to protect Isabel by living with her. He naively admires Lucy as 'an angel' (311), unmindful of the insidious sexual element in his earlier worship of Isabel as 'angel'. He later feels that 'some strange heavenly influence was near him, to keep him from some uttermost harm' (337–8), once Lucy is ensconced at the Apostles', though to Isabel's 'covertly watchful eye' he 'would seem to look upon Lucy with an expression illy befitting their singular and so-supposed merely cousinly relation' (337). Even in the death-cell he sees his predicament as merely the result of his refusal to disown and portion off Isabel (360), just as earlier he tries to accept his grief at the news of his mother's death as a part of the cost at which 'the more exalted virtues are gained' (286). After belatedly recognizing the incestuous nature of his attraction to Isabel, Pierre copes with the knowledge by shutting it out of his consciousness and continuing to deceive himself about his motives. In earlier Books Melville frequently comments on and analyzes Pierre's lack of awareness and his self-deception; now in the last four Books such commentary is notably lacking. Instead, Melville exalts his hero as consumed with devouring profundities, the result of his recent momentous experiences, even while Pierre is revealing a lack of profundity, a lack of perception, and an inability to face the truth of what he has actually experienced—limitations that are as dangerous as ever. While earlier Melville had commented incisively on Pierre's 'strange oversights and inconsistencies', he now fails to recognize a major contradiction in his characterization. He also forgets the origin of Pierre's book. Pierre announces to Isabel that he will 'gospelize the world anew' (273), but his new gospel is delusive, merely the result of his inability to accept himself as anything less than immaculate. Rather than recognizing that he is no longer virtuous, he proclaims that 'Virtue and Vice are trash!' (273). Melville makes no attempt to reconcile Pierre's initial evasion of truth as an author with his later supposed profundity. Nor does he make any attempt to explain the incongruity of Pierre's writing a blasphemous new gospel yet feeling protected by 'some strange heavenly influence' when Lucy joins him, though the incongruity makes Pierre seem more a simpleton than a man of profundity. . . .

These conflicting attitudes toward Pierre's behaviour are not final, meaningful ambiguities Melville has carefully worked towards, but abrupt, confusing contradictions, the ultimate results of his excessively personal sympathy for Pierre's frustrations as an author. The decision to make the hero an author, whenever it was made, led to some powerful writing in the second half of *Pierre*, particularly in the Enceladus vision. It also deprived Melville of a full sense of what he was doing, in the second half and in the novel as a whole. 'Two books are being writ', said Melville (304), referring to the bungled one Pierre is putting on paper to offer to the world's eyes and the 'larger, and the infinitely better' one 'for Pierre's own private shelf', the one being written in his soul as the other is written on paper. In *Pierre* itself two books were also written, the one up through Book XIV (and intermittently thereafter) which examined the growth of a deluded but idealistic soul when confronted with the world's conventionality, and the later one which expressed Melville's sometimes sardonic, sometimes embittered reflections on his own career. There was no successful fusion of the two. As the new obsession drained off Melville's psychic and creative energies, the original purpose was blighted. Under the circumstances, it may be wrong to think of what *Pierre* might have been: behind Melville there was no educated literary milieu, no available models, no shoptalk with other literary masters, no rigorously critical friend, no one to assure him of ultimate glory—nothing, in short, to help him hold to the pervading idea that impelled the first half of the book. Yet he had accomplished so much in this book that one becomes anguished as Melville's genius goes tragically to waste. The great epic of metaphysical whaling came tormentingly close to being succeeded within a few months by a Kraken-book, one of the finest psychological novels in world literature rather than merely the best psychological novel that had yet been written in English.

The Empire of Agoraphobia

Gillian Brown

"Bartleby the Scrivener, A Tale of Wall Street" puts into circulation the story of a man about whom "nothing is ascertainable." Because "no materials exist for a full and satisfactory biography of this man," the "few passages in the life of Bartleby" related by the narrator represent the life of Bartleby. Transforming this very impediment to biography into biographical copy, Herman Melville's 1853 story of the "unaccountable Bartleby" both thematizes and reproduces a market-economy ontology: Bartleby's history is a tale of the marketplace and, like other market productions, significant because circulating, effective because communicative and commercial.[1] Melville's entry into mass-magazine circulation after the commercial failures of *Moby-Dick* and *Pierre*, the tale exemplifies the mechanisms by which life in and of the marketplace is forwarded.

Unlike the moving copy the tale creates and disseminates, Bartleby himself is "a motionless young man" (45), "singularly sedate" (46), "stationary" (69). The curiosity "the inscrutable scrivener" provokes and the story he thus provides issue from this mysterious immobility, from "his great stillness" (53), his affinity to what is static in Wall Street: the walls of the buildings and offices where the circulation of property is ratified in deeds and titles, where changes in proprietorship are codified and copied. Amidst this conveyancing, Bartleby remains in his partitioned office cubicle—walled in, facing more walls through his window, in his own "dead-wall reveries" (56). This enigmatic stance by which Bartleby removes himself from circulation also occasions his biography; "Bartleby the Scrivener," a tale of a stationary man, thus includes within its commerce a protest against commerce, and moreover makes commerce of that protest, translating a wall into a scrivener, the scrivener's inscrutability into market reproduction.

Reiterating the market imperative to move, the circulatory fate of Bartleby demonstrates the crucial productivity of immobility. In the tautological procedures of the marketplace, Bartleby's static, even ahistorical, status, when

[1]Herman Melville, "Bartleby the Scrivener: A Tale of Wall Street," in *Great Short Works of Herman Melville*, ed. Warner Berthoff (New York, 1969), 39–40. Subsequent references are cited in parentheses in the essay.

transposed into literary currency, reprises life in the marketplace where movement is all. Melville's tale describes an itinerary of what might be called the immobility principle, the reproduction of circulation through tableaux of the stationary. Bartleby's arrested motion is one such tableau in the nineteenth-century American iconography of stillness featuring invalidism, woman, and home (and conflations of these) as predominant figures of restfulness.[2] The frail, sentimental heroine whose domestic angelicism marks her for death, imprinted in the American imagination by Harriet Beecher Stowe's 1852 invention of Little Eva—reproduced on the stage for the rest of the century—inaugurates and sustains this idealization of worldly retreat by a commercial society. Resembling the retreat of the invalid heroine into her home (Eva speaks of dying as going home to heaven), Bartleby's withdrawal invokes the domestic tableau in order to investigate its commercial peregrinations. How Bartleby's immobility moves is thus the story of how American culture deployed domestic stations and spaces of seclusion.

In order to understand how Bartleby's resistance ultimately enters and typifies commerce, or, to put it another way, how walls move, it is necessary first to see how and why, in nineteenth-century America, ordinarily mobile humans might become "dead-walls." The preeminent figure of immobility for the nineteenth century is the hysteric, whose strange postures freeze normal bodily motion and activity. While Freud derived a theory of female sexuality from hysteria, American doctors focused upon the characteristic hysterical symptoms of paralysis and nervous exhaustion. Nervous attitudes and hysterical presentations fit into a recurrent imagery of paralysis and exhaustion in American medical literature on nervous disorders. This discourse of immobility treats nervous poses and symptoms as social practices, as variant implementations of a customary iconography. Postulating an evolutionary psychology in which mental diseases accidentally resuscitate formerly useful animal instincts, William James in 1890 associated "the statue-like, crouching immobility of some melancholiacs" with the "death-shamming instinct shown by many animals," the self-preservative immobility of "the feigning animal." This instinctual etiology, James believes, explains "the strange symptom which has been described of late years by the rather absurd name of *agoraphobia.*" "When we notice the chronic agoraphobia of our domestic cats, and see the tenacious way in which many wild animals, especially rodents, cling to cover, and only venture on a dash across the open as a desperate measure," we are witnessing a prototype of the agoraphobic, who in "terror at the sight of any open place or broad street which he has to cross alone . . . slinks round the sides of the square, hugging the houses as closely as he can."[3]

[2]For an account of the icons of home and mother in popular nineteenth-century discourse see Mary Ryan's discussion of the 1850s rhetoric of domestic isolation and rest in *The Empire of the Mother: American Writing About Domesticity, 1830–1860* (New York, 1982), 97–115.

[3]William James, *The Principles of Psychology*, 2 vols. (1890; reprint ed., New York, 1950), 2:421–22.

This concern with the protection of walls and enclosures recurs throughout nineteenth-century case histories of agoraphobics appearing after the classification of agoraphobia as a nervous disease in 1873.[4] A Connecticut man treated by Dr. William A. Hammond "would not go out into the street unless he went in a carriage," and, "in passing from the vehicle to the door of a house, he required the support of two men—one on each side of him."[5] The agoraphobic dependence upon walls of some kind is epitomized in nineteenth-century medical literature by a story about Pascal. After a 1654 carriage accident in which he was thrown into the Seine, Pascal "had the morbid fear of falling into a large space." To protect himself from chasms he imagined at his side, Pascal ever afterward kept a screen beside him. Nineteenth-century French doctors posthumously diagnosed Pascal as agoraphobic. The agoraphobic dependence on enclosures or adjacent fortifications kept most sufferers within the walls of houses, safe from their terror of the street, where "everything was in motion."[6]

Many observers of the nineteenth-century American scene did not find such anxious house-hugging the anachronism James theorized but rather a symptom specific to the conditions of American economic life. The democratic opportunity and competition for economic advancement, the very mobility of American society, Alexis de Tocqueville worried in 1835, was apt to render the individual "stationary."[7] Agreeing with this evolution of anxiety from economic freedom, Dr. George M. Beard declared in 1881 that the recent inventions of steam power, the periodical press, and the telegraph, as well as developments in the sciences and the increased mental activity of women, "must carry nervousness and nervous diseases." New technologies of transportation and communication enable "the increase in amount of business" that has "developed sources of anxiety."[8] In the case of the agoraphobic man from Connecticut, Dr. Hammond noted that "there had been excessive emotional disturbance in business matters."[9] The anxieties and responsibilities of commerce, the famous Dr. S. Weir Mitchell believed, explain the "numerous instances of nervous exhaustion among merchants and manufacturers." According to Mitchell's notebooks of the 1880s, "manufacturers and certain classes of railway officials are the most liable to suffer from neural exhaustion";

[4]Dr. D. C. Westphal coined the term in an article discussing a case of fear of open places; *Journal of Medical Sciences* 19 (1873): 456. An earlier version of this article appeared in Germany in *Archiv für Psychiatrie* 1 (1871).

[5]William A. Hammond, *A Treatise on Insanity* (1883; reprint ed., New York, 1973), 419–22.

[6]Charles Bossut, ed., *Préface aux oeuvres de Blaise Pascal* (Paris, 1819), xxxii; and Louis-Françisque Lelut, *L'Amulette de Pascal* (Paris, 1846), quoted in Hammond, *A Treatise on Insanity.*

[7]Alexis de Tocqueville, *Democracy in America*, ed. Phillips Bradley, 2 vols. (New York, 1945), 2:146.

[8]George M. Beard, *American Nervousness, Its Causes and Consequences* (New York, 1881), 96–129.

[9]Hammond, *A Treatise on Insanity*, 422.

merchants and brokers are the next most likely sufferers.[10] In the latter half of the century, the railroad figured prominently in American, German, and French lawsuits for mental health damages; it appeared to have created a fear of itself, the new phobia of railway traveling.[11]

In these accounts of nervousness and anxiety, the mechanisms and modes of commerce ultimately immobilize the individual. Beard and Mitchell's association of such conditions with economic developments in nineteenth-century life reflects anxieties about the effects of commerce notable in literature ranging from medical advice books to popular magazines such as *Putnam's* where "Bartleby" first appeared. In this context agoraphobia, the anxiety and immobility occasioned by the space and scope of streets, by the appurtenances and avenues of traffic, is an anticommercial condition—literally, fear of the marketplace. The nosology of the condition as it emerged in America in the latter half of the century suggests, contrary to James, the aptness of the term *agoraphobia*; what inhibits the agoraphobe is the commerce that inhabits American life.

From the symptomatology of immobility observed in nervous cases, an agoraphobic disposition emerges in social and medical discourse as a hallmark of American personal life. The agoraphobic recourse when outside the house to the protection of interiors or companions or shielding edifices represents an effort to retain the stability and security of the private sphere. Reproducing the enclosure and stillness of home in the deportment of the individual, agoraphobia approximates domesticity, often proclaimed the nineteenth-century antidote to commercialism. The antagonism between self and world manifest in agoraphobia reflects and replays the opposition between home and market upheld by domestic ideology. By maintaining the integrity of the private sphere, this opposition sustains the notion of a personal life impervious to market influences, the model of selfhood in a commercial society. In his propinquity to walls and in his preference for his own impenetrable postures, Bartleby presents an extreme version of such a model: in "his long-continued motionlessness" he achieves an "austere reserve," the ideal of domesticity within Wall Street.

Just as hysteria translated into an anatomy of the self and its desires in Victorian society, agoraphobia furnished Victorian America with a paradigmatic selfhood associated with female experience—or more specifically, summarized and reproduced the tradition of selfhood established by domestic ideology. For nineteenth-century America, women signified the stability of the private sphere that Bartleby's wall-like stance exhibits, the standard of self-containment that the hysteric melodramatized. Thus the physicians who worried about the immobilizing effects of commerce direct much attention to

---

[10]S. Weir Mitchell, *Wear and Tear; or, Hints for the Overworked* (1887; reprint ed., New York, 1973), 63.

[11]See George Frederick Drinka's chapter on railway neuroses in *The Birth of Neurosis* (New York, 1984), 108–22.

preserving the tranquility of women and home, treating market-stricken men by attending to the maintenance of domestic womanhood. Both Beard and Mitchell decried nondomestic activity by women; Mitchell's *Wear and Tear; or, Hints for the Overworked* treats the deleterious effects of commerce with advice on women's health. "It will not answer to look only at the causes of sickness and weakness which affect the male sex," Mitchell believes, because "if the mothers of a people are sickly and weak, the sad inheritance falls upon their offspring." To strengthen mothers for the American future, Mitchell designed his famous rest cure for nervous diseases. After undergoing a regimen of constant bed rest and severely restricted activity, women patients were to return to tranquil lives as wives and mothers. The rest cure countered the marketplace with a fortified domesticity.[12]

This fortified domesticity finally fortified the marketplace. The interest of physicians in the immobilizing effects of the marketplace signifies not an antimarket program but a foregrounding of domesticity from other images of the stationary. As the symptomatology of immobility proliferates domestic attributes, its cure reiterates and recommends conventional domesticity. The aim of the rest cure, then, is not to limit market mobility but to reinforce a select domestic stillness, to underscore the healthy function of the stationary. In restricting women to bed, the rest cure in a sense demobilizes the domestic in order to recharge it for reproductive service to the market. This interdependence of domesticity with the market emerges with greater specificity in nineteenth-century feminist critiques of the rest cure. . . .

It is within these politics of agoraphobia, the dynamic between home and world manifested by consumption, that the meaning of Bartleby's negations and mysterious isolationism emerges. Bartleby, who in Elizabeth Hardwick's paraphrase "shuns the streets and is unmoved by the moral, religious, acute, obsessive, beautiful ideal of Consumption," insists upon a noncommercial domesticity.[13] In preferring "to be stationary" (69), Bartleby achieves an impenetrability the lawyer narrator cannot alter or enter. What the lawyer recognizes as Bartleby's complete self-possession—"his great stillness, his unalterableness of demeanor under all circumstances" (53)—obviates the very notion of exchange or intercourse, denying any form of commerce, including the conversation and charity the lawyer would readily extend.

In his agoraphobic responses, or rather lack of responsiveness, Bartleby follows female agoraphobic modes of evading domestic consumerism and repudiating intercourse between private and public realms. The encounter between the lawyer and the scrivener is one between two competing models

[12]S. Weir Mitchell, "The Evolution of the Rest Cure," *Journal of Nervous and Mental Diseases* (1904): 368–73.

[13]Elizabeth Hardwick, "Bartleby in Manhattan," in *Bartleby in Manhattan and Other Essays* (New York, 1984), 217–31. Another interesting aspect of "Bartleby" as an urban tale is its contemporaneous appearance with articles describing the emerging phenomenon of the urban poor and homeless. I am indebted to Hans Bergmann for this point.

of domesticity: commercial and truly agoraphobic. In this context, the narrator appears as a kind of Wall Street housekeeper; however, his domesticated business practices are undermined by Bartleby's renunciation of the domestic pretensions of the "eminently safe man" in his "snug business" on Wall Street (40).

Although the lawyer belongs "to a profession proverbially energetic and nervous, even . . . turbulent," he permits "nothing of that sort . . . to invade [his] peace." He attributes to his office "the cool tranquility of a snug retreat" (40). The business of the lawyer's domestic commercial sphere chiefly involves overseeing and compensating for the unhealthy gustatory habits of his copyists. Turkey drinks and cannot perform his duties during the afternoon; his fellow worker Nippers suffers from morning indigestion and doesn't work efficiently until afternoon. The office boy Ginger-nut seems to function mainly as "cake and apple purveyor for Turkey and Nippers" (45). For the lawyer, these concerns with food and drink are labor/management issues: what his employees consume directly affects what they produce. In this office in the image of home, the eccentricities of appetite are incorporated into the business routine.

Into this domestic colony on Wall Street comes the "motionless young man" Bartleby (45), who initially seems to suit perfectly and even optimize the narrator's domestic economy. The lawyer thinks "a man of so singularly sedate an aspect . . . might operate beneficially upon the flighty temper of Turkey and the fiery one of Nippers" (46). Bartleby's habits "at first" appear the model of balance between work and diet, consumption and production—his work *is* ingestion. "As if long famishing for something to copy," the lawyer notes, "he seemed to gorge himself on my documents . . . without pause for digestion" (46).

Indeed, Bartleby so much epitomizes for his employer the successful union of economic and individual attributes that his place in the office—in a screened corner of a partition, facing a window with a view only of a brick wall—makes a "satisfactory arrangement" in which "privacy and society were conjoined" (46). The lawyer thinks of Bartleby's office carrel as "his hermitage" (50), and Bartleby literalizes this domestic fantasy. His insistent denial of every request directed at him, his removal of himself into his "dead-wall reveries" (52), effectively achieves the hermitage and privacy that the lawyer imagines his establishment provides. Making the "office his constant abiding place and home" (56), Bartleby purifies his employer's domestic economy. While the lawyer attempts to domesticate business, to accommodate the fluctuations of production and consumption within the walls of his establishment, Bartleby seeks to empty the domestic of the economic, to establish an impregnable privacy. Counter-spirit to the Market Street Phantom, the "apparition of Bartleby" "haunting the building" (53, 68) enforces the rhetorical boundaries of the private sphere.

Making the office home in fact, Bartleby is a missionary agoraphobic, incongruously claiming the walls of Wall Street as the protective borders of the private domain, preferring to the congenial agoraphobia of the narrator a doctrinaire, absolute one whose primary feature is not so much that he "never went anywhere" but that, as the lawyer observes, "he never went to dinner" (50). Rather than follow, in the fashion of the lawyer, the logic of agoraphobia, which ultimately admits and embraces the market, Bartleby "lives without dining" (73), perfecting the agoraphobic condition in anorexia, where the borders between world and self are traced (and ultimately erased) on the individual body. This radical refusal to partake of, and participate in, the world makes Bartleby "self-possessed" (54) and impenetrable, the traditional goal of domestic life. Simultaneously fulfilling and negating the logic of agoraphobia—establishing selfhood in the extinction of commerce—anorexia secures the agoraphobic division of self from world, home from market. A strict and rigid observance of this division, anorexia realizes the hermitage agoraphobia cannot obtain; eliminating consumption, it halts agoraphobia's inevitable progress into the marketplace.

The anorexic, almost always a woman, avoids the world by refusing the most basic form of consumption. By starving herself she suppresses her menstrual cycle, shutting down the process of her own reproductive functions. She maintains in her body the fantasy of domesticity Bartleby enacts: a perfect self-enclosure. While anorexia hardly seems an ideal condition, it is the fulfillment of the ideal of domestic privacy, a state in which complete separation from the demands and supplies of the world is attained.

Anorexia, somewhat contrary to its name, is not the condition of being without desire but the enterprise of controlling desire. That is, the anorexic wants to not want and to this end tries not to consume, or to undo consumption. She devotes all her energy and efforts to regulating the passage of food to and from her body. Most anorexics do in fact succumb to eating binges and become bulimic, inducing expurgation after every meal. Or they adopt intensive exercise regimens and ingest large amounts of laxatives and diuretics. One anorexic reported to her therapist that she masturbated one hundred times each evening, believing the constant pressure would strengthen her sphincter muscles, thereby facilitating release of food through defecation.[14]

This effort to eliminate or control food frequently involves preoccupation with the buying, preparation, and serving of food. An anorexic will insist upon cooking for the family and produce elaborate meals whose consumption she supervises but herself forgoes. One anorexic was brought to treatment by her mother who was concerned about the weight gain her daughter was inflicting upon her. In this dedication to others' consumption, the anorexic bizarrely imitates the mother's housekeeping role. She thus controls the desire to consume that she recognizes as essential to the family. Another anorexic so

---

[14]Ira L. Mintz, "Psychoanalytic Therapy of Severe Anorexia: The Case of Jeanette," in *Fear of Being Fat: The Treatment of Anorexia Nervosa and Bulimia*, ed. C. Phillip Wilson et al. (New · York, 1983), 217–44.

insisted on having dominion over food that her wealthy father built her her own kitchen, separate from the kitchen where the family cook worked. Here the girl maintained her perfected domestic province, where she performed the central housekeeping role without consuming.[15] This case makes clear the anorexic's radical claim to domestic space, her Bartleby-like insistence on a privacy without commerce. The anorexic kitchen literalizes domestic ideals, perfecting domesticity in antidomesticity.

Anorexic practices, like agoraphobic strategies, manifest domestic functions in extreme forms. Not surprisingly, some recent analysts and interpreters of anorexia read in this hyperbolic condition a radical realization and indictment of cultural dictates upon women's bodies and functions. Anorexic body ideals seem to coincide with the contemporary valuation of female slenderness (another marketing of domesticity), prompting observers of anorexia to note the current "popularity" of this disease, its distinctive appeal to adolescent, middle-class girls. While cases of anorexia in the latter half of this century clearly reflect and address specific cultural values, the anorexic strategy in "Bartleby" stresses another agenda: the rejection of consumerist domesticity. Bartleby's anorexia would remove agoraphobia from domestic commerce, making impossible the connection between these diseases and domestic consumerism that nineteenth- and twentieth-century feminists and physicians variously register.

First recorded in a 1689 treatise on tuberculosis as "A Nervous Consumption," anorexia nervosa did not become a specific clinical entity until 1873, the same year agoraphobia was first classified, twenty years after the publication of "Bartleby."[16] The difficulty nineteenth-century doctors encountered in diagnosing anorexia, in identifying it as a specific disease, lay in the similarity between the symptoms of anorexia and consumption, now remembered as the great nineteenth-century disease. Though an incorrect paradigm for anorexia nervosa, the initial clinical classification of anorexia with consumption unwittingly points to the connection between these illnesses as metaphors, to the way the diseases, or the descriptions of the diseases, both exemplify economic models. Susan Sontag has pointed out the isomorphism between the economies of tuberculosis and nineteenth-century expanding capitalism. Tuberculosis exhibits "the negative behavior of nineteenth-century *homo economicus*: consumption; wasting; squandering of vitality."[17] The fluctuations characteristic of the illness—dramatic variations in appetite and energy—aptly repro-

[15]Hilde Bruch, *The Golden Cage: The Enigma of Anorexia Nervosa* (Cambridge, Mass., 1978), 75–77.

[16]Hilde Bruch, *Eating Disorders* (New York, 1973), 211–25. Before William Gull and Charles Lasegue introduced the nomenclature *anorexia nervosa* to eating disorders in 1873, Gull had recorded cases of female refusals to eat in 1868. Reports of similar cases date back to medieval times; Rudolph Bell and Caroline Bynum have identified anorexic behavior in the fasting of saints. See Rudolph M. Bell, *Holy Anorexia* (Chicago, 1985); Caroline Walker Bynum, "Fast, Feast, and Flesh," *Representations* 11 (Summer 1985): 1–25; and Bynum, *Holy Feast and Holy Fast: The Religious Significance of Food to Medieval Women* (Berkeley, 1987).

[17]Susan Sontag, *Illness as Metaphor* (New York, 1979), 5–41, 60–62.

duced marketplace disequilibrium and concomitant anxieties about saving and spending. Tuberculosis mysteriously consumed the body from within: the consumptive sufferer seemed to replicate upon the body an apocalyptic view of economic progress, a state of simultaneous voraciousness and exhaustion. No Camille-like martyred heroine to this economy, the anorexic chooses illness as a repudiation of the marketplace and an expression of self-control. A refusal to replicate the economy in the body, anorexia is the paradoxical antidote to consumption, the negative behavior of *femina economica*.

The anorexic enactment of the self-destructiveness of self-denial surpasses the deaths of angelic, tubercular heroines like Stowe's Little Eva and Louisa May Alcott's Beth, translating domestic angels into skeletal women. Taking to the limit the sentimental ideals of true womanhood, the anorexic appears the sentimental self-denying heroine par excellence. A macabre mockery of domesticity, anorexia, like agoraphobia and hysteria, appears to offer another figure of resistance to domestic ideology, another feminist type of the madwoman in the attic.[18]

But since the anorexic opposes the economy of consumption of both feminist and traditional versions of domesticity, the anorexic resists canonization as a sentimental or feminist heroine. Indeed, feminist visions of women in the world epitomize the commercial possibility in home/market relations from which the anorexic retreats. The circulation of the woman in "The Yellow Wallpaper" exhibits the tendency to mobility in agoraphobia that anorexia would eliminate. Unlike agoraphobic or hysteric stances, anorexic body language refuses to represent any form of commerce. A purging of agoraphobia, anorexia replaces the economy of consumption with abstinence. Disappearing from sight and space, the anorexic creates her own purified version of nineteenth-century tableaux of the stationary, an approach to complete privacy and stillness.

It is finally death, the termination of self, rather than self-circulation through the elimination of cultural obstructions, that anorexia seeks. This cult of death differs from popular sentimentalist celebrations of death like Harriet Beecher Stowe's glorification of Little Eva's consumption that circulated in nineteenth-century domestic literature.[19] Whereas sentimental death seeks

---

[18]Sandra Gilbert treats the literary representation of the feminist politics of anorexia in "Hunger Pains," *University Publishing*, Fall 1979. Two more recent feminist analyses link anorexia to the problematics of female identity following from mother-daughter relations. In *Starving Women: A Psychology of Anorexia Nervosa* (Dallas, 1983), analyst Angelyn Spignesi characterizes the anorexic as "our twentieth-century carrier" of the repressed female psyche. In denying the "principles of matter . . . she enacts in her disease the interpenetration of the imaginal and physical realms." This lack of demarcation between body and psyche, self and others, returns her to "the realm of the mother." Similarly focusing on the relation of the anorexic to the maternal, Kim Chernin reads anorexia as matricidal act, "a bitter warfare against the mother," enacted on the daughter's body; *The Hungry Self: Women, Eating, and Identity* (New York, 1985).

[19]Ann Douglas has aptly termed his sentimental cult of death "the domestication of death" and characterized it as a gesture by which women claimed a real estate society denied them; *The Feminization of American Culture* (New York, 1977), 240–72.

the world and an audience, demanding a public space in the world, anorexic death flees the world; the anorexic economy of self-denial redefines death as divestment from the marketplace. To realize the fantasy of controlling desire—to deny the existence of an outside, of anything exterior to the self— the anorexic inevitably must want to die. By rejecting the body she hates for its contiguity with the world, for its reminder of the desire to consume, the anorexic finally triumphs over desire. Paradoxically, her abstinence permits pure selfishness. Preferring not to eat, like Bartleby, she detaches herself from the world and finally from the body that borders it, the last semblance of walls contiguous with the world. In the logic of anorexia's perfection of agoraphobia, death best preserves the self.

These are the anorexic politics of Bartleby's radical employment of immobility. Stringently restricting the agoraphobic imagination to its ethic of immobility, Bartleby elaborates death as the best method of self-preservation. He leaves the world in order to keep himself. If properly understood, this choice of divestiture, despite the obvious disadvantages of the disappearing self, is a powerful one. What better critique of domestic difficulties than the decision to live no longer? But as inevitable as the cult of death is for the anorexic is the sentimentality of interpretation to which death is submitted and consequently misread. When Bartleby, entombed within the Tombs, sleeps "with kings and counsellors" (73), the narrator attempts to account for the bizarre life and death of his scrivener. In telling the scrivener's story, he accepts the invitation to investigate and interpret this successful agoraphobic. The "vague report" (73) he offers as an epilogue satisfies *his* curiosity about Bartleby's motivations. If Barleby worked in the Dead Letter Office in Washington, then his condition might be understood as a response to such close association with death. For do not dead letters "sound like dead men?" (73). Bartleby's condition seems to the narrator an intensified experience of human mortality. He therefore commemorates Bartleby's passage as a testament of the human tragedy, joining the man and the crowd in his closing lament, "Ah, Bartleby! Ah, humanity!" (74).

The narrator's sentimental closure to Bartleby's story links Bartleby with the very chain of existence he preferred to avoid. This conjunction of Bartleby with humanity—the agoraphobic's nightmare—also elides the differences between the domestic preferences of Bartleby and of his employer, thus diffusing the force of Bartleby's renunciation of commercial domesticity. By ignoring the alignment between circulation, life, and death that Bartleby signifies, the narrator's solution preserves the commerce his version of domesticity tacitly transacts. The narrator would have us believe that Bartleby, continually witnessing letters on doomed errands of life, speeding to death, suffered from an overexposure to death, when death is precisely what Bartleby sought. The very idea of an errand—of letters reaching their destination—is anathema to Bartleby, who evades every form of intercourse, whose preferences cannot even attach to an object. The anorexic tries to deny food and body of any relation by transforming objects of consumption into threatening, alien forces; she asserts the body's independence from the objects of its desires. Similarly, Bartleby detaches himself from things and all activities involving things, refusing even to commit himself to predicates that would signify subject-object relations, that would connect his negation to something external to himself. Bartleby hardly exemplifies the tragedy of death; his anorexia attests to the tragedy of circulation. What impels him, or rather what inters him, are not the disconnections caused by death but the connections produced by life.

The success of suicide missions depends on the proper interpretation of the suicidal intention. Bartleby's final act of refusal secures him no recognition for his cause, no canonization by fellow adherents. Despite the intended enunciation of the scrivener's death, the lawyer interprets the tragedy as a confirmation of his own sentimentality. Whereas Bartleby sought to dissociate himself from all forms of economy, the narrator returns the copyist to the sentimental economy. Imagining Bartleby among kings and counselors, the lawyer invokes Job's artificial death wish. In his lament on the misfortunes of his life, Job cries that he would have been at rest with kings and counselors if he had died in the womb, or if his birth and nurturance had been prevented by the knees and breasts.[20] This lament almost comically shifts both the responsibility for Job's unhappy life and its points of termination: the logic of his wish delivers him to a resting point only imaginable in history, only possible for having lived. So Job doesn't wish that he had never been born—but that is precisely what Bartleby wishes when he prefers not to. The lawyer would return Bartleby to history when Bartleby would prefer not to have sucked, to have aborted his existence altogether.

The lawyer's interpretation of Bartleby's death, the tale's circulation of Bartleby's life, subsumes the radical act into the chain of existence and chronicle of history, into literary currency. This final domestication implies that the elimination of the body achieves only partial secession from the commercial. Interpretation invades death's privacy, taking death as a communiqué. Bartleby's imagination of an aborted self, a broken circuit, offers to the sentimental imagination an annexation of the unknown, the widening boundaries of what we think of as the world and women's sphere. In the agoraphobic imagination structuring selfhood in a market economy, death becomes another province, another border to be crossed—the final domestic station to be mobilized. The narrator's attempt to find a transcendent meaning in the Bartleby enigma is thus precisely the triumph of sentimentalism and consumerism: the perpetuation of the preoccupation with private property and personal provinces.

Even death, whether imagined as an escape by Bartleby or invoked as a principle of coherence by the lawyer, repeats the expansion and contraction

[20]Job 3.11–16.

patterns of the various sects of domestic perfectionists. The agoraphobic structure of domestic ideology, which Bartleby takes to the limit, includes and utilizes mortality within the logic of home protection. The life and death of Bartleby recirculates the imagination of being besieged that persists in shaping and defining the economies of capitalism and of private life. Even in death, commerce continues; this is the errand of life on which letters speed to and from death.

Desert and Empire:
From "Bartleby" to "Benito Cereno"

Philippe Jaworski

"Poor fellow, poor fellow! thought I, he don't mean anything."
—*Bartleby*[1]

The Threshold of Tolerance

In answer to my advertisement, a motionless young man one morning stood upon my office threshold, the door being open, for it was summer. I can see that figure now—pallidly neat, pitiably respectable, incurably forlorn! It was Bartleby.[2]

Creature of the threshold, limit figure, Bartleby—when he appears, as soon as he appears, immobile within the unplaceable—is immediately relegated by the discourse to the irremediable status of absent to the world. "Incurably forlorn": his being-there locked inside the irrevocable distancing of abandonment. In the very moment when he has hardly even begun to respond (to the advertisement), he is already reduced—permanently reduced—to silence. Like the blacks of "Benito Cereno," Bartleby surfaces within a discourse which denies his being the character of Presence.

Nonetheless, the man of law appears to begin with the wish to inscribe the proximity of his copyist in space; he installs Bartleby in a corner of his office, behind a screen. An ambiguous proximity ("in a manner, privacy and society were conjoined" [100]), given that the scrivener, although placed within hearing range, is hidden from view: "I procured a high green folding screen, which might isolate Bartleby entirely from my sight, though not remove him from my voice" (100).

From Philippe Jaworski, "Le Proche et le Lointain: l'Eloignement de l'Autre." In: *Le Désert et l'Empire*, pp. 302–311. Copyright © 1991, Presses de l'École Normale Supérieure. Translation by Jim Hicks.

[1]Meaning, of course, "Poor fellow, he doesn't mean any harm," but also, "he doesn't *signify* anything, he has no meaning." In short, both inoffensive and, like Babo in the eyes of Delano, insignificant (120).

[2]All page references are to the following edition: *Herman Melville: Selected Tales and Poems*, ed. R. Chase. New York: Holt, Rinehart and Winston, 1950.

Thus, the first meaning of "privacy" is distance ("isolate"). But the term gradually changes in significance throughout the story, as shown in the following passage:

> Yes, Bartleby, stay there behind your screen, thought I; I shall persecute you no more; you are harmless and noiseless as any of these old chairs; in short, I never feel so private as when I know you are here. . . . Others may have loftier parts to enact; but my mission in this world, Bartleby, is to furnish you with office-room for such period as you may see fit to remain. (121)

Bartleby's proximity (and the assurance of it) has become for the narrator a measure of peace of mind, of personal comfort. But here again the gesture of the man of law is two-sided: at the same time as he designates his scrivener as a source of well-being (of *his* well-being), he does not make the decision to stop considering him as a sort of immovable item of furniture: "He remained as ever, a fixture in my chamber." Bartleby is a chair, and the only company which can be proposed to a chair is that of four walls.

Inside the limits of that territory where the principle of Sovereignty reigns, Bartleby, "the strange creature," the Inexplicable—representing an unsustainable paradox: an excess of want—is perceived in a contradictory manner by the Master. This explains why the latter resorts alternatively to either the discourse and practices of Power (threat, inquiry, dismissal) and to another behavior, another sort of commentary—tentative, disturbed, confused—one which suggests a temptation to know and to acknowledge. Nonetheless, no matter how much he forces himself to recognize the humanity of Bartleby (that unjustifiable Presence—but it is that, precisely that, which it is a question of admitting: "humanity" is undefinable, and unjustifiable, on the basis of its attributes), the Master is unable to broach that border which separates charity from hospitality. (This failure, in any case, is prefigured by the installation of the folding screen between himself and the scrivener. The voice is the instrument of Power: it is through this means [the given order] that the "boss" keeps in touch with his employee. On the other hand, the gaze—the means by which the Face is discovered—is blocked). . . .

Hospitality is an invitation to cross the threshold; charity, in contrast, knows only thresholds of tolerance. But it is precisely the wisdom of the charitable soul which is the sole asset that Bartleby's man of law has at his disposal:

> Aside from higher considerations, charity often operates as a vastly wise and prudent principle—a great safeguard to its possessor. (120)

It would be wrong to restrict the range of this admission: the charitable gesture is less directed toward the recognition of the Other than toward the preservation of Self. It refers, not to a conception of Being, but rather to a disposition of Having. All things taken *into account*, the truth of this "relation" (if such is the term) within the space of mastery brutally reappears in two passages where at first another lawyer, and then the neighbors, have the thought of demanding, from the boss, some *account* of his employee:

". . . really, the man you allude to is nothing to me—he is no relation or apprentice of mine, that you should hold me responsible for him."

In vain I persisted that Bartleby was nothing to me—no more than to any one else. In vain—I was the last person known to have anything to do with him, and they held me to the terrible account. (125)

He is *nothing* to me . . . he is nothing for me (or for anyone else): Bartleby *has* no *being*.

The Imperceptible

". . . a display of elegance which quite completed the insignificance of the small bare-headed Babo . . ." (55)

To move from "Bartleby" to "Benito Cereno" is to pass from the impossible perception—a perception which would be reception, greeting—of a foreign body installed in the walled space of System to the problem of apprehending the systematic (and systematically camouflaged) inversion of an order dependent on the System. The foreignness in need of domestication is no longer that of a scandalous Presence; instead, it is the strange sense of a masquerade whose very existence is attested to only by certain contradictory effects. However, even if the object of interrogation has changed its nature from one tale to the other, the observer's failure to comprehend that which is going on right before his eyes has its source in the same fundamental deficiency. Neither the man of law in "Bartleby" nor the good captain Delano is able to apprehend the real in any other manner than by passing through a perceptual grid, one based on formulaic subordination, a grid within which one element (the center, the reference, the model, the original, the matrix of meaning) holds the values and properties of Being, whereas another term, subordinate to the first, is relegated to inexistence and insignificance.

In "Bartleby" this formula is described in the two paragraphs which follow the introduction. There one finds a bit more than the narrator's self-portrait: it is the discourse itself—in and by which the copyist is to be "apprehended" (in all senses of the word: perceived, dreaded, captured)—which these lines set up. This discourse is organized around an economic principle: possession ("my *employés*, my business, my chambers" [92]); material comfort ("the cool tranquillity of a snug retreat . . . a snug business" [93]); concern for the preservation of wealth ("All who know me, consider me an eminently *safe* man" [93]); proximity to sources of Money ("I was not unemployed in my profession by the late John Jacob Astor; a name which, I admit, I love to repeat; for it hath a rounded and orbicular sound to it, and rings like unto bullion" [93]); love of gain ("It was not a very arduous office, but very pleasantly remunerative. . . . I had counted upon a life-lease of the profits" [93]). In a space where the Economic commands as law, where only that which can be counted and accumulated is recognized as (evidence of) Being, Bartleby is unable to find a place; Bartleby, a character for which the most one can say (after the moment in which the lawyer describes him as "a precious acquisition") is that he *is* there, still there.

In "Benito Cereno," the schema of subordination which determines Delano's gaze does not situate Being in a relation of absolute dependence in reference to Having. On the *San Dominick*, the events are played out inside a representation of the myth of difference between races. If Delano is fooled by the scenes staged by Babo (the rebel slave who has become the ship's master), it is because he is incapable of *seeing* the black man. Moreover, he fails to see him because, in his eyes, the Black *does not exist*.

Here, the insignificance of the black man, however, is not exactly of the same character as the "theological" version of the myth, according to which the Black is irremediably assimilated to Evil. In "Benito Cereno" (I refer of course to Delano's perspective), the Black is not purely and simply cast into the shadows of a malediction without remission, outside of human history, abandoned to the absolute exteriority of abjection or bestiality. In this particular context, some elements of the Enlightenment thought and evolutionary ideology have managed to add minor corrections—only minor corrections—to former prejudices. The Black appears in the *chiaroscuro* of the dawn of human progress—a progress for which the White, and the West (and still more precisely, the American democrat) constitute the meridian of achievement. Saved from the hell of reprobates, the Black is now free to begin the long path toward the midday sun. Thus, the only black man which the "benevolent" Delano is able to perceive is a black man that is *not yet* equal to the whites. In short, a psychological or political version of the myth follows, in place of the theological version (to which the discourse of slavery still resorts). In both cases, a single postulate orders the perspective: that of the difference between the races. . . .

First let us evoke the blindness of Delano. On the *San Dominick*, the American quickly notes the "good conduct" of Babo:

> No wonder that, as in this state [Benito Cereno] tottered about, his private servant apprehensively followed him. Sometimes the negro gave his master his arm, or took his handkerchief out of his pocket for him; performing these and similar offices with that affectionate zeal which transmutes into something filial or fraternal acts in themselves but menial; and which has gained for the negro the repute of making the most pleasing body-servant in the world; one, too, whom a master need be on no stiffly superior terms with, but may treat with familiar trust; less a servant than a devoted companion. (10)

The servile gesture transmuted . . . perhaps. It is, however, for the Spaniard alone, the other white Master, that he reserves his fraternal recognition: "a brother captain to counsel and befriend" (10). The expression "master and man," which constantly returns in the description of the pair Cereno-Babo, defines with fearsome irony the object of Delano's gaze: the man, the human in Babo, is the slave, or rather the domestic. This is progress: the black man is no longer the bad serf working down in the fields, out of the sight of the slave merchant, he is now the zealous and reliable valet, always within reach, who watches over the domestic comfort of the master of the house ("it was soon evident that, in taking his position, the black was still true to his master; since by facing him he could the more readily anticipate his slightest want" [56]). In short, the half of humanity that serves Man, that always comes second, after. . . .

Such a faithful fellow ("Don Benito, I envy you such a friend; slave I cannot call him" [16]), it would not be possible *to characterize him as a slave. . . .* But then, what is to be made of the offer which "the honest seaman" makes a short while later to the Spaniard: "Tell me, Don Benito . . . I should like to have your man here, myself—what will you take for him? Would fifty doubloons be any object?" (33). This wouldn't be a bad deal. Such "anxious" fidelity, can it then be bought, can virtue (that of the blacks) be corrupted?

The Black is humble . . . and has a smiling, good-natured mien. He is not dangerous. How could he be menacing, that adolescent still close to the state of nature, animated only by a few simple instincts? He moves within the realm of inception, at one extremity of that ladder of development of which the summit is occupied by the sun of Reason—on the *San Dominick*, incarnated by the plenitude of goodness in Delano ("the mild sun of Captain Delano's good-nature"). . . .

Decidedly there is, between blacks and whites, an essential difference:

The whites . . . by nature, were the shrewder race. A man with some evil design, would he not be likely to speak well of that stupidity which was blind to his depravity, and malign that intelligence from which it might be hidden? Not unlikely, perhaps. But if the whites had dark secrets concerning Don Benito, could then Don Benito be any way in complicity with the blacks? But they were too stupid. Besides, who ever heard of a white so far a renegade as to apostatize from his very species almost, by leaguing in against it with negroes? (39)

Questions, hypotheses, difficulties, adds the narrator—enigmas forming a labyrinth inside of which the good Delano, one more time, gets lost ("lost in their mazes"). That said, this passage is capital, and terrifying. Is it so very surprising that, in the following paragraph, the aged sailor busy in making inextricable knots turns over to Delano, to Delano alone, the duty of cutting the knot? This "knot," it seems apparent, is located in the observer's gaze.

Return for a moment to the passage above. It clearly shows how the theological version of the racial myth effectively gives way to its political version. Apparently, in a first stage, the instinct of Evil has become an attribute of the white race—and the Black has whitened. The operation of whitening, however, betrays the disquieting truth of the process. If the propensity toward Evil is an exclusive characteristic of the Master, it is because the latter has (and is) a conscience (and consciousness), pure and simple. As for the Black, he is *candid* only because he has none: he is, in an etymological sense, *stupid.*

The reference here . . . is to that which the interpretive narration of "Billy Budd" calls the "innocence" of Billy:

> . . . in Billy Budd intelligence such as it was, had advanced, while yet his simple-mindedness remained for the most part unaffected. . . . Besides, he had none of that intuitive knowledge of the bad which in natures not good or incompletely so foreruns experience. . . . (332)

> As it was innocence was his blinder. (334)

The blacks in "Benito Cereno" are also blind, would also be blind, in the estimation of Delano, to that depravation of which the spirit (of the whites) is capable ("that stupidity which was blind to his depravity" [39]). However, in this case, blindness is a form of stupidity and not innocence. Billy's immaturity (the "child-man" [332]) is decidedly different from that of Babo. In Billy, Being shines outward as a spiritual principle, it lives and vibrates in his native simplicity. In the case of Babo, conscience and consciousness still sleep, inert and lethargic.

Finally, let us note those reflections which come to the mind of the brave American at the moment when, in the cuddy, he observes Babo getting ready to give his master a shave:

> There is something in the negro which, in a peculiar way, fits him for avocations about one's person. Most negroes are natural valets and hair-dressers; taking to the comb and brush congenially as to the castanets, and flourishing them apparently with almost equal satisfaction. There is, too, a smooth tact about them in this employment, with a marvelous, noiseless, gliding briskness, not ungraceful in its way, singularly pleasing to behold, and still more so to be the manipulated subject of. And above all is the great gift of good-humor. (49)

A "natural valet," a "lively domestic," a "limited mind," gifted with a "susceptibility of bland attachment"—the inferiority of the black race is "indisputable" (49). Such is the truth which determines the American's gaze. The Black is above all an incompletely developed creature (puerile, immature, dependent), one that may be improved—through the contributions of whites:

> . . . it were strange, indeed, and not very creditable to us white-skins, if a little of our blood mixed with the African's, should, far from improving the latter's quality,

have the sad effect of pouring vitriolic acid into black broth; improving the hue, perhaps, but not the wholesomeness. (56)

Through such a postulate, the veil of appearance could not be torn away. To imagine a reversal of roles is altogether senseless; to see a black man *in the place* of a white is a sure sign of mental disorder:

> Not unaffected by the close sight of the gleaming steel, Don Benito nervously shuddered; his usual ghastliness was heightened by the lather, which lather, again, was intensified in its hue by the contrasting sootiness of the negro's body. Altogether the scene was somewhat peculiar, at least to Captain Delano, nor, as he saw the two thus postured, could he resist the vagary, that in the black he saw a headsman, and in the white a man at the block. But this was one of those antic conceits, appearing and vanishing in a breath, from which, perhaps, the best regulated mind is not always free. (51)

This failure to recognize the liberty of another man is the work of a classifying principle with clearly defined indices: an ordering of living history by slicing up time and space according to an evolutionary law; thought ruled by subordination, thought according to a grid. Once again we find all the themes associated with the desire for System; in the depths of Delano's gaze lies the outline of the city of Cain—this failure to recognize the Other does not have the Black for its sole object. The Spanish captain, elsewhere perceived within a relation of commercial rivalry, is for the American the characteristic product of a bizarre nation: "But as a nation—continued he in his reveries—these Spaniards are all an odd set; the very word Spaniard has a curious, conspirator, Guy-Fawkish twang to it" (43). The traces of an attitude which is violently suspicious toward the Latin world are particularly clear in the following passage, where the evocation of a possible fraud perpetrated by the Spaniard also causes an entire series of racial and social stereotypes and prejudices to emerge:

> The man was an imposter. . . . Benito Cereno—Don Benito Cereno—a sounding name. One, too, at that period, not unknown, in the surname, to supercargoes and sea captains trading along the Spanish Main, as belonging to one of the most enterprising and extensive mercantile families in all those provinces; several members of it having titles; a sort of Castilian Rothschild, with a noble brother, or cousin, in every great trading town of South America. The alleged Don Benito was in early manhood, about twenty-nine or thirty. To assume a sort of roving cadetship in the maritime affairs of such a house, what more likely scheme for a young knave of talent and spirit? But the Spanish was a pale invalid. Never mind. For even to the degree of simulating mortal disease, the craft of some tricksters had been known to attain. To think that, under the aspect of infantile weakness, the most savage energies might be couched—those velvets of the Spaniard but the silky paw of his fangs. (25)

During Delano's stroll through the starboard quarter-gallery (and during the reverie that accompanies it), another variation on the theme of discrimation appears. That "Venetian-looking water-balcon[y]" (37), covered at present with humid sea-moss, was formerly a theater of majestic spectacles: "he bethought him of the time when that state-cabin and this state-balcony had heard the voices of the Spanish king's officers" (37). Everything that surrounds Delano appears to reveal a faded grandeur: mosses, ruins, rust, decay—in a word, Decadence. And Delano the democrat, the republican, suddenly sees himself the prisoner of a deserted castle. On the path between eras (from the "Old World" to the "New"), the monarchic Latin world, with its glory and its pomp, is relegated to a past on the point of extinction. Moreover, it would not take much for yesterday's Empire to bring the new Elect down in its wake:

> Trying to break one charm, he was but becharmed anew. Though upon the wide sea, he seemed in some far inland country; prisoner in some deserted château . . .
>
> But these enchantments were a little disenchanted as his eye fell on the corroded main-chains. Of an ancient style, massy and rusty in link, shackle and bolt, they seemed even more fit for the ship's present business than the one for which she had been built. . . .
>
> Not unbewildered, again he gazed off for his boat. But it was temporarily hidden by a rocky spur of the isle. As with some eagerness he bent forward, watching for the first shooting view of its beak, the balustrade gave way before him like charcoal. Had he not clutched an outreaching rope he would have fallen into the sea. The crash, though feeble, and the fall, though hollow, of the rotten fragments, must have been overheard. (37–8)

A decline of the former masters, decadence of the bizarre nation. For the new Prince, the mastery of a tranquil and kindly order ("the quiet orderliness of the sealer's comfortable family of a crew" [12]), an order where the blacks would be, at best, only merry animals: "Captain Delano took to negroes, not philanthropically, but genially, just as other men to Newfoundland dogs" (50).

It is not one of the least ironies of the tale that, staged as a *fiction* ("the fictitious story dictated to the deponent by Babo" [82], as the chronicler indicates in resuming the conclusions of the tribunal), and essentially resting on the role of Babo ("performing the office of an officious servant with all the appearance of submission of the humble slave" [82]), this fiction managed, up to the end (since after all Delano's illumination is provoked by the Spaniard's leap into his boat), to mask the reality of the subversion in that, for the observer, the fiction expresses nothing other than *the truth of its own representations*. The story, moreover, won't have taught him anything. We need to forget, he says to Cereno: "the past is passed; why moralize upon it? Forget it. See, yon bright sun has forgotten it all, and the blue sea, and the blue sky; these have turned over new leaves" (90). The new blots out the old, the present the past. We can forget this atrocity, forget the Black: the Black leaves no traces.

Desert and Empire

The Empire is conquered space, it creates territory, complete with borders, a grid, protection. Boundaries, walls that insure the permanence of other limits, justifying the internal order, guarding the immutable. Differences, hierarchical arrangement of times and relations: high/low, inside/outside, before/behind, first/second. Subordination, prisons, machine. The reality of the Face disappears: representations reign, themselves ordered, classified.

On the *San Dominick*, in an enchanted revery, Delano imagines himself prisoner of a deserted castle, where his gaze discovers a desolate landscape: "empty grounds, and . . . vague roads, where never wagon or wayfarer passed" (38). Enraptured fascination or repulsion?

Beyond the surrounding walls the Desert begins. No paths, instead the principle of an interminable Way. No limits, instead a threshold which is always displaced, transferred, fleeing. No tyrannical order, instead a set of reference points always in need of reworking, a center that must still be replaced with no respite. No images or scales of the human, instead the continuous concept, processional: Man is unfolding everywhere, similar and different.

Writing desires the Desert as the sole horizon of its quest and its truth. Carceral architecture will yet become tombs, metallic dreams will still crumble. It is necessary to believe in the mirages that float above the ocean-like sands. They have less solidity than the stones in the walls, but they orient and constantly stir up the question of the wandering one toward the never-to-be-completed reality of the voyage, of phenomena. Movement, pause. The halts in the Desert are stations in the dwelling of Being—where the fire of the Face shines, the contemplated Face, shared as a gift.

"Am I my brother's keeper?" asked the first murderer (Gen. 4:9). The horror of Cain—the law of Empire—begins with the distancing of the Face.

Melville and Race

Arnold Rampersad

Herman Melville is slowly settling into our consciousness as one of the major commentators on race in the history of American literature, but the degree of his impact, like the precise nature of his meanings on the subject, is hard to ascertain. One useful way to measure both the impact of his ideas and his meanings on this subject might be to attempt to trace his influence on black American writers and intellectuals. Few Americans are more sensitive to race than black writers have been, and yet Melville has only recently begun to emerge as one of the more influential—or controversial—whites on this central question. Why has Melville failed to make an impact to rival that of Mark Twain or Faulkner, for example, especially when many readers consider him a more radical commentator on race?

In part, the answer has to do with the infamous obscuring of Melville's reputation in the 1880s and 1890s and down into the 20th century. In part, the answer lies in the difficulty of ascertaining his general position on race. Here, blacks were not helped by the mainstream of literary criticism, which is to say white scholars, critics, and teachers. In her landmark study *Shadow over the Promised Land: Slavery, Race, and Violence in Melville's America* (1980), Carolyn Karcher reminds us that "until the mid-1960s, there was almost no interest in Melville's racial views, and very little recognition of the prominent place that social criticism occupies in his writings." Even those critics who had identified themselves with strongly liberal or even radical social attitudes "insisted that a work like 'Benito Cereno,' for example, was not about slave revolt, but about good and evil." Furthermore, in this reading of "Benito Cereno," the fact that Melville makes whites represent good and blacks represent evil was said to have "no racial implications." The few critics who pointed out the racism of such assignations of symbolic value "accused Melville himself of racism."[1]

Resisting the temptation to be self-righteous by indulging in hindsight, one should face the difficulty posed by Melville's narratives on the question of race. Karcher herself, declaring that his views were not always consistent,

First printed in this volume. Printed by permission of the author.

[1]Carolyn L. Karcher, *Shadow over the Promised Land: Slavery, Race, and Violence in Melville's America* (Baton Rouge: Louisiana State University Press, 1980), p. ix.

called him "a refractory conformist and a reluctant rebel."[2] She argues only that "criticisms of slavery and racism" were "pressing concerns of his that he kept bringing up in his antebellum novels and tales." However, "in a few works—notably *Moby-Dick* and *The Confidence Man*" she boldly asserts, "slavery and race are crucial themes," the study of which "not only takes us to the heart of the text, but radically transforms our perceptions of its total meaning." Aldon Lynn Nielsen has made a similar point. Sometimes Melville seems to have had dubious racial views, in keeping with the intellectual world in which he lived. "But just as often he can be found puzzling out the way in which race appears in our representations to ourselves."[3]

Black writers and intellectuals were hardly reluctant to try to puzzle out the ways of racial representation; but there may have been other reasons for their relative blindness to Melville. For one thing, there are dominating elements in Melville's body of work that are at odds with the tradition of black fiction. The classic black fictional narrative was far more often than not a domestic tale, tied to racial and political ambitions but bound by middle class proprieties, including strong elements of sentiment, love, and marriage. And while Melville has something to offer in this line, it was not enough to make much of an impression. The author of *Typee* and *Omoo* and even *Moby-Dick* and *Billy Budd* encourages a fiction based on a sense of the author as voyager, rover, roamer, or even bum; a mixture of the bohemian spirit with adventurism in the Third World—something that had interested few black writers (for example, Langston Hughes, as one might infer from his autobiographies *The Big Sea* and *I Wonder as I Wander*). But the most daunting challenge presented by Melville lies in his merging of something like bohemianism with disturbing ideas about race. These ideas intimidated the black writer almost as much as they have challenged the white world, which recoiled from them in the 1850s and has only slowly come around to engaging them fully.

Not everyone flinched, and black writers of a more independent cast might have responded in kind. In his typically wild and yet inspired way, D. H. Lawrence caught more than a glimpse of Melville's radicalism on the subject of race. Melville "was a modern Viking. There is something curious about real blue-eyed people. They are never quite human. . . . In blue eyes there is sun and rain and abstract, uncreate element, water, ice, air, space, but not humanity." Melville in the South Seas, in *Typee* and *Omoo*, finds the Noble Savage and the ignoble white man. "Here at last," in *Typee*, "is Rousseau's Child of Nature and Chateaubriand's Noble Savage called upon and found at home. Yes, Melville loves his savage hosts. He finds them gentle, laughing lambs compared to the ravening wolves of his white brothers, left behind in

[2]Karcher, p. 3.
[3]Karcher, p. xi. Aldon Lynn Nielsen, *Reading Race: White American Poets and the Racial Discourse in the Twentieth Century* (Athens: University of Georgia Press, 1988), p. 15.

America and on an American whaleship. The ugliest beast on earth is a white man, says Melville."[4]

According to Lawrence, Melville cannot rest there. Unable finally to identify with the black savage, he also hated the white "renegade." Held by "a long thin chain" around his ankle connected to "America, to civilization, to democracy, to the ideal world. . . . It never broke. It pulled him back." At the same time, however, he saw clearly the end of civilization, which he recorded in *Moby-Dick*. "Doom! Doom! Doom!," Lawrence intones. "Something seems to whisper it in the very dark trees of America. Doom! / Doom of what? / Doom of our white day. We are doomed, doomed. And the doom is in America. The doom of our white day. / . . . Melville knew. He knew his race was doomed. His white soul, doomed. His great white epoch, doomed. Himself, doomed. The idealist, doomed. The spirit, doomed. / . . . What then is Moby-Dick? He is the deepest blood-being of the white race; he is our deepest blood-nature. . . . The last phallic being of the white man. Hunted into the death of upper consciousness and the ideal will."[5]

Early in this century, a few black writers, notably W. E. B. Du Bois in certain pieces, were intrigued by the idea of the death of the white race, the fall of white culture. Far more often, black writers have tiptoed around the subject, as for generations they tiptoed around the subject of the will among blacks to hatred and violence as the achieved consequence of white racism. Of course, all that timidity was to change, first with the publication of *Native Son* in 1940, then more explosively with the Black Power and the Black Consciousness movements of the 1960s and later.

Until Wright's novel, the blueprint for black fiction was that originated by Harriet Beecher Stowe in *Uncle Tom's Cabin* in 1853. (The fact that behind Stowe's novel, by her own admission, was the slave narrative only reinforced the centrality of her novel.) The black writer, in a real sense, had Stowe on one side and, on the other, Melville. Blacks almost always chose Stowe and her world: domestic, familial, womanly, religious, moral, separatist but apparently integrationist. Just as often they shunned Melville: nomadic, lonely, masculine, satanic, amoral, and (in the end, though different in the beginning) separationist. Du Bois openly admired Stowe; Langston Hughes comfortably published an introduction to *Uncle Tom's Cabin*. And why not? Her social radicalism came garbed distinctly in a highly moral, highly religious fabric, ideally suited for characterizations that involved submission, stoicism, or heroic sacrifice, as in her most memorable creations—black Uncle Tom and white Little Eva—as well as plots that moved inexorably toward success and fulfillment.

Thus a real landmark in African American literary and intellectual history is the celebrated attack on Mrs. Stowe by young James Baldwin in his June 1949

[4]D. H. Lawrence, *Studies in Classic American Literature*, in Edmund Wilson, ed., *The Shock of Recognition* (New York: Random House, 1955), pp. 1031, 1035.
[5]Lawrence, pp. 1041, 1060.

essay "Everybody's Protest Novel." Did Baldwin understand exactly what he
was doing in attacking Harriet Beecher Stowe? Probably not. His essay, an
attack on the protest novel in general, has always seemed to me in some way
misguided. *Uncle Tom's Cabin* is held to be "a very bad novel," one that is
"activated by what might be called a theological terror, the terror of damna-
tion; and the spirit that breathes in this book . . . is not different from that
spirit of medieval times which sought to exorcize evil by burning witches."
The essay closes with an attack on what might have been Baldwin's real target
all along—ironically, Richard Wright's *Native Son*, which is held to be another
protest novel steeped in race that disfigures the humanity of its black
characters in order to hew to the formula of protest. "Bigger is Uncle Tom's
descendant, flesh of his flesh, so exactly opposite a portrait that, when the
books are placed together, it seems that the contemporary Negro novelist and
the dead New England woman are locked together in a deadly, timeless
battle; the one uttering merciless exhortations, the other shouting curses."[6]

Without quite knowing it, I believe, Baldwin recognized something crucial
and yet debilitating in the relationship between Stowe's work and black
American literature. Whether Wright is most accurately seen as the inverse of
Stowe is another matter, for Wright may be seen as a Melvillian, in that
"Benito Cereno" forms a kind of prediction of *Native Son*, that is, with Babo
predicting Bigger Thomas. Babo and Bigger are alike in one supremely
important way. In spite of the consumerist elements in Bigger's make-up,
both men are largely without a sense of ambivalence about their attitude to
the white world and the America they know. The big difference between them
is that Bigger appears to have little that might be called mature, purposeful
political consciousness: Babo is much more self-possessed. Babo's gaze is fixed
on freedom and Africa, and militantly against the whites, America, and all its
works and pomps.

In 1949, Baldwin was not ready—far from it—for racial radicalism of such
extreme degree, for the displays of rage that would make him be received as a
prophet; otherwise he might have seen that Wright and *Native Son* deserved
to be linked to the American mid-nineteenth century world from which Stowe
had come, but in a different way. But clearly he knew that something was in
the wind. Interestingly, Baldwin comes to mind crucially in Aldon Lynn
Nielsen's discussion of Melville in *Reading Race: White American Poets and
the Racial Discourse in the Twentieth Century* (1988). Of the beheaded Babo,
Nielsen writes: "Babo's eyes gaze out from the text . . . in stark announcement, not only of the terror which the slavers must have anticipated, but of a
terror which must be faced by white culture generally, that dread that culture
must face of having the 'bad other' it has called into being suddenly break
through the abstraction of white description. Melville has forced just such a
rent in the veil of racial discourse." Here, in this rent, Nielsen sights and cites

---

[6]James Baldwin, *Notes of a Native Son* (Boston: Beacon, 1990), pp. 14, 22.

none other than Baldwin: "The real terror that engulfs the white world now is a visceral terror. . . . It's the terror of being described by those they've been describing so long."[7]

Within four years after Baldwin's essay, the matter of Melville and race as perceived by blacks would take a decisive turn in the work of two black intellectuals and writers. First came the young Ralph Ellison, who had by this point moved from orthodox Marxism toward his full realization as an artist with the publication in 1952 of his novel *Invisible Man*. Foregounding his admiration for Melville—unprecedented in African-American writing, as far as I know—Ellison chose as one of his two epigraphs the question of Amasa Delano to the morose Don Benito near the end of "Benito Cereno": " 'You are saved,' cried Captain Delano, more and more astonished and pained; 'you are saved: what has cast such a shadow upon you?' "

A year later, in 1953, the Trinidad-born writer C. L. R. James, well known as the author of *Black Jacobins* (about the Haitian revolution) and a brilliant disciple of Leon Trotsky, published *Mariners, Renegades and Castaways: The Story of Herman Melville and the world we live in*. This was the first book by someone steeped in the problems posed by race to attempt to take the measure of Herman Melville. Much of the work was written on Ellis Island, where James was detained by the Department of Immigration as an undesirable alien in spite of his militant anti-communism. To James, Melville is astonishingly prophetic of the world of the 1950s. Of *Moby-Dick* he writes: "The question of questions is: how could a book from the world of 1850 contain so much of the world of the 1950s?"[8] How did James see Melville on the question of race?

James had only a limited idea of exactly how much of the future world was prophesied by Melville. As a Trotskyist, he viewed race and nationalism, including black nationalism, as a kind of banality. His book is dedicated to his son, "who will be 21 years old in 1970 by which time I hope he and his generation will have left behind them forever all the problems of nationality." In his Marxist zeal, he failed to take Melville's full measure. James comes close, in linking *Moby-Dick* to 20th century history. After World War I, Germany "sought a theory of society and a program. . . . The national state *was* the one god without any hypocrisies or pretenses. The national race *was* the master race." When the Germans followed a totalitarian leader to their doom, Melville had foreseen it all. "That this is how the masses of men would sooner or later behave is what Melville was pointing out in 1851. Being a creative artist, he had seen it in terms of human personality and human relations, and therefore could only present it that way." Denouncing Stalin and communism, who triumphed over the Nazis along with the capitalists,

---

[7]Nielsen, p. 20.

[8]C. L. R. James, *Mariners, Renegades and Castaways: The Story of Herman Melville and the world we live in* (New York: Author, 1953), p. 80.

James sees Ahab as the "embodiment of the totalitarian type . . . concerned with two things only: 1) science, the management of things; and 2) politics, the management of men."[9]

Certainly James is alive to the ways in which Melville's depictions of blacks are an improvement on what had come before in American and European literature. Effortlessly, he links Melville to Stowe. "Melville, with his usual scientific precision, does not write of Negro slaves," says James. "He writes of the Negro race, civilized and uncivilized alike. Harriet Beecher Stowe, who wrote a few years before, wrote about Negroes, about Uncle Tom and Eva, who mean nothing today." He compares *Moby-Dick* to Cooper's *The Last of the Mohicans* and the age-old invocation of the noble savage. Queequeg is drawn first according to the stereotype of the noble savage; then Melville takes him in certain directions "or takes them [his black characters] over into the world he saw ahead." Melville's vision of race is embodied in his narrator Ishmael's, and is founded on a view of whiteness and of civilization as being corrupt and insupportable. Ishmael is "as isolated and bitter as Ahab and as helpless. He cannot stand the narrow, cramped, limited existence which civilization offers him. He hates the greed, the lies, the hypocrisy. Thus shut out from the world outside, he cannot get out of himself."[10]

So far, there is perhaps little remarkable about this analysis; little that is remarkable today, in any event. At *Benito Cereno*, however, James balks. He appreciates the elements that make it a *tour de force*; in fact, he, like other critics, uses precisely these elements to give weight to his final dislike of the tale. He faithfully presents the general enterprise of the story. Through Amasa Delano, Melville had "itemized every single belief cherished by an advanced civilization . . . about a backward people and then one by one showed that they were not merely false but were the direct cause of his own blindness and stupidity." And James sees the heroic character of the blacks and especially of their leader, and thus the radicalism of Melville: "As is usual with him, his protest is uncompromising, absolute. The Negroes fight to a finish, Babo is the most heroic character in Melville's fiction. He is a man of unbending will, a natural leader, an organizer of large schemes but a master of detail, ruthless against his enemies but without personal weakness. . . . Melville purposely makes him physically small, a man of internal power with a brain that is a 'hive of subtlety.' "[11]

And yet "Benito Cereno" illustrates "Melville's decline into the shallowness of modern literature. It is a propaganda story, a mystery, written to prove a particular social or political point." In execution it is excellent, but "propaganda stories are of necessity limited. Ahab, for example, is a new type of human being. Bartleby is not. Still less is Babo." Of the slave's heroism, "history tells us ten thousand such stories. Melville had ceased to be creative,

[9]James, pp. 11–13.
[10]James, pp. 133, 141.
[11]James, pp. 133–134.

and he had lost his vision of the future. Without such vision no writer can describe existing reality, for without it he does not know what is important or what is not, what will endure and what will pass."[12]

All of this is debatable. What must be debated is whether or not Babo is a "new type of human being" and whether Melville "had lost his vision of the future." And, of course, whether Melville had "ceased to be creative." Clearly Babo was not quite as new a figure as Ahab was; but I am not sure what black historical or literary personages James is referring to when he declared Babo not new. And yet one might see in Babo's homicidal desire for freedom, and his uncompromising hatred of Cereno and the whites, a kind of new black man. This man sees the world of blacks and the world of whites as irreconcilably separate. His head, chopped off and stuck on a pole in a public square, presents only hostility to the passing whites—or, as Melville put it, "met, unabashed, the gaze of the whites."

Here we have in James a collision between race analysis and class analysis, as well as a conflict between partisan racial feeling and James's essential sense of himself as an intellectual and a personality. By his own admission, he considered himself a "black European" and conceded that his "whole life was toward European literature, European sociology."[13] It is useful to remember the division between the Trotskyists and the Communist Party over the Black Nation question, with the Communists after 1928 advocating self-determination for American blacks and the Trotskyists advocating a similar degree of freedom—but only as a step toward the eventual goal of an interracial, international coalition. James is being faithful to his Trotskyist views in reading Melville in the way he does, and particularly so on the question of race. But it seems safe to say that he sacrificed prophesy in adhering to Trotskyist ideology, not to say dogma.

How did Ralph Ellison come to the point of citing "Benito Cereno" as an epigraph to *Invisible Man?* Surely the black writer engaging Melville, like any writer thoroughly engaging Melville, necessarily also engages what one might call the deep tradition of American literature. He or she must be happy in that engagement, which is to say that the black writer must bring respect and even a degree of reverence for long dead white writers; and such respect and reverence has not always been possible for the young black writer facing the national past. To this writer, the reputation of abolitionism, which one takes to represent the ultimate radicalism on the question of race in the mid-nineteenth century, does not sufficiently glamorize or even illuminate the past to warrant such devotion. Taken for granted is the absence of an intellectual force for liberty based on premises beyond abolitionism. Occasionally, however, someone probes deeply enough and discovers connections where connections were not supposed to exist. Such a figure, among black American

[12]James, p. 134.
[13]Cedric J. Robinson, *Black Marxism: The Making of the Black Radical Tradition* (London: Zed Press, 1983), p. 396.

writers facing the American mid-nineteenth century, was Ralph Waldo Ellison.

As early as 1945, in a review in *The New Republic* of the white writer Bucklin Moon's *Primer for White Folks*, Ellison looked at Melville and Melville's contemporaries and saw a group of writers with whom he obviously believed he had something in common. Between 1776 and 1876, he writes, "there was a conception of democracy current in this country that allowed the writer to identify himself with the Negro." Among those identifying were "Whitman, Emerson, Thoreau, Hawthorne, Melville and Mark Twain. For slavery (it was not called a 'Negro problem' then) was a vital issue in the American consciousness, symbolic of the condition of Man, and a valid aspect of the writer's reality." Only later was the question of blacks "pushed into the underground of the American conscience and ignored."[14]

The year after the appearance of *Invisible Man*, in his essay "Twentieth-Century Fiction and the Black Mask of Humanity," delivered at Harvard University, Ellison singled out Melville as representative of writers of the nineteenth century. The main difference between Melville and these writers, on the one hand, and the writers of Ellison's time, on the other, was "not in the latter's lack of personal rituals" but rather "in the social effect aroused within their respective readers." Melville's own ritual and rhetoric were based on "a blending of his personal myth with universal myths as traditional as any used by Shakespeare or the Bible." What is different is that "Melville's belief could still find a public object. Whatever else his works were 'about' they also managed to be about democracy. But by our day the democratic dream had become too shaky a structure to support the furious pressures of the artist's doubts. And as always when the belief which nurtures a great social myth declines, large sections of society become prey to superstition. For man without myth is Othello with Desdemona gone: chaos descends, faith vanishes and superstitions prowl in the mind."[15]

In his allusion to Othello and Desdemona, I would suggest, Ellison shows the extent to which the dilemma of the black writer facing the white American tradition is on his mind, and the nostalgia he feels for a vanished era, when the writer and the audience were far more at one than in our time—and the American writer was far more concerned with democracy and race than he or she was in 1953. In linking himself to the past, ironically, he opened his way into the future both ideologically and formally, as he explored racial alienation and created a structure that went beyond naturalism.

In breaking with naturalism, Ellison appears to have found his major support not so much in writers more contemporary with him than Wright or Dreiser but by moving backward toward Melville. Charles T. Davis has described Ellison's style in *Invisible Man* as one that is "always eclectic,

---

[14]Ralph Ellison, *Shadow and Act* (New York: Signet, 1966), pp. 107–108.
[15]Ellison, pp. 56–57.

changing to reflect the psychological shifts within his unnamed narrator." The style may be eclectic, but Davis reminds us that Ellison himself has spoken (in his interview called "The Art of Fiction" in *Paris Review* in 1955) of the three major parts of the novel being dominated respectively by naturalism, impressionism, and surrealism. "Even in the more naturalistic pages of *Invisible Man*," Davis wrote, "we find a Melvillian duality, a delight in playing with two equally valid but opposed physical realities."[16]

How did Melville facilitate Ellison's decisive modification of naturalism by impressionism and surrealism, and thus his self-liberation from both the "domestic" and bourgeois discourse of Harriet Beecher Stowe and the almost dogmatic naturalism of Wright and Dreiser? In the exchange between Amasa Delano and Don Benito Cereno in which Ellison found an epigraph to his novel, Melville revealed how much he understood of the vagaries of meaning inherent in the Africanist presence in the United States. When Delano asks Don Benito, "what has cast such a shadow upon you?" Don Benito's reply is "The negro." The "shadow" of the "negro" is death to Cereno, who gathers his mantle about him "as if it were a pall." Does Don Benito mean Babo, or all Negroes? I think the latter. Unacknowledged perhaps by most writers (George Washington Cable in *The Grandissimes* is perhaps an exception), the death-dealing shadow of blacks on whites in Melville is a concept, an image, which in its singularity is at least as powerful as the concept or image that, as a modification of Stowe's imaging of race, helped to define black writing in this century—Du Bois's concept and image of the "veil" in *The Souls of Black Folk*. (The artistic power of the image of the "shadow," which is crucial to my argument, is demonstrated deliberately in "Benito Cereno," of course, where it is the central, all-pervading image. Less centrally, it is also a powerful presence in *Moby-Dick*.)

A veil, Du Bois writes at the start of that book, separates blacks from whites in America. "After the Egyptian and Indian, the Greek and Roman, the Teuton and Mongolian, the Negro is a sort of seventh son, born with a veil, and gifted with second-sight in this American world, —a world which yields him no true self-consciousness, but only lets him see himself through the revelation of the other world. It is a peculiar sensation, this double-consciousness." The black American has "two souls, two thoughts, two unreconciled strivings; two warring ideals in one dark body, whose dogged strength alone keeps it from being torn asunder."[17]

Melville's shadow and Du Bois's veil are similar in one respect but paradoxical in other respects. From the point of view of blacks, the former (as

<hr />

[16]Charles T. Davis, "The Mixed Heritage of the Modern Black Novel," in Kimberly W. Benston, ed., *Speaking for You: The Vision of Ralph Ellison* (Washington, DC: Howard University Press, 1987), p. 276.

[17]W. E. B. Du Bois, *The Souls of Black Folk* (Chicago: A. C. McClurg, 1903), p. 3. Note that Aldon Lynn Nielsen (pp. 1–2) also discusses Du Bois's concept of the veil in the context of Melville, and identifies (p. 1) an additional prefiguring of *Invisible Man* (the "Battle Royal" episode) in *White Jacket*.

personified in Babo, or even Bigger Thomas, for example) speaks of unitary consciousness, the latter of a divided consciousness, out of which comes intrinsic drama but—by definition—the probability of political and cultural indecisiveness. For whites, however, the shadow operates as the veil does for blacks, in that it destabilizes unitary consciousness as well as political and cultural power. In another twist, if for the black writer divided consciousness, or the veil, is intrinsically dramatic, the shadow, on the other hand, presents a dead end in art even as it may represent a victory over whites. Thus the black writer, or the white writer completely sympathetic to blacks, who is possessed by a sense of the authenticity of unitary consciousness (again, as represented by Babo or Bigger) may face an end to art. C. L. R. James certainly saw the death-dealing shadow of the Negro as a dead end for Melville, one that signals the death of hope, of faith in humanity.

I would suggest that *Invisible Man* gains much of its power from Ellison's establishment of a working tension between the shadow and the veil, the death-dealing shadow and the ambivalent veil. Repudiating neither concept, Ellison instead lets them play off against one another, before coming down on the side of the veil, which is to say on the side of optimism, the party of hope, the promise of America. "For, like almost everyone else in our country," Invisible says at the end, "I started out with my share of optimism. I believed in hard work and progress and action, but now, after first being 'for' society and then 'against' it, I assign myself no rank or any limit. . . . My world has become one of infinite possibilities."[18] What expedites Ellison's fusion is his major borrowing from Melville—that is, the character of his narrator, who resembles no one else in previous fiction so much as he resembles Ishmael of *Moby-Dick.*

Invisible is black, Ishmael white, but both men feel the shadow of "the negro," or of race. The shadow falls across Ishmael but does not kill him, as it kills Don Benito. Rather does it open up the wellsprings of his humanitarian consciousness early in the novel, through Queequeg, whose coffin also saves him in the end. Ellison signals his debt to Melville when, in the prologue to *Invisible Man*, he reprises a moment in the second chapter of *Moby-Dick.* Looking for a place to sleep in New Bedford, Ishmael goes from one inn to another, finding them uncongenial and too expensive. In the darkness, he moves toward the inns near the water, knowing they would be cheapest. "Such dreary streets! blocks of blackness, not houses, on either hand, and here and there a candle, like a candle moving about in a tomb. At this hour of the night, of the last day of the week, that quarter of the town proved all but deserted." He comes to "a smoky light proceeding from a low, wide building, the door of which stood invitingly open." Entering, he stumbles over an ash-box. "Ha! thought I, ha, as the flying articles almost choked me, are these ashes from that destroyed city, Gomorrah?" Ishmael decides, jokingly, that

---

[18]Ralph Ellison, *Invisible Man* (New York: Random House, 1952), p. 498.

this must be an inn called "The Trap." However, he hears a voice inside and "pushed on and opened a second, interior door."

> A hundred black faces turned round in their rows to peer; and beyond, a black Angel of Doom was beating a book in the pulpit. It was a negro church; and the preacher's text was about the blackness of darkness, and the weeping and wailing and teeth-gnashing there.[19]

In the prologue to *Invisible Man*, Invisible recalls a prime moment of truth when he smoked marijuana and entered the spirit of music as for the first time: "I not only entered the music but descended, like Dante, into its depths." He hears an old woman singing a spiritual "as full of Weltschmerz as flamenco," and then a naked lightskinned black girl "pleading in a voice like my mother's" at her own auction. Then, at "a lower level" yet, he hears a shout: "Brothers and sisters, my text this morning is the 'Blackness of Blackness.' " And the congregation answers: "That blackness is most black, brother, most black. . . ."[20]

Thus Invisible crosses Ishmael's path, and enters his text; and thus Ishmael enters Invisible's text. Both men are innocents puzzling out the question of the meaning of blackness and whiteness. Ishmael's education begins with his encounter with Queequeg. The major steps in Ishmael's conversion may be seen in the following quotations. At first: "I felt a melting in me. . . . Wild he was; a very sight of sights to see; yet I began to feel myself mysteriously drawn towards him."[21] And then, as he and Queequeg walk together in public: "we did not notice the jeering glances of the passengers, a lubber-like assembly, who marveled that two fellow beings should be so companionable; as though a white man were anything more dignified than a white-washed negro."[22] And after Queequeg has shown himself to be far braver and far more competent than Ishmael could ever be: "From that hour I clove to Queequeg like a barnacle; yea, till poor Queequeg took his long last dive."[23]

If Ishmael's education begins with his meeting with Queequeg, then it might be said that Invisible's education begins with his meeting with Ishmael and Queequeg. By representing the humanity of blacks and the complexity of race and racism so acutely and generously in his text, Melville had empowered Ellison to insist on a place in the American literary tradition, no matter how racism tried to exclude him. It is good to remember where Invisible lives. He lives not in Harlem proper "but in a border area"; his building is rented strictly to whites, but "I live rent-free . . . in a section of the basement that was shut off and forgotten during the nineteenth century, which I discovered when I was trying to escape from Ras the Destroyer."[24] Ras

[19]Herman Melville, *Moby-Dick* (Boston: Houghton Mifflin, 1956), p. 28.
[20]*Invisible Man*, p. 12.
[21]*Moby-Dick*, p. 59.
[22]*Moby-Dick*, p. 65.
[23]*Moby-Dick*, p. 66.
[24]*Invisible Man*, p. 9.

personifies the destructive excesses of cultural nationalism, from which Ellison, through Invisible, escapes by clinging to a notion of cultural inheritance and tradition based on an appreciation of the relevance of nineteenth-century American writing to his own desires as a writer.

Invisible Man could not have been written by someone without such a sense, although the novel looks forward technically and ideologically as readily as it looks backward. In other words, Ellison's novel exemplifies the spirit of T. S. Eliot's essay "Tradition and the Individual Talent," in which Eliot stresses the interrelationship of the living and the dead. No wonder, then, that the other epigraph to *Invisible Man* is from Eliot (from *The Cocktail Party*). The special challenge, as I have said, was for a black writer to find part of his tradition among whites; Ellison must have had few illusions about how Eliot viewed blacks and black culture. Ellison himself made a distinction between family and ancestors. Langston Hughes and Richard Wright were family; Eliot and Hemingway and Melville, presumably, were ancestors. He was surely not the first person—and absolutely not the first artist—to exalt his ancestors over his family.

Ellison's sense of tradition was not shared by the next generation of black writers, those who matured—if that is the right word—in the 1960s. Breaking with the white past, with white people, was the hallmark of the Black Power movement and of the Black Arts movement, of which the major leader, as an artist and a theorist, was almost certainly LeRoi Jones, later Amiri Baraka. And yet Melville evidently meant something to Jones before he became Baraka and as he was trying to become him. In 1962, in a lecture entitled "The Myth of 'Negro Literature,' " Jones heaped scorn on most black writing as being little more than the effluence of bourgeois mentalities bent on aping mediocre white writers while avoiding the best. Only Toomer, Wright, Ellison and Baldwin, he declared, had created any examples of writing "that could succeed in passing themselves off as 'serious' writing. . . . That is, serious, if one has never read Herman Melville or James Joyce."[25]

This is hardly evidence of influence, but it is clear that Baraka and the Black Power movement would have understood Babo in his murderous hatred of Don Benito, indeed, identified with him; and excoriated Amasa Delano as the embodiment of fantastic white liberal values (notably the famed American value called "innocence"). All of which, it seems to me, Melville fairly anticipated. And yet C. L. R. James was surely right in seeing the bleakness of it all, how destructive of art such radicalism is—art, that is, that depends on America (black or white) for its audience. Generally without saying so, the African-American literary tradition has recognized this problem and effected a compromise with the past—a stern compromise, but a compromise nevertheless. The work of the leading black writers since the 1960s reflects this carefully negotiated truce with the American literary tradition. The echoes of

[25]LeRoi Jones, *Home: Social Essays* (New York: Morrow, 1966), p. 107.

Melville himself are there in the work of John Edgar Wideman, and Barbara Chase-Riboud, and of course in Charles Johnson. And Melville has figured prominently in the work by the preeminent black writer today, Toni Morrison, in her attempt as a cultural interpreter to affect our sense of the American literary tradition—that is, to amplify the insights and intuitions of Ralph Ellison and others on this question.

Although what one might call a deep nationalism—a commitment to the "ancient properties" of black peoples—is an indispensable feature of Morrison's work, it is a feature surrounded by her sense of the necessity of a broader, deeper view of tradition and responsibility. She has best articulated her thoughts on this question in her essay "Unspeakable Things Unspoken: The Afro-American Presence in American literature" (1989). There, she proposes to engage the multiple debates concerning the canon in American literature "in order to suggest ways of addressing the Afro-American presence in American Literature that require neither slaughter nor reification—views that may spring the whole literature of an entire nation from the solitude into which it has been locked."[26] And Melville is central to her project.

Admiring Michael Rogin's subversive genealogy: *The Politics and Art of Herman Melville* (1983), she differs from him, however, in identifying not slavery but the fabrication and idealization of whiteness as ideology, as the cause of Melville's alienation in his lifetime. "If the whale is more than blind, indifferent Nature unsubduable by masculine aggression," Morrison suggests, "we can consider the possibility that Melville's 'truth' was his recognition of the moment in America when whiteness became ideology. And if the white whale is the ideology of race, what Ahab has lost to it is personal dismemberment and family and society and his own place as a human in the world. The trauma of racism is, for the racist and the victim, the severe fragmentation of the self, and has always seemed to me a cause (not a symptom) of psychosis. . . .

> Ahab . . . is navigating between an idea of civilization that he renounces and an idea of savagery he must annihilate, because the two cannot co-exist. The former is based on the latter. What is terrible in its complexity is that the idea of savagery is not the missionary one: it is white racial ideology that is savage and if, indeed, a white, nineteenth-century, American male took on not abolition, not the amelioration of racist institutions or their laws, but the very concept of whiteness as an inhuman idea, he would be very alone, very desperate, and very doomed. Madness would be the only appropriate description of such audacity. . . . What I am suggesting is that he was overwhelmed by the philosophical and metaphysical idea that had its fullest manifestation in his own time in his own country, and that that idea was the successful assertion of whiteness as ideology."[27]

Quoting liberally from the chapter "The Whiteness of the Whale," Morrison stresses that "Melville is not exploring white *people*, but whiteness idealized."

[26]Toni Morrison, "Unspeakable Things Unspoken: The Afro-American Presence in American Literature," *Michigan Quarterly Review* (Winter 1989): 1.
[27]Morrison, pp. 15–16.

He is neither "engaged in some simple and simple-minded black/white didacticism" nor was he "satanizing white people." Melville's final observation on whiteness "reverberates with personal trauma. 'This visible [colored] world seems formed in love, the invisible [white] spheres were formed in fright.' The necessity for whiteness as privileged 'natural' state, the invention of it, was indeed formed in fright."[28]

Finally, she uses Father Mapple's sermon to measure the radicalism of *Moby-Dick*:

> To question the very notion of white progress, the very idea of racial superiority, of whiteness as privileged place in the evolutionary ladder of humankind, and to meditate on the fraudulent, self-destroying philosophy of that superiority, to "pluck it out from under the robes of Senators and Judges," to drag the "judge himself to the bar," —that was dangerous, solitary, radical work. Especially then. Especially now. To be "only a patriot to heaven" is no mean aspiration in Young America for a writer—or the captain of a whaling ship.

Embracing both white and black writers, Morrison's tribute to Melville is unequivocal: "To this day no novelist has so wrestled with its subject."[29]

For a number of reasons, some of them almost inscrutable, Melville saw into the heart of America on the question of race. He saw how the concept of innate white superiority—of whiteness as absolute—had been constructed out of economic and political pressures and desires in a "new" world, in which Europeans had come up against a native population and an imported African presence and redefined themselves according to those pressures. He saw not only the complex psychological consequences for whites but the ways in which the newly constructed ideology of whiteness would shape and invade the entire apparatus of signification, from color of skin to color in art to standards of facial beauty and far beyond into virtually every aspect of culture.

And I think he also clearly saw something of the complex psychological consequences for blacks, and the ways in which they would become, or had already become, entangled in the apparatus of signification designed to keep them in perpetual servitude. For daring to put these ideas in fiction, Melville was punished with neglect, silence, and then misappropriation and misinterpretation. He instead should be seen as one of the principal interpreters of the American obsession with race and commitment to racism, an artist to whose work we should turn for a fair measure of illumination and guidance.

[28]Morrison, p. 16.
[29]Morrison, p. 18.

"Benito Cereno" and
New World Slavery

Eric J. Sundquist

In the climactic scene of "Benito Cereno," after the terrified Spanish captain has flung himself threateningly into Captain Delano's boat, followed by his servant Babo, dagger in hand, Melville writes: "All this, with what preceded, and what followed, occurred with such involutions of rapidity, that past, present, and future seemed one." The revelation of Babo's true design, as his disguise of dutiful slave falls away to reveal a "countenance lividly vindictive, expressing the centered purpose of his soul," is mirrored in the countenance of Delano himself, who, as if "scales dropped from his eyes," sees the whole host of slaves "with mask torn away, flourishing hatchets, and knives, in ferocious piratical revolt."[1] The masquerade staged by Babo and Benito Cereno to beguile the benevolent Delano probes the limits of the American's innocence; at the same time it eloquently enacts the haltingly realized potential for slave rebellion in the New World and, in larger configuration, the final drama of one stage in New World history.

The American, the European, and the African, yoked together in the last crisis as they are throughout the pantomime of interrupted revolution that constitutes Melville's story, play parts defined by the climactic phase slavery in the Americas had entered when Melville composed his politically volatile tale during the winter and spring of 1854–55. The American Civil War reduced New World slavery to Cuba and Brazil; it brought to an end the threatened extension of slavery throughout new territories of the United States and Caribbean and Latin American countries coveted by the South. In the 1850s, however, the fever for such expansion was at a pitch, and Melville's tale brings into view the convulsive history of the entire region and epoch—from the Columbian discovery of the Americas, through the democratic revolutions in the United States, Haiti, and Latin America, to the contemporary crisis over the expansion of the "Slave Power" in the United States. "In

From *Reconstructing American Literary History*, edited by Sacvan Bercovitch, Cambridge, Mass.: Harvard University Press. Copyright © 1986 by the President and Fellows of Harvard College.

[1]"Benito Cereno," *Great Short Works of Herman Melville*, ed. Warner Berthoff (New York: Harper and Row, 1969), pp. 294–295.

1860 pressures, past, present, and future, blasted the Union apart," writes Frederick Merk in his study of manifest destiny.[2] Unable to see the future but nonetheless intimating its revolutionary shape, Melville adds to these recent national pressures an international structure of exceptional scope and power, such that past, present, and future do indeed seem one aboard the *San Dominick*.

"Benito Cereno's" general significance in the debates over slavery in the 1850s is readily apparent; moreover, Melville's exploitation of the theme of balked revolution through an elaborate pattern of suppressed mystery and ironic revelation has helped draw attention to the wealth of symbolic meanings the slave revolt in San Domingo in the 1790s would have for an alert contemporary audience. Even so, the full implications of Melville's invocation of Caribbean revolution have not been appreciated, nor the historical dimensions of his masquerade of rebellion completely recognized.

In changing the name of Benito Cereno's ship from the *Tryal* to the *San Dominick*, Melville gave to the slave revolt a specific character that has often been identified. Haiti, known as San Domingo (Saint-Domingue) before declaring its final independence from France in 1804 and adopting a native name,[3] remained a strategic point of reference in debates over slavery in the United States. Abolitionists claimed that Haitian slaves, exploiting the upheaval of the French Revolution, had successfully seized the same Rights of Man as Americans two decades earlier; whereas proslavery forces claimed that the black revolution led to wholesale carnage, moral and economic degradation, and a political system that was (in the words of the British minister to Haiti in the 1860s) "but a series of plots and revolutions, followed by barbarous military executions." The outbreak of revolution in 1790 produced a flood of white planter refugees to the United States, some 10,000 in 1793 alone, most of them carrying both slaves and tales of terror to the South. Thereafter, especially in the wake of Nat Turner's bloody uprising in 1831 and the emancipation of slaves in British Jamaica in the same year, Haiti came to seem the fearful precursor of black rebellion throughout the New World. When Melville altered the date of Amasa Delano's encounter with Benito Cereno from 1805 to 1799, he accentuated the fact that his tale belonged to the age of democratic revolution, in particular the period of violent struggle

[2]Leon Howard, *Herman Melville: A Biography* (Berkeley: University of California Press, 1951), pp. 218–222; Frederick Merk, *Manifest Destiny and American Mission in American History* (1963; rpt. New York: Vintage-Random, 1966), p. 214.

[3]In English and American usage of the nineteenth century, the entire island at times and even after the revolution the western half (a French possession since the seventeenth century) was often designated San Domingo or St. Domingo. The Spanish, eastern half (the Dominican Republic after 1844) was usually designated Santo Domingo, as was the principal city founded by the Columbian expeditions and named in memory of Columbus's father, Dominick.

leading to Haitian independence presided over by the heroic black general
Toussaint L'Ouverture. . . .[4]

Were the noble and humane Toussaint the only representative figure of the
Haitian revolution, fears of slave insurrection in the United States might not
have taken on such a vicious coloring. The black activist William Wells Brown
compared him in an 1854 lecture not only to Nat Turner ("the Spartacus of the
Southampton revolt") but also to Napoleon and Washington—though with the
withering irony that whereas Washington's government "enacted laws by
which chains were fastened upon the limbs of millions of people," Toussaint's
"made liberty its watchword, incorporated it in its constitution, abolished the
slave trade, and made freedom universal amongst the people." Brown's lecture
on San Domingo, subtitled "Its Revolutions and Its Patriots," adopted the
familiar antislavery strategy of declaring the San Domingo uprising the model
for an American slave rebellion that would bring to completion the stymied
revolution of 1776. When Americans contemplated what would happen if the
San Domingo revolt were "reenacted in South Carolina and Louisiana" and
American slaves wiped out "their wrongs in the blood of their oppressors,"
however, not Toussaint but his successor as general-in-chief, Dessalines,
sprang to mind. Whatever ambivalent gratitude might have existed toward
Haiti for its mediating role in the United States' acquisition of Louisiana was
diluted by the nightmarish achievement of independence under Dessalines,
whose tactics of deceitful assurance of safety to white landowners, followed by
outright butchery, enhanced his own claim that his rule would be initiated by
vengeance against the French "cannibals" who have "taken pleasure in bathing
their hands in the blood of the sons of Haiti." When he made himself emperor
in 1804 Dessalines wore a crown presented by Philadelphia merchants and
coronation robes from British Jamaica; but in the histories of San Domingo
available in the early nineteenth century, both these ironies and unofficial
economic ties to the island tended to be forgotten amid condescending
accounts of his pompous reign and the frightful bloodshed that accompanied
it. Although a sympathetic writer could claim in 1869 that the independence
of Haiti constituted "the first great shock to this gigantic evil [slavery] in
modern times," what Southerners in particular remembered were accounts of
drownings, burnings, rapes, limbs chopped off, eyes gouged out,
disembowelments—the sort of Gothic violence typified by an episode in
Mary Hassal's so-called *Secret History; or, The Horrors of St. Domingo*
(1808), in which a young white woman refuses the proposal of one of

4Spenser St. John, *Hayti, or the Black Republic* (London: Smith, Elder, 1884), p. x; C. L. R.
James, *The Black Jacobins: Toussaint L'Ouverture and the San Domingo Revolution*, rev. ed.
(New York: Vintage Books, Random House, 1963), p. 127; Clement Eaton, *The Freedom-of-
Thought Struggle in the Old South*, rev. ed. (New York: Harper and Row, 1964), pp. 89–90;
Eugene D. Genovese, *From Rebellion to Revolution: Afro-American Slave Revolts in the Making
of the New World* (1979; rpt. New York: Vintage Books, Random House, 1981), pp. 35–37, 94–96;
Winthrop D. Jordan, *White over Black: American Attitudes toward the Negro, 1550–1812* (1968;
rpt. New York: Norton, 1977), pp. 375–402.

Dessalines' chiefs: "The monster gave her to his guard, who hung her by the throat on an iron hook in the market place, where the lovely, innocent, unfortunate victim slowly expired."[5]

While Hassal's "history" both in form and substance more resembles such epistolary novels as *Wieland*, its account of the Haitian trauma is hardly more sensational than the standard histories and polemics of the day. Antislavery forces for good reason hesitated to invoke Haiti as a model of black rule; even those sympathetic with its revolution considered its subsquent history violent and ruinous. Until the 1850s, moreover, most Americans agreed with assessments holding "that specious and intriguing body, the society of the *Amis des Noirs*," responsible for the rebellion and subsequent descent of the island "into the lowest state of poverty and degradation." What Bryan Edwards asserted of the British West Indies in 1801 remained persuasive in the United States for decades: if encouragement is given to those "hot-brained fanaticks and detestable incendiaries, who, under the vile pretense of philanthropy and zeal for the interests of suffering humanity, preach up rebellion and murder to the contented and orderly negroes," the same "carnage and destruction" now found in San Domingo will be renewed throughout the colonial world. Precisely the same fears permeated the South, even in exaggerated form after Jamaica itself was added to the list of revolutionized colonies in 1831. Lasting paranoia among slaveholders about abolitionist responsibility for slave unrest thus continually referred back to San Domingo and became, according to David Brion Davis, "an entrenched part of master class ideology, in Latin America as well as the United States." Implicit in the assumption of abolitionist conspiracy, of course, is a doubt of the slaves' own ability to organize and carry out a revolt, a doubt contradicted by any of the slave revolutionaries Melville might have had in mind—by Toussaint, by Dessalines, by Nat Turner, by Cinque (the notorious leader of the revolt aboard the slave ship *Amistad*), and by Mure, the original of his own Babo.[6]

When the sixty-three slaves aboard Benito Cereno's ship revolted, killing twenty-five men, some out of simple vengeance, they especially determined to murder their master, Don Alexandro Aranda, "because they said they could not otherwise obtain their liberty." To this Melville's version adds that the

[5]William Wells Brown, *St. Domingo: Its Revolutions and Its Patriots* (Boston: Bela Marsh, 1855), pp. 23, 36–38, 32–33; James, *Black Jacobins*, pp. 370–374; Charles MacKenzie, *Notes on Haiti, Made During a Residence in that Republic*, 2 vols. (London: Colburn and Bentley, 1830), II, 61; Jonathan Brown, *The History and Present Condition of St. Domingo*, 2 vols. (Philadelphia: William Marshall, 1836), II, 152–154, 147–148; Mark B. Bird, *The Black Man; Or, Haytian Independence* (New York: American News Co., 1869), pp. 60–61; Mary Hassal, *Secret History; or, The Horrors of St. Domingo* (Philadelphia: Bradford and Inskeep, 1808), pp. 151–153.

[6]James Franklin, *The Present State of Hayti* (London: John Murray, 1828), pp. 90–96, 409–410; Bryan Edwards, *An Historical Survey of the Island of Saint Domingo* (London: John Stockdale, 1801), p. 226; David Brion Davis, *The Slave Power Conspiracy and the Paranoid Style* (Baton Rouge: Louisiana State University Press, 1969), p. 35.

death would serve as a warning to the other seamen; not only that, but a warning that takes the form of deliberate terror. Aranda's body, instead of being thrown overboard, as in reality it was, is apparently cannibalized and the skeleton then "*substituted for the ship's proper figure-head—the image of Cristobal Colon, the discoverer of the New World,*" from whose first contact with the New World in Hispaniola—that is, San Domingo—flowed untold prosperity and human slavery on an extraordinary scale. The thirty-nine men from the *Santa Maria* Columbus left at the north coast base of Navidad on Hispaniola in 1492 were massacred by the natives after quarreling over gold and Indian women; on his second voyage in 1494 Columbus himself took command, suppressed an Indian uprising, and authorized an enslavement of Indians to work in the gold fields that was destined to destroy—by some estimates—close to one million natives within fifteen years.[7] . . .

[There is a] further coincidence, its irony commonplace by Melville's day, that "Hayti, the first spot in America that received African slaves, was the first to set the example of African liberty."[8] It is this coincidence and its ironic origins that are illuminated by Babo's symbolic display of the skeleton of a modern slaveholder in place of the image of Columbus. Along with the chalked admonition, "*Follow your leader,*" it too appears to Delano at the climactic moment when Benito Cereno and Babo plunge into his boat and the piratical revolt is unveiled; but the benevolent American, self-satisfied and of good conscience, remains oblivious to the end to the meaning of Babo's terror and to the murderous irony summoned up in Melville's symbolic gesture. Like those of Aranda, the sacred bones of Columbus, rumored still in 1830 to have been lodged in the cathedral of Santo Domingo before being transferred to Havana upon the Treaty of Basle in 1795, might well join those of the millions of slaves bound for death in the New World. Of them is built Benito Cereno's decaying ship as it drifts into the harbor of the Chilean island of Santa Maria: "Her keel seemed laid, her ribs put together, and she launched, from Ezekiel's Valley of Dry Bones."[9]

Delano, as Jean Fagan Yellin suggests, may portray the stock Yankee traveler in plantation fiction, delighted by the warm patriarchal bond betweeı

---

[7]Amasa Delano, *Narrative of Voyages and Travels in the Northern and Southern Hemispheres* (Boston: E. G. House, 1817), p. 336; see also Harold H. Scudder, "Melville's *Benito Cereno* and Captain Delano's Voyages," *PMLA*, 43 (1928), 502–532; Melville, *Benito Cerino*, p. 310; John Edwin Fagg, *Cuba, Haiti, and the Dominican Republic* (Englewood Cliffs, N.J., Prentice-Hall, 1965), pp. 114–115; Brown, *History and Present Condition of St. Domingo*, I, 22–33; Edwards, *Historical Survey of the Island of Saint Domingo*, p. 208; Samuel Eliot Morison, *Admiral of the Ocean: A Life of Christopher Columbus* (Boston: Little, Brown, 1942), pp. 297–313, 423–438.

[8]Melville, *Benito Cereno*, pp. 246, 240; H. Bruce Franklin, *The Wake of the Gods: Melville's Mythology* (Stanford: Stanford University Press, 1963), pp. 136–150; Gloria Horsley-Meacham, "The Monastic Slaver: Images and Meaning in 'Benito Cereno,' " *New England Quarterly*, 55, no. 2 (June 1983), 261–266; George Bancroft, *History of the United States of America*, 10 vols. (New York: Appleton and Co., 1885), I, 121–125.

[9]MacKenzie, *Notes on Haiti*, pp. 263–266; Melville, *Benito Cereno*, pp. 296, 241.

the loyal, minstrel-like slave and his languid master; he may even, like Thomas Gray, who recorded and published Nat Turner's *Confessions*, penetrate the violent center of that relationship and yet prefer to ignore its meaning. Recognizing that "slavery breeds ugly passions in man" but banishing from mind the significance of that realization, Delano is a virtual embodiment of repression, not simply in the sense that he puts down the revolt aboard the *San Dominick* and thereby restores authority that has been overturned, but also in the sense that his refusal to understand the "shadow" of the Negro that has descended upon Benito Cereno is itself a psychologically and politically repressive act.[10]

Melville borrows Amasa Delano's trusting disposition and generosity directly from the captain's own account, which records that the *"generous captain Amasa Delano"* much aided Benito Cereno (and was poorly treated in return when he tried to claim his just salvage rights), and was saved from certain slaughter by his own "kindness," "sympathy," and "unusually pleasant" temperament. A passage earlier in Delano's *Narrative* might also have caught Melville's eye: "A man, who finds it hard to conceive of real benevolence in the motives of his fellow creatures, gives no very favourable testimony to the public in regard to the state of his own heart, or the elevation of his moral sentiments." The self-serving nature of Delano's remarks aside, what is notable is the manner in which Melville may be said to have rendered perversely ironic the entire virtue of "benevolence," the central sentiment of abolitionist rhetoric and action since the mid-eighteenth century. Delano's response is not "philanthropic" but "genial," it is true—but genial in the way one responds to Newfoundland dogs, natural valets and hairdressers, and minstrels set "to some pleasant tune." Delano's "old weakness for negroes," surging forth precisely at Melville's greatest moment of terrifying invention, the shaving scene, is the revolutionary mind at odds with itself, energized by the ideal of fatherly humanitarianism but, confounded by racialism, blind to the recriminating violence they hold tenuously in check. Like that most eloquent advocate of benevolence, Harriet Beecher Stowe, for whom "the San Domingo hour" would be ushered in only by slaves with "Anglo Saxon blood . . . burning in their veins," Delano himself is emblematic of the paralyzed American revolution, at once idealistic and paternalistic, impassioned for freedom but fearful of continuing revolution.[11] . . .

As it happened, American hegemony in the New World was increased rather than retarded by the Civil War. From Melville's perspective, however,

---

[10]Jean Fagan Yellin, *The Intricate Knot: Black Figures in American Literature, 1776–1863* (New York: New York University Press, 1972), pp. 215–227; Melville, "Benito Cereno," pp. 283, 314.

[11]Delano, *Narrative of Voyages*, pp. 337, 323, 73; David Brion Davis, *The Problem of Slavery in Western Culture* (Ithaca: Cornell University Press, 1966), pp. 333–390; Melville, *Benito Cereno*, pp. 278–279; Harriet Beecher Stowe, *Uncle Tom's Cabin* (New York: Penguin, 1981), p. 392; cf. George Fredrickson, *The Black Image in the White Mind: The Debate on Afro-American Character and Destiny, 1817–1914* (New York: Harper and Row, 1971), pp. 97–129.

the nature and extent of future American power remained a function of the unfolding pattern of anticolonial and slave revolutions in the Americas. Even though slaves fought at different times on opposing sides, the national revolutions of South and Central America in the early part of the century helped undermine slavery throughout the region (in most cases, slaves were not freed immediately upon independence but legislation abolishing slavery was at least initiated—in Mexico, Uruguay, Chile, Argentina, and Bolivia in the 1820s; in Venezuela and Peru in the 1850s). The end of slavery in the British West Indies in 1833 and in the Dutch and French Islands in 1848 left the United States more and more an anomaly, its own revolutionary drama absurdly immobilized. Thus, when extremists of Southern slavery later sought to tie an extension of the peculiar institution to new revolutions in a policy of manifest destiny in Latin America, they ignored the decline of colonial rule on the one hand and on the other the trepidations expressed by one of the best known of South American revolutionaries, Francisco Miranda, who wrote as early as 1798:

> as much as I desire the liberty and independence of the New World, I fear the anarchy of a revolutionary system. God forbid that these beautiful countries become, as did St. Domingue, a theatre of blood and of crime under the pretext of establishing liberty. Let them rather remain if necessary one century more under the barbarous and imbecile oppression of Spain.

Miranda's plea expresses well the paradox of New World liberation and of the United States' continued, expanding enslavement of Africans between 1776 and 1860. Drawn by the territorial dreams opened by Louisiana, the post-Revolutionary generation advocated expansion through a conscious policy of America's manifest destiny to revolutionize the continent—eventually the entire hemisphere—spreading Anglo-Saxon free institutions, as one writer put it, from the Atlantic to the Pacific and "from the icy wilderness of the North to . . . the smiling and prolific South." That dreams of a global millennium ever exceeded reality is less relevant here than the fact that the harsh conflict between dream and reality was anchored in the wrenching paradox that had come to define New World revolution itself: would it advance freedom or increase slavery? At the time of "Benito Cereno's" publication, the question was concentrated in the Caribbean, where the energy of manifest destiny had been redirected after its initial efforts had failed to bring "All Mexico" into the United States orbit.[12] The region offered in miniature an emblem of the hemisphere in its historical revolutionary moment, with the remnants of Spain's great empire, free blacks who had revolutionized their

---

[12]Genovese, *From Rebellion to Revolution*, pp. 119–121; C. Duncan Rice, *The Rise and Fall of Black Slavery* (1975; rpt. Baton Rouge: Louisiana State University Press, 1976), pp. 262–263; Miranda quoted in Salvador de Madariaga, *The Fall of the Spanish American Empire* (London: Hollis, Carter, 1947), pp. 322–323; James Bennett, quoted in Merk, *Manifest Destiny and Mission*, p. 46; Merk, pp. 180–214.

own nation, and American expansionist interests all in contention. Melville's tale does not prophecy a civil war but rather anticipates, as at the time it might well have, an explosive resolution of the conflict between American democracy, Old World despotism, and Caribbean New World revolution. . . .

Melville's portrayal of Babo would have aroused memories of notorious American slave rebels like Gabriel Prosser, Denmark Vesey, and Nat Turner, all of them in one faction of the public mind artful and vicious men prompted to their deeds by madness, dreams of San Domingo, or—what was much the same thing—abolitionist propaganda. Turner in particular was perceived to be deranged, the victim of apocalyptic hallucinations. In contrast, Babo is a heroic figure—though full of that "art and cunning" the real Delano attributed to all African slaves. Melville's depiction of his ferocity and cruelty, his comparison of Babo to a snake and his followers to wolves, and most of all his attribution to him of great powers of deception—these characteristics make Babo fearsome and commanding at the same time. His masquerade of devotion to Benito Cereno concisely portrays the complexly layered qualities of rebellion and submission—of "Nat" and "Sambo" roles—that historians have detected among the accounts of slave behavior, and it is a virtual parody of Thomas Wentworth Higginson's observation in an 1861 essay on Turner: "In all insurrections, the standing wonder seems to be that the slaves most trusted and best used should be the most deeply involved." Higginson goes on to quote James McDowell, member of the Virginia House of Delegates, who remarked in the historic 1832 debates over emancipation and colonization that Southern paranoia was prompted by the "suspicion that a Nat Turner might be in every family; that the same bloody deed might be acted over at any time and in any place; that the materials for it were spread through the land, and were always ready for a like explosion."[13] . . .

Melville's most significant moment of invention in "Benito Cereno," the shaving scene, brings to a climax of terror the "juggling play" that Babo and Benito Cereno have been "acting out, both in word and deed," before him. The "play of the barber" compresses Delano's blind innocence, Cereno's spiritual fright, and Babo's extraordinary mastery of the scene's props and actors into a nightmare pantomime symbolic of the revenge of New World slaves upon their debilitated masters. The cuddy, with its "meagre crucifix" and "thumbed missal," its settees like an "inquisitor's rack" and its barbering chair that seems "some grotesque engine of torment," is a scene defined by symbols of Spain's violent Catholic history. Babo's use of the Spanish flag as a

[13]Seymour L. Gross and Eileen Bender, "History, Politics, and Literature: The Myth of Nat Turner," *American Quarterly*, 23, no. 4 (October 1971), 487–518; Delano, *Narrative of Voyages*, p. 550; Melville, "Benito Cereno," pp. 295, 299; John W. Blassingame, *The Slave Community: Plantation Life in the Antebellum South*, rev. ed. (New York: Oxford University Press, 1979), pp. 192–248; Thomas Wentworth Higginson, "Nat Turner's Insurrection," *Travellers and Outlaws: Episodes in American History* (Boston: Lee and Shepard, 1889), pp. 322–325; cf. Genovese, *From Rebellion to Revolution*, pp. 116–117, and Herbert Aptheker, *American Negro Slave Revolts* (New York: International Publishers, 1952), pp. 293–324.

barber's apron, which through his agitation unfolds "curtain-like" about his master, heightens Delano's playful affection for "the negro" and coordinates the personal and historical dramas of vengeance that are acted out—dramas that Delano, as he often does, unwittingly or unconsciously glimpses but fails fully to comprehend:

> Setting down his basin, the negro searched among the razors, as for the sharpest, and having found it, gave it an additional edge by expertly stropping it on the firm, smooth, oily skin of his open palm; he then made a gesture as if to begin, but midway stood suspended for an instant, one hand elevating the razor, the other professionally dabbling among the bubbling suds on the Spaniard's lank neck. Not unaffected by the close sight of the gleaming steel, Don Benito nervously shuddered; his usual ghastliness was heightened by the lather, which lather, again, was intensified in its hue by the contrasting sootiness of the negro's body. Altogether the scene was somewhat peculiar, at least to Captain Delano, nor, as he saw the two thus postured, could he resist the vagary, that in the black he saw a headsman, and in the white a man at the block. But this was one of those antic conceits, appearing and vanishing in a breath, from which, perhaps, the best regulated mind is not always free.

The conceit of decapitation—uniting Jacobin terror, the Inquisition, and slave vengeance—has here more actuality than the literal barbering that is taking place. It epitomizes Melville's masterful employment throughout the tale of metaphors whose submerged meaning momentarily exceeds in truth their literal contexts, only to be forced—repressed—once again beneath the conscious surface of Delano's mind and the story's narrative. The entire tale, most of all its revolutionary import, is similarly repressed by the legalistic documents and the executions of the slave rebels that codify Delano's putting down of the piratical revolt. Yet in that very act the fullest rebellious power, like the energy of the unconscious, is released in Melville's questioning of the moral authority of such documents and tribunals. . . .

Among the constellation of historical and contemporary issues Melville invoked in the drama of the *San Dominick*, present concern over the sporadic war between Haiti and the Dominican Republic is central for several reasons. From the mid-1840s on, claims had been made by Frederick Douglass and others that Haiti would be annexed to protect American (slave) interests. Now threats to the Dominican Republic—another Texas—seemed to offer a suitable excuse. The significance of the whole island was heightened by the simultaneous crisis over the Kansas-Nebraska Act and the "Africanization of Cuba," a purported plot by Spain and Britain to free slaves and put blacks in power. In retrospect, the fact that the South spent energy on the battle for Kansas that it might otherwise have directed toward Cuba, a territory of greater value to it, does not contradict the fact that at the time *both* seemed possible. Franklin Pierce's May 1854 interdiction against filibustering in Cuba was based on his reports that Cuba was too well protected and on the great Northern pressure brought to bear on him as a result of his conciliation of

Slave Power in signing the Kansas-Nebraska Act the day before. Cuba, in addition, would have been too much. If the South, in David Potter's words, "sacrificed the Cuban substance for the Kansas shadow," it did not do so intentionally. Besides, the fears of endless slave expansion that Theodore Parker voiced in "The Nebraska Question" were still echoed a year later in an essay on "The Kansas Question" appearing in the October 1855 issue of *Putnam's* in which *"Benito Cereno's"* serialization began. Kansas, the essay maintained, was still but the next step in the spread of slavery to Mexico, the Amazon, and eventually back to Africa. In the long run, the conjunction of Kansas and Cuba devastated both the Democratic Party and the idea of popular sovereignty; crushed the South's dream of a Caribbean empire; lost a territory destined to be of strategic importance to the United States in later years; rekindled fears about the spread of Haitian terror and counterbalancing proslavery plots against that republic; and at the same time sparked premonitions of the greater domestic convulsion to come. "The storm clouds of [war over] slavery were gathering so fast in the South," wrote John Bigelow to Charles Sumner after an 1854 visit to Haiti, "that writing letters about Hayti seemed like fiddling while the country was burning."[14]

Melville's tale circles continually around a plot against himself that Delano vaguely suspects Benito Cereno to be meditating, perhaps with the aid of Babo and the slaves. But Delano's own blindness and its psychological significance should not overshadow the secondary effects Melville surely counted on. Purported plots of slaves against their masters were outstripped at the time by fears of the two other "plots" we have touched on—that of the South to expand its power and that of Cuba to be Africanized. The supposed conspiracy of 1853 between Spain and Britain to end slavery and the slave trade in Cuba and promote armed black rule produced calls from Cuban and American slaveholders for American intervention. New Spanish policies liberalizing slave laws, combined with the seizure in February 1854 of the American steamer *Black Warrior* on a violation of port regulations, accelerated both legal and extralegal maneuvering to obtain Cuba before it became, as a State Department agent, Charles W. Davis, wrote in March 1854, another "Black Empire" like Haiti, "whose example they would be proud to imitate" in destroying the wealth of the island and launching "a disastrous bloody war of the races." The height of imperialistic rhetoric came after the crisis had passed and attempts to force a purchase of Cuba had failed, in the

[14]Dexter Perkins, *The Monroe Doctrine, 1826–1867* (Baltimore: Johns Hopkins University Press, 1933), pp. 253–317; Charles Callan Tansill, *The United States and Santo Domingo, 1798–1873: A Chapter in Caribbean Diplomacy* (Baltimore: Johns Hopkins University Press, 1938), pp. 137–212; Logan, *Diplomatic Relations,* pp. 238–292; Basil Rauch, *American Interest in Cuba, 1848–1855* (New York: Columbia University Press, 1948), pp. 280–294; David M. Potter, *The Impending Crisis, 1848–1861* (New York: Harper and Row, 1976), pp. 177–198, quote at p. 198; Robert E. May, *The Southern Dream of a Caribbean Empire, 1854–1861* (Baton Rouge: Louisiana State University Press, 1973), pp. 21–75; "The Kansas Question," *Putnam's Monthly,* 6 (October 1855), 425–433; John Bigelow, quoted in Logan, *Diplomatic Relations,* p. 281.

notorious Ostend Manifesto of October 1854, which declared that Cuba belonged "naturally to that great family of States of which the Union is the providential nursery" and that the United States would be justified "in wresting it from Spain . . . upon the very same principle that would justify an individual in tearing down the burning house of his neighbor if there were no other means of preventing the flames from destroying his own home." The issue of Cuba, that is to say, was couched in the familiar rhetoric that Lincoln would exploit, combining the domestic language of the revolutionary fathers and that of slaveholding paternalism. And it brought together just those threats Delano perceives aboard the *San Dominick*: Spanish misrule and deterioration, and threatened black insurrection and liberation.[15]

The South's—and the Pierce administration's—plan to "rescue" Cuba from black rule presupposed the decay of the Spanish empire and its replacement by an Anglo-Saxon empire in the western hemisphere. Peculiar to the South's version of manifest destiny, of course, was the extension of slavery and the shift of national power geographically to the south. This, perhaps, more than any single point of reference such as Haiti or Cuba, alerts us to the complex dimensions of the actions dramatized in "Benito Cereno." The Southern dream of a Caribbean empire reached its most extreme formulations in somewhat later documents such as Henry Timrod's "Ethnogenesis," William Walker's *The War in Nicaragua*, and Edward Pollard's *Black Diamonds Gathered in the Darkey Homes of the South*, published in 1861, 1860, and 1859, respectively, but based on sentiments common throughout the decade. Pollard, for example, claimed southern expansion was not a sectional issue but one involving "the world's progress, and who shall be the founders of its greatest empire of industry." Eventually, he maintained, the seat of the Southern Empire would be in Central America; control of the West Indies, the isthmuses of Central America, and the production of the world's cotton and sugar would complete America's destiny:

> What a splendid vision of empire! How sublime in its associations! How noble and inspiriting the idea, that upon the strange theater of tropical America, once, if we may believe the dimmer facts of history, crowned with magnificent empires and flashing cities and great temples, now covered with mute ruins, and trampled over by half-savages, the destiny of Southern civilization is to be consummated in a glory brighter even than that of old, the glory of an empire, controlling the commerce of the world, impregnable in its position, and representing in its internal structure the most harmonious of all systems of modern civilization.

Walker, too, in one chapter of the account of his filibustering career in Sonora and Nicaragua, celebrated the destined rejuvenation of Central and South

15Rauch, *American Interest in Cuba*, pp. 275–277; Philip S. Foner, *A History of Cuba and Its Relations with the United States*, 2 vols. (New York: International, 1963), II, 75–85; Charles W. Davis quoted in Foner, II, 81–82; "Ostend Manifesto," *Documents of American History*, 2 vols. in 1, ed. Henry Steele Commager (New York: F. S. Croft, 1934), I, 333–335.

America. The effort the South wasted on the "shadow" of Kansas, Walker wrote, could have brought her the "substance" of Central America, a territory necessary to protect slavery, to raise the African from darkness and teach him the "arts of life," and to forestall the spread of degeneracy that has occurred in Haiti and Jamaica.[16]

Walker among others adopted in his rhetoric a new ideology of progress that paternalized the remnants of Spain's American empire. He believed too that popular sovereignty could be applied as effectively to the Caribbean and Central America as to Kansas, and that expansion was necessary to complete the republican defeat of dying European monarchism. (So extreme did this idea become in the early 1850s that at one point Louis Kossuth, the enthusiastically courted hero of the 1848 Hungarian revolution, became embroiled in a southern plot to invade Haiti on the pretext that Soulouque was a czarist agent.) "Empire" became a common word in discourse about the region—not only among such slave interests as the Knights of the Golden Circle, which promoted a Gulf circle of power drawing together New Orleans, Havana, Yucatan, and Central America, but remarkably also among black American colonizationists such as J. Dennis Harris, who proposed to build an "Anglo-African Empire" in Haiti, a mulatto utopia, and James T. Holly, who imagined a similar regeneration originating in Haiti, "the Eden of America," and overspreading the whole world.[17]

Although such visions counted for little against the South's need to stabilize its economic and political power, they accentuate from a different angle the paradisial dream that the Americas continued to represent. California gold, the dream's great symbol in this period, would soon so enrich the nation, claimed *De Bow's Review* in 1854, that no possible investment would be equal to it but the cultivation of the entire western hemisphere. Lying between two of the great valleys of the world, the Mississippi and the Amazon, the Gulf would link the most productive regions of the earth, and by unlocking trading access to the wealth of the Pacific Basin (China, Australia, California) make the Atlantic in the modern world what the Mediterranean was "under the reign of the Antonies in Rome." Given the continued dissolution of European

[16]A. Curtis Wilgus, "Official Expression of Manifest Destiny Sentiment Concerning Hispanic America, 1848–1871," *Louisiana Historical Quarterly*, 15, no. 3 (July 1932), 486–506; Edward A. Pollard, *Black Diamonds Gathered in the Darkey Homes of the South* (New York: Pudney and Russell, 1859), pp. 106–115; William Walker, *The War in Nicaragua* (Mobile: S. H. Goetzel, 1860), pp. 251–280.

[17]C. Stanley Urban, "The Ideology of Southern Imperialism: New Orleans and the Caribbean, 1845–1860," *Louisiana Historical Quarterly*, 39, no. 1 (January 1956), 48–73; Donald S. Spencer, *Louis Kossuth and Young America: A Study of Sectionalism and Foreign Policy, 1848–1852* (Columbia: University of Missouri Press, 1977), pp. 166–169; May, *Southern Dream*, pp. 148–150; Mannix and Cowley, *Black Cargoes*, pp. 266–274; J. Dennis Harris, "A Summer on the Borders of the Caribbean Sea," (1860) in Howard H. Bell, *Black Separatism and the Caribbean, 1860* (Ann Arbor: University of Michigan Press, 1970), p. 172; James T. Holly, "A Vindication of the Capacity of the Negro Race Demonstrated by Historical Events of the Haytian Revolution," in Bell, *Black Separatism*, p. 64.

political power and possession of Cuba, Santo Domingo, and Haiti, the United States might control the Gulf and through it the world: "Guided by our genius and enterprise, a new world would rise there, as it did before under the genius of Columbus." This new Columbian vision had a price, however, one which the circular argument of the writer for *De Bow's* did little to hide:

> Heretofore, the great difficulty in civilizing the barbarian races of the world has been to procure cheap and abundant clothing for them. A naked race must necessarily be a wild one. To Christianize or civilize a man, you must first clothe his nakedness. In the three millions of bags of cotton the slave labor annually throws upon the world for the poor and the naked, we are doing more to advance civilization and the refinement of life than all the canting philanthropists of New and Old England will do in centuries.

As the author noted, "slavery and war have [always] been the two great forerunners of civilization."[18]

Of course the utopian schemes of the South now seem precisely that; but as the possibilities of renewed Caribbean revolution and civil conflict in the United States unfolded in the 1850s, they too served to focus with critical symbolic significance the historical and contemporary role of San Domingo in the question of slavery. Lincoln's diplomatic recognition of Haiti in 1862 ensured the island's harassment of Confederate privateers, and black rule was hardly an issue between the two governments once the South seceded; moreover, the Caribbean and Latin America ceased for the time being to be of pressing national interest once the issue of slavery was resolved and a transcontinental railroad completed later in the decade.[19] The disappearance from view of the region until conflicts fifty and a hundred years later brought it back into the public mind has contributed to the general disregard of its critical role in "Benito Cereno." Still, there can be little doubt as to Melville's richness of allusion and dramatic enactment, his masterful exploitation of the revolutionary spirit locked in the heart of the American New World, in this most troubled and explosive tale of America's antebellum destiny.[20]

[18]"Destiny of the Slave States," *De Bow's Review*, 17, no. 3 (September 1854), 280–284; cf. Eugene Genovese, *The Political Economy of Slavery: Studies in the Economy and Society of the Slave South* (New York: Vintage Books, Random House, 1967), pp. 243–274.

[19]Logan, *Diplomatic Relations*, pp. 293–314; Montague, *Haiti and the United States*, pp. 85–88.

[20]A revised and expanded version of this essay appears in Eric J. Sundquist, *To Wake the Nations: Race in the Making of American Literature* (Cambridge, MA: Harvard University Press, 1993).

Melville's Geography
of Gender

Robyn Wiegman

Perhaps more than any other writer, Herman Melville has been perceived as *the* American master of male bonding narratives, a writer obsessively devoted to sentimental renderings of life among men. But while his work often features a male couple or fraternity, Melville's depiction of the bond cannot be read as simple affirmation, especially his exploration of 1855, "The Paradise of Bachelors and the Tartarus of Maids." Here, in a paradigmatic rendering of the ideological structures of gender, class, and race underlying the male bond, Melville is far more skeptical than in his earlier works where, for instance, Ishmael and Queequeg sleep "in our hearts' honeymoon . . . a cosy, loving pair" (*Moby-Dick* 54). In its structure and theme, this two-sided tale demonstrates a broader pattern of representation in American culture in which the mythology of the male bond serves to reiterate America's cultural rhetoric of "raceless, classless possibility" (Baker 65). Most importantly, Melville's critique of the ideological structures fashioning the fraternity occupies an exemplary moment in nineteenth-century American cultural production, foregrounding the tensions of a social order increasingly fond of portraying itself as the standard of democracy for the world.

This standard is contingent, as the classic representational scene of the male bond affirms, on the diffusion of cultural hierarchies of difference *among men*, a diffusion often achieved by casting the bond in seemingly uncivilized realms where the oppressive systems of culture can be suspended. For this reason, the bond is frequently envisioned as culturally innocent, beyond the reaches of civilization, on ships, in forests, on deserted islands, across long empty prairies—all those places Huck was seeking when he lit out with Jim for the territory. But no matter how far the fraternity goes, it cannot escape, because it is ideologically dependent upon, the hierarchical structure underlying all patriarchal relations: sexual difference. As the most stable feature of the male bond, gender—either the image of woman or the evocation of the feminine space of otherness—gives the bond its cultural power, providing a

From *American Literary History*, 1 (4): 735–753, 1989. Copyright © 1989, Oxford University Press and reprinted with permission.

seemingly natural, essential difference against which the masculine can define itself. In diffusing the bond's internal hierarchies of race, class, and sexuality, gender articulates not only power relations between men and women, but also those among men, establishing the masculine as internally cohesive, as itself without difference.

Such a cultural homogenization of differences among men is brought into ironic relief in "The Paradise of Bachelors and the Tartarus of Maids" where the idyllic world of men together—appropriately called Paradise—is depicted in its seeming disconnection to the industrial nightmare of Tartarus, the frozen landscape of dominated and doomed women. Through the confluence between these segregated spheres, the diptych quite stunningly reveals how the rhetoric of the male bond is forged across a discourse of sexual difference that functions to veil class and race hierarchies among men. . . . By using the diptych to analyze how differences are constructed, maintained, and disguised, we can begin to reconsider both Melville's canon and the literary/critical tradition defined by such fraternities, not to claim their disruption of patriarchal power, or simply to cite their complicity with it, but to understand how the male bond functions as both a product and a process of nineteenth-century American culture.

Melville exposes the bond's reiteration of a privileged masculine perspective in "The Paradise of Bachelors and the Tartarus of Maids," creating, as he often does, an unreliable narrator, one whose attraction to the repressed homosexuality of the bachelor world ensures his complicity in the structures of difference governing Paradise. While Richard Fogle describes Paradise as "the highest art" (46), Melville's manipulation of the narrative voice reveals the bachelors' intellectual and moral bankruptcy, preventing any simple equation of the narrator's perspective with Melville's own. By exploring the seemingly separate Tartarian world of female sacrifice and re/production that underlies the male bond, Melville critiques the structure of Paradise: its predication on a masculine point of view that veils its hierarchical and exclusionary nature through the myth of the democratic equality of the male bond. Only in considering the narrator's capitulation to this mythos can the difficulties in decoding the diptych be resolved, for it is the romance of men without women that most clearly prevents the narrator from deciphering the ideology of his own discourse.

In particular, the narrator cannot interpret the implications of his own description of Paradise and Tartarus as "counterpart[s]" (214). While they are indeed counters to one another—on one side exists the masculine, symbolized by the repressed homosexuality of Paradise, and on the other is the feminine, marked by the nightmare geography of compulsory heterosexuality—they fail to reflect their opposites equally; instead they duplicate the asymmetrical representational economy of gender in which woman's difference is articulated by and subsumed into the masculine. In its structural replication of the binary system of gender, Melville's diptych thus reveals the very problem of gender itself: that all difference in this system designates the space of "origin"—the masculine—which represents woman only as a mirror for the phallus, as the reflection of masculine wholeness. For Luce Irigaray, this homogeneity of gender, the "hom(m)osexual," underwrites patriarchal culture: "The exchanges upon which patriarchal societies are based take place exclusively among men. Women, signs, commodities, and currency always pass from one man to another. . . . Thus all economic organization is hom-(m)osexual. That of desire as well, even the desire for women. Woman exists only as an occasion for mediation, transaction, transition, transference, be-tween man and his fellow man, indeed between man and himself" (192–93).

While Irigaray sees points of collapse between an organizational hom(m)o-sexuality and genital desire given the same name, the structure she describes goes beyond any simple account of sexual activity by characterizing the representational economy as one that simultaneously posits woman's differ-ence and recuperates that difference as signifier of itself. Contrary to appear-ance, then, compulsory heterosexuality is not the articulation of a *heteros* economy but the foundation of a homogenized masculine economy. Thus the diptych's sexual organization—metaphoric homosexuality in Paradise and mechanized heterosexuality in Tartarus—evokes the asymmetry of gender, for all desire reverts to the masculine vocabulary itself. As Jane Gallop says, "[t]here is no real sexuality of the *heteros*," for "a woman in a heterosexual encounter will not be able to represent her difference" (66, 74).

The diptych's discursive method of equating homosexuality with the mas-culine and compulsory heterosexuality with the feminine is foregrounded through the metaphors of sexual intercourse that open each section. H. Bruce Franklin has noted that Paradise is found via the symbolic landscape of the male homosexual act: "Going to it, by the usual way, is like stealing from a heated plain into some cool, deep glen, shady among harboring hills" (202). The deep glen, a symbolic anus, is found beyond the din and soil of Fleet Street where the Benedick tradesmen "with ledgerlines ruled along their brows, thinking upon rise of bread and fall of babies," are ruled by monogamous heterosexuality. To transcend both the monogamous and the heterosexual, one must "adroitly turn a mystic corner—not a street—glide down a dim, monastic way, flanked by dark, sedate, and solemn piles, and still wending on, give the whole care-worn world the slip, and, disentangled, stand beneath the quiet cloisters of the Paradise of Bachelors" (202). As the symbolic language of the male homosexual act, the narrator's description establishes desire for the masculine as the preeminent rule of Paradise—as he tells us, the bachelors "had no wives or children to give an anxious thought" (209). In opposing the homoeroticism of Paradise to monogamous heterosexu-ality, the diptych quickly establishes a fundamental distinction of the male bond: cast as scene of masculine freedom, it exists outside of society, apart from women and children, those who can most threaten the solidarity of male companionship. Defined in such a way, the bond is culturally innocent, a "natural" formation, not a gendered structure crucial to cultural constructions of difference.

In repressing his awareness of the symbolic contours of Paradise, the narrator concentrates on the various pleasures offered by this "charming, most delectable" place (202), pleasures that contradict the democratic ethos of the male bond by clarifying how it is predicated on a class hierarchy. Specifically, the narrator is drawn to the spectacle of commodification and consumption that signifies the bachelor world. As he tells us, "nothing do you know . . . till you dine among the banded Bachelors, and see their convivial eyes and glasses sparkle. Not dine in bustling commons . . . but tranquilly, by private hint, at a private table; some fine Templar's hospitably invited guest" (203). While the narrator is momentarily aware of the bachelors' consumption as a "moral blight"—"the worm of luxury crawled beneath their guard . . . and the sworn knights-bachelors grew to be but hypocrites and rakes"—he still asserts that "the Templar's fall has but made him all the finer fellow" (203, 204). This reconstruction of the scene from one of degeneracy to superiority is necessary to the full functioning of the male bond, for it allows the narrator to displace his own momentary critique of Paradise's hedonistic obsessions.

The narrator's partnership in the bachelors' corruption, his repression of the sources of their leisure and subsequent absorption of their class values, is depicted best in his (mis)perception of the waiter, whom he ironically names Socrates: "All these manoeuvrings of the forces were superintended by a surprising old field-marshal (I can not school myself to call him by the inglorious name of waiter), with snowy hair and napkin, and a head like Socrates. Amidst all the hilarity of the feast, intent on important business, he disdained to smile. Venerable man!" (207). While the narrator wants to read the waiter's demeanor simply as a refusal to participate in the "hilarity" of the dinner, it is "Socrates' " exclusion from the paradisiacal male bond that renders him silent; existing only insofar as he tends to their appetites, his real name, like the class structure underlying Paradise, is forever repressed. When the narrator writes, "I am quite sure, from the scrupulous gravity and austerity of his air, that had Socrates, the field-marshal, perceived aught of indecorum in the company he served, he would have forthwith departed without giving warning" (208), he portrays his misunderstanding of "Socrates' " loyalty and the economic necessity governing the waiter's servitude. "What the narrator mistakes for Socrates' decorum," Ray Browne writes, "is actually disgust" (223).

As the representative of the invisible servant class that upholds the bachelor Paradise, Socrates, recalling Plato's Symposium, also undermines the narrator's view of the intellectual atmosphere of the gathering. This silent philosopher represents a tradition of inquiry absent from the "Senate of the Bachelors"; their conversation results only in emotional and philosophical sterility: "Pain! Trouble! As well talk of Catholic miracles. No such thing.— Pass the sherry, sir.—Pooh, pooh! Can't be!—The port, sir, if you please.

Nonsense; don't tell me so.—The decanter stops with you, sir, I believe" (209). This world replicates the tradition of the Symposium but without its philosophical debate; the key intellectual figure is now reduced to silence and subservience. While Marvin Fisher rightly sees that "Socrates . . . asks no irritating questions, leads men to no unseen truths," he misreads the class implications of Melville's critique by contending that this ironic philosopher "helps them to lose themselves, rather than know themselves, by supplying an endless array of bottles" (75). The agency of the bachelors' corruption cannot be displaced onto the servant class, for, as Carolyn Karcher has noted, Paradise's existence is based on the labor of this anonymous populace (124). In describing Paradise as "the very perfection of quiet absorption of good living, good drinking, good feeling, and good talk. We were a band of brothers" (209), the narrator invokes the mythology of the male bond, repressing the hierarchical systems constructing such democratic fraternities.

Not only does Melville undercut the narrator's idealization of the bachelor world by exposing its reliance on class, but he also isolates race as a hierarchical structure underwriting the male bond. The narrator's description of the "cloisters" of Paradise symbolically connects it with the American system of slavery by invoking southern gentility: "Dear, delightful spot! Ah! when I bethink me of the sweet hours there passed, enjoying such genial hospitalities beneath those time-honored roofs, my heart only finds due utterance through poetry; and, with a sigh, I softly sing, 'Carry me back to old Virginny!' " (205). Evoking the "southern plantation idyll, with its images of carefree hosts, hospitable mansions, and convivial gatherings" (Karcher 122), the narrator's description links Paradise with "old Virginny" and America's Peculiar Institution. In this way, the diptych captures the ideological compatibility of the class and slave systems, their necessity in maintaining the privileged realm of the bachelor paradise. By presenting race and class hierarchies as repressed aspects of the male bond, Melville shows the exclusionary cultural ideology that underlies the bond's existence as a celebrated construction. Thus absorbed in the superficial brotherhood of the bachelor world, Melville's narrator is blind to its affirmation and replication of cultural hierarchies.

For the narrator, the height of the bachelors' brotherhood is expressed in the ritualistic consumption of the Jericho horn, which serves as the instrument for the bachelors' sexual rite, their "consummation" of brotherly conviviality. Passing it around the table, each man inserts "his thumb and forefinger into its mouth," thereby taking snuff, the symbolic aromatic sperm to the "noble main horn" (209). The narrator responds to this ritual with delight— "Capital idea this, thought I" (209)—and as the evening begins to break up, he admits, "I was the last lingerer" (210). While the overtly phallic and sexual connotations of this ritual are unacknowledged by the narrator, they clearly develop the homosexual metaphor that fashions the first half of the diptych, demonstrating the particular confluences at this moment in cultural production between the homosexual and that broader structure Eve Kosofsky Sedgwick calls "homosocial," that is, "social bonds between persons of the same sex" (1); as she explains, "in any male-dominated society, there is a special relationship between male homosocial (*including* homosexual) desires and the structures for maintaining and transmitting patriarchal power: a relationship founded on an inherent and potentially active structural congruence" (25). According to Sedgwick, this active congruence is disrupted in Anglo-American culture in the late nineteenth century with the medical/ psychological designation of "homosexuality" as a discrete sexual practice, a designation whose consequences are not only widespread homophobia but, later in the twentieth century, the articulation of a politicized homosexual identity.

Such historicizing of sexualities is important in considering Melville's diptych where the cultural distinctions we now make between homosexuality and other kinds of male bonds are not as discontinuous. In this sense, [Robert K.] Martin's reading of the bachelors' phallic ritual as transforming homosexual love "into homosocial 'fraternity' with its implicit misogyny" (105) misses the way in which Melville's metaphoric use of the male body links, structurally, both the homosexual and the homosocial as manifestations of the (same) masculine position by emphasizing a patriarchal obsession with "the seen"— that which visibly marks difference. In the paradisiacal male bond, equality within this space, regardless of its metaphoric sexuality, is achieved through the adulation of the male body where the phallus is the supreme signifier not only of the circuit of the male bond but also of the representational economy itself. It is precisely the exclusion of women, their metaphoric "lack," that establishes the necessary space for constructing these masculine relations, for the female articulates, as Irigaray says, "[t]he negative, the underside, the reverse of the only visible and morphologically designatable sex organ . . . the penis" (26). In this economy of the visible, all masculine desire is not simply equalized but universalized. For this reason, Irigaray contends that "hom(m)o-sexuality" regulates the sociocultural order (192–93).

While Irigaray's reading of patriarchal relations is fundamental to a structuralist paradigm of woman's theoretical absence in representational systems, this model is itself constructed at the expense of any notion of historical change, thereby replicating the very way in which the discourse of sexual difference works historically to mask differences within homosocial bonds— that is, class, race, and sexuality as sites of contestation among men. By positing a monolithic masculine economy, Irigaray reproduces the mystification at the heart of the patriarchal system where, through the discourse of sexual difference—a discourse contingent on the economy of the visible— relations between men can be portrayed as stable, as themselves not dependent on difference. For this reason, Sedgwick's work is an important intervention in feminist analyses of patriarchal relations, for she isolates how, for instance, in the nineteenth century, "the emerging pattern of male friendship, mentorship, entitlement, rivalry, and hetero- and homosexuality was in an intimate and shifting relation to class; and . . . [how] no element of that pattern can be understood outside of its relation to women and the gender system as a whole" (1). This connection between gender and other constructions of difference is central to Melville's critique of Tartarus where, through the representation of woman's lack, the narrator can recreate the mythology of the male bond as the locus both for masculine wholeness and democratic possibility itself.

Given the narrator's absorption in the pleasures of the all-male Paradise, it seems inevitable that when he turns to Tartarus he encounters the landscape of a grotesque female body, one that elicits in him castration fear. Moving from "bright farms" to "bleak hills" (210), the narrator penetrates—in the masculine imaginary of heterosexual intercourse—a "Dantean gateway" (211), a dark hellish entrance into the vagina. His metaphoric contact with the female body makes him imagine the past phallic power of his surroundings, those "primitive times when vast pines and hemlocks superabounded throughout the neighboring region," but now, "[b]rittle with excessive frost, many colossal tough-grained maples, snapped in twain like pipe-stems, cumbered the unfeeling earth" (212). His stark description of the alabaster world of female labor, the flip side of the Edenic bachelor temple, defines the female body as both castrated and castrating; her body is responsible for the symbolic death associated with masculine entry into the heterosexual, a death that can only be overcome, as the diptych demonstrates, through the reconstitution of the male bond.

Revealing himself to be a seedsman who has planted "through all the Eastern and Northern States" (211), the narrator is the symbolic semen in this grim, castrating female landscape. Significantly, his first words in Tartarus are a metaphoric penetration: "is there no shed hereabouts which I may drive into?" (214). In this heterosexual economy, women, like sheds, function as sheaths for the phallus, the colonized space of masculine desire. As the narrator's description of the women's role in the factory process demonstrates, the heterosexual evokes the asymmetry of the gender system, becoming—like woman—signifier of the masculine itself: "In one corner stood some huge frame of ponderous iron, with a vertical thing like a piston periodically rising and falling. . . . Before it—its tame minister—stood a tall girl, feeding the iron animal with half-quires of rose-hued note-paper which, at every downward dab of the piston-like machine, received in the corner the impress of a wreath of roses" (215). In their subservience to the "piston-like machine," the women bear the stamp of the phallus, the wreath of roses—classic image of romance linked now with death—connecting the heterosexual with the loss of life and self. Without their own master signifier, women can only enter the representational system through a process that first affirms their castration and then forces them to wear the mark of it by becoming symbols of the phallus itself. In Tartarus, the women's very blankness is symptomatic of their inability to be represented except as or by the phallic, making them the tame ministers to the expansion of a masculine economy.

The homogeneity of the heterosexual economy is enacted not only through the representational erasure of the factory women, but also by the narrative of the paper-making process. Requiring only a miraculous nine minutes, the paper is made through a symbolic replication of human gestation, prompting Michael Paul Rogin to see the mechanization as "monstrous, sexual, maternal" (204). But, as Cupid shows the narrator, the paper begins not in the female rag room but in the symbolic male body, "two great round vats . . . full of a white, wet, whoolly-looking stuff" (218). It pours "from both vats into that one common channel yonder, and so goes, mixed up and leisurely, to the great machine," a colossal structure housed in a room "stifling with a strange, blood-like, abdominal heat" (218). The sexual geography of this description reenacts the heterosexual from the masculine point of view, revealing the heterosexual as a structure that the male bond both creates and promotes. While the female body is essential to such a production, any power women might yield over their reproductive processes is subsumed by the masculine, by the primacy of his seminal contribution. At the end of the process, when the paper drops from the machine "as of some cord being snapped" (220), the mechanical reproduction of the heterosexual as a replication of the asymmetry of gender is complete: the male creates, the female, as the sheath for the phallus, incubates. The two halves of Melville's diptych thus exist as gendered evocations of the same economy; what initially appear as separate male and female worlds are in fact the product of a homogenizing masculine point of view, one that constructs democracy and equality only in the privileged space of a masculine paradise.

The narrator's commentary on this description of the paper-making process marks Tartarus as compulsory re/production. Struck "by the inevitability . . . in all its motions," the narrator wonders, "Does [the machine] never stop—get clogged?" Cupid assures him that "It *must* go" (221). Locked in the biological "necessity" of the heterosexual body, the spermatic "pulp can't help going" (221). This "metallic necessity, the unbudging fatality" of the machine, awes the narrator, making "the thing I saw so specially terrible" (221). As the representation of the heterosexual, the machine takes over female selfhood in its unbudging fatality, the numbing necessity of the masculine economy reproducing itself by colonizing woman's difference. This is not, then, as Wilma Garcia contends, a "parody of fertility experienced by women torn from the domestic environment and nurturing instincts natural to their sex" (68), for the implicit critique of this world is based on the women's subservience to the re/production of the heterosexual economy, an economy Melville sees as violently exploitative in its commodification of women's labor. To view the factory women's virginity as the epitome of their oppression, as Garcia suggests, reinscribes the heterosexual imperative and displaces the complementary relationship between the homosociality of Paradise and the compulsory heterosexuality of Tartarus.

When "something latent, as well as something obvious" recalls the Temple Bar, the narrator makes his only commentary on his narrative form: "Though the two objects did by no means completely correspond, yet this partial inadequacy but served to tinge the similitude not less with the vividness than the disorder of a dream" (213). Instead of evoking the similarity in the hierarchical arrangements both within and between Paradise and Tartarus, the narrator misinterprets his discursive design: "the marvelous retirement of this mysterious mountain nook fastened its whole spell upon me . . . and I said to myself, 'This is the very counterpart of the Paradise of Bachelors, but snowed upon, and frost-painted to a sepulchre' " (214). Tartarus is indeed a tomb, but one created by the cultural heterosexual imperative that, sending women to their literal and symbolic deaths, is the counterpart of the homosociality of Paradise. In this way patriarchal culture claims the female body as its product, while its real desires are directed toward itself. In reifying the patriarchal origins of the women's role in Tartarus, the narrator's discourse replicates the ideological mystification necessary for reproducing patriarchal culture.

Significantly, it is through the male bond that the narrator can negotiate Tartarus without fully recognizing its cultural implications, even though, in contrast to his decidedly obtuse passage through Paradise, he has moments of connection. As he says early on, "Machinery—that vaunted slave of humanity—here stood menially served by human beings. . . . The girls did not so much seem accessory wheels to the general machinery as mere cogs to the wheels" (215–16). But in his initial confrontation with a mill girl, whose face is so shockingly "pale with work, and blue with cold," he seeks refuge in the social intercourse he knows best: "is there no man about?" (214), he asks. Rescued for the first of three times by one of the two men in the factory world, the narrator maintains his naive masculine point of view, a critical perspective that cannot account for the "strange emotion" that overtakes him in Tartarus. While he notices the women's "agony dimly outlined on the imperfect paper," his awareness is short-lived, for Cupid, "with the protecting air of a careful father" (221), rushes him outside. This male-aided escape allows the narrator to reconstruct the scene so that he can tell Old Bach, foreman and significantly the "principal proprietor," that "Yours is a most wonderful factory. Your great machine is a miracle of inscrutable intricacy" (222).

Where class distinctions might pose a separation or distance between the men in Tartarus, the visibility of the factory women's difference mediates between them, healing their own potential differences and establishing the necessary norm from which a seemingly homogenized masculine can continue to construct itself. Through his capitulation to the rhetoric of the bond, the narrator smooths over potential disruptions caused by class differences between the men and himself. As Sedgwick writes, "in the presence of a woman who can be seen as pitiable or contemptible, men are able to exchange power and to confirm each other's value even in the context of the remaining inequalities in their power" (160). As Melville's diptych reveals, hierarchical structures are necessary to the perpetuation of the male bond; articulated from a privileged masculine point of view, the bond functions to recuperate social tensions among men. Bonding with Cupid and Old Bach—the only bonding to take place in Tartarus—guarantees the narrator's denial of the hierarchical structures implicit in Paradise and Tartarus and enables him to lend his economic approval to female oppression by purchasing the symbolic children of their labors, the envelopes.

The purchase of these envelopes—to be "stamped, and superscribed with the nature of the seeds contained" (211–12)—presents the products of the "heterosexual" economy as ones specifically owned and circulated by men. This means the narrator can claim the production, and reproduction, of the female body as his own, for within such a circuit, woman's labors are exchanged as commodities, the production of her body bereft of value unless superscribed by the masculine. The commodification of her labor thus defines her body as his territory, the ground for his insemination and consumption. Looking at the piles of paper "dropping, dropping, dropping" from the machine, the narrator thinks of how "[a]ll sorts of writings would be writ on those now vacant things—sermons, lawyers' briefs, physicians' prescriptions, love-letters, marriage certificates, bills of divorce, registers of births, death-warrants, and so on, without end" (220). Indeed, all social discourse will be written on the blank pages of female labor. In this way, the structure of the male bond articulates a system of exchange through the heterosexual imperative that paradoxically reinforces a hom(m)osexual economy while repressing its reliance on both the biological and economic reproduction of the female body. Women's exclusion from its privileged space is therefore both the mark of the gender system and its excess—an excess that can only be contained by repression or expulsion.

While women's exclusion operates as the bond's basic ideological assumption, Melville's diptych is particularly important in capturing the changing patriarchal economy of the nineteenth century, its transformation of women's labor from compulsory reproduction to factory production. By constituting women's difference as a class oppression, the full range of women's labor could be tied to an economic system in which their bodies served as commodities in a circuit of exchange defined by men. The major trope of the patriarchal family—the colonization of women's reproduction in the name of the Father—is enacted in the factory, through the large-scale production of commodities; women's labor thus becomes not only the essential though invisible support of the family, but the underlying assumption of the economy as well. In articulating the connection between reproduction and production, Melville's depiction of the changing configuration of gender at mid-century isolates a broader pattern in American culture, one that had begun in the first moments of industrialization, and one whose legacy remains with us today. . . .

In exposing the rehabilitative force of the mythology of the male bond, Melville's story importantly reveals the complicity among categories of gender, race, class, and sexuality that shape social relations in nineteenth-century American culture. But most crucially, his text directs us beyond the standard account of patriarchy as coterminous with sexual difference and toward an understanding of its organizational structure as deeply reliant on the intersection among various hierarchical formations. These intersections result in complex configurations that vary not only across time but within specific historical contexts, demonstrating the extent to which cultural power is neither monolithically produced nor monolithically maintained. In its evocation of these premises, the mythology of the male bond works to dehistoricize the cultural terrain, eclipsing the distance between democratic rhetoric and specific configurations of difference. One of the stunning achievements of American patriarchal organization is its use of the gendered ideology of the male bond to negotiate differences among men—the mythos of men together providing an efficient point of access for creating and maintaining patriarchal power.

Works Cited

Baker, Houston, Jr. *Blues, Ideology, and Afro-American Literature: A Vernacular Theory.* Chicago: U of Chicago P, 1984.

Browne, Ray B. *Melville's Drive to Humanism.* Lafayette, IN: Purdue U Studies, 1971.

Fisher, Marvin. *Going Under: Melville's Short Fiction and the American 1850s.* Baton Rouge: Louisiana State UP, 1977.

Fogle, Richard. *Melville's Shorter Tales.* Norman: U of Oklahoma P, 1960.

Franklin, H. Bruce. *The Victim as Criminal and Artist: Literature from the American Prison.* New York: Oxford UP, 1978.

Gallop, Jane. *The Daughter's Seduction: Feminism and Psychoanalysis.* Ithaca: Cornell UP, 1982.

Garcia, Wilma. *Mothers and Others: Myths of the Female in the Works of Melville, Twain, and Hemingway.* New York: Peter Lang, 1984.

Irigaray, Luce. *This Sex Which Is Not One.* 1977. Trans. Catherine Porter with Carolyn Burke. Ithaca: Cornell UP, 1985.

Karcher, Carolyn. *Shadow Over the Promised Land: Slavery, Race, and Violence in Melville's America.* Baton Rouge: Louisiana State UP, 1980.

Martin, Robert K. *Hero, Captain, and Stranger: Male Friendship, Social Critique, and Literary Form in the Sea Novels of Herman Melville.* Chapel Hill: U of North Carolina P, 1986.

Melville, Herman. *Moby-Dick.* 1850. New York: Norton, 1967.

———. "The Paradise of Bachelors and the Tartarus of Maids." *Great Short Works of Herman Melville.* Ed. Warner Berthoff. New York: Harper, 1966.

Rogin, Michael Paul. *Subversive Genealogy: The Politics and Art of Herman Melville.*
    New York: Knopf, 1983.
Sedgwick, Eve Kosofsky. *Between Men: English Literature and Male Homosocial
    Desire.* New York: Columbia UP, 1985.

Revolutionary Fathers
and Confidence Men

Michael Paul Rogin

[In *The Confidence-Man*, Melville] imagined, for the first and last time, a world without the mythic fathers. The *Fidèle* was no oceangoing whaler, pirate ship, or man-of-war. It was a riverboat steamer, exclusively under the sway of the marketplace masquerade. *Israel Potter* exhausted the heritage of Melville's revolutionary grandfathers. *The Confidence-Man* turned to the business world of his father. Because there were no sacred fathers on the *Fidèle*, Melville was free to examine the real sources of his father's demise. His medium, the masquerade, was his message.

An "Anacharsis Cloots Congress" gathers on the steamship *Fidèle* in St. Louis, to travel down the Mississippi. "Here reigned the dashing and all-fusing spirit of the West, whose type is the Mississippi itself, which, uniting the streams of the most distant and opposite zones, pours them along, helter-skelter, in one cosmopolitan and confident tide." The crew of the *Pequod* also comprised an Anacharsis Cloots deputation. In *Israel Potter* "the Western spirit is, or will yet be . . . the true American one." (195) The democratic, Western mixture of peoples promised to free Gansevoort and Herman Melville from the sepulcher of their father. It offered them, through the appropriation of savage power, a regeneration through violence. Anacharsis Cloots and the Western spirit have turned inside out on the *Fidèle*. The democratic West of *The Confidence-Man* has "exterminated . . . the hunted generations of wolves . . . ; which would seem cause for unalloyed gratulation, and is such to all except those who think that in new countries, where the wolves are killed off, the foxes increase."[1]

Foxes are the hunters who appear when the West is cleared of wolves. They are everywhere on the *Fidèle*. "Farm-hunters and fame-hunters; heiress-hunters, gold-hunters, buffalo-hunters, bee-hunters, happiness-hunters, truth-hunters, and still keener hunters after all these hunters" comprise

From *Subversive Genealogy: The Politics and Art of Herman Melville* by Michael Paul Rogin. Copyright © 1979, 1980, 1983 by Michael Paul Rogin. Reprinted by permission of Alfred A. Knopf, Inc.

[1]Herman Melville, *The Confidence-Man* (New York, 1964 [1857]), pp. 10, 15. Subsequent page numbers in the text refer to this edition.

the passenger list on the Mississippi riverboat. (*The Confidence-Man*, 15) The *Fidèle*'s Western spirit is the spirit of the main chance. The overthrow of the fathers has liberated from its "civilized externals" not the "savage at heart"[2] who strikes through the mask, but the masquerading confidence man.

The *Confidence-Man* undercuts not only Western savagery but also Christian regeneration. Redburn and White-Jacket's American nature redeemed the Hebraic father's law with New Testament love. Melville had always attacked philanthropists, who dispensed charity in the name of Jesus. Beginning with *Pierre* he launched an attack on charity, itself. Pierre promised Isabel the charity that his mother and her minister refused Delly Unser, but his love was as contaminated as their coldness. The Wall Street lawyer offered "charity" to Bartleby as a substitute for human commitment. A plea for charity introduces the confidence man.

On April Fool's Day, a deaf-mute dressed in cream colors appears on board the *Fidèle*. "He had neither trunk, valise, carpet-bag, nor parcel . . . no badge of authority about him, but something quite the contrary." (9–10) The deaf-mute wore a white fur hat "with a long fleecy nap," such as Gansevoort Melville had once manufactured. This "unencumbered traveller" who carries no luggage (to recall Melville's letter to Hawthorne) will not be stopped at the "Custom House." He calls attention, on the contrary, to a confidence man who is crossing "the frontier."[3]

The deaf-mute stops in front of a placard "offering a reward for the capture of a mysterious imposter . . . recently arrived from the East." "As if it had been a theatre-bill, crowds were gathered about the announcement." The man in cream colors holds up a small slate next to the placard, on which he has written, " 'Charity thinketh no evil,' " "so that those who read the one might read the other." He erases his first message, and writes various others also preaching charity. (9–11) Shortly thereafter, a crippled black man begs for charity from the passengers. Is Black Guinea the man in cream colors wearing another disguise? Is he the "mysterious imposter," preaching charity to fleece the passengers?

A "sour-faced person, it may be some discharged custom-house officer," makes that charge. (17–18) Black Guinea is "some white operator," he insists. "Looks are one thing, and facts are another." (20) Having introduced the unencumbered traveler of his letter to Hawthorne, Melville next brings forth a custom-house officer to stop him. This custom-house inspector has been fired, however, and he limps along on a wooden leg. His custom house is a ruined monument of republican political authority, the last that will appear in the tale. When Major Melvill was a custom-house inspector, he stood watch over the new nation. He guarded it against merchants who mislabeled their

---

[2]Melville, *Israel Potter*, p. 159.

[3]Merrell R. Davis and William Gilman, eds., *The Letters of Herman Melville* (New Haven, 1960), p. 125. Cf. Chapter 3.

imports, or who did not pay their duties. The major's removal marked the transformation of the custom house; instead of guarding republican virtue, it offered business promotion and political charity. The custom-house officer in *The Confidence-Man* has no authority at all. No one listens to him, and he has a wooden leg as well. The damaged leg in Melville's fiction has removed from Tommo, the son, to Ahab, the father, to this discharged custom-house grand-father. The emblem of the crippled, impotent self has gone to rest at the revolutionary origins of authority. The custom-house man is a "foiled wolf." (22) One of the "hunted generation of wolves," exterminated by the foxes, he speaks as the last Mohawk.

The custom-house man's suspicion of Black Guinea is met with resentment. "Have you no charity, friend?" asks a Methodist minister who has served in the Mexican War. "Charity is one thing, and truth is another," responds the custom-house officer. (20) His mistrust of the appearance of charity suits a man driven from the custom house, and his wooden leg makes him misan-thropic as well. The passengers on the *Fidèle* prefer the "Wall Street spirit" of confident enterprise to the lethargic and suspicious "clerk-shops" of the "custom-house." (48)

The wooden-legged man reappears a bit later in the day, to question Black Guinea's authenticity again. This time he tells the story of a man who formed the idea of a faithful wife from a theatrical performance, married the specta-cle, and failed to recognize his wife's infidelity. "Does all the world act? Am *I*, for instance, an actor?" asks the confidence man. "To do is to act; so all doers are actors," responds the custom-house officer. (39) He is collapsing action in the world into acting in the theater, and repudiating both. Near the end of the novel, Melville contrasts acting to the "custom-house counter" again. He is defending his tale against those who demand "severe fidelity to real life" in "a work of amusement." Now the custom house stands, as it did in Hawthorne's Custom-House sketch, for the dullness of ordinary life. Fiction, by contrast, should "allow people to act out themselves with that unreserve permitted to the stage." Such fiction will provide "even for more reality, than real life itself can show." It will give "nature, too; but nature unfettered, exhilarated, in effect transformed. . . . the people in a fiction, like the people in a play, must dress as nobody exactly dresses, talk as nobody exactly talks, act as nobody exactly acts. It is with fiction as with religion; it should present another world, and yet one to which we feel the tie." (190)[4]

As in "The Two Temples," theater replaces religion as redemptive of ordinary life. Custom-house "fidelity to real life," insisting that packages be opened for inspection, is set against the masquerade on the *Fidèle*. Theater provides freedom from life's demands for fidelity. The young Melville, speak-

---

4Cf. Nathaniel Hawthorne, "The Custom House: Introductory to the Scarlet Letter," *The Scarlet Letter* (New York, 1959 [1849]), pp. 15–53, and chap. 9 of *Subversive Genealogy*, "The Custom House: Introductory to Billy Budd."

ing as a rover and romancer, had repudiated the baggage of social life which stopped him at the frontier. The narrator of *The Confidence-Man* also seems to be contrasting real, social life to an artistic fairy land. The stage is contrasted to the custom house, however, not to escape from actual life, but to describe the character of real life once the custom house has withdrawn its political authority from the world. The confidence man's masquerade is no more an escape from life than Melville's *Piazza Tales* were romances. The masquerade rather calls attention to the fictionalized, self-constructed character of American life. The confidence man exposes the absent core of marketplace reality itself.

Status, family, historically rooted relationship, and the insignias of dress marked a person's identity in traditional, stable societies. Modern strangers who came together to buy, to sell, and to persuade revealed themselves by their performances. The performing self in public was not expected to act like the natural self at home. Nevertheless, relations of exchange among strangers in public required confidence in the reliability of appearances; there were good reasons, in antebellum America, not to have it.[5] . . .

On the one hand, marketplace motives threatened to swallow up politics, religion, and family life. On the other hand, the marketplace itself required mutual confidence and was vulnerable to confidence games. Markets, since they did not root their participants in a shared, traditional ground, depended on trust in appearances. "Confidence is the indispensable basis of all sorts of business transactions," explains the confidence man. (136) "Destroyers of confidence" (55) ruined the value of the stock of the Black Rapids Coal Company, he complains. But he makes this appeal to confidence in order to sell worthless stock. His trickery indicates that it was as dangerous to have confidence as to refuse it. Men deceived others to advance their own fortunes by calling on their victims to trust them. Then they were victimized in turn. The hunger for advantage invariably overcomes suspiciousness on the *Fidèle*, but the effect on the reader is quite the opposite. Once the "fiction of depression" (55) is refuted, promises the confidence man, "confidence will be more than restored." (29) Were "the fiction of depression" a reality, it would not simply destroy the value of investments; it would drive men insane. "I have been in mad-houses full of tragic mopers, and seen there the end of suspicion," the Methodist minister warns the custom-house man. (22) To trust was to be gulled, to mistrust was to go mad. Sanity required a trust in appearances that placed one in the power of confidence men.

Confidence games not only raised doubts about the motives of others; they also corroded the cognitive reliability of perception. David Brion Davis has attributed the antebellum preoccupation with conspiracies and secret power to pervasive role-playing in a mobile, acquisitive society. Actors moved in a constructed world, and they were torn between a devouring suspiciousness

5Cf. Richard Sennett, *The Fall of Public Man* (New York, 1977), pp. 64–72, 161–91.

and a need for symbolic reassurance. Ahab, devoured by mistrust, struck through the pasteboard mask to expose the hidden reality. Republicans and Southern fire-eaters in the latter 1850s also hunted secret conspiracies which constricted their freedom. But Melville had exhausted the artistic possibilities of heroic, monomaniacal claims to individual freedom.

As the Republican party glorified the free market, in opposition to chattel slavery, Melville investigated the sort of freedom that actually resided there. The confidence man did not, like Ahab, attack a single, projected source of hidden power. Instead he entered a world hungry to trust and appropriated it. He did not strike through the "pasteboard signs" (11) of the other travelers; he used their methods to defeat them. As the confidence man reassured his fellow-passengers, to expose and exploit them, he sowed a "terrible doubt of appearances" in the reader. The confidence man, in a world without the fathers, resorted to manipulation. He abandoned open rebellion for a more primitive, indirect assault on basic trust.

Basic trust is at the origins of an ego's sense of well-being in the world. It originates in the relationship of trust between mother and infant, without which there can be neither a stable sense of self nor a confident relation to the world. To undermine basic trust is to throw the self back into primitive, mistrustful, ego-dissolving anxieties. Unable to defeat and become the father, the confidence man became the mother instead.[6]

The confidence man appears in a variety of disguises in the first half of the novel. He convinces one passenger after another that to fail to give him money is to reveal a corrosive suspicion of the world. "Have you no confidence in dis poor ole darkie?" he asks. (22) "Trust me." (33) "Confidence may come too late." (36) Put "confidence in the world's charity." (49) "Could you put confidence in *me*, for instance?" (51) "Do you feel quite yourself again? Confidence restored?" (74) "But again I say, you must have confidence." (88) "My conscience is peaceful. I have confidence in everybody." (100) The repeated refrain is enough to drive the reader mad.

Each passenger who regains confidence becomes a victim. What is at stake for these victims increases at each encounter, from the pennies (and buttons) thrown in charity into Black Guinea's mouth; to the personal charity given the man with the weed; to the organized charity invented by the man in the gray coat; to the business frauds perpetrated by the man with the ledger book; to the medicine sold the invalid by the herb doctor; to the restoration of the misanthrope's confidence in servant boys by the man with the brass plate. First the financial stakes increase; then the confidence man plays with

---

6Cf. Perry Miller, *The Life of the Mind in America from the Revolution to the Civil War* (New York, 1965), p. 211; Alexander Mitscherlich, *Society Without the Father* (London, 1969); Christopher Lasch, *The Culture of Narcissism* (New York, 1978), pp. 31–51; Ann Douglas, *The Feminization of American Culture* (New York, 1977), pp. 319–20; Erik H. Erikson, *Childhood and Society* (Middlesex, Eng., 1965 [1950]), pp. 239–43; R. D. Laing, *The Divided Self* (Middlesex, Eng., 1965), pp. 39–61.

physical illness and ontological mistrust. The confidence man spreads deception for its own sake. As he draws the other passengers into his fictions, he reveals the fictitious character of their own stories. They, like him, construct self-justifying fictions about their lives. As the confidence man shifts from one disguise to another, in apparent self-effacement, he gains the power to appropriate their stories. But the role-player's power of absolute self-aggrandizement, as Stephen Greenblatt has said of Iago, affirms absolute vacancy. The protean quality of the confidence man calls into question the self underneath his disguises. And as the reader hunts for the real confidence man, he is drawn into the charade.[7]

The reader begins *The Confidence-Man* in confusion. He does not know whether the man in cream colors is the mysterious imposter, or whether one of them is (both of them are?) Black Guinea. Neither the man in cream colors nor Black Guinea has a face. Neither has a character. Both are known by their clothing alone. That will be true for all the characters on the *Fidèle*, those that seem to be the confidence man in disguise, and those that do not. Since clothing provides no clues to the actual individuality of the wearer, the confidence man can change clothing and identity at will. But his costume changes invite the reader to solve the puzzle of his identity and discover the single trickster underneath the characters he plays.

Black Guinea lists several men, identifiable by their dress, who will vouch for his authenticity. (19) The attentive reader will take Black Guinea as the confidence man, and his list as a list of the costumes in which he will show himself. At first, the characters do appear in the order announced by Black Guinea, and each departs before his successor. The reader thinks he has discovered a single, manipulating self under the various costumes. He begins to feel, after the bewildering introduction, that he has solved the puzzle of the book. Unlike the gullible participants on the *Fidèle*, the reader believes he has seen through the confidence game. He imagines himself exempt from the conditions established by the novel. He shares the confidence man's confidence that he can manipulate others (or observe their manipulation) while remaining detached himself.

There are unsettling premonitions, however, that the reader is also falling victim to a confidence game. Black Guinea has listed a man in a yellow vest after the herb doctor; no such figure appears. Perhaps he is the man in cream colors who began the book, or the boy with the tattered yellow coat near its end. But these two characters (or are they one?) appear out of Black Guinea's order. That is not so surprising, after all. If Black Guinea is the confidence man, why should he be telling the truth? The entrance of Charles Noble and

[7]Cf. Nancy Limprecht, "Repudiating the Self-Justifying Fiction: C. B. Brown, N. Hawthorne, and H. Melville as Anti-Romancers," unpublished Ph.D. dissertation, University of California, Berkeley, 1977, pp. 528–56; Stephen J. Greenblatt, *Renaissance Self-Fashioning from More to Shakespeare* (Chicago, 1980), pp. 233–37.

the cosmopolitan, however, marks a decisive shift in the novel. Their appearance will suggest that the invitation to discover the single, authentic confidence man is another confidence game.

The cosmopolitan appears in a "vesture barred with various hues" (139); he wears the costume of a court-jester. He tells the misanthrope, "Life is a picnic *en costume*; one must take a part, assume a character, stand ready in a sensible way to play the fool." (141) The custom-house officer called the *Fidèle* a "ship of fools" (21); the cosmopolitan is at its center. In the colors of the rainbow and the persona of a fool, he seems to have merged all the confidence man's disguises into one. Black Guinea, however, had listed a man in a violet robe. The cosmopolitan's robe is multicolored. Charles Noble wears no robe, but he has a violet vest. Which is the confidence man? Has he split in two? The violet-robed man is followed by a soldier in Black Guinea's list. He is not followed by a soldier in the story. A man wearing a "grimy old regimental coat" (99) does appear earlier in the novel. Masquerading as a soldier, he claims to be a confidence man who gets charity by feigning as war wounds injuries received in prison. His brother, he claims, was buried beneath a hickory bier. (103) But the soldier converses with the confidence man playing the part of an herb doctor, and is finally gulled by him. If there is a single confidence man, he cannot be both the soldier and the herb doctor. Is this a forewarning that the confidence man's self will split, as it seems to with Noble and the cosmopolitan? The reader drawn into the masquerade, who feels he has gained the confidence of the actor playing the role and the author writing the play, discovers he is another victim.

The problematic identity of the confidence man spreads to the other characters, just as Bartleby's language infects the lawyer and his employees. All the characters on the *Fidèle* wear costumes; none has a self. "A modest man thrust out naked into the street, would he not be abashed? Take him in and clothe him; would not his confidence be restored?" the cosmopolitan asks the barber. (239) He is defending clothing in the name of the authenticity of wigs, to assuage the barber's anxiety that men are not what they seem. Men are not what they seem on the *Fidèle*, but that is not because they have true selves hidden under their clothing. There are only the costumes with no one inside. Clothes have lost their connection to a self, even to a hidden one revealed by the clues they provide. Once clothing is cut loose from its moorings in the self, the unembodied interior dissolves. *Pierre* and *Bartleby* imagined a split between exterior and interior. There is only an absent self on the *Fidèle*.

Melville's fiction before *Moby-Dick* proposed a straightforward division between the self on the one hand, its inherited or official costume on the other. But Melville's protagonists also use clothing to express their relationships to their inherited or self-assumed identities. Redburn's hunting-jacket and White-Jacket's cloak could be cast off, after they had served their purposes. After White-Jacket liberated himself from his costume, Ahab's "dignity" needed "no robed investiture." Costumes return in *Israel Potter* and *Benito Cereno*; they now function as deliberate disguises. Israel wears various disguises, but cannot escape his own identity. Don Benito is forced to disguise himself in his own uniform. His self is thereby permanently deformed, tortured by the insignia of its own identity. Don Benito cannot, like White-Jacket or Israel Potter, simply throw off his costume. He has become what he recognized that his uniform represents him to be, a master in the power of a slave. *The Confidence-Man* frees the self from its clothing once again. But the apparent freedom of the confidence man's detached self dissolves the self that is free. The distinction between stage performance and stable identity breaks down. There is no longer a character who plays different roles, but only costumes and performances, designating a character no longer there. As Peter Schlemihl lost his shadow to the devil, so the confidence man sells his body. His masquerade shatters the illusion of a single, hidden self, detached and manipulative behind the scenes.[8]

Masquerade might seem to belong to fiction, the self to life. Characters in fiction, Melville agrees, are "mere phantoms which flit along a page, like shadows along a wall." Readers demand consistency in fictional characters. But, asks Melville, "Is it not a fact, that, in real life, a consistent character is a *rara avis?*" Having read a novel which satisfactorily unravels "the tangled web of some character," "the studious youth will still run risk of being too often at fault upon actually entering the world." (75–77) A realist novel with stable characters, for Melville, is poor preparation for life. Better to stay on one side of the wall, and watch the shadows play upon it. Melville offers the phantom-like confidence man not as an escape from life, but as preparation for the fictive, chameleonlike character of life itself.

"The author who draws a character, even though . . . at different periods, as much at variance with itself as the butterfly is with the caterpillar into which it changes, may yet, in so doing, be not false but faithful to facts." (75) Melville's simile suggests the mutability of identity, but his syntax turns the butterfly back into the caterpillar. In *Moby-Dick* the "gilded velvets of butterflies" are illusions, painted by the harlot of nature; Bentham's "skeleton" is inside the "chrysalis" of the whale's padded body.[9] Both those images insist on the priority of the physical body against romantic and scientific efforts to escape it. By transforming the butterfly into the caterpillar, Melville is suggesting a similar point in *The Confidence-Man*, that fiction aims at beauty, while life goes the other way, but metamorphosis still means connection, in *Moby-Dick*; in *The Confidence-Man* it means dissolution. If one is "faithful to Facts" on the *Fidèle*, the body is no more real than its veils.

Melville calls into question the singleness of the confidence man's identity in the first half of his tale. In the second, he undermines individualism in another way. The confidence man has (or men have) appeared in several

---

[8]Greenblatt, pp. 251–52.
[9]Melville, *Moby-Dick* (New York, 1956), pp. 163, 215.

disguises in the first half of the story. The cosmopolitan remains a single character, present throughout the novel's second half. But while the confidence man would be self-sufficient (if he had a self), the cosmopolitan demands relationships with the other characters. Interdependence is the theme beneath the longest story within *The Confidence-Man*, the story which divides the book in two, Charles Noble's account of the Indian-hater.

It seems perverse to claim that Noble's tale of Colonel Moredock concerns interdependence. Colonel Moredock, the Indian-hater, appears to be the single, unexterminated lone wolf in Melville's tale. He makes no pretense of love or charity; he has "little or no confidence." (150) He leaves society, and is independent of human relations. In contrast to the smiling, manipulative confidence man, the Indian-hater displays his vengeful rage. Set against the confidence man's false exteriors, he seems the lone figure of integrity in the novel, a descendant of the sailor Jackson, and of Ahab.

The typical Indian-hater is a backwoodsman, according to Charles Noble, who "having with his mother's milk drank in small love for red men," has received "some signal outrage from them." (157) He broods on his injury in nature's solitude, and seeks revenge. "With the solemnity of a Spaniard turned monk, he takes leave of his kin." (158) His desire for vengeance removes him from normal social intercourse. He "renounce[s] ambition, with its objects—the pomps and glories of the world." (163) He has no use for philanthropy. "Under the guise of amity" toward Colonel Moredock's family, Indians won "their confidence" and killed them. (156) Moredock spends his solitary life stalking and killing Indians.

"Charity, charity!" responds the cosmopolitan to Charles Noble's account. (164) Noble has described the Indian-hater to explain why the "misanthrope" from Missouri has rejected the cosmopolitan's "philanthropy." (138) "The vice consists in a want of confidence," agrees the cosmopolitan, (165) but he cannot believe that the misanthropic "Ishmael" (146) on the *Fidèle* is genuinely full of hate. "His outside is but put on. Ashamed of his own goodness," according to the cosmopolitan, the misanthrope pretends to anger. (164) The cosmopolitan first tries to interpret misanthropy as just another disguise. Then he goes further. Colonel Moredock, he insists, was "either misanthrope or nothing; . . . and . . . as for this Indian-hating in general, I can only say of it what Dr. Johnson said of the alleged Lisbon earthquake, 'Sir, I don't believe it.'" (164–65) This Candide-like disavowal of Colonel Moredock undercuts itself, however, since the Lisbon earthquake was perfectly real. "*I* admire Indians," insists the cosmopolitan, differentiating himself from the Indian-hater. (148) His refusal even to believe in the Indian-hater seems to establish Colonel Moredock's reality, independent of and opposed to the confidence man.

All we know of Colonel Moredock, however, we know from another confidence man, Charles Noble. . . . Moreover, even Noble refuses to vouch for his account of the Indian-hater; he attributes it to his friend, Judge Hall. "I have . . . given you, not my story, mind, or my thoughts, but another's," he concludes. (162) Judge Hall is James Hall, from whose *Wilderness and the Warpath* Melville took his account of the Indian-hater. Hall claimed actually to have encountered such a man in a frontier store, "so different from the noisy mirth and thoughtless deportment of those around him, that I could not help observing him. . . . There were indications of openness and honesty, that forbade distrust." Hall had confidence in his Indian-hater. He set him off from the other frontiersmen, and from himself (as a naive, Eastern youth) as well. Melville seems to follow his lead. By describing Moredock at fourth remove, however (Hall, the narrator, and Noble intervene between the author and the Indian-hater), Melville dissolves the boundaries between confidence man and Indian-hater that he appears to establish. One can have no confidence that *The Confidence-Man's* Indian-hater is as noble as Noble describes him. Noble's disavowal of responsibility for his story, moreover, allows him to create sympathy for Moredock without appearing to endorse his brutality. Indians, he acknowledges, object to the backwoodsman's portrayal, "but whether, on this or any point, the Indians should be permitted to testify for themselves, to the exclusion of other testimony, is a question that may be left to the Supreme Court." The court had ruled that other men had the right to testify, to the exclusion of Indians. Noble's apparently judicious conclusion places legal authority behind the Indian-hater.[10]

Charles Noble stands in the same relation to Moredock as does the "gentleman with gold sleeve-buttons" to his Negro slave, and Mark Winsome to his disciple, Egbert. Each of these masters, as Joyce Adler points out, has a servant to do his dirty work for him. The "good man" keeps his white kid gloves clean because he can "sin by deputy." (42–43) He gives charity to the confidence man for the Seminole widows and orphans, victims of a war fought so that men like him could acquire Indian land. The good man needs the Indian-hater to cleanse the West of its wolves and open it up to confidence men. The philanthropist who gives charity to Indians is twinned with the backwoodsman who murders them.[11]

From *Typee* through *Pierre*, savages stand as authentic opponents of civilized life. They end, in *The Confidence-Man*, as manufactured justifications for it. "Though held as a sort of a barbarian, the backwoodsman would seem to America what Alexander was to Asia—captain of the vanguard of conquering civilization. (153) Charles Noble, who speaks those words, sees the Indian-hater as a "Pathfinder, provider of security to those who come after him." Asia had Alexander; America has Colonel Moredock. Cooper's epic representative of the American Adam has turned into a vengeful killer. For Jacksonian expansion, and in *Redburn* and *Moby-Dick*, the frontier promised

[10]James Hall, *The Wilderness and the Warpath* (New York, 1849), pp. 138–51 (quoted p. 139); Joyce Sparer Adler, "Melville on the White Man's War Against the American Indian," *Science and Society*, XXXVI (Winter 1972), 426, 429–30.

[11]Adler, *Science and Society*, XXXVI, 421, 438.

to redeem a failed marketplace at home. The Indian-hater's West is a fictive creation, invented by the foxes.

Colonel Moredock is twinned with the confidence man as well. The Indian-hater acts openly on vengeful feelings, which the confidence man satisfies by manipulation. Both, in different ways, take revenge on humankind. As brutalized murderer, as Noble's puppet, and as his double, the Indian-hater is a triply useless alternative to the marketplace. Moredock's symbiosis with Noble exhausts the regenerative possibilities of the frontier. It also introduces the decisive shift in *The Confidence-Man.*

Moredock's isolation seems to free him from the contaminated relationships on the *Fidèle.* But the doubleness of Noble and Moredock, like the dissolution of the single confidence man, points to the problem of relationships in the story. The confidence man disappears after he sells the misanthrope a nonexistent servant. The cosmopolitan replaces him. He tries to convert the misanthrope to philanthropy, and fails. The confidence man defrauds his victims and leaves them; the cosmopolitan seeks ongoing connections. The confidence man is a success; the cosmopolitan is a failure.

The confidence man sells (fictitious) products; his victims buy self-esteem, riches, health, or support. He also solicits for charities, making appeals which at once compartmentalize business and charity, and make them equivalent. The confidence man brings "the Wall Street spirit" to charity. (41, 48) By making charity a business, he allows men to aid Indians and blacks without committing themselves to personal attachments. The cosmopolitan, by contrast, wants loans. Asked to enter into a relationship that will tie them to the figure they aid, Charles Noble and Egbert refuse. The cosmopolitan wants to ground personal ties in financial obligations. He wants to reconnect the family, the marketplace, and friendship. But the cosmopolitan will most probably be absent from the friendships for which he pleads. Since we have no confidence he will repay the loans, his project does not simply uncover a web of mistrust, but creates it.

"I give away money, but never loan it," announces Egbert, "a well-dressed, commercial-looking gentleman of about thirty." (203, 208) He explains, "The negotiation of a loan is a business transaction. And I will transact no business with a friend . . . a true friend has nothing to do with loans; he should have a soul above loans." (208)

Egbert is applying the lesson he has learned from his "Master," Mark Winsome. He is using Winsome's "Essay on Friendship" (210) to refuse to befriend the cosmopolitan. The essay on friendship to which Melville refers was actually written by Thoreau. "The Friend asks no return," wrote Thoreau. "We do not wish for friends to feed and clothe our bodies—neighbors are kind enough for that—but to do the like office to our spirits." Thoreau wanted to preserve a realm of pure friendship uncontaminated by material need. Such friendship, Melville suggests, avoids the tangible, reciprocal obligations that tie actual friends together. In the name of preserving a realm of pure spirit, the "transcendental philosophy" (206) of Egbert and Winsome allows capitalism to take its course. It liberates the marketplace from the constraints of personal loyalty. Winsome and Egbert are parodies of Emerson and Thoreau.[12]

Capitalists lend money at interest, not out of love. The modern doctrine of usury, Benjamin Nelson explains, eliminates the special, tribal obligations (which joined friend to friend, in *The Merchant of Venice*, and Jew to Jew). Proponents of usury do not assert, as Egbert says he does not, "that, in the hour of need, a stranger is better than a brother." (209) Rather, they end the distinction between financial practices appropriate within a brotherhood, and those permitted toward strangers. As Egbert explains, "A loan of money at interest is a sale of money on credit. To sell a thing on credit may be an accommodation, but where is the friendliness?" (208) In Thoreau's words, "Friendship is not so kind as is imagined. . . . When the Friend . . . treats his Friend like a Christian, or as he can afford; then friendship ceases to be friendship, and becomes charity." Egbert and Thoreau separate personal bonds from monetary interests.[13]

Family, merchant capitalism in eighteenth-century America merged kinship networks and business practices. Nineteenth-century jurists like Lemuel Shaw justified capitalism with paternalist, communal rhetoric. But the judge's willingness to hold capitalists to paternal standards only went so far. Shaw did not want employers to have to assume toward their workers the sort of obligations that masters traditionally owed their apprentices. In *Farwell v. Boston and Worcester Railroad*, a decision with enormous consequences, Shaw distinguished between the two relations. His "fellow-servant" doctrine, in *Farwell*, was the mirror image of Winsome's "Essay on Friendship."[14]

Traditionally masters were responsible for the family members, servants, and apprentices who lived in their households. *Farwell* distinguished masters and apprentices from employers and workers. Shaw ruled that a factory-owner, unlike a master, was not liable for injuries sustained by his workers on the job. The "fellow-servant" doctrine presumed that other employees were responsible for any negligence. *Farwell* allowed the injured worker to sue his "fellow-servants."[15]

Farwell utilized the ideology of marketplace equality to deny inequality in the factory. "By elevating the paradigm of contract to its supreme place in nineteenth-century legal thought," writes Morton Horwitz, Shaw freed em-

---

[12]Henry D. Thoreau, *A Week on the Concord and Merrimack Rivers* (Boston, 1867), pp. 274–93. Quoted passages are on pp. 282–83, 286.

[13]Benjamin Nelson, *The Idea of Usury, from Tribal Brotherhood to Universal Otherhood* (Princeton, 1949); Thoreau, p. 292.

[14]Morton J. Horwitz, *The Transformation of American Law, 1780–1860* (Cambridge, Mass., 1977), pp. 207–10.

[15]Ibid.; Leonard W. Levy, *The Law of the Commonwealth and Chief Justice Shaw* (Cambridge, Mass., 1957), pp. 166–77.

ployers from responsibility for the conditions under which their workers labored.[16] Shaw spoke for pure business, Egbert for pure friendship. Together they emancipated the economy from personal obligation. Together they dissolved the claims of paternal responsibility which had united the market to the home. Together they turned their backs on the confidence game which, placing family loans at the mercy of strangers, had destroyed Allan Melvill.

The ur-story underneath *The Confidence-Man* is the bankruptcy, madness, and death of Allan Melvill. He is the missing person behind the novel's confidence games. Melville placed the history of his family at the center of one of his fictions for the first time since *Pierre*. Neither *Pierre* nor *The Confidence-Man* repeats the autobiographical claims of Melville's fiction before *Moby-Dick*, however, and neither is straightforward family history. *Pierre* recounts the autobiography Melville did not live. *The Confidence-Man* offers neither the actual history of Allan Melvill, nor a novelistic account of his life, but alludes to his fate in fragments. Allan Melvill's life makes the fictional fragments of *The Confidence-Man* whole.

A trajectory drawn from *Redburn* through *Pierre* and "I and My Chimney" charts the collapse of Melville's idealization of his father. The defenses which Melville had erected to protect himself from seeing that father—from Redburn's heroic merchant, to Pierre's "pious imposture," to the Bunker Hill monument in the public world and the chimney at home—have all come tumbling down. *The Confidence-Man* depicts the business world in which Allan Melvill was at once guilty participant and pathetic victim. *The Confidence-Man*, which concerns the consequences of the absence of authority, is Melville's novel about his father.

One episode, in particular, evokes Allan Melvill's fate. To dramatize Winsome's "Essay on Friendship," Egbert and the cosmopolitan stage a scene. They play "two friends, friends from childhood, bosom-friends; one of whom, for the first time, being in need, for the first time seeks a loan from the other." (207) The cosmopolitan plays "Frank," the friend who needs money; Egbert plays "Charlie" (an echo of Charlie Noble), the friend who has it. To explain his refusal to lend "Frank" money, "Charlie" tells him "at second-hand" (214) of the fate of China Aster. "Why don't you have confidence, China Aster?" asks his friend, Orchis, forcing a loan upon him. (217) China Aster, dreaming he can improve his candlemaking business, accepts the money. He involves his family in debt, signs a "secret bond" with a moneylender, (221) and cannot repay his former friend. Faced with imminent bankruptcy, China Aster goes mad and dies. "Old Prudence" and "Old Plaintalk," friends of China's father and reincarnations of the custom-house man, place an epitaph on China's tombstone: HE WAS RUINED BY ALLOWING HIMSELF TO BE PERSUADED, AGAINST HIS BETTER SENSE, INTO THE FREE INDULGENCE OF CONFIDENCE. . . ." The epitaph and the tale point to Allan Melvill.

[16]Horwitz, p. 209.

Like the other members of his clan, Allan Melvill exploited his family connections for financial gain. Judge Shaw speculated in land with Peter Gansevoort. Peter did business with the Van Schaicks on his mother's side of the family, and with the Sanford brothers of his first wife. Such financial ties were peripheral for Shaw and Gansevoort; they dominated Allan Melvill's life. He created a familial joint-stock company, centered on himself and with unlimited liability for all of its members. Allan Melvill is like one of the characters in the first half of *The Confidence-Man*, whose misplaced trust makes them the confidence man's victims. He is, like those characters, a failed confidence man himself. But his loans also implicate him, as China Aster is implicated, in an ongoing, fatal web of mistrust.[17]

Major Melvill, the Inspector of the Boston Custom House, set up his son in business. Allan could, he wrote, "rely with confidence in any absolute emergency" on his father. But Allan foresaw no emergencies. "The confidence you have placed in me shall never be forfeited," he wrote the Major. I "always hope for the best, and all I trust will yet go well," Allan explained to Peter Gansevoort, but the "want of confidence" in trade troubled him from the beginning. The repeated incantation of "confidence" in the tale of Melvill the son imitates the obsession of Melvill the father.[18]

Allan Melvill cited his confidence to justify borrowing money from both his father and his brother-in-law. Within a few years, however, he was writing Peter a "*confidential* letter," which "should be destroyed," describing his business troubles. Allan wanted another loan. But the shift in his language, from "confidence" to "confidential," signaled Allan's transformation from a man who had trust to the organizer of a masquerade. In 1827 Allan Melvill became a confidence man.[19]

Allan formed in 1827 a "confidential connection" with secret business associates. He reported his progress to Peter Gansevoort, in several "confidential" letters and conversations. "It is entirely a *confidential* connection with Persons combining every qualification but money," Allan explained. He supplied the capital; by keeping his connection confidential, he could endorse the firm's notes as if they were not his own. "My name will not appear in the firm, which will enable them to use my endorsement when necessary," Allan told his worried brother-in-law. "The whole affair will take over *sub rosa*, and in entire confidence among all parties, for I have even now the best grounded

[17]Lemuel Shaw to Peter Gansevoort, Nov. 2, 1831, Jan. 1, 1843, Peter Gansevoort to Lemuel Shaw, Feb. 14, 1849, The Gansevoort-Lansing Collection, New York Public Library (hereafter abbreviated GL). I have not recorded the dates of the Sanford and Van Schaick correspondence with Peter Gansevoort.

[18]Allan Melvill to Peter Gansevoort, Dec. 11, 1818, GL; Allan Melvill to Thomas Melvill, Nov. 11, 1818, Melville Collection, Berkshire Athenaeum.

[19]Allan Melvill to Peter Gansevoort, June 10, 1823, June 23, 1823, GL. In addition to Melvill's correspondence, I have relied on T. Walter Herbert, *Moby-Dick and Calvinism* (New Brunswick, N.J., 1977), pp. 47–53.

assurance, that all *is safe* and *secret*, and with heaven's blessing will remain so." "While nothing has transpired to create suspicion or create alarm, implicit faith is reposed in your friendship and discretion."[20]

Allan had deceived his own confidential partners, however. He did not have the capital he had promised them, and he had to borrow it from Peter. He had tried to obtain money elsewhere, "without communicating my confidential matter," and failed. If his brother-in-law did not help him, Allan wrote, the project "will *explode* to my utter disgrace." "My honour, dearer than life itself, will be forfeited," Allan despaired, if Peter refused to advance him $10,000. "If you do, which kind Heaven in mercy avert, I should know not whither in this world to turn for succour in the very crisis of my fate, and all, all may be lost to me forever." Without Peter's help, Allan would fall "prey to a brace of harpies instigated by the spirit of gain and . . . self interest." "If you value my present welfare and future existence, disappoint me not I beseech you," pleaded Allan. "As you esteem me, and *love our dear Maria*, do not I conjure you as a friend and Brother, disappoint me in the *utmost need*.[21]

"Help, help, Charlie, I want help!" says the cosmopolitan. (212) "Charlie! speak as you used to, tell me you will help me."(214) Charlie refuses to lend money to Frank, his friend "from childhood up," without receiving "security" in return. (210) "You may indeed implicitly and confidentially rely on my honour for security," Allan replied to Peter. "Under Providence my chief salvation in all emergencies, [my honor] shall never be polluted by a breach of confidence to a Brother, who has so generously pledged in my behalf the entire faith of *himself and friends*." One of the friends to whom Allan referred had endorsed Allan's notes. "I shall always be proud of his confidence," Allan responded. He also asked his brother-in-law for "a *confidential* list of those persons in Albany, Troy &tc., whom you still esteem trustworthy," as prospective clients for his firm. "You shall have the details in *confidence*," he assured Peter, as he swore that the business was prospering. "Many compliment it in my hearing *without dreaming of my connection*. . . . My concern of course is a confidential secret." Allan pledged never again to ask Peter for money; he broke that promise within months.[22]

Allan was constructing a net of confidential relationships for his own self-aggrandizement. It trapped him instead. Allan's failure offered "Charlie" good reason to refuse "Frank's" pleas for a loan. Unlike Melville's confidence man, however, Melville's father shared the trust on which he tried to capitalize. He was completely enmeshed, financially and psychologically, in his own confidence game. Allan's commitment to his family and his reputation was no

[20]Allan Melvill to Peter Gansevoort, Jan. 17, 1827, Feb. 8, 1827, Feb. 10, 1827, GL.

[21]Allan Melvill to Peter Gansevoort, Feb. 10, 1827, Feb. 23, 1827, March 30, 1827, March 31, 1827, GL.

[22]Allan Melvill to Peter Gansevoort, March 2, 1827, March 27, 1827, March 30, 1827, April 4, 1827, April 10, 1827, Oct. 23, 1827, GL.

charade. He manipulated others from family absorption and weakness, not from detachment, self-awareness, and strength. Instead of being the director in control of a confidence game, he became its victim.

Allan Melvill gave his father's and brother-in-law's money to associates who had gained his confidence. The arrangement was a peculiar one, he admitted to Peter. "Unknown in the Books . . . it is a matter of equity rather than law, of feeling rather than policy." Allan rejected Peter's plea that he sign a written agreement. Such a legal contract, he explained, showed a "want of confidence" in his friends. Allan could rely on their "uncommon friendship."[23]

The cosmopolitan wanted to convince the ship's barber to rely on friendship, too, and give haircuts on trust. Cleverer than Allan Melvill, he signed a written contract with the barber, agreeing "to make good to the last any loss that may come from his trusting mankind." The barber agreed, in return, to take down his sign advertising NO TRUST. The cosmopolitan had no intention of honoring the agreement, to be sure, but all he got out of it was a free shave. The cosmopolitan did not get a loan from Egbert; Allan Melvill got loans from Peter Gansevoort, and was shorn. He insisted to Peter that he was not "beguiled by, as you think 'high hope as ardent anticipation,' deceived by false appearances or insensible to sad reality."[24] He was wrong. His confidence in appearances was misplaced, and the confidential partnership in which he placed his trust lost his money. Its failure not only bankrupted Allan; it also threatened the prosperity of the Melvill and Gansevoort clans.

When the firm of A. Brinkerhoff failed, it was rumored that Brinkerhoff owed $20,000 "to [his] family, chiefly confidential." Allan wrote that it "must be a severe mortification to a Family, so sensitive on the subject—and which probably caused the death of the senior Partner." The very next year Allan borrowed more money from his father, and then fled New York to escape his unpaid debts. He borrowed again from Peter, but that money also failed to stave off bankruptcy. Confidential family debts, to a family member "so sensitive on the subject," drove Allan Melvill (like China Aster) to madness and death.[25]

Allan's confidential partnership, he had written Peter, "seems to have been inspired by HIM who directs all mortal events." "My humble yet ardent confidence, in the constant protection, and eventual bounty of our almighty Parent . . . sustained me in a fearful and protracted struggle which would otherwise have overwhelmed the boldest spirit and the stoutest heart." Allan's bankruptcy raised doubts not simply about the confidence he had reposed in his fellows, but about his confidence in God. The "divine Parent" he created in his own image turned out to be a confidence man, too. "To distrust the creature," says the cosmopolitan, "would imply distrust of the Creator." (255)

[23]Allan Melvill to Peter Gansevoort, March 10, 1828, GL.
[24]Ibid.
[25]Allan Melvill to Peter Gansevoort, Jan. 20, 1829, GL.

Allan's failure brought down around him the entire structure of basic trust he had created, extending from the "almighty Parent" through his family-connected business relations into the interior of his own psyche. His fate confirmed the custom-house officer's warning against confidence. But Allan's loss of confidence brought him, as the minister had warned the custom-house officer that it would, to madness.[26]

"Horror . . . overwhelmed" Allan Melvill on his deathbed, in the words that he read from Psalms 55:5. But face to face with his father's history at last, Melville insulated himself from its horror. He did not tell the story whole, with living characters who were destroyed, but in pieces and at "second-hand." The characters who suffer from the confidence man, in the first half of the tale, are not real. "You are the fact in a fiction," Thoreau's "true and not despairing Friend will address his friend." Friends "Charlie" and "Frank" are fictions within a fiction. China Aster is fictitious on a third level of remove, for he is Charlie's invention. In exposing the fictitious character of Allan's relationships, Melville retold his father's story as if nothing were at stake. *The Confidence-Man* flees from the painful intimacy that tied Pierre to Isabel, the lawyer to Bartleby, and Benito Cereno to Babo into fragmented, fictitious, disassociated bonds that are more painful yet.[27]

We can imagine Peter Gansevoort as Charlie warning Allan Melvill (as Frank) against Allan's fate. With retrospective knowledge, Peter can foretell Allan's future (as China Aster) and warn him against it. But Charlie is too self-serving to have Frank's interest at heart, and Frank's need is put on. Pretending to be "Frank" when he pleads with Charlie for a loan, the cosmopolitan plays the desperation on stage that Allan experienced in life. The cosmopolitan, or so we think, does not really need the loan; when it is refused, he seems "disdainfully to throw off the character he had assumed." But Egbert, reminded of the familiar lines, "All the world's a stage . . . and one man in his time plays many parts," is "at a loss to determine where exactly the fictitious character had dropped, and the real one, if any, resumed." (231)

The cosmopolitan imitates Allan Melvill's suffering. Since he has no real character, it does not cost him anything. Unlike Melvill, he does not get his loans. He is saved, by the absence of financial and personal commitments, from Melvill's actual pain. The confidence man imitates Melvill's confidence game, and succeeds where Melvill failed. As the author recreating his father's story, Melville also acquired power that his father had lost. Detaching the masquerade from the suffering self, and depicting all relations through the prism of his father, Melville at once avoided judging his father, and distanced himself from Allan Melvill's weakness and pain. The son could succeed as trickster where the father had failed. But the anesthetizing price of his power

---

[26] Allan Melvill to Peter Gansevoort, Feb. 10, 1827, March 2, 1827, March 10, 1828, GL.
[27] Herbert, pp. 52–53; Thoreau, pp. 285–86.

as author is an absent self, and so the masquerade consumes both the confidence man and his creator.

Allan Melvill was not the pillar of rectitude he seemed; his son saw him in every man. The "studious youth . . . entering the world" is saved from being disappointed in his belief in a "consistent character" if he reads all characters as "mere phantoms." (75, 77) Allan's fate spoke to relationships in a market society, and so *The Confidence-Man* illuminates not only Melville's failed father, but the society which swallowed him up. But the author's way of rendering that society swallows him up with his father. Petrification, saving the self by insulating it from experience, monumentalizes identity to protect it. The masquerade which replaces the monument does not free the self from stone but dissolves it. The self saved from dangerous commitments in life disappears into its role. The son of a failed clothing importer has made clothing all that there is.

Melville had the power to retell his father's story in 1856. It was all the power he had. His isolation from a reading public, and from any literary or political movement as well, threw him back into his past. Melville's historic family was as cut off from contemporary recognition as he was, and so the burden of supporting it fell on him alone. Taking on that burden intensified both Melville's hostility to his readers and his ambivalence toward his family. Trapped by a paralyzing anger he could not openly express, Melville cries out in *The Confidence-Man* against the unsettling absence of commitment in his story.

At the novel's end, "a boy in the fragment of an old linen coat, bedraggled and yellow," (252) has sold a lock, a money belt, and a detector of counterfeit money to an old man. The old man clutches these objects, which belie his professed confidence as they exploit it. "A perverse man" has wanted to extinguish the last lamp in the stateroom. The steward warns him that it "was not becoming" "in a place full of strangers, to show oneself anxious to produce darkness." The cosmopolitan puts out the lamp nonetheless, "and kindly led the old man away." (260) *The Confidence-Man* ends with the cosmopolitan leading the bewildered ancient into darkness.

"Something further may follow of this masquerade," the narrator concludes. (260) Read as a comment confined to the book, the last sentence of the novel predicts a performance in darkness, which no one will see. But the last sentence of *The Confidence-Man* also leads the author and his readers out of the novel and into life. Reality has been absorbed into the fictitiousness of the text. The masquerade to follow will be staged in life, by "mere phantoms which flit along a page, like shadows along a wall." (75) Melville has turned the walls which had imprisoned his protagonists into stage props for shades. . . .

The Confidence-Man was the last piece of Melville's prose to appear in print while he lived, for thirty-five more years. Melville had written steadily and with increasing concentration for a decade. He did not publish another word for a decade more.

Billy Budd: After the Homosexual

Eve Kosofsky Sedgwick

Under the general rubric of the "Epistemology of the Closet," I have been suggesting that the current impasse within gay theory between "constructivist" and "essentialist" understandings of homosexuality is the most recent link in a more enduring chain of conceptual impasses, a deadlock between *universalizing* and *minoritizing* accounts of the relation of homosexual desires or persons to the wider field of all desires or persons. Not the correctness or prevalence of one or the other side of this enduring deadlock, but rather the persistence of the deadlock itself has been the single most effectual feature of the important twentieth-century understandings of sexuality whether hetero or homo, and a determining feature too of all the social relations routed, in this sexualized century, through understandings of sexuality. This deadlock has by now been too deeply constitutive of our very resources for asking questions about sexuality, for us to have any realistic hope of adjudicating it in the future. What we can understand better are the structuration, the mechanisms, and the immense consequences of the incoherent dispensation under which we now live. . . .

The crisis of sexual definition whose terms, both minoritizing and universalizing, were crystallizing so rapidly by 1891 provides the structure of *Billy Budd*. There is *a homosexual* in this text—a homosexual person, presented as different in his essential nature from the normal men around him. That person is John Claggart. At the same time, *every* impulse of *every* person in this book that could at all be called desire could be called homosexual desire, being directed by men exclusively toward men. The intimate strangleholds of interrepresentation between that exemplar of a new species, the homosexual man, and his thereby radically reorganized surround of male erotic relations seem to make it irresistible to bring to *Billy Budd* all *our* intimate, paralyzing questions about the essential truths of "homosexuality." . . .

But if *Billy Budd* won't tell us whether it is of the essence of male homosexual desire to wash across whole cultures or to constitute a distinct minority of individuals, neither will it answer the crucial question of a potentially utopian politics that, again, it all but forces us to ask. Is men's desire for other men the great preservative of the masculinist hierarchies of Western culture, or is it among the most potent of the threats against them? *Billy Budd* seems to pose the question frontally. The male body lovely to male eyes: is this figure "the fighting peacemaker"¹ precious to a ship's captain, the "cynosure" [1359] of male loves whose magnetism for his fellows ("they took to him like hornets to treacle" [1356]) can turn the forecastle that had been a "rat-pit of quarrels" (1356) into "the happy family" (1357) of commercial or warlike solidarity? Or to the contrary, does his focusing of male same-sex desire render him the exact, catalytic image of revolution—of that threat or promise of armed insurrection that, an early draft says, embodies "a crisis for Christendom not exceeded . . . by any other recorded era" (1476n.1405.31), and under the urgency of whose incessant evocation the narrative proceeds?² *Billy Budd* is unequivocal about the hierarchy-respecting inclinations of its hero. But these notwithstanding, it remains for the very last moments of the novella to show whether his ultimate effect on the personnel of the man-o'-war *Bellipotent* will be to trigger violent revolt or, in the actual denouement that is reclaimed from mutiny by a seeming hair's breadth, to reconsolidate the more inescapably the hierarchies of discipline and national defense. . . .

The only barely not aleatory closeness of shave by which, at the end of *Billy Budd*, the command of the *Bellipotent* averts mutiny should warn us again: this is a dangerous book to come to with questions about the *essential nature* of men's desire for men. A book about the placement and re-placement of the barest of thresholds, it continues to mobilize desires that could go either way. A better way of asking the question might then be, What are the operations necessary to deploy male-male desire as the glue rather than as the solvent of a hierarchical male disciplinary order?

But first, we need to reconstruct how we have gone about recognizing the homosexual in the text.

---

¹Herman Melville, *Pierre; Israel Potter; The Piazza Tales; The Confidence Man; Uncollected Prose; Billy Budd* (New York: Library of America, 1984), p. 1357. Further citations from *Billy Budd* will be given by page number in the text.

²Note that I am *not* here distinguishing the peaceable trader *Rights of Man* from the man-o'-war *Bellipotent*. The merchant marine and the military navy are two distinct faces of the same national polity; Billy Budd is desired by each community, and for approximately the same potentials in him. The hierarchies of the *Rights of Man*, and its forms of enforcement, are vastly less exacerbated than those of the *Bellipotent*, but both are hierarchical, and the symbiosis between the two systems makes any attempt to disjoin them symbolically a difficult one.

It may be worth adding that if, as this chapter will argue, the last third of *Billy Budd* is a symptomatic Western fantasy about a life *after the homosexual*, the *Rights of Man* parts correspondingly represent the fantasy of life *before the homosexual*—before, that is, the specification of a distinct homosexual identity. To the extent that it is a fantasy of *before*, it is also already structured, therefore, by a full and self-contradictory notion of *the homosexual*.

Knowledge/Ignorance; Nature/Unnatural

In the famous passages of *Billy Budd* in which the narrator claims to try to illuminate for the reader's putatively "normal nature" (1382) the peculiarly difficult riddle of "the hidden nature of the master-at-arms" Claggart (riddle on which after all, the narrator says, "the point of the present story turn[s]" [1384]), the answer to the riddle seems to involve not the substitution of semantically more satisfying alternatives to the epithet "hidden" but merely a series of intensifications of it. Sentence after sentence is produced in which, as Barbara Johnson points out in her elegant essay "Melville's Fist," "what we learn about the master-at-arms is that we cannot learn anything":[3] the adjectives applied to him in chapter 11 include "mysterious," "exceptional," "peculiar," "exceptional" again, "obscure," "phenomenal," "notable," "phenomenal" again, "exceptional" again, "secretive." "Dark sayings are these, some will say" (1384). Indeed. These representationally vacant, epistemologically arousing place-markers take what semantic coloration they have from a parallel and equally abstract chain of damning ethical designations—"the direct reverse of a saint," "depravity," "depravity," "depravity,"—"wantonness of atrocity," "the mania of an evil nature"—and from the adduced proximity, in a perhaps discarded draft of the next chapter, of three specific, diagnostic professions, law, medicine, and religion, each however said to be reduced to "perplexing strife" by "the phenomenon" that can by now be referred to only, but perhaps satisfactorily, as "it" (1475n.1384.3).[4] And, oh by the way, "it" has something to do with—"it" is prone, in the double shape of envy (antipathy, desire) to being fermented by—the welkin eyes, dyed cheeks, supple joints, and dancing yellow curls (1385) of a lad like Billy Budd. . . .

What *was*—Melville asks it—the matter with the master-at-arms? If there is a full answer to this question at all then there are two full answers. Briefly these would be, first, that Claggart is depraved because he is, in his desires, a pervert, of a sort that by 1891 had names in several taxonomic systems although scarcely yet, in English, the name "homosexual"; or, second, that Claggart is depraved not because of the male-directed nature of his desire, here seen as natural or innocuous, but, rather, because he feels toward his own desires only terror and loathing (call this "phobia"). The relation between these possible two answers—that Claggart is depraved because homosexual, or alternatively depraved because homophobic—is of course an odd problem.

3Barbara Johnson, "Melville's Fist: The Execution of *Billy Budd*," *Studies in Romanticism* 18 (Winter 1979): 567–99; quoted from p. 582.

4"Pride," indeed, "envy," and "despair," nouns that could be substantive, are finally produced as if in explanation—but produced also as if synonymous with one another, and as part of a stylized biblical/Miltonic scenario ("serpent," "elemental evil") that barely if at all fails to resubmerge their psychological specificity in the vacant, bipolar ethical categories of the preceding two chapters. To the degree that the three nouns mean each other, they mean nothing but the category "evil"—a category whose constituents then remain to be specified.

Suffice it here to say that either could qualify him for, and certainly neither would disqualify him from, a designation like "homosexual."

Arguably, however, there can be no full or substantive answer at all to the question; even as it invokes the (stymied) expertise of certain taxonomic professions, the narrative has nonetheless gone to considerable lengths to invite the purgative reading that "Melville's Fist" exemplarily performs, the reading in which Claggart represents a pure *epistemological essence*, a form and a theory of knowing untinctured by the actual stuff that he either knows or comprises. Claggart, in this reading, "is thus a personification of ambiguity and ambivalence, of the distance between signifier and signified, of the separation between being and doing. . . . He is properly an ironic reader, who, assuming the sign to be arbitrary and unmotivated, reverses the value signs of appearances."[5]

That Claggart displays, as indeed he does prominently, the allegorical label of a certain pure epistemological extremity is not, however, enough to drive doctor, lawyer, clergyman, once summoned, from their place of consultation at the door of the text. Rather, doesn't it associate the abstractive epistemological pressure Claggart embodies *with* the diagnostic specifications—diagnostic and therefore demeaning—of these institutions of expertise?[6] The rhetorical impaction here between a thematically evacuated abstraction of knowledge and a theoretically jejune empiricism of taxonomy effects, I believe, finally a crossing whereby the (structurally generalized) vessels of "knowledge itself" do come to take their shape from the (thematically specified) thing known, or person knowing. The shape taken—the form of knowledge that represents at the same time "knowledge itself" and a diagnosable pathology of cognition, or the cognition of a diagnosable pathology—must, in accordance with the double presentation of Claggart's particular depravity, be described by some such condensation as "homosexual-homophobic knowing." In a more succinct formulation, paranoia.

Urbane/Provincial; Innocence/Initiation; Man/Boy

I have described this crossing of epistemology with thematics as a "rhetorical impaction." The adjective is appropriate because such a crossing can be effected only through a distinctive *reader*-relation imposed by text and narrator. The inexplicit compact by which novel-readers voluntarily plunge into worlds that strip them, however temporarily, of the painfully acquired cognitive maps of their ordinary lives (awfulness of going to a party without knowing anyone) on condition of an invisibility that promises cognitive exemp-

---

[5]Johnson, "Melville's Fist," p. 573.

[6]In, however, a metonymy none the less durable for its apparent contingency; none the less efficient for the logical contradiction between diagnosis on the one hand and, on the other, the epistemological imperative to uncouple from one another "being and doing."

tion and eventual privilege, creates, especially at the beginning of books, a space of high anxiety and dependence. In this space a reader's identification with modes of categorization ascribed to her by a narrator may be almost vindictively eager. Any appeal, for instance, to or beyond "knowledge of the world" depends for its enormous novelistic force on the anxious surplus of this early overidentification with the novel's organizing eye. "Worldly" or "urbane" is par excellence one of those categories that, appearing to be a flatly descriptive attribution attached to one person, actually describes or creates a chain of perceptual angles: it is the cognitive privilege of the person described over a separate, perceived world that is actually attested, and by a speaker who through that attestation lays claim in turn to an even more inclusive angle of cognitive distancing and privilege over both the "urbane" character and the "world." The position of a reader in this chain of privilege is fraught with promise and vulnerability. The ostentatious presumption by the narrator that a reader is similarly entitled—rather than, what in truth she necessarily is, disoriented—sets up relations of flattery, threat, and complicity between reader and narrator that may in turn restructure the perception of the conformation originally associated with the "worldly.". . .

Billy Budd enforces, through the reader's drama of disorientation and tentative empowerment, an equation between cognitive mastery of the world in general and mastery of the terms of homoerotic desire in particular.

> But for the adequate comprehending of Claggart by a normal nature these hints are insufficient. To pass from a normal nature to him one must cross "the deadly space between." And this is best done by indirection.
>
> Long ago an honest scholar, my senior, said to me in reference to one who like himself is now no more, a man so unimpeachably respectable that against him nothing was ever openly said though among the few something was whispered, "Yes, X— is a nut not to be cracked by the tap of a lady's fan. You are aware that I am the adherent of no organized religion, much less of any philosophy built into a system. Well, for all that, I think that to try and get into X—, enter his labyrinth and get out again, without a clue derived from some source other than what is known as 'knowledge of the world'—that were hardly possible, at least for me."
>
> . . . At the time, my inexperience was such that I did not quite see the drift of all this. It may be that I see it now. (1382)

Where the reader is in all this is no simple matter: where, after all, can the reader wish to be? The terrorism wielded by the narrator's mystifications makes the role of "normal" incomprehension at once compulsory and contemptible. The close frame of a male-homosocial pedagogy within which alone the question of X— can be more than whispered (though still not so much as asked), but "*against*" which the question of X— must be all the more sharply distinguished, is specified as a bygone possibility at the same time as it is teasingly proffered by the narrator to the reader. Knowledge of X—, in an image whose ghastliness is scarcely mitigated by its disguise as commonplace, is presented as a testicular violence against him, while to fail to crack his nut is oneself to be feminized and accessorized. The worst news, however, is that knowledge of X— and " 'knowledge of the world' " turn out to be not only not enough, but more dangerous than no knowledge at all: to know X— is not, after all, to deliver the single *coup* of the nutcracker but, rather, with a violence suddenly made vulnerability "to get into X—, enter his labyrinth"— requiring the emergency rescue of some yet more ineffable form of cognition to prevent the direst reversal of the violent power relations of knowledge.

The reader, thus, is invented as a subject in relation to the "world" of the novel by an act of interpellation that is efficacious to the degree that it is contradictory, appealing to the reader on the basis of an assumed sharing of cognitive authority whose ground is hollowed out in the very act of the appeal. The reader is both threatened with and incited to violence at the same time as knowledge. This is also the rhetorical structure of a pivotal moment of the plot of *Billy Budd*. The sudden blow by which Billy murders Claggart in their confrontation under the eye of Vere is preceded by two interpellatory imperatives addressed by Vere to Billy. The first of these instructs Billy, " 'Speak, man! . . . Speak! defend yourself!' " The second of them, brought home to Billy's body by Vere's simultaneous physical touch, is " 'There is no hurry, my boy. Take your time, take your time' " (1404). It is possible that Billy could have succeeded in making himself intelligible as either "man" or "boy." But the instruction to him to defer as a boy, simply juxtaposed on the instruction to expedite as a man, "touching Billy's heart to the quick" also ignites it to violence: "The next instant, quick as the flame from a discharged cannon at night, his right arm shot out, and Claggart dropped to the deck." It is, of course, at this moment of Claggart's murder that Billy has been propelled once and for all across the initiatory threshold and into the toils of Claggart's phobic desire. The death of the text's homosexual marks, for reasons we must discuss later, not a terminus but an initiation for the text, as well, into the narrative circulation of male desire.

In *Billy Budd's* threatening staging, then, *knowledge of the world*, which is linked to the ability to recognize same-sex desire, while compulsory for inhabitants and readers of the world, is also a form of vulnerability as much as it is of mastery. Some further, higher, differently structured way of knowing is required of the person who would wish for whatever reason to "enter [Claggart's] labyrinth *and get out again*." We have already suggested, in a formulation that will require more discussion, that the form of knowledge circulated around and by Claggart ought to be called paranoia. If that is true, then what form of knowledge can in this world be distinguished from paranoia, and how?

Cognition/Paranoia; Secrecy/Disclosure

If it is justifiable to suggest that the form of knowledge—one marked by his own wracking juncture of same-sex desire with homophobia—by which Claggart is typically known to others is the same as that by which he himself knows others, that records the identifying interspecularity and fatal *symmetry* of paranoid knowledge. To know and to be known become the same process. . . .

The projective mutual accusation of two mirror-image men, drawn together in a bond that renders desire indistinguishable from predation, is the typifying gesture of paranoid knowledge. "It takes one to know one" is its epistemological principle, for it is able, in Melville's phrase, to form no conception of an unreciprocated emotion (1387). And its disciplinary processes are all tuned to the note of police entrapment. The politics of the agent provocateur makes the conditions of Claggart's life and consciousness; as we shall see, if there is a knowledge that "transcends" paranoia, it will also be reflected, in *Billy Budd*, in a politics that claims both to utilize and to "place" the paralytic mirror-violence of entrapment that Claggart embodies.

Both the efficacy of policing-by-entrapment and the vulnerability of this political technique to extreme reversals depend on the structuring of the policed desire, within a particular culture and moment, as an open secret. The particular form of the open secret on the *Bellipotent* is the potential among its men for mutiny. Not an alternative to the plot of male-male desire and prohibition in *Billy Budd*, the mutiny plot is the form it takes at the (inseparable) level of the collective. The early evocations of mutiny in the novella suggest that the difficulty of learning about it is like the difficulty of learning about such scandalous secrets as proscribed sexuality. Both are euphemized as "aught amiss." As with that other " 'deadly space between' " (1382), the terms in which mutiny can be described must be confined to references that evoke recognizant knowledge in those who already possess it without igniting it in those who may not. Claggart's exquisite responsiveness to epistemological pressures from both above and below comes from the symmetrical undecidability of his own position between being stigmatized agent and stigmatized object of military compulsion: whether he himself came under sway of naval discipline voluntarily, as a result of impressment, or as a result of blackmail, for instance, is left carefully undecidable. . . . And naturally, the resources of the master-at-arms for understanding the men over whom he is to exercise discipline replicate so faithfully the disciplinary imperative itself that they can convey to him nothing but mirrorings of the panic of his own position. . . .

A more ingenuous and less paranoid personality structure than Billy's, we are repeatedly informed, it would be impossible to imagine. Who could be more immune to paranoid contagion than a person with no cognition at all? Yet even the determined resistance posed by Billy's stupidity can be made, under the right pressure of events, to answer actively as a mirror to the exactions of paranoid desire. In Robert K. Martin's acute summary of the murder itself, for instance,

> Claggart's desire for Billy is not only a desire to hurt Billy, but also a desire to *provoke* Billy, so that *he* (Claggart) can be raped by Billy. His false accusation

achieves this purpose by finally provoking Billy to raise his arm. . . . When Billy strikes Claggart, he in some way fulfills Claggart's desire: Claggart dies instantly, at last possessed by that which he has sought to possess.[7]

Discipline/Terrorism

It is easy to forget, however, that the pressure under which Billy and Claggart are finally, in the scene of Claggart's murder, faced off as if symmetrically against one another is not simply the pressure of Claggart's position and desire. Rather, it is the pressure of *Vere's mobilization of Claggart's position and desire.* I mean to argue that the force and direction of paranoid knowing—of, in the past century, the homophobic/homosexual momentum around men's desire for men—are manipulable, though not reliably so, by certain apparently nonparanoid processes of reframing and redefinition affecting the binarisms we are discussing, and exemplified by Captain Vere.

One useful distinction to adduce, though as an opposition it will prove no more absolute than those others we already have in play, could be between two structures of enforcement. From the inefficient, paranoiacally organized structure we have already discussed, symmetrical and "one-on-one," based on entrapment and the agent provocateur, *Billy Budd* suggests that it may be possible to differentiate another: the more efficient because spectacular one of exemplary violence, the male body elevated for display. "War looks but to the frontage, the appearance. And the Mutiny Act, War's child, takes after the father" (1416), Vere reflects, railroading Billy's death sentence through his drumhead court. The bodies of executed men already preside over the prehistory of the book, where discipline after the Great Mutiny is shown to have been "confirmed only when its ringleaders were hung for an admonitory spectacle to the anchored fleet" (1477*n*.1405.31). The sacrificial body of Lord Nelson, both in life and in death, has itself been an admonitory spectacle of great magnetism. . . .

Of course, at a more routine level but scarcely less grievous, there is the galvanizing effect on Billy of the brutal public ritual of flogging that he sees enacted on his own ship. . . . The association of Captain Vere with on the one hand the cognitive category of discipline, and on the other the physical image of the single human body elevated from the common horizon of view, is stamped by the story even on his firmamental nickname, "Starry Vere." This comes, we are told, from lines in "Upon Appleton House,"

This 'tis to have been from the first
In a domestic heaven nursed,
Under the discipline severe
Of Fairfax and the starry Vere.
(1370)

[7]Martin, *Hero, Captain, and Stranger,* p. 112.

Again, the inflexibility of Vere's converse is attributed by the narrator to a constitutional "directness, sometimes far-reaching like that of a migratory fowl that in its flight never heeds when it crosses a frontier" (1372). Vere's discipline is thus associated with physical elevation in two ways. First, his preferred form of discipline depends, as we have seen, on positioning some male body not his own in a sacrificial "bad eminence" of punitive visibility, an eminence that (in his intention) forms the organizing summit of what thereby becomes a triangle or pyramid of male relations, a "wedged mass of upturned faces" (1427), the men at whom the spectacle is aimed being braced by their shared witness of it into a supposedly stabilized clutch of subordination. In another version of Vere's disciplinary triangle, however, his own seeing eye, not the looked-upon body of some other man who has been made an example of, makes the apex of the disciplinary figure.

The defining example of this latter tableau is the way Vere chooses to handle Claggart's insinuations to him about Billy Budd: he cannot rest until the stage is set on which he may stand "prepared to scrutinize the mutually confronting visages" (1403) of the two men who are or are soon to be locked in a mutually fatal knot of paranoid symmetry. The geometric symmetry of their confrontation seems to be essential to Vere's achieving the elevated distance to which he aspires. At the same time, it is Vere's desire to adjudicate from such a disciplinary distance, one defined by its very difference from the mutual confrontation of symmetrical visages, that completes the mutuality and entirely *creates* the fatality of the paranoid knot of Claggart and Billy Budd.[8] At the crudest level, had Vere been content either to hear the two men's depositions separately or to grant them an official hearing—to confront each with his own visage, or each with the collective visage of a court-martial, rather than each with the other's visage under Vere's "impartial" eye—then neither of the men would have been murdered.

Vere's discipline both requires and enforces the paranoid symmetry against which it is defined, then, just as it will not dispense with the system of police entrapment whose squalid techniques provide at once foil and fodder for the celestial justice-machine.[9] It is Vere's "judicious" justice that solders Billy into

[8]And even after Claggart's death, Vere's fine sense of space persists in keeping the two men confronted: his drumhead court takes place in a room flanked by two "compartments," in one of which Claggart's body lies, "opposite that where the foretopman remained immured" (1406).

[9]Indeed, there is some suggestion that Vere's transcendent, "judicious" urbanity may be enabled by, or even indistinguishable from, a paranoid relation—"strong suspicion clogged by strange dubieties" (1402)—precisely to Claggart's relation to the crew. The same man who is rendered suspicious by Claggart's protective suggestion that Billy's "daisies" might conceal "a man trap" (1400) apprehends Claggart himself, in turn, as part of a gestalt of submerged dangers the very recognition of which could enmesh him the more fatally in their operations:

[L]ong versed in everything pertaining to the complicated gun-deck life, which like every other form of life has its secret mines and dubious side, the side popularly disclaimed, Captain Vere did not permit himself to be unduly disturbed by the general tenor of his subordinate's report.

Furthermore, if in view of recent events prompt action should be taken at the first

the vis-à-vis from which—with the incitement of Vere's generous contradictory address and the ignition of his kindly digital touch—neither Claggart nor Billy will emerge alive. . . .

Majority/Minority; Impartiality/Partiality

The disciplinary triangle whose apex is the adjudicating eye, or the one capped by the exemplary object of discipline: these are only pseudo-alternative formations, to the degree that the same agent, Captain Vere, is in charge of the circulation of characters from one positioning to another. How steady his hand seems on this kaleidoscope—how consistent his desire! His hungers and his helmsmanship he wields together with a masterful economy. The desires of Captain Vere are desires of the eye:

> Now the Handsome Sailor as a signal figure among the crew had naturally enough attracted the captain's attention from the first. Though in general not very demonstrative to his officers, he had congratulated Lieutenant Ratcliffe upon his good fortune in lighting on such a fine specimen of the *genus homo*, who in the nude might have posed for a statue of young Adam before the Fall. . . . The foretopman's conduct, too, so far as it had fallen under the captain's notice, had confirmed the first happy augury, while the new recruit's qualities as a "sailor-man" seemed to be such that he had thought of recommending him to the executive officer for promotion to a place that would more frequently bring him under his own observation, namely, the captaincy of the mizzentop, replacing there in the starboard watch a man not so young whom partly for that reason he deemed less fitted for the post. (1400–1401)

The casting of sky-eyed Billy in the generic role of the "Handsome Sailor" has suggested from the beginning of the story his ocular consumability as a figure lofted high in the field of vision, "Aldebaran among the lesser lights of his constellation" (1353), "a superb figure, tossed up as by the horns of Taurus against the thunderous sky" (1354). When Claggart, unobserved, glimpses "belted Billy rolling along the upper gun deck," his repertoire of responses is circumscribed and ineffectual: "his eyes strangely suffused with incipient feverish tears" (1394), setting in motion again the embittering cycle of "pale ire, envy, and despair" (1457n.1384.14). Captain Vere, on the other hand, desires not to hold Billy but to behold him, for while Claggart "could even have loved Billy but for fate and ban" (1394), to Vere the "stripling" whom his instinctive fantasy is to (denude and) turn to marble must remain a mere "specimen" of "the right stuff" (1400–1401). In contrast to Claggart's toilsome enmeshments, Vere's eye sees in Billy a clean-cut stimulus to his executive

---

palpable sign of recurring insubordination, for all that, not judicious would it be, he thought, to keep the idea of lingering disaffection alive by undue forwardness in crediting an informer. (1399)

aptitudes, the catalyst of a personnel-management project to get the magnificent torso hoisted up to "a place that would more frequently bring him under his own observation." If there are frustrations entailed in Vere's system of supplying his eye with sustenance, those have to do only with the contingency and mutability of particular, embodied flesh: unlike marble or the platonic abstraction *genus homo*, particular lads grow "not so young" and become "partly for that reason" unfitted to the prominent "watch."

Impossible not to admire the deftness with which Captain Vere succeeds in obviating his frustrations and assuring the fulfillment of his desire. Billy displayed, Billy aloft in "a place . . . under his own observation," Billy platonized, Billy the "pendant pearl" (1434), Billy who won't grow old. The last third of the novella, the shockingly quick forced-march of Billy to the mainyard gallows and his apotheosis there: wholly and purely the work of Captain Vere, these represent the perfect answer to a very particular hunger.

It is time to pause here, perhaps, and ask explictly what it means to have found in Claggart the homosexual in this text, and in Vere its image of the normal. Just as the Uranian disciplinary justice of "Starry" Vere depends on the same paranoid policial clinch that it defines itself by transcending, Vere's supposedly impartial motivations toward Billy Budd are also founded on a Claggart-like partiality as against which, however, they as well are imperiously counterposed. Claggart's "partiality" and Vere's "impartiality": perhaps rather than being mutually external opposing entities, X versus non-X, desire versus non-desire, "partial" and "impartial" are meant to relate here instead as *part* to *whole*: Claggart's impotent constricted desire gnawing at his own viscera, Vere's potent systemic desire outspread through all the veins and fault lines of naval regulation. The most available term for Claggart's desire may be "private"; for Vere's, "public." But what do these designations mean?

Public/Private

. . . One of the most consequential intuitions of Melville's talent was how like the space of a sailing ship could be to that of the Shakespearean theatre. Each of these (all-male) venues made graphic the truth that the other architectural vernaculars of the nineteenth century, at any rate, conspired to cover over: that the difference between "public" and "private" could never be stably or intelligibly represented as a difference between two concrete classes of physical space. Instead, on shipboard as on the boards, the space for those acts whose performative efficacy depended on their being defined as either private or public had to be delineated and categorized anew for each. . . . The same space on deck, after all, may be treated as a space of work, of promiscuous society, of converse, of business, of solitude—depending on the original investment of authority, and the continual draughts of it thereafter, of the person who claims the right to define the space. . . . When Vere determines, therefore, that the measure required for the continuance of this encounter "involve[s] a shifting of the scene, a transfer to a place less exposed to observation" (1402), he is responding to a range of difficult imperatives by manipulating a range of sensitive binarisms. In addition to the discomfort of having to maintain by exertion of willpower an impermeable interlocutory space within a physical space that is actually awash with people, he is also responding to the double bind constituted by the status of mutiny in his navy as an open secret. . . . Along with stage-managing the physical space of the encounter over the charged threshold from open-air to closed-door . . . and its informational space over the threshold from demonstrative to secret, Vere has also activated yet another public/private threshold, the threshold between acts done on the responsibility of the person and acts done in the name of the state, between the official and the unofficial.

At whatever point in the story Vere may tacitly have decided on the fate he has in mind for Billy Budd, it is within an instant after the death of Claggart under these stressed and equivocal circumstances that he first utters aloud his declaration of purpose: "the angel must hang!" (1406). In accomplishing that project Vere can scarcely depend on the narrow channel of strict official procedure, since according to that, as the surgeon reflects, "The thing to do . . . was to place Billy Budd in confinement, and in a way dictated by usage, and postpone further action in so extraordinary a case to such time as they should rejoin the squadron, and then refer it to the admiral" (1406–7). For Vere, however (as indeed, it turns out, for his superiors), "martial duty" (1409), which refers to the overarching conjunction of his mutiny panic with his visual desire, represents a higher law than the merely tactical facilities of official usage; and what "martial duty" dictates is a rhetorical tour de force by which the line between the official and the unofficial can be danced across back and forth, back and forth in a breathtakingly sustained choreography of the liminal, giving the authority of stern collective judgment and the common weal to what are, after all, the startlingly specific sensory hungers of a single man.

Thus, "reserving to himself . . . the right of maintaining a supervision of it, or formally or informally interposing at need," Vere "summarily" convenes a drumhead court, "he electing the individuals composing it" (1409). His desire in choosing them is to find men "altogether reliable in a moral dilemma involving aught of the tragic" (1409)—that is to say, men who can be persuaded from the beginning, as a matter of definition, that this is a story that *is* tragic: one that must inevitably end with death, and with a death of a certain exemplary altitude and gravity. In constructing that death as—against all the odds—inevitable, Captain Vere has to do not only the police but the judge, witness, defense, and D.A. in different voices, always, however, trading on his prerogatives of position as the captain of the vessel, as well. If Captain Vere, as prosecution witness, happens to respond to testimony by the accused with the more than witnesslike affirmation "I believe you, my man," it will scarcely occasion surprise that Billy can address him only as "your honor" (1410). Billy's unwavering trust in him, on which the smoothness of the official proceedings also depends, comes, however, from viewing him in the wholly unofficial light of "his best helper and friend" (1411). As witness, as "coadjutor" (1414), as commanding officer, as best friend to the defendant, as chief prosecutor, as final judge, as consoler and explainer and visitant, and at the last as chief executioner and chief mourner, Vere contrives by his ceaseless crossing of these lines of oppositionality and of rank not to obscure such demarcations but to heighten them and, by doing so, to heighten the prestige of his own mastery in overruling them.

Sincerity/Sentimentality

Ann Douglas ends her jeremiad against "the feminization of American culture" with a climactic celebration of *Billy Budd,* choosing this particular text because *Billy Budd* represents in her argument the precise opposite of the category of the sentimental. Ann Douglas's *Billy Budd* is Captain Vere's *Billy Budd*: Vere is not only its "fair-minded" hero but its God. And in Douglas's account Captain Vere shares with the story itself a "remoteness" that only enhances the "essential fairness" of each; *his* virtue of a spacious judiciousness is *its* virtue of a spacious judiciousness.[10]

What most characterizes the exemplary nonsentimentality of the novella *Billy Budd* and of Captain Vere, according to Douglas, is the total scrupulousness with which each respects the boundaries between the public and the private. "Everything has its place," Douglas writes approvingly. "Melville respects his characters' privacy." Vere, analogously, operating "on the impersonal, even allegorical plane," is absolved of having any "personal" motivation for his sacrifice of Billy. And his divine stature is guaranteed by the complete impermeability that is said to obtain between his own public and private lives. "His action in condemning Budd is analogous to the Calvinist Deity's in sacrificing Christ. Vere suffers in private for the fact that he has pulled off a totally public gesture." Thus, he and the story become, in Douglas's argument, the perfect antithesis to a century-long process of sentimental degradation of American culture, a process in the course of which public and private have become fatally confused.

Douglas's reading of Captain Vere is a powerful one in the sense that it records sharply an effect that Vere and his text do powerfully generate. It might be called the privacy effect: the illusion that a reader of *Billy Budd* has witnessed a struggle between private and public realms that are distinguished

---

[10]All the material quoted is from Ann Douglas, *The Feminization of American Culture* (New York: Alfred A. Knopf, 1977; rpt. ed., New York: Avon/Discus, 1978), pp. 391–95.

from one another with quite unusual starkness. Vere is the character who seems most identified with and responsible for the austerity of this definitional segregation, and as readers we habitually celebrate or deprecate Vere according to whether or not we approve of so scrupulous a segregation, or of so absolute a denegation of the private in favor of the public realm so demarcated. . . .

I hope I have already said enough about the incoherence of the public/ private duality aboard the *Bellipotent*, and about the sinuosity of Captain Vere's relation to it, to suggest that the creation by this text and this character of this intense a *privacy effect* is a stunning fictional achievement. How is the trick done? How, for instance, do readers come to be convinced that we know that "*Vere suffers in private*" for his "public" gesture?

For the most part, we receive this information in the same way the officers and crew receive it. . . . We know that "Vere suffers in private" because Vere suffers in private in public. We know, furthermore, that Vere suffers in secret and in silence, by the operatic volubility and visibility with which he performs the starring role of Captain *agonistes*. Rather than seek out a private space for what may be his private suffering (as if there were private space aboard the *Bellipotent*—as if there were private space anywhere), Vere instead sets out to reorganize his immediate, populous community through a piece of theatre by which he himself may come to embody, in his speech and in his very physique, the site of definitional struggle between public and private. Through this act of daring, Vere is conclusively confirmed in his judicial authority by dramatizing, for a subjected audience, his own body as the suffering site of categorizing division. "Sentimentality" can serve as a name for one side, the ejected side, of the category division embodied in him—and, at the same time, as a name for the overarching strategy that is here deployed around him. . . .

To Vere, to the story, and to the little world of the *Bellipotent* two things are happening together, then, in the wake of the death of Claggart. First, Vere is increasingly impelled toward a strategy of dramaturgic embodiment. The uses he needs to make of the categories "public" and "private," and the increasing stress and visibility of his doing so, evoke in him a new, almost Nixonian verve and recklessness in exploiting and transgressing their boundaries. The fact that his resource for doing so is to organize a theatrical ritual around the liminal sufferings of not only Billy's body but his own, however, subjects him to a vulnerability entirely new to him. That is a vulnerability, not to the already accounted-for-suffering or self-division he embodies, but to the exactions of embodiment itself. As an object of view—for his officers and men, but most of all for the narrative itself—the Nixonized Vere becomes subjected, in a way that he cannot, after all, bring under single-handed control, to the indignities of taxonomy, circulation, and ocular consumption. Nixonlike, he is most taxonomically vulnerable at the very moments when his strategy of embodiment is working most powerfully: competence and craziness, or discipline and desire, seem dangerously close to one another as they become manifest through the staged body.

The terms of Vere's taxonomy, circulation, consumption have been set by *the preexistence of a homosexual in the text.* Yet, until the death of the homosexual, those terms had seemed sufficiently stabilized by their attachment to that painstakingly minoritized, exploitable figure, and to the induced symmetries between him and the also objectified Billy. As soon as Billy has killed Claggart, however, the circuit of objectification gapes open to envelop Vere as well. . . .

Wholeness/Decadence; Utopia/Apocalypse

Repeatedly, the narrative fulcrum of *Billy Budd*, when the story is read as an account of the interplay between minoritizing and universalizing understandings of homo/heterosexual definition, has turned out to be the moment of the death of Claggart, the man through whom a minority definition becomes visible. What are we to make of so cruel a fact? *Billy Budd* is a document from the very moment of the emergence of a modern homosexual identity. But already inscribed in that emergent identity seems to be, not only the individual fatality that will metamorphose into the routine gay suicides and car crashes of the twentieth-century celluloid closet,[11] but something more awful: the fantasy trajectory toward a life *after the homosexual.*

Now slides the silent meteor on, and leaves
A shining furrow, as thy thoughts in me.[12]

The spatialized counterposition of characters we posed in the first half of our analysis should not obscure the narrative fact: the glamorized, phosphorescent romantic relations between Vere and the doomed Billy constitute the shining furrow of the disappearance of the homosexual. From the static tableau of Vere's discipline we moved on to look for temporality and change in Vere himself, in his ambitions, his strategies, his presentation, his fate—as, against a heaven already denuded of its minority constellation, Vere, like Billy, set his sights toward that greater majority, the dead, that Claggart had already joined.

From at least the biblical story of Sodom and Gomorrah, scenarios of same-sex desire would seem to have had a privileged, though by no means an exclusive, relation in Western culture to scenarios of both genocide and omnicide. That sodomy, the name by which homosexual acts are known even

---

[11]See Vito Russo, *The Celluloid Closet: Homosexuality in the Movies*, revised ed. (New York: Harper & Row, 1987), esp. the devastating "Necrology," pp. 347–49.

[12]Alfred, Lord Tennyson, "The Princess," sec. 7, in Tennyson, *Poetical Works*, ed. Geoffrey Cumberledge (London: Oxford University Press, 1941), p. 197.

today to the law of half of the United States and to the Supreme Court of all of them, should already be inscribed with the name of a site of mass extermination is the appropriate trace of a double history. In the first place there is a history of the mortal suppression, legal or subjudicial, of gay acts and gay people, through burning, hounding, physical and chemical castration, concentration camps, bashing—the array of sanctioned fatalities that Louis Crompton records under the name of gay genocide, and whose supposed eugenic motive becomes only the more colorable with the emergence of a distinct, naturalized minority identity in the nineteenth century. In the second place, though, there is the inveterate topos of associating gay acts or persons with fatalities vastly broader than their own extent: if it is ambiguous whether every denizen of the obliterated Sodom was a sodomite, clearly not every Roman of the late Empire can have been so, despite Gibbon's connecting the eclipse of the whole people to the habits of a few. Following both Gibbon and the Bible, moreover, with an impetus borrowed from Darwin, one of the few areas of agreement among modern Marxist, Nazi, and liberal capitalist ideologies is that there is a peculiarly close, though never precisely defined, affinity between same-sex desire and some historical condition of moribundity, called "decadence," to which not individuals or minorities but whole civilizations are subject. Bloodletting on a scale more massive by orders of magnitude than any gay minority presence in the culture is the "cure," if cure there be, to the mortal illness of decadence.

If a fantasy trajectory, utopian in its own terms, toward gay genocide has been endemic in Western culture from its origins, then, it may also have been true that the trajectory toward gay genocide was never clearly distinguishable from a broader, apocalyptic trajectory toward something approaching omnicide. The deadlock of the past century between minoritizing and universalizing understanding of homo/heterosexual definition can only have deepened this fatal bond in the heterosexist *imaginaire*. In our culture as in *Billy Budd*, the phobic narrative trajectory toward imagining a time *after the homosexual* is finally inseparable from that toward imagining a time *after the human*; in the wake of the homosexual, the wake incessantly produced since first there *were* homosexuals, every human relation is pulled into its shining representational furrow.

Fragments of visions of a time *after the homosexual* are, of course, currently in dizzying circulation in our culture. One of the many dangerous ways that AIDS discourse seems to ratify and amplify preinscribed homophobic mythologies is in its pseudo-evolutionary presentation of male homosexuality as a stage doomed to extinction (read, a phase the species is going through) on the enormous scale of whole populations.[13] The lineaments of openly genocidal malice behind this fantasy appear only occasionally in the respectable

[13]These reflections were stimulated by an opportunity, for which I am grateful, to read Jeffrey Nunokawa's unpublished essay, "*In Memoriam* and the Extinction of the Homosexual."

media, though they can be glimpsed even there behind the poker-face mask of our national experiment in laissez-faire medicine. A better, if still deodorized, whiff of that malice comes from the famous pronouncement of Pat Robertson: "AIDS is God's way of weeding his garden." The saccharine lustre this dictum gives to its vision of devastation, and the ruthless prurience with which it misattributes its own agency, cover a more fundamental contradiction: that, to rationalize complacent glee at a spectacle of what is imagined as genocide, a proto-Darwinian process of natural selection is being invoked—in the context of a Christian fundamentalism that is not only antievolutionist but recklessly oriented toward universal apocalypse. A similar phenomenon, also too terrible to be noted as a mere irony, is how evenly our culture's phobia about HIV-positive blood is kept pace with by its rage for keeping that dangerous blood in broad, continuous circulation. This is evidenced in projects for universal testing, and in the needle-sharing implicit in William Buckley's now ineradicable fantasy of tattooing HIV-positive persons. But most immediately and pervasively it is evidenced in the literal bloodbaths that seem to make the point of the AIDS-related resurgence in violent bashings of gays—which, unlike the gun violence otherwise ubiquitous in this culture, are characteristically done with two-by-fours, baseball bats, and fists, in the most literal-minded conceivable form of body-fluid contact.

It might be worth making explicit that the use of evolutionary thinking in the current wave of utopian/genocidal fantasy is, whatever else it may be, crazy. Unless one believes, first of all, that same-sex object-choice across history and across cultures is *one thing* with *one cause*, and, second, that its one cause is direct transmission through a nonrecessive genetic path—which would be, to put it gently, counter-intuitive—there is no warrant for imagining that gay populations, even of men, in post-AIDS generations will be in the slightest degree diminished. Exactly *to the degree* that AIDS is a gay disease, it's a tragedy confined to our generation; the long-term demographic depredations of the disease will fall, to the contrary, on groups, many themselves direly endangered, that are reproduced by direct heterosexual transmission.

Unlike genocide directed against Jews, Native Americans, Africans, or other groups, then, gay genocide, the once-and-for-all eradication of gay populations, however potent and sustained as a project or fantasy of modern Western culture, is not possible short of the eradication of the whole human species. The impulse of the species toward its own eradication must not either, however, be underestimated. Neither must the profundity with which that omnicidal impulse is entangled with the modern problematic of the homosexual: the double bind of the definition between the homosexual, say, as a distinct *risk group*, and the homosexual as a potential of representation within the universal.[14] As gay community and the solidarity and visibility of

---

[14]Richard Mohr, in "Policy, Ritual, Purity: Gays and Mandatory AIDS Testing," *Law, Medicine,*

gays as a minority population are being consolidated and tempered in the forge of this specularized terror and suffering, how can it fail to be all the more necessary that the avenues of recognition, desire, and thought between minority potentials and universalizing ones be opened and opened and opened?

---

and Health Care (forthcoming), makes a related linkage, with a more settled hypothesis about the directionality of causation:

> AIDS social coercion has become a body accelerated under the gravitational pull of our anxieties over nuclear destruction. Doing anything significant to alleviate the prospects of the joint death of everything that can die is effectively out of the reach of any ordinary individual and indeed of any political group now in existence. So individuals transfer the focus of their anxieties from nuclear omnicide to AIDS, by which they feel equally and similarly threatened, but about which they think they can do something—at least through government. AIDS coercion is doing double duty as a source of sacred values and as a vent for universal anxieties over universal destruction.

Melville's Fist:
The Execution of *Billy Budd*

Barbara Johnson

The Plot Against the Characters

. . . No consideration of the nature of character in *Billy Budd* . . . can fail to take into account the fact that the fate of each of the characters is the direct reverse of what one is led to expect from his "nature." Billy is sweet, innocent, and harmless, yet he kills. Claggart is evil, perverted, and mendacious, yet he dies a victim. Vere is sagacious and responsible, yet he allows a man whom he feels to be blameless to hang. It is this discrepancy between character and action that gives rise to the critical disagreement over the story: readers tend either to save the plot and condemn Billy ("acceptance," "tragedy," or "necessity"), or to save Billy and condemn the plot ("irony," "injustice," or "social criticism").

In an effort to make sense of this troubling incompatibility between character and plot, many readers are tempted to say of Billy and Claggart, as does W. Y. Tindall, that "each is more important for what he is than what he does. . . Good and bad, they occupy the region of good and evil."[1] This reading effectively preserves the allegorical values suggested by Melville's opening chapters, but it does so only by denying the importance of the plot. It ends where the plot begins: with the identification of the moral natures of the characters. One may therefore ask whether the allegorical interpretation (good vs. evil) depends as such on this sort of preference for "being" over "doing," and, if so, what effect the incompatibility between character and action may have on the allegorical functioning of *Billy Budd*.

Interestingly enough, Melville himself both invites an allegorical reading and subverts the very terms of its consistency when he writes of the murder: "Innocence and guilt personified in Claggart and Budd in effect changed places."[2] Allowing for the existence of personification but reversing the rela-

From *Studies in Romanticism*, 18.4. Copyright © 1979, Trustees of Boston University.

[1]"The Ceremony of Innocence," in R. M. McIver, ed., *Great Moral Dilemmas in Literature, Past and Present* (New York: Harper & Row, 1956), p. 75.

[2]Melville, *Billy Budd*, in *"Billy Budd, Sailor," and Other Stories*, ed. H. Beaver (New York: Penguin Books, 1967), p. 380. Unless otherwise indicated, all references to *Billy Budd* are to this edition, which reprints the Hayford and Sealts Reading Text.

tion between personifier and personified, positioning an opposition between good and evil only to make each term take on the properties of its opposite, Melville thus sets up his plot in the form of a chiasmus:

Billy —————————————— Innocence
Claggart ————————————— Guilt

This story, which is often read as a retelling of the story of Christ, is thus literally a cruci-fiction—a fiction structured in the shape of a cross. At the moment of the reversal, an instant before his fist shoots out, Billy's face seems to mark out the point of crossing, bearing "an expression which was as a crucifixion to behold" (p. 376). Innocence and guilt, criminal and victim, change places through the mute expressiveness of Billy's inability to speak.

If *Billy Budd* is indeed an allegory, it is thus an allegory of the questioning of the traditional conditions of allegorical stability. The fact that Melville's plot requires that the good act out the evil designs of the bad while the bad suffer the unwarranted fate of the good indicates that the real opposition with which Melville is preoccupied here is less the static opposition between evil and good than the dynamic opposition between a man's "nature" and his acts, or, in Tyndall's terms, the relation between human "being" and human "doing."

Curiously enough, it is precisely this question of "being" versus "doing" that is brought up by the only sentence we ever see Claggart directly address to Billy Budd. When Billy accidentally spills his soup across the path of the master-at-arms, Claggart playfully replies, "Handsomely done, my lad! And handsome *is* as handsome *did* it, too!" (p. 350; emphasis mine). The proverbial expression "handsome *is* as handsome *does*," from which this exclamation springs, posits the possibility of a continuous, predictable, transparent relationship between "being" and "doing." It supposes that the inner goodness of Billy Budd is in harmonious accord with his fair appearance, that, as Melville writes of the stereotypical "Handsome Sailor" in the opening pages of the story, "the moral nature" is not "out of keeping with the physical make" (p. 322). But it is precisely this continuity between the physical and the moral, between appearance and action, or between "being" and "doing," that Claggart questions in Billy Budd. He warns Captain Vere not to be taken in by Billy's physical beauty: "You have but noted his fair cheek. A mantrap may be under the ruddy-tipped daisies" (p. 372). Claggart indeed soon finds his suspicions confirmed with a vengeance; when he repeats his accusation in front of Billy, he is struck down dead. It would thus seem that to question the continuity between character and action cannot be done with impunity, that fundamental questions of life and death are always surreptitiously involved.

In an effort to examine what it is that is at stake in Claggart's accusation, it might be helpful to view the opposition between Billy and Claggart as an opposition not between innocence and guilt but between two conceptions of language, or between two types of reading. Billy seemingly represents the perfectly *motivated* sign; that is, his inner self (the signified) is considered transparently readable from the beauty of his outer self (the signifier). His "straightforward simplicity" is the very opposite of the "moral obliquities" or "crookedness of heart" that characterizes "citified" or rhetorically sophisticated man. "To deal in double meanings and insinuations of any sort," writes Melville, "was quite foreign to his nature" (p. 327). In accordance with this "nature," Billy reads everything at face value, never questioning the meaning of appearances. He is dumbfounded at the Dansker's suggestion, "incomprehensible to a novice," that Claggart's very pleasantness can be interpreted as its opposite, as a sign that he is "down on" Billy Budd. To Billy, "the occasional frank air and pleasant word *went for what they purported to be*, the young sailor never having heard as yet of the 'too fair-spoken man' " (pp. 365–66; emphasis mine). As a reader, then, Billy is symbolically as well as factually illiterate. His literal-mindedness is represented by his illiteracy because, in assuming that language can be taken at face value, he excludes the very functioning of *difference* that makes the act of reading both indispensable and undecidable.

Claggart, on the other hand, is the very image of difference and duplicity, both in his appearance and in his character. His face is not ugly, but it hints of something defective or abnormal. He has no vices, yet he incarnates evil. He is an intellectual, but uses reason as "an ambidexter implement for effecting the irrational" (p. 354). Billy inspires in him both "profound antipathy" and a "soft yearning." In the incompatibility of his attitudes, Claggart is thus a personification of ambiguity and ambivalence, of the distance between signifier and signified, of the separation between being and doing: "apprehending the good, but powerless to be it, a nature like Claggart's, . . . what recourse is left to it but to recoil upon itself" (p. 356). As a reader, Claggart has learned to "exercise a distrust keen in proportion to the fairness of the appearance" (p. 364). He is properly an ironic reader, who, assuming the sign to be arbitrary and unmotivated, reverses the value signs of appearances and takes a daisy for a mantrap and an unmotivated accidental spilling of soup for an intentional sly escape of antipathy. Claggart meets his downfall, however, when he attempts to master the arbitrariness of the sign for his own ends, precisely by falsely (that is, arbitrarily) accusing Billy of harboring arbitrariness, of hiding a mutineer beneath the appearance of a baby.

Such a formulation of the Budd/Claggart relationship enables one to take a new look not only at the story itself, but at the criticism as well. For, curiously enough, it is precisely this opposition between the literal reader (Billy) and the ironic reader (Claggart) that is reenacted in the critical readings of *Billy Budd* in the opposition between the "acceptance" school and the "irony" school. Those who see the story as a "testament of acceptance" tend to take Billy's final benediction of Vere at face value; as Lewis Mumford puts it, "As Melville's own end approached, he cried out with Billy Budd: God Bless Captain Vere! In this final affirmation Herman Melville died."[3] In contrast,

[3]*Herman Melville* (New York: Harcourt, Brace & World, Inc., 1929), p. 357.

those who read the tale ironically tend to take Billy's sweet farewell as Melville's bitter curse. Joseph Schiffman writes: "At heart a kind man, Vere, strange to say, makes possible the depraved Claggart's wish—the destruction of Billy. " 'God bless Captain Vere!' Is this not piercing irony? As innocent Billy utters these words, does not the reader gag?" (p. 133). But since the acceptance/irony dichotomy is already contained within the story, since it is obviously one of the things the story is *about*, it is not enough to try to decide which of the readings is correct. What the reader of *Billy Budd* must do is to analyze what is at stake in the very opposition between literality and irony. . . .

Three Readings of Reading

It is no doubt significant that the character around whom the greatest critical dissent has revolved is neither the good one nor the evil one but the one who is explicitly presented as a *reader*, Captain Vere. On some level, readers of *Billy Budd* have always testified to the fact that it is reading, as much as killing, that is at the heart of Melville's story. But how is the act of reading being manifested? . . .

It seems evident that Billy's reading method consists in taking everything at face value, while Claggart's consists in seeing a mantrap under every daisy. Yet in practice, neither of these methods is rigorously upheld. The naive reader is not naive enough to forget to edit out information too troubling to report. The instability of the space between sign and referent, normally denied by the naive reader, is called upon as an *instrument* whenever that same instability threatens to disturb the *content* of meaning itself. Billy takes every sign as transparently readable as long as what he reads is consistent with transparent peace, order, and authority. When this is not so, his reading clouds accordingly. And Claggart, for whom every sign can be read as its opposite, neglects to doubt the transparency of any sign that tends to confirm his own doubts: "the master-at-arms *never suspected the veracity*" (p. 357) of Squeak's reports. The naive believer thus refuses to believe any evidence that subverts the transparency of his beliefs, while the ironic doubter forgets to suspect the reliability of anything confirming his own suspicions.

Naiveté and irony thus stand as symmetrical opposites blinded by their very incapacity to see anything but symmetry. Claggart, in his antipathy, "can really form no conception of an *unreciprocated* malice" (p. 358). And Billy, conscious of his own blamelessness, can see nothing but pleasantness in Claggart's pleasant words: "Had the foretopman been conscious of having done or said anything to provoke the ill-will of the official, it would have been different with him, and his sight might have been purged if not sharpened. As it was, innocence was his blinder" (p. 366). Each character sees the other only through the mirror of his own reflection. Claggart, looking at Billy, mistakes his own twisted face for the face of the enemy, while Billy, recognizing in Claggart the negativity he smothers in himself, strikes out.

The naive and the ironic readers are thus equally destructive, both of themselves and of each other. It is significant that both Billy and Claggart should die. Both readings do violence to the plays of ambiguity and belief by forcing upon the text the applicability of a universal and absolute law. The one, obsessively intent on preserving peace and eliminating equivocation, murders the text; the other, seeing nothing but universal war, becomes the spot on which aberrant premonitions of negativity become truth. . . .

In order to analyze what is at stake in Melville's portrait of Vere, let us first examine the ways in which Vere's reading differs from those of Billy Budd and John Claggart:

1. While the naive/ironic dichotomy was based on a symmetry between *individuals*, Captain Vere's reading takes place within a social *structure:* the rigidly hierarchical structure of a British warship. While the naive reader (Billy) destroys the other in order to defend the self, and while the ironic reader (Claggart) destroys the self by projecting aggression onto the other, the third reader (Vere) subordinates both self and other, and ultimately sacrifices both self and other, for the preservation of a political order.

2. The apparent purpose of both Billy's and Claggart's readings was to determine *character:* to preserve innocence or to prove guilt. Vere, on the other hand, subordinates character to action, being to doing: "A martial court," he tells his officer, "must needs in the present case confine its attention to the *blow's consequence*, which consequence justly is to be deemed not otherwise than as the *striker's deed*" (p. 384).

3. In the opposition between the metaphysical and the psychoanalytical readings of Billy's deed, the deciding question was whether the blow should be considered accidental or (unconsciously) motivated. But in Vere's courtroom reading, both these alternatives are irrelevant: "Budd's intent or non-intent is nothing to the purpose" (p. 389). What matters is not the cause but the consequences of the blow.

4. The naive or literal reader takes language at face value and treats signs as *motivated*; the ironic reader assumes that the relation between sign and meaning can be *arbitrary* and that appearances are made to be reversed. For Vere, the functions and meanings of signs are neither transparent nor reversible but fixed by socially determined *convention*. Vere's very character is determined not by a relation between his outward appearance and his inner being but by the "buttons" that signify his position in society. While both Billy and Claggart are said to owe their character to "Nature," Vere sees his actions and being as meaningful only within the context of a contractual allegiance:

Do these buttons that we wear attest that our allegiance is to Nature? No, to the King. Though the ocean, which is inviolate Nature primeval, though this be the element where we move and have our being as sailors, yet as the King's officers lies our duty in a sphere correspondingly natural? So little is that true, that in receiving

our commissions we in the most important regards ceased to be natural free agents.
When war is declared are we the commissioned fighters previously consulted? We
fight at command. If our judgments approve the war, that is but coincidence.
(p. 387)

Judgment is thus for Vere, a function neither of individual conscience nor of
absolute justice but of "the rigor of martial law" (p. 387) operating *through*
him.

> 5. While Billy and Claggart read spontaneously and directly, Vere's reading often
> makes use of precedent (historical facts, childhood memories), allusions (to the
> Bible, to various ancient and modern authors), and analogies (Billy is like Adam,
> Claggart is like Ananias). Just as both Billy and Claggart have no known past, they
> read without memory; just as their lives end with their reading, they read without
> foresight. Vere, on the other hand, interrogates both past and future for interpreta-
> tive guidance.

> 6. While Budd and Claggart thus oppose each other directly, without regard for
> circumstance or consequence, Vere reads solely in function of the attending
> historical situation: the Nore and Spithead mutinies have created an atmosphere
> "critical to naval authority" (p. 380), and, since an engagement with the enemy fleet
> is possible at any moment, the *Bellipotent* cannot afford internal unrest.

The fundamental factor that underlies the opposition between the metaphysical Budd/Claggart conflict on the one hand and the reading of Captain Vere on
the other can be summed up in a single word: history. While the naive and
the ironic readers attempt to impose upon language the functioning of an
absolute, timeless, universal law (the sign as *either* motivated *or* arbitrary),
the question of *martial* law arises within the story precisely to reveal the law
as a *historical* phenomenon, to underscore the element of contextual mutability in the conditions of any act of reading. Arbitrariness and motivation, irony
and literality, are parameters between which language constantly fluctuates,
but only historical content determines which proportion of each is perceptible
to each reader. Melville indeed shows history to be a story not only of events
but also of fluctuations in the very functioning of irony and belief:

> The event *converted into irony for a time* those spirited strains of Dibdin. . . .
> (p. 333)

> Everything is *for a term venerated* in navies.
> (p. 408)

The opposing critical judgments of Vere's decision to hang Billy are divided, in the final analysis, according to the place they attribute to history in
the process of justification. For the ironists, Vere is misusing history for his
own self-preservation or for the preservation of a world safe for aristocracy.
For those who accept Vere's verdict as tragic but necessary, it is Melville who
has stacked the historical cards in Vere's favor. In both cases, the conception of
history as an interpretive instrument remains the same: it is its *use* that is

being judged. And the very fact that Billy Budd criticism itself historically moves from acceptance to irony is no doubt itself interpretable in the same historical terms.

Evidence can in fact be found in the text for both pro-Vere and anti-Vere judgments:

> Full of disquietude and misgiving, the surgeon left the cabin. Was Captain Vere suddenly affected in his mind?
> (p. 378)

> Whether Captain Vere, as the surgeon professionally and privately surmised, was really the sudden victim of any degree of aberration, every one must determine for himself by such light as this narrative may afford.
> (p. 379–80)

> That the unhappy event which has been narrated could not have happened at a worse juncture was but too true. For it was close on the heel of the suppressed insurrections, an aftertime very critical to naval authority, demanding from every English sea commander two qualities not readily interfusable—prudence and rigor.
> (p. 380)

> Small wonder then that the *Bellipotent's* captain . . . felt that circumspection not less than promptitude was necessary. . . . Here he may or may not have erred.
> (p. 380)

The effect of these explicit oscillations of judgment within the text is to underline the *importance* of the act of judging while rendering its outcome undecidable. Judgment, however difficult, is clearly the central preoccupation of Melville's text, whether it be the judgment pronounced *by* Vere or *upon* him.

There is still another reason for the uncertainty over Vere's final status, however: the unfinished state of the manuscript at Melville's death. According to editors Hayford and Sealts,[4] it is the "late pencil revisions" that cast the greatest doubt upon Vere; Melville was evidently still fine-tuning the text's attitude toward its third reader when he died. The ultimate irony in the tale is thus that our final judgment of the very reader who takes history into consideration is made problematic precisely by the intervention of history: by the historical accident of the author's death. History here affects interpretation not only within the content of the narration but also within the very production of the narrative. And what remains suspended by this historical accident is nothing less than the exact signifying value of history itself. Clearly, the meaning of "history" as a feature distinguishing Vere's reading from those of Claggart and Budd can in no way be taken for granted.

---

[4]Editors' Introduction, *Billy Budd, Sailor* (Chicago: University of Chicago Press, 1962); see esp. pp. 34–35.

Judgment as Political Performance

> When a poet takes his seat on the tripod of the Muse, he cannot control his thoughts. . . . When he represents men with contrasting characters he is often obliged to contradict himself, and he doesn't know which of the opposing speeches contains the truth. But for the legislator, this is impossible: he must not let his laws say two different things on the same subject.
>
> —Plato, *The Laws*

In the final analysis, the question is not: what did Melville really think of Captain Vere? but rather: what is at stake in his way of presenting him? What can we learn from him about the act of judging? Melville seems to be presenting us less with an *object* for judgment than with an *example* of judgment. And the very vehemence with which the critics tend to praise or condemn the justice of Vere's decision indicates that it is judging, not murdering, that Melville is asking us to judge.

And yet Vere's judgment *is* an act of murder. Captain Vere is a reader who kills, not, like Billy, *instead* of speaking, but rather, precisely *by means of* speaking. While Billy kills through verbal impotence, Vere kills through the very potency and sophistication of rhetoric. Judging, in Vere's case, is nothing less than the wielding of the power of life and death through language. In thus occupying the point at which murder and language meet, Captain Vere positions himself precisely astride the "deadly space between." While Billy's performative force occupies the vanishing point of utterance and cognition, and while the validity of Claggart's cognitive perception is realized only through the annihilation of the perceiver, Captain Vere's reading mobilizes both power and knowledge, performance and cognition, error and murder. Judgment is precisely cognition functioning as an act. It is this combination of performance and cognition that defines Vere's reading not merely as historical but as *political*. If politics is defined as the attempt to reconcile action with understanding, then Melville's story offers an exemplary context in which to analyze the interpretive and performative structures that make politics so problematic.

That the alliance between knowledge and action is by no means an easy one is amply demonstrated in Melville's story. Vere indeed has often been seen as the character in the tale who experiences the greatest suffering: his understanding of Billy's character and his military duty are totally at odds. On the one hand, cognitive exactitude requires that "history" be taken into consideration. Yet what constitutes "knowledge of history"? How are "circumstances" to be defined? What sort of causality does "precedent" imply? And what is to be done with overlapping but incompatible "contexts"? Before deciding upon innocence and guilt, Vere must define and limit the frame of reference within which his decision is to be possible. He does so by choosing the "legal" context over the "essential" context: "In a *legal view* the apparent victim of the tragedy was he who had sought to victimize a man blameless; and the indisputable deed of the latter, *navally regarded,* constituted the most heinous of military crimes. Yet more. The *essential right and wrong* involved in the matter, the clearer that might be, so much the worse for the responsibility of a loyal sea commander, inasmuch as he was not authorized to determine the matter on that *primitive* basis" (p. 380). Yet it is precisely this determination of the proper frame of reference that dictates the outcome of the decision: once Vere has defined his context, he has also in fact reached his verdict. The very choice of the *conditions* of judgment itself constitutes a judgment. But what are the conditions of choosing the conditions of judgment?

The alternative, it seems, is between the "naval" and the "primitive," between "Nature" and "the King," between the martial court and what Vere calls the "Last Assizes" (p. 388). But the question arises of exactly what the concept of "Nature" entails in such an opposition. In what way, and with what changes, would it have been possible for Vere's allegiance to be to "Nature"? How can a legal judgment exemplify "primitive" justice?

In spite of his allegiance to martial law and conventional authority, Vere clearly finds the "absolute" criteria equally applicable to Billy's deed, for he responds to each new development with the following exclamations:

"It is the divine judgment of Ananias!"
(p. 378)

"Struck dead by an angel of God! Yet the angel must hang!"
(p. 378)

"Before a court less arbitrary and more merciful than a martial one, that plea would largely extenuate. At the Last Assizes it shall acquit."
(p. 388)

"Ay, there is a mystery; but, to use a scriptural phrase, it is a 'mystery of iniquity,' a matter for psychological theologians to discuss."
(p. 385)

This last expression, which refers to the source of Claggart's antipathy, has already been mentioned by Melville's narrator and dismissed as being "tinctured with the biblical element": "If that lexicon which is based on Holy Writ were any longer popular, one might with less difficulty define and denominate certain phenomenal men. As it is, one must turn to some authority not liable to the charge of being tinctured with the biblical element" (p. 353). Vere turns to the Bible to designate Claggart's "nature"; Melville turns to a Platonic tautology. But in both cases, the question arises: what does it mean to seal an explanation with a quotation? And what, in Vere's case, does it mean to refer a legal mystery to a religious text?

If Vere names the Absolute—as opposed to the martial—by means of quotations and allusions, does this not suggest that the two alternative frames of reference within which judgment is possible are not Nature and the King, but rather two types of textual authority: the Bible and the Mutiny Act? This is not to say that Vere is "innocently" choosing one text over another, but the nature of "Nature" in a legal context cannot be taken for granted. Even Thomas Paine, who is referred to by Melville in his function as proponent of "natural" human rights, cannot avoid grounding his concept of nature in Biblical myth. In the very act of rejecting the authority of antiquity, he writes: "The fact is, that portions of antiquity, by proving every thing, establish nothing. It is authority against authority all the way, till we come to the divine origin of the rights of man, at the Creation. Here our inquiries find a resting-place, and our reason a home."[5] The final frame of reference is neither the heart nor the gun, neither Nature nor the King, but the authority of a Sacred Text. Authority seems to be nothing other than the vanishing-point of textuality. And Nature is authority whose textual origins have been forgotten. Even behind the martial order of the world of the man-of-war, there lies a religious referent: the *Bellipotent*'s last battle is with a French ship called the *Athée*.

Judgment, then, would seem to ground itself in a suspension of the opposition between textuality and referentiality, just as politics can be seen as that which makes it impossible to draw the line between "language" and "life." Vere, indeed, is presented precisely as a reader who does not recognize the "frontier" between "remote allusions" and current events:

> In illustrating of any point touching the stirring personages and events of the time he would be as apt to cite some historic character or incident of antiquity as he would be to cite from the moderns. He seemed unmindful of the circumstance that to his bluff company such remote allusions, however pertinent they might really be, were altogether alien to men whose reading was mainly confined to the journals. But considerateness in such matters is not easy to natures constituted like Captain Vere's. Their honesty prescribes to them directness, sometimes far-reaching like that of a migratory fowl that in its flight never heeds when it crosses a frontier.
> (p. 341)

Yet it is precisely by inviting Billy Budd and John Claggart to "cross" the "frontier" between their proper territory and their superior's cabin, between the private and the political realms, that Vere unwittingly sets up the conditions for the narrative chiasmus he must judge.

As was noted earlier, Captain Vere's function, according to many critics, is to insert "ambiguity" into the story's "oversimplified" allegorical opposition. Yet at the same time, it is precisely Captain Vere who inspires the most vehement critical oppositions. Captain Vere, in other words, seems to mobilize simultaneously the seemingly contradictory forces of ambiguity and polarity.

[5]Thomas Paine, *The Rights of Man* (Garden City, N.Y.: Anchor Press, 1973), p. 303.

In his median position between the Budd/Claggart opposition and the acceptance/irony opposition, Captain Vere functions as a focus for the *conversion* of polarity into ambiguity and back again. Interestingly, he plays exactly the same role in the progress of the plot. It is Vere who brings together the "Innocent" Billy and the "guilty" Claggart in order to test the validity of Claggart's accusations, but he does so in such a way as to effect not a clarification but a reversal of places between guilt and innocence. Vere's fatherly words to Billy are precisely what triggers the ambiguous deed upon which Vere must pronounce a verdict of "condemn *or* let go." Just as Melville's readers, faced with the ambiguity they themselves recognize as being provided by Vere, are quick to pronounce the Captain vicious *or* virtuous, evil *or* just; so, too, Vere, who clearly perceives the "mystery" in the "moral dilemma" confronting him, must nevertheless reduce the situation to a binary opposition.

It would seem, then, that the function of judgment is to convert an ambiguous situation into a decidable one. But it does so by converting a difference *within* (Billy as divided between conscious submissiveness and unconscious hostility, Vere as divided between understanding father and military authority) into a difference *between* (between Claggart and Billy, between Nature and the King, between authority and criminality). A difference *between* opposing forces presupposes that the entities in conflict be knowable. A difference *within* one of the entities in question is precisely what problematizes the very *idea* of an entity in the first place, rendering the "legal point of view" inapplicable. In studying the plays of both ambiguity and binarity, Melville's story situates *its* critical difference neither within nor between, but precisely in the very question of the *relation between the two* as the fundamental question of all human politics. The political context in *Billy Budd* is such that on all levels the differences *within* (mutiny on the warship, the French revolution as a threat to "lasting institutions," Billy's unconscious hostility) are subordinated to differences *between* (the *Bellipotent* vs. the *Athée*, England vs. France, murderer vs. victim). This is why Melville's choice of historical setting is so significant: the war between France and England at the time of the French Revolution is as striking an example of the simultaneous functioning of differences within and between as is the confrontation between Billy and Claggart in relation to their own internal divisions. War, indeed, is the absolute transformation of *all* differences into *binary* differences.

It would seem, then, that the maintenance of political authority requires that the law function as a set of rules for the regular, predictable misreading of the "difference within" as a "difference between." Yet if, as our epigraph from Plato suggests, law is thus defined in terms of its repression of ambiguity, then it is itself an overwhelming example of an entity based on a "difference within." Like Billy, the law, in attempting to eliminate its own "deadly space," can only inscribe itself in a space of deadliness.

In seeking to regulate the violent effects of difference, the political work of cognition is thus an attempt to *situate* that which must be eliminated. Yet in the absence of the possibility of knowing the locus and origin of violence, cognition itself becomes an act of violence. In terms of pure understanding, the drawing of a line *between* opposing entities does violence to the irreducible ambiguities that subvert the very possibility of determining the limits of what an "entity" is:

> Who in the rainbow can draw the line where the violet tint ends and the orange tint begins? Distinctly we see the difference of the colors, but where exactly does the one first blendingly enter into the other? So with sanity and insanity. In pronounced cases there is no question about them. But in some supposed cases, in various degrees supposedly less pronounced, to draw the exact line of demarcation few will undertake, though for a fee becoming considerate some professional experts will. There is nothing nameable but that some men will, or undertake to, do it for pay.
> (p. 379)

As an act, the drawing of a line is not only inexact and violent: it is also that which problematizes the very possibility of situating the "difference between" the judge and what is judged, between the interests of the "expert" and the truth of his expertise. What every act of judgment manifests is not the value of the object but the position of the judge within a structure of exchange. There is, in other words, no position from which to judge that would be outside the lines of force involved in the object judged.

But if judging is always a *partial* reading (in both senses of the word), is there a place for reading beyond politics? Are we, as Melville's readers, outside the arena in which power and fees are exchanged? If law is the forcible transformation of ambiguity into decidability, is it possible to read ambiguity *as such*, without that reading functioning as a political act?

Even about this, Melville has something to say. For there is a fourth reader in *Billy Budd*, the one who "never interferes in aught and never gives advice" (p. 363): the old Dansker. A man of "few words, many wrinkles," and "the complexion of an antique parchment" (p. 347), the Dansker is the very picture of one who understands and emits ambiguous utterances. When asked by Billy for an explanation of his petty troubles, the Dansker says only, "Jemmy Legs [Claggart] is down on you" (p. 349). This interpretation, entirely accurate as a reading of Claggart's ambiguous behaviour, is handed down to Billy without further explanation: "Something less unpleasantly oracular he tried to extract; but the old sea Chiron, thinking perhaps that for the nonce he had sufficiently instructed his young Achilles, pursued his lips, gathered all his wrinkles together, and would commit himself to nothing further" (p. 349). As a reader who understands ambiguity yet refuses to "commit himself," the Dansker thus dramatizes a reading that attempts to be as cognitively accurate and as performatively neutral as possible. Yet however neutral he tries to remain, the Dansker's reading does not take place outside the political realm:

it is his very refusal to participate in it, whether by further instruction or by direct intervention, that leads to Billy's exclamation in the soup episode ("There now, who says Jemmy Legs is down on me?"). The transference of knowledge is not any more innocent than the transference of power. For it is precisely through the impossibility of finding a spot from which knowledge could be all-encompassing that the plays of political power proceed.

Just as the attempt to "know" without "doing" can itself function as a deed, the fact that judgment is always explicitly an act adds a further insoluble problem to its cognitive predicament. Since, as Vere points out, no judgment can take place in the *Last* Assizes, no judge can ever pronounce a Last Judgment, in order to reach a verdict, Vere must determine the consequences not only of the fatal blow, but also precisely of his own verdict. Judgment is an act not only because it kills, but because it is in turn open to judgment:

> "Can we not convict and yet mitigate the penalty?" asked the sailing master. . . .
> "Gentlemen, were that clearly lawful for us under the circumstances, consider the consequences of such clemency. . . . To the people the foretopman's deed, however it be worded in the announcement, will be plain homicide committed in a flagrant act of mutiny. What penalty for that should follow they know. But it does not follow. Why? They will ruminate. You know what sailors are. Will they not revert to the recent outbreak at the Nore?"
> (p. 389)

The danger is not only one of repeating the Nore mutiny, however. It is also one of forcing Billy, for all his innocence, to repeat his crime. Billy is a politically charged object from the moment he strikes his superior. He is no longer, and can never again be, plotless. If he were set free, he himself would be unable to explain why. As a focus for the questions and intrigues of the crew, he would be even less capable of defending himself than before, and would surely strike again. The political reading, as cognition, attempts to understand the past; as performance, it attempts to eliminate from the future any necessity for its own recurrence.

What this means is that every judge is in the impossible position of having to include the effects of his own act of judging within the cognitive context of his decision. The question of the nature of the type of historical causality that would govern such effects can neither be decided nor ignored. Because of his official position, Vere cannot choose to read in such a way that his reading would not be an act of political authority. But what Melville shows in *Billy Budd* is that authority consists precisely in the impossibility of containing the effects of its own application.

As a political allegory, Melville's *Billy Budd* is thus much more than a study of good and evil, justice and injustice. It is a dramatization of the twisted relations between knowing and doing, speaking and killing, reading and judging, which make political understanding and action so problematic. In the subtle creation of Claggart's "evil" out of a series of spaces in knowledge, Melville shows that gaps in cognition, far from being mere absences, take on the performative power of true acts. The *force* of what is not known is all the more effective for not being perceived as such. The crew, which does not understand that it does not know, is no less performative a reader than the Captain, who clearly perceives and represses the presence of "mystery." The legal order, which attempts to submit "brute ·force" to "forms, measured forms," can only eliminate violence by transforming violence into the final authority. And cognition, which perhaps begins as a power play against the play of power, can only increase, through its own elaboration, the range of what it tries to dominate. The "deadly space" or "difference" that runs through *Billy Budd* is not located *between* knowledge and action, performance and cognition: it is that which, within cognition, functions as an act: it is that which, within action, prevents us from ever knowing whether what we hit coincides with what we understand. And this is what makes the meaning of Melville's last work so . . . *striking*.

Post-Scriptum: A Whale Sights Men

Antonio Tabucchi

Always so frantic, with long, frequently waving appendages. And not round enough, without the grandeur of achieved and sufficient forms, but with instead a tiny, motile head, in which all of their strange life appears concentrated. They arrive sliding over the sea, although they don't swim (almost as if they were birds), and they cause death, with fragility and a graceful ferocity. Silent for long periods, they then shout among themselves with improvised fury, with a tangle of noise that is almost invariable and that lacks the essential perfection of our sounds: calls, love, and cries of mourning. Their love must be pitiful: bristly, immediate, even brusque—without a soft blanket of fat and fostered by their wiry or threadlike nature (which doesn't allow for either the heroic difficulty of unions or for the magnificent, tender challenge of achieving them).

They don't love water, and they fear it—why they frequent it isn't easy to understand. Like us, they travel in herds; however, they don't take females with them, one may assume that the females remain elsewhere, although they have yet to be sighted. Sometimes they sing, but only for themselves, and their song is not a call but rather a sort of longing. They tire quickly and, when the sun goes down, they stretch out on the small islands which guide them about, and perhaps they fall asleep or watch the moon. They slide away in silence, and you realize they are sad.

Chronology of Important Dates

1819	Herman Melville born August 1, New York City, third child (second son) of Allan Melvill, importer and merchant of Scottish descent, and Maria Gansevoort, daughter of General Peter Gansevoort, a hero of the American Revolution and member of a prominent Albany family.
1825–29	Attends New-York Male High School.
1829–30	Attends Columbia Grammar School, New York, beginning September 1829.
1830	Father fails in business, and family moves to Albany in October.
1830–31	Attends Albany Academy, October 1830 to October 1831.
1832	Father dies, January 28, in debt.
1832–34	Works as clerk at the New York State Bank in Albany.
1834–35	Works on his uncle Thomas's farm near Pittsfield, Mass.
1835–37	Works in Albany as bookkeeper and clerk in his brother's fur business. Attends Albany Classical School in 1835; returns to Albany Academy, September 1, 1836, to March 1, 1837.
1837	Brother's business fails, April. Teaches in Sikes District School near Pittsfield for the fall term. Returns to Albany at the end of the year.
1838	Moves with family to nearby Lansingburgh in the spring. Returns briefly to his uncle's farm in the autumn. Back in Lansingburgh in November, studies surveying at the Lansingburgh Academy.
1839	Two sketches, "Fragments from a Writing Desk," published pseudonymously in *Democratic Press and Lansingburgh Advertiser*, May. Sails from New York to Liverpool and back as crew member on the trading ship *St. Lawrence*, June 5 to October 1.
1839–40	Teaches school in Greenbush, N.Y., and briefly (late May 1840) in Brunswick, N.Y.

Chronology compiled by G. Thomas Tanselle for *Herman Melville: Typee, Omoo, Mardi*, © 1982, The Library of America. Reprinted by permission of The Library of America.

1840   Visits his uncle Thomas in Galena, Ill., in the summer, accompanied by his friend, Eli Fly. Travels on a Mississippi River steamer before returning to the East. In autumn searches for a job in New York.

1841–42   Sails from New Bedford harbor, January 3, 1841, on the maiden voyage of the whaling ship *Acushnet*, bound for the South Seas. On July 9, 1842, deserts the *Acushnet* with Richard Tobias Greene at Nuku Hiva in the Marquesas.

1842   After a month in the Taipi valley, sails August 9 on the Australian whaling ship *Lucy Ann*; at Tahiti, is sent ashore with others as mutineer; escapes with John B. Troy in October; the two explore Tahiti and Eimeo and work on a potato farm.

1842–43   Sails on the Nantucket whaling ship *Charles and Henry* from November 7, 1842, through April 27, 1843; is discharged at Lahaina in the Hawaiian Islands, May 2, and takes various jobs in Honolulu.

1843–44   Enlists in the United States Navy in Honolulu; sails August 19, 1843, aboard the frigate *United States*, on which his superior and friend is John J. Chase; arrives in Boston October 3, 1844—having been away nearly four years—and is discharged October 14. Returns to Lansingburgh.

1845   Works on manuscript of a book based on his adventures in the Marquesas; it is rejected by Harper & Brothers in New York but is accepted by John Murray in London, through the efforts of his brother Gansevoort, secretary of the American Legation there.

1846   *Narrative of a Four Months' Residence among the Natives of a Valley of the Marquesas Islands* published by John Murray in London, February 26; published by Wiley & Putnam in New York, under the title *Typee*, about March 20. A "Revised Edition" published in New York in August.

1847   *Omoo* published by Murray in London, March 30, and by Harper & Brothers in New York, about May 1. Marries Elizabeth Shaw, daughter of Chief Justice Lemuel Shaw of the Massachusetts Supreme Court, August 4, and moves to Manhattan.

1847–50   Publishes anonymous reviews (including "Hawthorne and His Mosses," August 1850) and satirical pieces, the former in the *Literary World*, edited by his friend Evert A. Duyckinck, and the latter in *Yankee Doodle*, edited by a member of Duyckinck's circle, Cornelius Mathews.

1849   A son, Malcolm, born, February 16. *Mardi* published by Richard Bentley in London, March 16, and by Harper in New York, April 14. *Redburn* published by Bentley in London, September 29, and by Harper in New York, November 14.

1849–50   Makes a trip to London (to visit publishers) and the continent, October 11, 1849, to February 1, 1850.

1850   *White Jacket* published by Bentley in London, January 23, and by

Harper in New York, March 21. Meets Nathaniel Hawthorne at a picnic near Pittsfield, Mass., August 5, and they become friends. Borrowing money from his father-in-law, Melville purchases a farm (which he names "Arrowhead") near Pittsfield, September 14, and his family is in residence there by early October.

1851   *Moby-Dick* published by Bentley in London, October 18 (under the title *The Whale*), and by Harper in New York, November 14. A second son, Stanwix, born, October 22.

1852   *Pierre* published by Harper in New York, August 6, and by Sampson Low in London in November.

1853   Melville's family and friends, concerned about his health, attempt unsuccessfully during the spring to secure a consulship for him. A daughter, Elizabeth, born, May 22. From about this time, and through the next quarter-century, his wife's family worries about her life with Melville, involving financial insecurity and his recurrent depression.

1853–56 Publishes fourteen tales and sketches in *Putnam's Monthly Magazine* and *Harper's New Monthly Magazine.*

1855   *Israel Potter* published by G. P. Putnam in New York in early March (having been serialized in *Putnam's Monthly Magazine,* July 1854–March 1855) and—without authorization—by George Routledge in London in May. A second daughter, Frances, born, March 2.

1856   *The Piazza Tales,* consisting of five of the *Putnam's* pieces and a newly written introductory sketch, published by Dix & Edwards in New York in late May and distributed in England by Sampson Low.

1856–57 Takes a trip (financed by his father-in-law) for his health, sailing for Glasgow October 11, 1856; visits Hawthorne in Liverpool; then tours the Holy Land, Greece, and Italy; returns to Liverpool and, on May 5, 1857, begins the voyage back to New York, arriving May 20.

1857   *The Confidence-Man* published by Dix & Edwards in New York, April 1, and by Longman, Brown, Green, Longmans & Roberts in London in early April.

1857–60 Goes on the lecture circuit for three seasons, lecturing the first season on "Statues in Rome," the second on "The South Seas," and the third on "Traveling."

1860   Embarks May 28 for San Francisco on the clipper ship *Meteor* as a guest of the captain, his brother Thomas; returns via Panama, arriving in New York on November 12.

1861   Travels to Washington in March to attempt to secure a consular appointment. Father-in-law dies. Family spends the winter in New York.

1863   Leaves Pittsfield permanently in October, trading "Arrowhead" for his brother Allan's New York house at 104 East 26th Street.

1864   Visits his cousin Col. Henry Gansevoort in an army camp on the Virginia front, April.

1866   Publishes some Civil War poems in *Harper's*. A collection of his war poems, *Battle-Pieces and Aspects of the War*, published by Harper, August 23. Appointed a deputy inspector of customs at the port of New York, December 5.

1867   In the spring, Melville's wife's family and her minister discuss the possibility of a legal separation between her and Melville (whom they regard as insane). Their son Malcolm dies by his own pistol, September 11.

1876   The long poem *Clarel* published (at his uncle Peter Gansevoort's expense) by Putnam in early June.

1878   Melville's wife inherits money from the estate of her aunt, Martha Marett.

1885   Resigns position as customs inspector, December 31.

1886   Son Stanwix dies in San Francisco, February 23.

1887   Receives his last royalty statement from the Harper firm, March 4, there having been no printings of his books since 1876; some copies of *Typee, Mardi, Redburn, Pierre,* and *Battle-Pieces* are still in stock, but *Omoo, White-Jacket,* and *Moby-Dick* are out of print. (The total sales of these eight books during Melville's lifetime amounted to about 35,000 copies in the United States and 16,000 in Britain; his lifetime earnings from all his books came to about $5900 from the United States and $4500 from Britain.)

1888   *John Marr and Other Sailors* privately printed at the De Vinne Press in an edition of 25 copies.

1891   *Timoleon* privately printed at the Caxton Press in May in an edition of 25 copies. Dies September 28, leaving a number of poems and *Billy Budd* in manuscript.

Bibliography

Herman Melville is one of the most written about writers in the English language. Obviously no six- or seven-book bibliography can represent the depth or the range of this literature. Instead of attempting this impossible task, I have listed a set of works and recommendations to serve as guides to further research.

Bibliographies

Bryant, John, ed. *A Companion to Melville Studies*. New York: Greenwood Press, 1986.
———. *Melville Society Extracts*. Published quarterly by the Melville Society of America.
Hayashi, Tetsumaro, ed. *Herman Melville: Research Opportunities and Dissertation Abstracts*. Jefferson, NC: McFarland & Company Inc., 1987.
Higgins, Brian, ed. *Herman Melville: An Annotated Bibliography. Volume I: 1846–1930*. Boston: G. K. Hall & Co., 1979.
———. *Herman Melville: A Reference Guide, 1931–1960*. Boston: G. K. Hall, 1987.
Phelps, Leland R., ed. *Herman Melville's Foreign Reputation: A Research Guide*. Boston: G. K. Hall, 1983.

Biographies

Howard, Leon. *Herman Melville*. Berkeley: University of California Press, 1951. Mainly concerned with establishing the facts of Melville's life and career. Howard's biography was intended to complement Leyda's log.
Leyda, Jay. *The Melville Log: A Documentary Life of Herman Melville, 1819–1891*, 2 volumes. New York: Harcourt, 1951. As the title indicates, this provides a plethora of facts, whose significance is to be determined.
Weaver, Raymond. *Herman Melville: Mariner and Mystic*. New York: George H. Doran Company, 1921. The first biography, and very influential in creating the somewhat melodramatic persona of Melville that has prevailed still today.

Editions

Hayford, Harrison, ed. *Herman Melville: Pierre, Israel Potter, The Confidence Man, Tales, and Billy Budd.* New York: The Library of America, 1984.

———. *The Writings of Herman Melville: The Northwestern-Newberry Edition.* 13 volumes published, 15 planned. Evanston and Chicago: Northwestern University Press and The Newberry Library, 1968–.

Tanselle, G. Thomas, ed. *Herman Melville: Redburn, White-Jacket, Moby Dick.* New York: The Library of America, 1983.

———. *Herman Melville: Typee, Omoo, Mardi.* New York: The Library of America, 1982.

Contemporary Reviews

Branch, Watson G., ed. *Melville: The Critical Heritage.* Boston: Routledge & Kegan Paul, 1974.

Hayes, Kevin, and Hershel Parker, eds. *Checklist of Melville Reviews.* Evanston, IL: Northwestern University Press, 1991.

Selected Criticisms

Berthoff, Warner. *The Example of Melville.* Princeton, NJ: Princeton University Press, 1962.

Brodhead, Richard H. *Hawthorne, Melville, and the Novel.* Chicago: University of Chicago Press, 1976.

———. *The School of Hawthorne.* New York: Oxford University Press, 1986.

Brown, Gillian. *Domestic Individualism: Imagining Self in 19th Century America.* Berkeley: University of California Press, 1990.

Cameron, Sharon. *The Corporeal Self: Allegories of the Body in Melville and Hawthorne.* Baltimore: Johns Hopkins University Press, 1981.

Charvat, William. *The Profession of Authorship in America, 1800–1870.* Columbus: Ohio State University Press, 1968.

Dimock, Wai-chee. *Empire for Liberty: Melville and the Poetics of Individualism.* Princeton, NJ: Princeton University Press, 1988.

Douglas, Ann. *The Feminization of American Culture.* New York: Alfred A. Knopf, 1977.

Dryden, Edgar A. *Melville's Thematics of Form.* Baltimore: Johns Hopkins University Press, 1968.

Feidelson, Charles. *Symbolism and American Literature.* Chicago: University of Chicago Press, 1953.

Herbert, T. Walter. *Marquesan Encounters: Melville and the Meaning of Civilization.* Cambridge, MA: Harvard University Press, 1980.

———. *Moby-Dick and Calvinism.* New Brunswick, NJ: Rutgers University Press, 1977.

James, C. L. R. *Mariners, Renegades, and Castaways: The Story of Herman Melville and the World We Live In.* New York, 1953.

Jehlen, Myra. *American Incarnation: The Individual, The Nation, and the Continent.* Cambridge, MA: Harvard University Press, 1986.

Karcher, Carolyn L. *Shadow over the Promised Land: Slavery, Race, and Violence in Melville's America.* Baton Rouge: Louisiana State University Press, 1980.

Lawrence, D. H. *Studies in Classic American Literature.* Reprinted New York: Viking Press, 1964.

Leverenz, David. *Manhood and the American Renaissance.* Ithaca, NY: Cornell University Press, 1989.

Levin, Harry. *The Power of Blackness: Hawthorne, Poe, Melville.* New York: Alfred A. Knopf, 1958.

McWilliams, John P. *Hawthorne, Melville, and the American Character: A Looking-Glass Business.* New York: Cambridge University Press, 1984.

Martin, Robert K. *Hero, Captain, Stranger: Male Friendship, Social Critique, and Literary Form in the Sea Novels of Herman Melville.* Chapel Hill: University of North Carolina Press, 1986.

Matthiessen, F. O. *American Renaissance.* New York: Oxford University Press, 1941.

Miller, Perry. *The Raven and the Whale: The War of Wits and Words in the Era of Poe and Melville.* New York: Harcourt, Brace, and World, 1956.

Olson, Charles. *Call Me Ishmael.* San Francisco: City Lights, 1947.

Rogin, Michael Paul. *Subversive Genealogy: The Politics and Art of Herman Melville.* New York: Alfred A. Knopf, 1983.

Simpson, David. *Fetishism and Imagination: Dickens, Melville, Conrad.* New York: Cambridge University Press, 1984.

Sten, Christopher, ed. *Savage Eye: Melville and the Visual Arts.* Kent, OH: Kent State University Press, 1991.

Thomas, Brook. *Cross-Examinations of Law and Literature: Cooper, Hawthorne, Stowe, and Melville.* New York: Cambridge University Press, 1987.

Zoellner, Robert. *The Salt Sea Mastodon: A Reading of Moby-Dick.* Berkeley: University of California Press, 1973.

Notes on Contributors

SACVAN BERCOVITCH is Charles H. Carswell Professor of English and American Literature at Harvard. He is the author of *The American Jeremiad* (1979) among other books, and most recently *The Rites of Assent: Transformations in the Symbolic Construction of America* (1993).

LEO BERSANI is the Class of 1950 Professor of French at the University of California, Berkeley, and the author, most recently, of *Arts of Impoverishment: Beckett, Rothko, Resnais* (written with Ulysse Dutoit).

MITCHELL BREITWIESER teaches American literature at the University of California, Berkeley. He is the author of *Cotton Mather and Benjamin Franklin: The Price of Representative Personality* (1984) and of *American Puritanism and the Defense of Mourning: Religion, Grief, and Ethnology in Mary White Rowlandson's Captivity Narrative* (1990).

RICHARD BRODHEAD is Housum Professor of English at Yale University and Dean of Yale College. He is the author of *Hawthorne, Melville, and the Novel* (1976), *The School of Hawthorne* (1986), and *Cultures of Letters: Scenes of Reading and Writing in Nineteenth-Century America* (1993).

GILLIAN BROWN, Associate Professor of English at the University of Utah, is the author of *Domestic Individualism: Imagining Self in Nineteenth-Century America* (1990). Her forthcoming work, *The Consent of the Governed*, concerns ideas of agency and accountability in American culture.

WAI-CHEE DIMOCK is an Associate Professor of English at Brandeis University. She is the author of *Empire for Liberty: Melville and the Poetics of Individualism* (1988), and of a forthcoming book on American literature, law, and political theory titled *Cognition and History*.

EDGAR A. DRYDEN is the editor of the *Arizona Quarterly* and the author of *Melville's Thematics of Form* (1968), *Nathaniel Hawthorne: The Poetics of Enchantment* (1977), and *The Form of American Romance* (1988).

JIM HICKS, who has recently received his Ph.D. in Comparative Literature from the University of Pennsylvania and teaches at the University of Massachusetts in Boston, worked closely with the editor on all aspects of this collection. His knowledge of the scholarship and his critical understanding have been essential to its completion.

BRIAN HIGGINS, Professor of English at the University of Illinois at Chicago, has compiled a two-volume bibliography of writings about Melville and wrote the annual chapter on Melville for *American Literary Scholarship* from 1984–1989.

PHILIPPE JAWORSKI teaches American literature at the Université Paris VII. He is the author of *Melville. Le Désert et l'Empire* (1986). He has edited two collections of critical essays on Melville and is currently working on the four-volume Pleiade edition of Melville's works.

MYRA JEHLEN is Board of Governors Professor of Literature at Rutgers University. She is the author of *American Incarnation: the Individual, the Nation and the Continent* (1986) and *The Literature of Colonization* in the Cambridge Literary History of the United States.

BARBARA JOHNSON is Professor of English and Comparative Literature at Harvard University. She is author of *The Critical Difference* (1980) and *A World of Difference* (1987) and editor, most recently, of *Freedom and Interpretation: Oxford Amnesty Lectures 1992* (1993).

HERSHEL PARKER, H. Fletcher Brown Professor at the University of Delaware, is associate general editor of *The Writings of Herman Melville* and is currently completing a two-volume biography of Melville.

DONALD PEASE holds the Ted and Helen Geisel Chair of the Humanities at Dartmouth University. He is the author of *Visionary Compacts* (1987) and the general editor for the New Americanists series at Duke University Press.

ARNOLD RAMPERSAD is Woodrow Wilson Professor of Literature at Princeton University, and director of its Program in American Studies. He is the author of the two-volume *Life of Langston Hughes* (1986, 1989) and, most recently, *Days of Grace: a Memoir*, with Arthur Ashe (1993).

MICHAEL ROGIN teaches political science at the University of California, Berkeley. His books include *Fathers and Children: Andrew Jackson and the Subjugation of the American Indian* (1975) and *Ronald Reagan, the Movie and Other Episodes in Political Demonology* (1987).

EVE KOSOFSKY SEDGWICK, the Newman Ivey White Professor of English at Duke University, is the author, most recently, of *Between Men* (1985) and *Epistemology of the Closet* (1990).

ERIC J. SUNDQUIST is Professor of English at UCLA. His recent books include *To Wake the Nations: Race in the Making of American Literature* (1993), *The Hammers of Creation: Folk Culture in Modern African American Fiction* (1992), and, as editor, *Frederick Douglass: New Literary and Historical Essays* (1990).

ANTONIO TABUCCHI teaches Portuguese literature at the University of Siena. He is the author of, among other books, the novel *Notturno Indiano*; *I Volatili Del Beato Angelico*; a critical study of Fernando Pessoa; and, most recently, of *Sogni di Sogni* (1992).

ROBYN WIEGMAN, Assistant Professor of Women's Studies and English at Indiana University, has recently co-edited *Who Can Speak? Identity and Critical Authorship* (University of Illinois Press). Her book, *Economies of Visibility*, investigates race and gender in the United States.

BRYAN J. WOLF is the Director of Graduate Studies in the American Studies Program at Yale and author of the forthcoming *The Invention of Seeing: Painting and Ideology in Vermeer, Wright, Homer and Eakins.*